BROADWAY BABYLON

GLAMOUR, GLITZ, AND GOSSIP ON THE GREAT WHITE WAY

BOZE HADLEIGH

BACK STAGE BOOKS
AN IMPRINT OF WATSON-GUPTILL PUBLCATIONS
New York

Senior Editor: Mark Glubke
Project Editor: Gary Sunshine
Interior Design: Julie Duquet
Production Manager: Salvatore Destro

First published in 2007 by Back Stage Books,
an imprint of Watson-Guptill Publications,
Nielsen Business Media,
a division of The Nielsen Company
www.watsonguptill.com

Library of Congress Control Number: 2006937256

ISBN: 13: 978-0-8230-8830-0
ISBN: 10: 0-8230-8830-8

First printing 2007

Printed in the United States of America
1 2 3 4 5 6 7 8 9 / 13 12 11 10 09 08 07

To Ronnie . . . and to all
the plays and musicals
we've loved before

CONTENTS

ACKNOWLEDGMENTS

My mother sometimes wished me to get a PhD, as my father had done—for a professor, it's mandatory. This book is the closest I'd want to get: a "PhD" in Broadway history. The project was long, massive, and fascinating. Researching it was an education, but a joyful one: putting it together was lengthy and necessarily interrupted (on three continents!). My trimmed-down manuscript finally weighed in at 642 typewritten pages when sent to Back Stage Books for further trimming by other hands.

Over the years I've relished theatre books by others—from A to Ken Mandelbaum and Ethan Mordden to Z for Zadan, Craig—and it's shocking to realize that Broadway is now only a fraction as musically, journalistically, and socioeconomically influential as three or four decades ago. Even so, the dimmer memories survive colorfully in my mind.

Speaking of which, there are several to thank, starting as always with my partner and associate Ronald Boze Stockwell. And my sister Linda for a multitude of clippings. My originating editor, Mark Glubke, my current editor, Bob Nirkind, and my copy editor, Michèle LaRue. Gary Sunshine, my project editor, enthusiastically helped shape and diet down this book. Producer Ben Bagley wanted to do a book together, and died much too soon. Truman Capote encouraged me, as did Sandy Dennis, Charlie Earle, Richard Condon, and Chad Oberhausen.

Thanks to Bea Arthur, Robert Clary, Frederick Combs, David Cravatts, Bette Davis, Mitch Douglas, Dody Goodman, Julie Harris, Arthur Laurents, Cameron Mackintosh, Rose Marie, Jim Pinkston, Charles Nelson Reilly, George Rose, Maureen Stapleton, Kenzo Tanaka, and Frederick Ziffel (no relation to Arnold's father).

It's a surprise and delightful treat that my book *Bette Davis Speaks* is being turned into a play, *A Couple of Bettes*, by screenwriter-producer Dan Gordon, to star the talented Linda Gray. Coincidence: Boze is (I am), of course, a character in the three-person play, and one of Bette's early films included a character first-named Boze: *The Petrified Forest*, based, like so many screen classics, on a Broadway play. (Leslie Howard and Humphrey Bogart costarred in the stage and movie versions.)

As with nearly every star of Hollywood's golden era, Ms. Davis came to motion pictures via the theater, with Broadway experience and acclaim in her pocket. Sadly, she remarked that fewer young actors than ever were taking that route. "Acting schools, commercials, and even television," she declared, "are not a substitute. When you have worked on Broadway, you have been tested in fire. You have worked with the best, with professional discipline and glowing self-confidence—if not at the start of the run, then by its end. Broadway improves any actor."

Although about half of my seventeen books have been the basis of TV programs or documentaries here and abroad, that one of them will be that living, breathing, and actable thing, A Play, is particularly gratifying.

Now, on with the show!

"When you are away from old Broadway you are only camping out."
—GEORGE M. COHAN,
composer of "Give My Regards to Broadway"

"Broadway is the performance side of the American character."
—GWEN VERDON
(*Damn Yankees, Sweet Charity*)

*"If all the world's a stage, Broadway is center stage
with a baby pink spotlight."*
—producer GEORGE ABBOTT at 105

PREFACE

Theater is Acting. In person, in sequence, and for a live audience. It is not a pre- packaged product, like performing for the camera—little or big screen. Real actors tread the boards, and real theater stars—in the United States—play Broadway. Once the mecca of American entertainment, Broadway—and to a lesser but vital extent Off-Broadway—remains the pinnacle of play and stage musical entertainment in this country.

Although "the Great White Way" no longer yields a majority of popular culture's hit songs, it retains an enduring mystique and glamour, and occasionally creates a new star, such as 4' 11" full-sized 2003 Tony-winner Marissa Jaret Winokur, who pre-award already had a post–*Hairspray* TV series deal. Notwithstanding a depressed economy and lingering decline in tourism since 9/11, the 2005–2006 Broadway season set an all-time record of $861.6 million. If Broadway is no longer a habit, it's now an Event—an expensive one—and its more-famous shows are eagerly awaited from coast to coast and in between.

A Broadway hit like *The Producers* can revitalize a fading screen career, like Matthew Broderick's; and as with *Hairspray* or *The Producers*, a musical format—America's gift to the world—can resurrect and re-commercialize a straight play or film from long ago. The challenge and prestige of Broadway still lure movie stars with integrity, such as Hugh Jackman, who dazzlingly proved his versatility and earned a Tony for his performance in *The Boy from Oz*, playing fellow Australian Peter Allen, who flopped big-time as an American gangster in an earlier musical. Not all projects are potentially tuneful; *Carrie*, the Stephen King musical, was a legendary disaster.

It's worth remembering that during the McCarthy witch hunts and blacklists, it was on Broadway and in theater generally where a writer, performer, director, etcetera, whose politics Congress or the White House disapproved of, could find work when none was available in TV or on screen. The stage has always been more welcoming and inclusive, also more daring and innovative, than the mass media.

Broadway Babylon is an affectionate, hopefully entertaining, and informative overview of Broadway past and present. It is necessarily selective and by choice nonchronological. "Oh, my God! Not another stage textbook," shuddered Bea Arthur over the telephone. No way, I assured her. (The LA–based trouper, 80, had just returned from touring her one-woman Broadway show in England and South Africa.)

The death, specifically Broadway's, of the American theater has been repeatedly predicted. However, despite the incursions of television, cable, video, DVD, computer games, etcetera, Broadway still pulsates with energy, creativity, and glamorous appeal, for its spectacles, artists, and immediacy are timeless and fill a need that has endured some 2,500 years, ever since Thespis stepped out of the chorus to seize audiences' attention and touch their dreams.

1

BROADWAY IS . . .

"Broadway is what I do at night."—ETHEL MERMAN

"Broadway is my kinda town."—FRANK SINATRA

"Broadway is the ultimate live event for people who think."—MADONNA (*Speed the Plow*)

"Broadway is where writers are respected . . . the inverse of Hollywood." —writer-director GARSON KANIN (*Born Yesterday*)

"Broadway is where faded movie stars go to try."—DEAN MARTIN

"Broadway is . . . thrilling!"—LIZA MINNELLI

"Broadway is an acquired taste that most Americans haven't acquired. But give it time."—choreographer MICHAEL BENNETT (*A Chorus Line*)

"Broadway is the opportunity to see fabulous people fly or flub."—director-choreographer JOE LAYTON (*George M!*)

"Broadway is nowhere near being an endangered species. . . . In America's biggest, most sophisticated city, top-notch entertainment is still required. . . . The out-of-towners love it too. It's a big reason they come to New York."—ROSIE O'DONNELL

"Broadway is the biggest challenge in the field of entertainment." —KATHARINE HEPBURN, who starred and even sang in the musical *Coco*

"Broadway is to entertainment what adrenalin is to your body."—HUGH JACKMAN (*The Boy from Oz*)

"Broadway is innovative, so sometimes others pinch our ideas. . . . I did a play about a witch who falls in love with a mortal [*Bell, Book and Candle*]. Just a few years after the movie version, the small screen appropriated my premise with a comedy series called *Bewitched*."—JOHN VAN DRUTEN, playwright and stage director (*The King and I*)

"Broadway is . . . a puzzlement."—YUL BRYNNER, who triumphed as the King but flopped as Odysseus

"Broadway is about audiences . . . about expectation. I know that Broadway audiences expect more. And they get more."—MARIETTA BITTER ABEL, who played the harp in the orchestra pit at countless Broadway shows and was married to actor Walter Abel

"Broadway is for me the great what-might-have-been. I'd done stage work, of course, but when I was going to move to New York and really concentrate on the stage, I got offered the part of Ward Cleaver and I accepted. It was steady work from about 1957 to 1963, but it typecast me . . . [and] today the work I did on stage is practically all forgotten."—HUGH BEAUMONT of *Leave It to Beaver*

"Broadway is certainly friendlier and more egalitarian than out in Los Angeles. I was a character actor before I became blacklisted, and in LA stars and character actors almost never mix socially. In New York I had several starry friends. It was natural."—VICTOR KILIAN, later known as Grandpa the Fernwood Flasher on TV's *Mary Hartman, Mary Hartman*

"Broadway is more humane. It's more realistic. In the movies, you're only as good as your last project. In the theater, you're as accepted as your biggest success. So you can be Michael Bennett or Carol Channing, years later, and still be celebrated because of *A Chorus Line* or *Hello, Dolly!*"—DICK VAN DYKE (*Bye Bye Birdie*)

"Broadway is the most exciting thing I have done. . . . In Spain, everyone knows Hollywood movies; not everyone likes them. But everyone has heard of Broadway, and most people think it is something exciting and special, even intellectually."—ANTONIO BANDERAS, who made his Broadway bow in a 2003 revival of the musical *Nine*

"Broadway is somewhat intimidating to us [English], due to its size, the emphasis on budgets and profits, and the preferably unfriendly critics." —SIR JOHN GIELGUD

"Broadway is a hoot. I love it. . . . Thank goodness an actor's never too old to play Broadway."—KATHLEEN FREEMAN, Tony nominated in her final role, in *The Full Monty*

"Broadway is glamour. It's the best! And you have to be at your best when you're on it."—VIVIAN VANCE, who worked on Broadway before *I Love Lucy*

"Broadway is magic. Or should I say, can be magic."—NATHAN LANE

"Broadway is craft. It's rehearsal, blood, sweat, and tears. And then more rehearsal."—playwright JOHN HERBERT (*Fortune and Men's Eyes*)

"Broadway is the source of the best actors. Trained ones willing to put in the time and pay dues. Broadway actors used to look down on film people. . . . The only actors I look down on are those who put the word 'star' above 'actor.'"—Hollywood director BILLY WILDER

"Broadway is a challenge at any age. Probably more at my age, which is one reason to do it. It's still a thrill to face a live audience. . . . I love [*Our Town*], because I made my stage debut in it in 1939, a small part, yet a thrill for me. Now I play the stage manager."—PAUL NEWMAN, who played a two-month Broadway engagement in 2002–2003

"Broadway is stressful if it's your career. . . . The only ones who don't really care and worry much are stars who sail in from the movies or television and then sail out again."—legendary gypsy CATHRYN DAMON, best known for TV's *Soap*

"Broadway is just too goddamn critical. It's so scary. Every time I go back there people stop me on the street and ask, 'When are you coming back to Broadway?' But it's too painful, with all you have to go through, and I've had too much rejection. Sometimes I wake up and I can't believe I've been doing this for 30 years. . . . How does anyone come up with a hit?"—KAREN MORROW, talented singer-actress and almost-star

"Broadway is difficult to keep succeeding at. A hit is seldom followed by another hit. I had *The Miracle Worker*, with all the awards and the movie [version] . . . [then] in 1962 I played a girl in the same general vein—with an incurable heart ailment—but that (*Isle of Children*) was no hit at all. So then I stayed away from Broadway for forty-one years, is all."—PATTY DUKE

"Broadway is the epitome—the very heart, soul, and essence of the entertainment business. There is a magic that comes over you even if you walk along the streets and look up at the marquee. In a word, Broadway was, is, and always will be 'it.'"—ROSE MARIE (*The Dick Van Dyke Show*), who appeared four times on the Great White Way

"Broadway is the Big Apple an actor wants a bite of! I moved to New York at nineteen, studied, played nightclubs. Broadway was the big goal. Even a small role on Broadway is a dream come true. The smallest roles still have hundreds of kids competing for them. Everyone wants a piece of that dream."—NELL CARTER (*Ain't Misbehavin'*)

"Broadway is where you put it all to work . . . the best of your talents and what you learned from your teachers. One of my coaches used to say, 'If you make it big, remember even so to act during the dog's feet.' He was Russian; he meant the 'pawses.'"—JIM BACKUS (*Gilligan's Island*)

"Broadway is The Big Street. It's big-time and big theatres. By gum, if you dare play there, you better be big or have something big to offer."—RICHARD KILEY (*Man of La Mancha* and TV's *Ally McBeal*)

"Broadway is the most expensive entertainment medium in the history of the world. Including Lakers games."—basketball fan JACK NICHOLSON

"Broadway is predicated on the dollar. On profit. It's a little more mercenary than theater anywhere else."—columnist and TV host ED SULLIVAN

"Broadway is theater, but more so. More commodified, and therefore less honest. Theater has a better reputation than it deserves, I think because those who make theater are so vulnerable, they struggle so hard, and they desire so much. And almost no one gets rich from theater, so we tend to think of it as a place for progressive ideas, that it's more hopeful and pure than it really is."—playwright/novelist SARAH SCHULMAN

"Broadway is presenting fewer shows . . . [it's] economics. But I don't think diminished quantity always means diminished quality."—MARY WICKES (the 1979 *Oklahoma!* revival)

"Broadway is, I suppose, still 'the Fabulous Invalid.' Someone said that a very long time ago. It's always been true. It's always been about too much expense, too little audience, . . . a balancing act. But it's still there."—SIR LAURENCE OLIVIER

"Broadway is people. And it should stay people, not special effects. . . . Ethel Merman's voice was a special effect. So was Richard Rodgers' music. And Zero Mostel's expressions. Et cetera. On and on. People. Special people did all that—not machines or lights."—MAXENE ANDREWS (*Over There*) of the Andrews Sisters

"Broadway is still where you can see the most exciting spectacles and actors—and in some cases stars making spectacles of themselves."—DAVID CARROLL (*Grand Hotel*)

"Broadway is where American actors can actually, really, flat-out act."—DAME
MAGGIE SMITH

"Broadway is and always has been full of narcissists and egotists. And that's just
the critics."—former playwright WOODY ALLEN

"Broadway is maddening. Till opening night. Then it's joyous or heartbreaking,
depending on the damned critics."—RAUL JULIA (*Nine*)

"Broadway is about proving and stretching yourself."—RAQUEL WELCH,
who took over for Lauren Bacall in *Woman of the Year*

"Broadway is star power. Which one doesn't have to be a star, going in, to dis-
play."—BOB FOSSE

"Broadway is, or it was, where they could send out the girl from the sticks to
replace the ailing leading lady and she'd come back a star. Well, it happened
to Shirley MacLaine from Virginia. In other words, Broadway was a place
to dream."—director ROBERT MOORE (*Woman of the Year*)

"Broadway is where every actor, singer, or dancer should perform at least once
in a lifetime. It's unforgettable."—ANDY GRIFFITH, who twice starred on
Broadway

"Broadway is what people-pleasing actors aspire to. . . . A Broadway audience's reaction is immediate and energizing. Movie actors are so much further removed from humanity and reality."—DEBORAH KERR (*Tea and
Sympathy*)

"Broadway is no longer the acme of American culture, just as New York is no
longer the real capital of America, which it was when America had more
culture."—composer JULE STYNE (*Gypsy, Funny Girl*)

"Broadway is no longer the innovator. Broadway has become the showcase. It
is the end stop rather than the beginning. Where once most plays started
on Broadway and went out into the world, Broadway has become the final
stop on a journey that might begin in a workshop Downtown and then
go to Seattle or Chicago and then come back. Theater has been decen-
tralized."—critic and author HOWARD KISSEL

"Broadway is the best theater audience. . . . New York is the only city in the
United States that has an old theater culture . . . like London. . . . It's a theater town . . . [But] it's important to remember that *Angels in America* is not
a play that could have been created for Broadway. This play exists because
of the regional not-for-profit theater movement. Most serious, important
theater in this country is created at regional theaters, including some in

New York City, like Lincoln Center and the Public."—playwright TONY
KUSHNER

"Broadway is a marketplace. . . . A lot of people are unhappy about the Tony
[Awards ceremony] because it does not recognize a lot of Off-Broadway
productions. [Some] say that the most creative productions on
Broadway today, with the exception of a couple of things, come from
Off-Broadway . . . [but] are not nominated for Tonys because they're Off-
Broadway."—playwright CRAIG LUCAS (*Prelude to a Kiss*)

"Broadway is not all of the theater in New York. Not by a long shot. As my
friend Jason Robards Jr. used to say, you can often see better plays Off-
Broadway."—AL LEWIS (Grandpa on TV's *The Munsters*), who costarred
with Robards in Circle in the Square's *The Iceman Cometh*

"Broadway is like military life. They run an act to the minute, using a stop-
watch. I remember once knocking ten seconds off an act because the
director insisted. At least in motion pictures you can run a few days over
the schedule. Broadway is all high finance, a five-hundred-to-one shot
that you'll make it. That's why there's so much pressure and no freedom."—O'Neill devotee and two-time Oscar-winner JASON
ROBARDS JR.

"Broadway is . . . I mean this about theater in general, it means freedom to me.
As a girl—a total tomboy—I wanted to be an aviatrix, to be that high and
that free and far away from boredom. On stage, that is exactly what I do.
I'm complete, yet I'm somebody else. Stage acting is the most freeing
activity I know."—actress and Actors' Equity Association President
COLLEEN DEWHURST

"Broadway is magic time! It may be childish, but I love to see a curtain going
up, and to this day [1997], when it rises, I want to be on that stage. Now
my theater life is over, but I go all the time and I'm a wonderful audience.
The curtain goes up, the bank of lights in the balcony comes on, and off
we go. It's heaven!"—JONATHAN HARRIS (*Lost in Space*'s Dr. Smith),
stage and TV actor

"Broadway is the most nerve-wrackingly glorious place on earth to work. . . .
I just wish it could be the other way 'round of what it is: that far more
people saw the musicals and plays than the movie versions!"—BEATRICE
ARTHUR (*Mame* and its non-hit movie version)

"Broadway is what excitement builds to, if you write songs."—composer
EUBIE BLAKE

"Broadway is what outsiders have created. And Tin Pan Alley, which supplied the music. . . . Mostly Jews, also gays . . . Catholics. Not wishing to insult white Protestant heterosexuals, but clearly their talents lie in making money and rules, not art."—NICHOLAS DANTE, co-writer, *A Chorus Line*

"Broadway is fairer, more realistic, more decent than it used to be. Today you can be openly gay or lesbian and have a stage career and win Tonys, like Nathan Lane and Cherry Jones. Mere decades ago, you couldn't present gay or lesbian characters on a New York stage or serve a drink in a bar to 'a known homosexual.' Those good old days were not."—Tony- and Emmy-winner MICHAEL JETER

"Broadway is the one medium, and art, that has said and done the most about AIDS, while other media, as well as political and religious institutions, have shamefully neglected this national tragedy and challenge."—GREGORY PECK

"Broadway is more 'all-American' than ever before. The price for this—in Hollywood too—is less glamour and diversity of types, accents, outlooks, and less perspective. Look at the golden age of Broadway or of the movies—if you hadn't had the European presence you did, behind the scenes as well as on, you wouldn't have had a golden age."—*A Chorus Line* co-writer JAMES KIRKWOOD

"Broadway is producing, or yielding, more and more cookie-cutter people. Clone people or actors. Somehow, the bigger our population, the more alikeness in the younger people."—legendary producer CHERYL CRAWFORD

"Broadway is big enough for b-i-g personalities. . . . Merman and Channing were too large for movies, forget TV. Broadway dotes on the bigger-than-life and the outrageous. At its best, Broadway is terrifically glamorous and outrageous."—GEORGE BURNS in 1983

"Broadway is not the happy habit it was. You'd go back each season to see your favorite stars in new shows. Stars can go away for years now, in between stage projects."—producer ALEXANDER COHEN

"Broadway is for people with longer attention spans. Seeing a play or musical is in several ways a commitment. Theatre is the ne plus ultra of Going Out. It's something to congratulate oneself on. You know, in America they don't really watch TV anymore—they watch 'what else is on.'"—writer-announcer ALISTAIR COOKE

"Broadway is partly about responsibility to language. . . . Plays come at you more through the ear than the eye. A play is ninety percent an auditory experience. I don't trust people to pay the attention they should. . . . There's the issue of the reduced attention span. People used to be able to listen to and comprehend an entire paragraph at a time."—three-time Pulitzer Prize–winning playwright EDWARD ALBEE

"Broadway is not about writing about what you know. Broadway is imagination unleashed. Lerner and Loewe wrote about Scotland and ancient England. Rodgers and Hammerstein wrote about Siam and Oklahoma. Why limit yourself?"—lyricist E.Y. HARBURG ("Over the Rainbow")

"Broadway is *for* the creator. It respects writers. In Hollywood when my play *Me* was produced [in 1973 with Geraldine Fitzgerald and Richard Dreyfuss], they congratulated me not because I wrote a play, but because I directed it. Hollywood always values the interpreter over the creator." —ex-TV star GARDNER MCKAY (*Adventures in Paradise*)

"Broadway is what I should have focused on. . . . My real love as an actor is Shakespeare. I should have gone to England, maybe. . . . One of the ruder people I worked with, who later gave up the stage for the silver screen— silver tarnishes, remember?—once said I had a future in the theatre because I had a face long enough to wrap twice around my neck! I should've followed the creep's advice."—JOHN CARRADINE

"Broadway is where a commercially successful and stereotyped actor can try something else. Nobody in [Hollywood] could see me in a mental institution, but on Broadway I starred in *One Flew Over the Cuckoo's Nest*, and it was great. . . . I never got to make the movie, and my role won [Jack] Nicholson the Oscar."—KIRK DOUGLAS

"Broadway is more impressive to someone from the Midwest. Two of the biggest thrills of my lifetime were on Broadway . . . when I played the lead's best friend in *Tea and Sympathy* and got nominated for 'best supporting' by the New York Drama Critics, and then when I took over the lead in *Bus Stop*, by William Inge. Those two had more of an impact on me than later when I found out *Bewitched* was the number-one-rated [TV] show for the season."—DICK YORK (the first Darrin)

"Broadway is wonderful! Like Berlin was. Before Hitler, of course."—LOTTE LENYA (*Cabaret*)

"Broadway is the most, it's just the heights. It's intoxicating. . . . After Broadway, everything else is poverty."—DOLORES GRAY (*Carnival in Flanders*)

"Broadway is the collision of talent and maximum publicity in a medium free of popcorn."—LARRY KERT (*West Side Story, Company*)

"Broadway is, at its best, words and music that blend and elevate."—critic VINCENT CANBY

"Broadway is good writing or diverting performers. One or the other. Both can happen, but don't expect it—be happily surprised. And grateful." —HOWARD CRABTREE, singer, dancer, designer, and former chorus boy

"Broadway is the illusion that everyone up there on the stage is having the time of their lives."—PEGGY CASS, Agnes Gooch in *Auntie Mame*

"Broadway is, like the [*Chicago*] song says, 'razzle-dazzle.' People want to believe. They want to be transported out of a grimy, gritty world. So . . . you razzle-dazzle 'em."—ROBERT PRESTON (*The Lion in Winter*, *The Music Man*)

"Broadway is where I was happiest."—musical star MARY MARTIN

"Broadway is, or used to be, America's showplace. The national circus."—LEE REMICK (*Anyone Can Whistle*)

"Broadway is more blatant than ever. And when an ecdysiast says that, you know it's gotten a mite raw! True, it *was* less truthful. But there wasn't actual nudity, just promises. Early on, I was in a traveling chorus show which cleaned up because we were billed as '50 Beautiful Girls! . . . 45 Gorgeous Costumes!'"—GYPSY ROSE LEE

"Broadway is just reflective of the bigger picture. . . . Bringing back *The Graduate* as a play isn't [about] nostalgia or reviving a classic movie. It's trading on the nudity of its star actress. . . . More people will go see *Take Me Out* now that it's won the Best Play Tony, but the big lure wasn't just drama or the outing theme, but athletes showering naked on stage. Shock, or nudity, is what it now takes to sell a show and get people inside. A good show's not enough. You gotta have a gimmick, and it's either major names or spectacles or major nudity."—Monte Carlo columnist DELPHINE ROSAY

"Broadway is and has always been more creative and daring than Hollywood, and I put it down to there being no studio heads in charge of the theater. Those were very uncreative, uneducated, frightened, conformist men, and it all revolved around safe formulas for the masses. Pro-commerce and anti-controversy."—Tony-winner RODDY McDOWALL

"Broadway is, thank goodness, non-akin to the movie world. In several aspects. . . . Broadway tries to cast for ability rather than type . . . [and] Broadway will even praise you, when warranted."—HOWARD DA SILVA, the original Jud in *Oklahoma!*, who was later blacklisted in Hollywood

"Broadway is like family. In the theater there's a kind of closeness, whether it's the stage manager or rehearsal pianist, the head carpenter or the star. All are family."—composer JOHN KANDER (*Cabaret*, *Chicago*)

"Broadway is not as culpable as other branches of entertainment that caved in—shockingly easily—to right-wing political witch hunters. After I was blacklisted for TV and movies, my career was revivified by Broadway, as was my friend Zero Mostel's."—JACK GILFORD (*A Funny Thing Happened on the Way to the Forum*)

"Broadway is something that evolves. Back in the '50s, early '60s, you couldn't have put on *Cabaret*. Today [1966] it's a hit, and an issue. And high time, too. When it no doubt gets revived someday, it may be even more daring, with more layers revealed."—prophetic *Cabaret* star BERT CONVY

"Broadway is also, even primarily, a venue for plays that question and enlighten. Such works are tough to get on . . . difficult to get an audience. But such a play, when it attains Broadway and finds its audience—and gets media attention—can become very significant and influential. . . . Broadway can magnify an idea."—three-time Tony-winner IRENE WORTH

"Broadway is a gamble. Obviously. For producers. Regardless, audiences usually win."—producer DAVID MERRICK

"Broadway is, sooner or later, bankers waiting in the wings."—Oscar-winning lyricist and Broadway director HOWARD ASHMAN

"Broadway is not always on the money. At least when I was young. Fancy, titling a play *The Brown Danube*! I was in it, but people wanted it *blue*. . . . I remember fondly the plays I did in the 1930s. I remember them as clearly as *King Kong* because what you do live, in person, with an audience, remains vivid in your memory. . . . Two of my husbands won Academy Awards for screenwriting, and they'd never have titled a movie *The Brown Danube*!"—FAY WRAY (born 1907) in 2003, on the seventieth anniversary of *King Kong*

"Broadway is the top of the heap . . . the big mountain peak you aim for. One of my most memorable and fulfilling times, though a helluva lot of work, was doing *The Music Man* in Chicago at the Shubert Theatre. The only thing that could have topped it would have been to take the show to Broadway. That's the big aim, and the height of prestige."—FORREST TUCKER, film (*Auntie Mame*) and TV (*F Troop*) actor

"Broadway is laying it on the line. You can't fake memorization. You can't substitute a good camera angle or a close-up for talent and a good voice." —DAVID DUKES (*Bent*, *M. Butterfly*)

"Broadway is a way of life. It's a world and schedule of its own . . . and you become a night owl, almost—in a wonderful, exhilarating way—like a vampire, just waiting for the night, to do your thing. You're eager to get on stage and live and perform deeply, in the moment."—CHITA RIVERA

"Broadway is alive. Film is dead—not commercially, [but] artistically. When you watch film, it's done and over. The audience is not and never can be involved the same way as in a play. Theatre is alive. Anything can happen. It can absorb you. Things can go wrong or wonderfully right. With a play or a musical, there's chemistry between audience and players. There is no chemistry toward a film."—Tony-winning costume designer PATRICIA ZIPPRODT (*Cabaret, Sweet Charity*)

"Broadway is footprints in the sand—a truism. But therefore more exciting, and thereafter more nostalgic."—ANGELA LANSBURY

"Broadway is certainly not dying, as I've read for years in American periodicals. It's just that Hollywood is taking over, almost monopolizing, American entertainment. And Broadway today is almost no American actor's goal. It's what actors resort to when Hollywood won't use them. It's not that way in England. We do stage, film, and television. Of course they're all in one city. But theater is absolutely still part of the actor's package. Nor do any of us, while working on the stage, expect to become wealthy. Which helps keep ticket prices at a decent level."—Tony winner SIR NIGEL HAWTHORNE

"Broadway is, you know, unlike Hollywood, it's a place where lack of talent is not enough."—ANITA MORRIS (*Nine*)

"Broadway is first and foremost about promise. It's the promise of entertainment, and the promise, or illusion, of youth."—*Rent* creator JONATHAN LARSON

The Dying Theater

"The American theater is on its last beloved legs. . . . In ten years there will be nothing but the Theatre Guild and one or two similar organizations. . . . We are being mechanized out of the theater by the talkies and radio and by people who prefer convenience to beauty."—actress JANE COWL in 1929

"The poor old theater is done for. . . . There will be nothing but 'talkies' soon."—GEORGE BERNARD SHAW in 1930

"Talking pictures will [by 1941] take the place of theater as we know it today."—theatrical designer NORMAN BEL GEDDES in 1931 (daughter Barbara played J.R.'s mother on *Dallas*)

"Television may kill the movies, but I doubt it. It is killing off plays, which used to be called the aspirin of the middle classes."—writer WOLCOTT GIBBS in 1959

"Broadway is dead, and if not dead, dying. Don't ask for my pity!"—DANNY KAYE after the closing of his musical *Two by Two* (1970)

"Broadway is dead, long live the new Broadway."—ELAINE STRITCH

Broadway Economics

"You can make a killing in the theater, but you can't make a living."—playwright ROBERT ANDERSON (*Tea and Sympathy, I Never Sang for My Father*)

"The Federal Theatre Project was part of a programme to provide jobs for the unemployed [and] financed over 800 different productions between 1935 and 1939. Many of them were 'living newspaper' documentaries, dealing with the plight of American farmers or the homeless. . . . [But] the level of social criticism in the 'living newspapers' eventually led to the programme being closed down."—*The Oxford Illustrated History of Theatre*

"Theater purists shouldn't scoff when somebody who's climbed up the ladder in Hollywood heads back to New York and does a play. Such a one is no less an actor . . . [and] is obviously less indolent than some, and brings in added revenue and patrons. The economics of stardom are undeniable when measured in a theater's box office."—movie and stage star JOHN GARFIELD

"The English keep producing my plays and they also keep producing Tennessee's plays and O'Neill's plays and a lot of other people's plays that never see the light of day here [in the United States] from one decade to the next. I'm not sure but that a broader audience isn't brought into the theater by the fact that the National [Theatre] exists, the prices are pretty reasonable, and so on and so forth."—playwright ARTHUR MILLER in 1996

"It's scary to have a bottom line of profit that you have to watch each week. It cost close to $170,000 a week to run *Angels in America* on Broadway. You had to sell that many tickets or more, and that got to be frightening. There are repertory theaters in Europe where *Angels* has been running now for two or three years, and it draws half audiences. But it doesn't matter. That's a much nicer way of doing it."—playwright TONY KUSHNER

"The impact of AIDS has been felt on Equity's health insurance fund, which is losing $1,000,000 a month. Changes in eligibility guidelines will be made which will leave as many as 4,500 part-time actors without health coverage."—*Variety*, February 15, 1993, pg. 89

"In February [2003], New Yorkers got their first glimpse of [Matt] Cavanaugh, his Western shirt flapping open, abs flexed as he rides a mechanical bull, on the show's posters. . . . No doubt recognizing that women and gay men are Broadway's primary ticket buyers, the producers had decided to rest the $5 million production's print-advertising campaign squarely on the broad shoulders of a [Broadway] newbie."—*Time Out New York* on the musical of the 1980 John Travolta film *Urban Cowboy*

"Each decade produces more flops than the previous decade, and for the most basic of reasons: the cost of Broadway keeps rising, so shows have to run longer to pay off. . . . The 1960s is the last decade in which the Broadway musical held a stable position in American civilization. During this time, the music changed (to rock), the status of Most Privileged Art changed (to cinema), and the capitalization minimums changed (to prohibitive)."—Broadway historian ETHAN MORDDEN

"The [1980s] was to be dominated by three imported British musicals and the talents of two English showmen: Andrew Lloyd Webber and Cameron Mackintosh [producer of *Cats, The Phantom of the Opera,* and *Les Miserables*]. . . . He introduced the limited-advance booking methods of the West End—permitting a few months' advance ticket sales to a hit show in order to keep the ticket tight—and raised the level of theater advertising to new heights. These three shows revolutionized Broadway theatergoing and cloned international companies of themselves, creating an aura of celebration regarding the original New York and London productions. . . . In the absence of exciting homegrown American musicals, the tri-state area of approximately fifteen million people selected *Cats, Les Miz,* or *Phantom* as the one [Broadway] event they had to experience on their birthday, anniversary, honeymoon, prom night, etc."—producer STUART OSTROW

"We were these mad people with a Shakespearean director [Trevor Nunn] and these boring old poems going into the worst theater in London. All the people who were our normal sources of money, 90% of them turned us down. We ended up with over 200 small investors. The show has been averaging a 200% profit since the return of capital—that's 200% per year for over 15 years."—CAMERON MACKINTOSH on *Cats*

"At the nervous London premiere, [producer] David Merrick told Mackintosh that he'd be prepared to swap the British rights to *42nd Street* for the American rights to *Cats*. It was, ostensibly, a generous offer: *42nd Street* was a proven smash. . . . But a wary Mackintosh declined, and was right to do so; by the end of 1990, *42nd Street* , Broadway's biggest hit of the '80s, had earned $10 million. *Cats's* box-office receipts were 510,809,266 pounds sterling."—author MARK STEYN in *Broadway Babies Say Goodnight*

"In terms of box-office receipts, a typical week shows 87% of the gross comes from musicals (*Variety*, February 9, 1993, p. 83). Owners of multiple theatres count on the long-running musicals for survival."—footnote from *Broadway Theatre* by ANDREW B. HARRIS

"Commerce owns theater much more than it used to. The costs are preposterous. . . . When we did *Virginia Woolf* in 1962, our total cost to open the production was $42,000. Off-Broadway, we produced Beckett's *Krapp's Last Tape* with my *Zoo Story* for $3,000."—EDWARD ALBEE in 2002

"I still say, under the right circumstances, every theater in the so-called Broadway area could be full within two or three years, if the price of tickets was brought down and a couple of other things were done. This is not some natural consequence. This is a result of a certain set of sociological courses which can be remedied."—ARTHUR MILLER in 1986

"[The mega-musical] came during a recession in England and America. Between 1970 and mid 1992, the dollar and pound had both fallen by over 65% against the D-mark and yen, and wholesale prices had risen twice as fast as in Japan and Germany. . . . [But] *Les Misérables* was advertised in the 1990s as 'The Show of All Shows' and 'The Musical Sensation.' 'Fight to get a ticket,' the public was told. . . . In 1970 the best seats for musicals in New York City were around $10, in 1980 $22.50, and in 1990 $55."—*The Oxford Illustrated History of Theatre*

"The Andrew Lloyd Webber shows were pioneers in marketing techniques like issuing the hit record before the show opened. . . . *Aspects of Love* was Webber's one Broadway flop. It lost $8 million in its New York run. . . . As with most Webber musicals, it followed up with a concert version, profitably touring the United States."—DENNIS MCGOVERN and DEBORAH GRACE WINER in the 1993 book *Sing Out, Louise!*

"The British musicals' extraordinary success continues after 16 years; they occupy the best Broadway houses and have caused a backup of productions wanting to play New York. With the exception of Stephen Sondheim, American musicals' dramatists were stifled, and the Broadway landlords did little or nothing to bolster their hopes, being contented with the prospect of having their flagship theatres filled into the millennium."—STUART OSTROW in his 1999 book *A Producer's Broadway Journey*

"The Broadway musical used to be capitalism's most joyous money-spinner. Today's musicals are the closest that business comes to fooling all of the people all of the time."—CHARLES NELSON REILLY (actor, *How to Succeed in Business Without Really Trying*; director, *The Nerd*)

"It's one of the tragic ironies of the theater that only one [person] in it can count on steady work—the night watchman."—TALLULAH BANKHEAD in her memoirs

Their All for Their Art

"*Wildcat* was a very mixed experience for me . . . If I could have done *Mame* as a musical play, it might have made the movie better. I'd have been terrified to sing and dance again on Broadway, but I'd have forced myself. I'd have given it everything. Back during *Wildcat* I didn't have a supportive husband behind me."—LUCILLE BALL

"I think most actors would literally break a leg to be in a Broadway hit show. Or an arm *and* a leg."—CAROL BURNETT

"I sweat blood when I'm on that stage. Later, I sometimes feel ten years older."—ROBERT PRESTON (*The Lion in Winter*, *The Music Man*)

"Once you become known as a functioning, contributing, and rewarded part of the Broadway scene, there's a lot less of being liked for yourself and a lot more of being disliked, or even hated, for who you are. Or more to the point, for what you've achieved."—MICHAEL BENNETT, director-choreographer (*A Chorus Line*)

"For a killer role, a really terrific comeback role and vehicle with all the right ingredients, I'd give up my house, if not its contents. . . . I wouldn't go back unless it's absolutely terrific. It's too easy to break your heart over Broadway."—ANTHONY PERKINS (*Greenwillow*)

"Whenever I've been on Broadway, I've had to try very hard to forget that I'm in a foreign country, and try to remember that the stage—an actor's home—is universal."—SIR JOHN GIELGUD

"When you sign on to be in a play, you temporarily give up the sanity in your life. Your schedule, your habits, your diet, everything—they all go out the window for the duration."—ROSIE O'DONNELL (*Grease*)

"Forget going out for lunch, for starters . . . and the ladies who lunch, or dinner parties! Part of the so-called glamour of starring on Broadway is having to eat by yourself a lot."—ETHEL MERMAN

"A play, let alone a musical, is terribly demanding. It just has to come first in your energies and attention. You can do that, for a while. Eventually, I had to put my family first. . . . It simply and unfortunately is more difficult for an actress."—ANGELA LANSBURY, four-time Tony winner

"The stage is completely absorbing. Very different from camera work. In a play you must be prepared to sacrifice your private life as well as a regular schedule. Not that I entirely sacrificed my private life, but I would have. And I've always liked my private life."—CHRISTOPHER HEWETT, of TV's *Mr. Belvedere*, who costarred in the movie *The Producers* and on Broadway in the 1959 musical *First Impressions*, based on Jane Austen's *Pride and Prejudice*

"The concentration required is just tremendous, total. This is the real acting, the essence of it. And acting on Broadway is the most paranoiac kind of theater acting. You feel as if every theatergoer in the Western world is watching you, that's all."—CHRISTOPHER REEVE (*The Fifth of July* and *A Matter of Gravity*)

"You'll more readily try something completely bizarre on Broadway than you might in a movie. I mean, makeup galore and lipstick on my nipples—I do that on Broadway (as the Emcee in *Cabaret*), but would I do it on the screen?"— ALAN CUMMING, Tony winner for *Cabaret*

"When you're starting out, you do anything, because it's Broadway. Broadway used to get national attention, automatically. . . . When you look back, it's sort of amusing how intense one was about it, and it's not even something that's permanent, like a motion picture."—BARBRA STREISAND (*Funny Girl*

"I have to give up my art for my art. When I starred in *Fiddler on the Roof*, I couldn't possibly give to my painting the same loving attention that Picasso does to his. Which is only because he doesn't have to act too."
—ZERO MOSTEL

"When I'm on stage, I am, of course, ageless. But I pay for it afterwards. It drains you . . . afterwards, I feel every year of my age. Until I'm back on stage."—BEATRICE ARTHUR (*Mame* and her own one-woman show in 2001–2002)

"I'd have given five years of my life if [*The New York Times* critic] Clive Barnes had been struck by lightning the day after he wrote that smug, bigoted review that insulted many of my theatergoers and much of the population, besides."—JOHN HERBERT, Canadian playwright. Barnes opined that if one liked Sal Mineo's production of Herbert's *Fortune and Men's Eyes*, one needed a psychiatrist. The openly gay John Herbert lived to 75.

"Broadway critics are notorious. When you're being judged by them, you'd gladly relinquish a major portion of a stellar salary for a good notice." —DIANA RIGG. John Simon famously wrote of Rigg's nude scene in *Abelard and Heloise* in 1970, "Diana Rigg is built like a brick mausoleum with insufficient flying buttresses."

"I practically go celibate when I'm performing on Broadway. It takes that much out of you."—RICHARD BURTON (*Hamlet* and *Camelot*)

"If you're not behind the scenes and not in the chorus, working on Broadway comes down to a big choice. That is, if you're gay. The choice is: your career or your integrity. It's smoother sailing if you lie and play it straight, but it's soul killing and it creates paranoia. . . . If you have a love relationship, the denials and pretense hurt you and your partner, besides. . . . At least it's not as bad as the movies, where the top Hollywood requirement, even more than looks nowadays, is lying low if you're gay or bi." —ROBERT LA TOURNEAUX, best known as Cowboy in 1968's *The Boys in the Band*

"Yes, I'm gay—when I'm on that stage. If the role required me to suck off Horst, I'd do it. But I didn't consider it a bold move."—*Rolling Stone* interview with pre-Hollywood RICHARD GERE, while he was in the Broadway production of *Bent*, about Nazi persecution of gays

2

Q&A

Q: *What is "Broadway"?*
A: Some say it's as much an invention as a geographic entity. Broadway and 42nd Street is the center of a five-block circle comprising much of the "legitimate" theater district. Writer Damon Runyon described Broadway as "a crooked and somewhat narrow street trailing from the lowest tip of Manhattan Island to the city limits of Yonkers and beyond."

"Broadway" stands for first-class theater, not that it has a monopoly on quality, and Off-Broadway—and more occasionally Off-Off-Broadway—are included in this book. Broadway was a farm with a manure dump in the early 1700s, at which time New York City already had two theaters. One represented the British Crown, the other Dutch settlers and those favoring home rule.

Q: *What's the most unusual coincidence involving a famous actor?*
A: Possibly the eeriest or most ironic coincidence involved acclaimed tragedian Edwin Booth, an elder brother of President Lincoln's assassin, John Wilkes Booth. Edwin was at a railway depot in Jersey City, en route to Philadelphia near the end of the Civil War. The conflict caused habitual crowds at train stations, and as the vehicle started to move, Edwin suddenly dropped his valise to seize a tall young man by the coat collar as he fell off the platform. Edwin hauled him up to safety. The grateful youth, recognizing the celebrity, exclaimed, "That was a narrow escape, Mr. Booth." The youth was Abraham's son Robert Lincoln.

Q: *What is a thespian?*

A: It's now a generic word for actor. But Thespis of Icaria (or Icarus) was an actual Greek actor who made his stage bow at a dramatic festival honoring the god Dionysus over 2,500 years ago and won the laurel-leaf crown. To honor this deity of wine and revelry, audiences attended plays while under the influence—even though Greek plays (and later, Roman ones) began in the morning.

Greeks called an actor "the answerer," for he responded to the chorus. Our word "hypocrite" evolved from the Greek for acting, that is, playing a part. Greek moralists often criticized actors for telling *lies*—that is, saying lines. Thespis is considered the first individualistic actor. He shifted the emphasis away from the chorus and onto the actor. He focused on tragedies and created characterization. He accustomed Greeks to plots and conflict, where previously they'd listened to recitations.

Q: *Who was the first playwright?*

A: The earliest playwright whose work has survived is Aeschylus (525?–456 B.C.E.). He reportedly wrote some 22 tetralogies, of which four complete parts of some four-parters, three quarters of one, and a few assorted fragments of others remain. Aeschylus was the first of Greek tragedy's Big Three; Sophocles and Euripides were more inclined to challenge theatrical conventions. However, before Aeschylus, Greek plays featured one actor, who played several parts in turn. This playwright initiated writing for two actors and the chorus—young Sophocles added a third actor.

Aeschylus also reduced the chorus from 50 to 12, added simple properties ("props") and painted backdrops, and introduced oratorio into drama.

Q: *How big was the Greek influence on (our) theater?*

A: It can be gauged by such words of Greek origin as: theater, drama, tragedy, comedy, also scene, episode, character, dialogue, music, mime, and chorus. Athenians called a producer "choregos," a provider of the chorus. Over the millennia, "choregos" became associated more with chorus lines and the dance. In the first half of the twentieth century choreographers were usually known as dance directors. Unlike modern producers, those of ancient Greece weren't in it for the money. Wealthier citizens were tapped to produce plays at dramatic festivals, a nonprofit honor viewed as a civic duty.

Q: *Who was the first theatergoer among English-speaking rulers?*

A: Charles II (c. 1660–1685) was the first to attend public performances. Elizabeth I (c. 1558–1603) was a theatrical devotee but didn't go public with her pleasures. From 1649 to 1660, Britain was without a monarch, ruled by Oliver Cromwell and the Puritans, religious fundamentalists who abolished the theater.

Q: *When did actors first get into trouble in the US?*
A: In 1665, three actors in the American colonies—in Accomac County, Virginia (named after Elizabeth, the Virgin Queen)—were arrested for putting on a play. *Ye Beare and Ye Cubbe* was written by one of the trio, which was acquitted. Christianity generally frowned on plays; any entertainment not devised or controlled by the Church was suspect. Also, European Puritans didn't move to America so much for religious freedom—which they usually had at home—as for the ability to impose their minority religious views on others.

P.S. Virginia was less fanatical than several other colonies, hence the acquittal on the potentially grave charge of mounting a play.

Q: *We know that colonial America, influenced by the Puritans, was anti-theater. Did this change after independence?*
A: Some. Henry Ward Beecher was a famous preacher and pamphleteer in 1870s America. In his thundering sermons he often denounced theatergoing as a "sin"—never mind that he became involved in an adultery scandal. But during one sermon, he admitted to the lesser sin, declaring, "Yes, I have been to the theater." Jaws dropped. "Mr. Beecher," he repeated, "has been to the theater. Now, if you will all wait until you are past seventy years of age and will then go and see Joseph Jefferson in *Rip Van Winkle*, I venture the risk that it will not affect your eligibility for heaven, if you do nothing worse."

P.S. One of Beecher's sisters became more lastingly famous: Harriet Beecher Stowe wrote the anti-slavery novel *Uncle Tom's Cabin*. Abraham Lincoln called her "the little woman who wrote the book that started this great war!"

Q: *When did performance spaces shift from outdoor to indoor?*
A: Greek and Roman amphitheaters were, of course, open air. And matinees meant just that: performances commenced in the morning. By the Elizabethan era, public theaters—like Shakespeare's Globe—were partly open to the heavens, and performances began in the afternoon. Renaissance Europe favored the comfort of indoor shows, which no matter the time of day necessitated developing the art of stage lighting.

Q: *Who was the most famous actress with the shortest career?*
A: Nell Gwyn (1650–1687), who acted for six years. Purportedly the daughter of a madam and possibly herself a prostitute, she was for a time an orange seller at London's famous Drury Lane Theatre. At fourteen she debuted on stage. She earned fame playing fast women—for, as Mrs. Patrick Campbell, another English actress, said a few hundred years later, "A good woman is a dramatic impossibility."

Gwyn also got laughs in comedy and excelled at "trouser roles" (wearing male clothing). But when Charles II chose her for his mistress, she left the stage for good (if not for good). Nell continued building her fortune, though on his deathbed Charles supposedly implored his brother, next in line to the throne, "Don't let poor Nelly starve." At Gwyn's death, she was worth £100,000, or some $6 million today.

Q: *Did anyone ever become a Broadway star via a striptease?*
A: Of course it was a mock striptease, but dancer Joan McCracken, who'd appeared in *Oklahoma!*, became a star in choreographer Agnes de Mille's 1944 hit *Bloomer Girl*. McCracken played a maid-of-all-work and performed a comical 1861-style striptease that audiences loved. A mock strip had also made a star of Mary Martin in the 1938 *Leave It to Me*, via Cole Porter's vampy "My Heart Belongs to Daddy."

P.S. McCracken was at one point married to Bob Fosse, later to fellow dancer and future novelist Jack Dunphy. When novelist Truman Capote met Dunphy, he was smitten and determined to have him. Capote theorized that anyone, if you concentrated on that person long and intensely enough, could be *had*. Dunphy left McCracken and the stage, and he and Capote became a couple for the rest of their lives.

Q: *Who was the oldest practicing playwright?*
A: George Bernard Shaw (1856–1950), at ninety-three. But his 1949 play *Buoyant Billions* was not a hit.

Q: *Who was the father of the American musical?*
A: Don't assume. Some would say the "father" was a mother: playwright-actress-novelist-lyricist Susanna Haswell Rowson (1762–1824). Only one of her plays exists in its entirety. By age twenty, she'd failed as a governess, so being of a literary bent, she wrote *Victoria*, an epistolary novel. Her most popular book, *Charlotte Temple*, was continuously in print from 1795 to 1906, with two further printings after World War II. But though the novel had over two hundred editions, it didn't make Ms. Rowson rich, for there were no copyright laws then, and royalties didn't exist.

The Englishwoman eventually found herself on the stage in the new United States. That led to writing plays, one of which was *Slaves in Algiers; or, a Struggle for Freedom* (1794), a farce with music. Via this work, set on the Barbary Coast of what is now Libya and involving American sailors captured and enslaved by Muslim pirates, Rowson became—on June 30, 1794—the first female playwright to be produced professionally in America, and "the mother of the American musical." (The musical's events were based on real-life ones.

The pirates sent a demand for ransom to Congress; the US refused, and finally American forces headed "to the shores of Tripoli.")

Susanna Haswell Rowson died in Boston in 1824, her theatrical successes long past, but her personally unprofitable novels still widely read. Sadly, her pioneering and musicals had never been held in high esteem; rather than being reviewed on their own merits they'd been treated as novelties, remarkable chiefly because of their distaff authorship

P.S. The first American actor to go into politics was, of course, a stage actor. John Howard Payne had also been a prolific playwright and was one of the first American actors to star in England, as Hamlet (age twenty-two). His play *The Fall of Algiers* was inspired by an incident in Susanna Rowson's *Slaves in Algiers*, but he's best remembered for the song "Home, Sweet Home," from his play *Clari, the Maid of Milan*. Payne became American consul to Tripoli once it re-established diplomatic relations with the USA.

Q: *Since* Chicago *was based on a real story, why wasn't this musical done sooner, especially since there had been a movie starring Ginger Rogers as* Roxie Hart *in 1942?*
A: The antics of two murderesses inspired a 1920s Broadway comedy and the '40s film—not one of Rogers's big hits—but wasn't generally viewed as the stuff of musical comedy, which until *Cabaret* (1966) was a typically light and fluffy genre. Besides, rights to redo *Chicago* were held by *Chicago Tribune* reporter Maurine Dallas Watkins, whose headline had read "Woman Plays Air Jazz as Victim Dies." After she became a fundamentalist Christian she refused anyone seeking to resurrect her play, *Chicago*, which she felt glamorized and trivialized murder. When Watkins died a recluse worth $2 million in 1969, she had so faded from memory that the *New York Times* ran no obituary.

Of course the perfect composer-lyricist team to bring *Chicago* to Broadway in the 1970s was Kander and Ebb, who'd done the dark and acclaimed *Cabaret*. *Chicago*'s initial reviews during its out-of-town Philadelphia run were negative, but Philly audiences liked it, and it became a bigger hit after returning to the Great White Way in 1996—it's currently the longest-running revival in Broadway history. (The film version won the Best Picture Academy Award in 2003.)

Q: *Do all composers accept that it goes with the territory when a song is dropped from a musical prior to its New York opening?*
A: Songs are routinely dropped. Some composers protest, most are resigned to it, and some seem to comply sweetly, like Jerry Herman. But some object vigorously, no one more so than lyricist Carolyn Leigh. She and composer Cy Coleman did the music for *Little Me* (1962), based on Patrick Dennis's post–*Auntie Mame* novel. Coleman decided during a Philadelphia tryout to drop a song, whereupon the enraged Leigh left the theater, found the nearest police-

man, and dragged him backstage, where she demanded he arrest Coleman. (This, during a performance.) It was Coleman and Leigh's last show together.

Q: *What was the oddest musical ever?*
A: Oddity is in the mind of the beholder, but *Lieutenant* is surely a contender. The 1975 rock opera focused on the massacre by American forces at My Lai during the Vietnam War. Its songs included "Kill" and "Massacre." It lasted nine performances.

Q: *Who "invented" musical comedy?*
A: The consensus is Jacques Offenbach. Before he left his native Cologne for Paris in 1833, musical theater was usually opera or its imitators, or carnival playlets performed with new lyrics on traditional melodies. Thus, a German invented musical comedy in France, and Broadway perfected it, specifically via Jewish, gay, and/or European-émigré composers.

Q: *Is a musical's title crucial to its success?*
A: Basically, a rose is a rose. A 1925 musical originally titled *My Fair Lady* became *Tell Me More* (who remembers that?), while *Lady Liza* and *The Talk of London* was finally called *My Fair Lady* (1956). Would the originally intended *East Side Story* have been any less successful than *West Side Story*? Or the mega-flop *Breakfast at Tiffany's* have been any more successful under its first moniker of *Holly Golightly*?

Q: *Who was Broadway's most prolific and successful librettist?*
A: Harry B. Smith was the most prolific. He had three hundred shows and six thousand songs. But how successful was he? Today his one somewhat-remembered song is "The Sheik of Araby," typically heard as an instrumental, minus Smith's lyrics. In most businesses, quantity and quality aren't synonymous. In his heyday, Smith wasn't as celebrated as several of his less-prodigious contemporaries.

Q: *What theatrical agent had the longest career?*
A: Nat Day (1886–1982) began his stage career in variety in 1898, then went into the agency business in 1904 and stayed in it for seventy-seven years. Coincidentally, he at one time shared an office floor on London's Oxford Street with the later-discovered serial killer Dr. Crippen, and actually booked Crippen's wife for various engagements.

Q: *Why is wearing green in a play considered bad luck?*
A: Before the twentieth century, a green spotlight, or "limelight," was used to

pick out the star. If said star wore green, the result was semi-invisibility—the true actor's nightmare.

Q: *Why do actors consider* Macbeth *such an unlucky play?*
A: Many productions of "the Scottish play," as it's referred to by those who won't say its name, have been plagued by injuries, disasters, even deaths. Sir John Gielgud's 1942 production saw the deaths of four actors. (Its designer later killed himself.) *Macbeth* is associated with black magic, and to quote from it in an actor's dressing room is deemed very unlucky. The antidote is to go outside, turn around three times, spit, knock thrice on the door, and beg readmittance. (This is also the antidote, minus spitting, for whistling in a dressing room.)

Q: *Did an actor ever kill a critic?*
A: Probably not. But in 1936 Orson Welles staged *Macbeth* for the Negro Division of the Federal Theatre. The setting was switched to the Caribbean, and the witches' magic to voodoo. After a scathing review by Percy Hammond of the *New York Herald Tribune*, some of the cast held an all-night voodoo ceremony to get back at Hammond. Three days later he died.

Q: *Was a critic ever actually killed?*
A: Yes, but it was in France in 1945 and Robert Brasillach had collaborated with the Germans. While a critic and editor, he'd called for the executions of Resistance actors and vented his anti-Semitic hatred. He was finally executed at the fort of Montrogue, France, aged 35.

Q: *Who is or was the most mean-spirited Broadway critic?*
A: It's not John Simon—surprise. By consensus, it seems to have been one William Winter, the *New York Tribune*'s drama critic from 1865 to 1909. One reason for his ongoing grouch may have been his weekly salary of $50, the least of any head of a New York paper's drama department. Besides his dubious taste, Winter had many hates, including foreigners. Such great European actresses as Duse, Bernhardt, and Rejane he labeled and libeled as "foreign strumpets," and the pioneering Norwegian playwright Henrik Ibsen he deemed "a reformer who calls you to crawl with him into a sewer, merely to see and breathe its feculence."

Speaking of bigotry, the often-sour Heywood Broun detested *Abie's Irish Rose*, a comedy about a Jewish-Catholic marriage. In 1922 he wrote that it was "So cheap and offensive that it might serve to unite all the races of the world in a common hymn of hate." Broun was certain, or hoped, it would be a flop. The record-breaker ran for 2,327 performances and was revived in 1954.

Q: *Apart from losing money, did a flop play ever set a record?*

A: The longest-running flop in theater history was *The Ladder* (1926), a drama of reincarnation. It ran for seventeen months in New York—at a loss of a then-monumental $750,000—because it was backed by Texas oil tycoon Edgar B. Davis. By late 1927 tickets were free, yet *The Ladder* played to mostly empty houses. Undaunted, Davis later opened it again in Boston. Wags called it the play that wouldn't die.

Q: *Is there any way of telling that a play will be bad?*

A: George Jean Nathan, critic for the *American Mercury*, *Vanity Fair*, *Newsweek*, *Theatre Arts*, etcetera, believed there were various giveaways, such as: "When, as the curtain goes up, you hear newsboys shouting, 'Extra, extra!'" Or "The moment anyone puts anything into a drawer with a furtive look." And "Any mystery play in which, at the very start, someone remarks that the nearest house is two miles away." Plus "In four cases out of five, when at the rise of the curtain the wife is writing a letter and the husband, in an easy chair, is reading a newspaper."

Nathan eschewed one-star shows, particularly the one-woman variety: "A woman talking steadily for two hours is hardly my idea of entertainment whether in the theater or in private." In the wake of *Oklahoma!*'s success, he noted, "It seems that the moment anyone gets hold of an exclamation point these days, he probably sits down and writes a musical show around it." About improvisation he felt, "An actor without a playwright is like a hole without a doughnut."

Known to friends as difficult, to others as impossible, Nathan held that "No chronically happy man is a trustworthy critic."

Q: *Why are classics that get made into musicals often given new titles?*

A: Sometimes it's obvious, as with Henry Fielding's *Rape Upon Rape*, which became *Lock Up Your Daughters* (1959). Or T.S. Eliot's *Old Possum's Book of Practical Cats*—just *Cats* was more practical. In some cases, an original word was judged noncommercial, like "prejudice" in Jane Austen's *Pride and Prejudice*, which became *First Impressions* in 1959. Or "cry" in Alan Paton's *Cry the Beloved Country*, which became the lyrical *Lost in the Stars* (1949).

It's frequently assumed most people have forgotten or never knew the original sources, which some Broadway producers view as free material with time-tested value. On the other hand, whose bright idea was it to rename the still-popular and beloved *Little Women* *A Girl Called Jo*?

Q: *How could a musical of* Gone with the Wind *fail to be a financial success?*

A: The musical version, which made its American bow in Los Angeles, closed en route to Broadway, a fiasco in its native land. In 1966 a nonmusical play of

Margaret Mitchell's novel had its world premiere in Tokyo, in a nine-hour production. It was a huge hit. The Japanese who owned the stage rights to the book then decided a musical *GWTW* might be as or even more popular. They commissioned Harold Rome to compose it and Joe Layton to stage it. It opened in Japan in 1970 as *Scarlett*.

It was next unleashed on the West: In 1972 *Gone with the Wind* opened in London, not New York, because of lower costs and less-caustic critics. Though the musical version had returned to the better-recognized title, it was still minus the film's extremely famous theme music. The critics were divided, but Londoners made up their own minds, and *GWTW* ran a year, thanks partly to out-of-towners and tourists. Predictably, the clutch of American critics who went to London to review it slammed it. Even so, an American debut in Atlanta was planned.

Instead it opened in 1973 in LA, then San Francisco, with Lesley Ann Warren as Scarlett and former *Bonanza* star Pernell Roberts as Rhett Butler. A ten-city tour was planned, with a Broadway opening in 1974. However, the British producer was reportedly horrified by the dreadful west coast reviews, and *GWTW* didn't leave California (although in 1976 it opened in Dallas and toured three cities before sinking).

The US and UK musical ran two and a half hours, versus the 222-minute movie and the four-hour Japanese *Scarlett*. Many people agreed that June Ritchie in London gave a magnificent performance as Scarlett, Broadway historian Ken Mandelbaum even claiming that it rivaled Vivien Leigh's—repeated eight times weekly. The fact remains that huge numbers of people in Tokyo, London, and elsewhere enjoyed the musical (also, in Japan, the nonmusical), but New Yorkers, excepting a handful of professional hard-boiled eggs, didn't get a chance to see or enjoy for themselves.

Q: *What was the longest consecutive performance in one role?*
A: One tends to think of Yul Brynner, post-Hollywood, returning to the stage in *The King and I* over and over again. But this record is held by James O'Neill (1848–1920), father of playwright Eugene. He enacted the Count of Monte Cristo over six thousand times between 1883 and '91, then returned to the role in later life.

Q: *Why was Eugene O'Neill sometimes called the only major playwright on Broadway?*
A: Because he was born in Times Square on October 16, 1888, at 43rd Street and Broadway, at the Barrett House (later the Cadillac Hotel). Much of his childhood was spent in hotels while his father toured.

Q: *Do nonprofessional playwrights ever have big successes with a play or plays?*
A: Everyone from Picasso to Pope John Paul II has tried their hand at writing a play—and getting it produced. Though there are occasional fluke successes—e.g., comic actor Steve Martin—generally the successful playwright is a full-time professional. In his *Desire Caught by the Tail*, Picasso made all of his characters die at the end from inhaling the fumes of fried potatoes. Friends who attended the Spaniard's play agreed that Pablo should stick to his day job.

Q: *Who was the first female manager of an important American theatre and what's her relationship to a current movie star?*
A: Louisa Lane Drew (1820–1897) began as a child actress and married her third husband—fellow thespian John Drew—in 1850. She mothered two actors—another John Drew and Georgiana Drew. "Georgie" married pugilist-turned-actor/playwright Maurice Barrymore, and gave birth to three stars: Lionel, Ethel, and John Barrymore—the latter grandfather to Drew Barrymore, who began as a child actor. For thirty years beginning in 1861, Louisa ran her own theatre, the Arch Street, in Philadelphia, and appeared opposite leading actors like Edwin Booth and Irish comedian Tyrone Power. She was a much-admired actress-manager, capable in all aspects of her business, such as carpentry, in which she sometimes instructed apprentices.

Q: *Who founded the first American acting "dynasty"?*
A: It wasn't long-lived, and it wasn't the first, but the Booth family had a significant impact. Junius Brutus Booth (1796–1852) was English, like most of 19th-century America's celebrated actors. He was father to Junius Brutus Jr. (1821–1883), Edwin (1833–1893), and John Wilkes (1839–1865). Fortunately for Junius Sr., he didn't live to see his youngest son become a presidential assassin. Booth *père* was an alcoholic and sometime rowdy. His aquiline profile was renowned, but in his 40s his nose was broken during a fight. Post-Profile, a fan told Booth she couldn't "get over" his nose. He snapped back, "No wonder, madame, for the bridge is gone."

John Wilkes Booth was killed soon after murdering Abraham Lincoln. His act drove his much-more successful brother from the stage for four years. Edwin Booth was one of the first American actors to earn an international reputation and become a star in England, where Stateside actors were considered second-rate. In 1869 Booth opened the $1 million Booth Theatre in New York City, which showcased him in Shakespearean roles. Its failure bankrupted the actor in 1873 and he had to tour extensively in the United States and United Kingdom, specializing in Shakespeare.

Edwin's Gramercy Park home became headquarters for The Players, the club he founded that was a combination social haven (gossip was officially discouraged) and museum of theatrical heirlooms. It later produced theatricals featuring professional actors, and helped separate Edwin's reputation and Shakespearean legacy from his brother's murderous rage. (Booth was biographed in the 1954 film *Prince of Players*, starring Richard Burton.) One of Edwin's closest friends was the scion of an equally long-lived major acting dynasty: comedian Joseph Jefferson III, famous for his portrayal of Rip Van Winkle.

Q: *Isn't nepotism much less common on Broadway than in Hollywood?*
A: Less, anyway, and more often behind the scenes. For instance, take the 1964 28-show-a-week musical spectacular *Wonderworld*, which played the New York World's Fair for 250 performances. It costarred Chita Rivera and Gretchen Wyler, with music by Jule Styne. The lyrics were by his older son, Stanley—the son also musicalizes.

Oscar Hammerstein II had a producer brother named Reginald, likewise Angela Lansbury, whose brother Edgar produced *Godspell* and her turn as Mama Rose in *Gypsy* (music by Jule Styne, lyrics by the unrelated Stephen Sondheim).

Q: *Who was America's first star actress?*
A: Charlotte Cushman (1816–1876) was an assertive eldest child who hated housework and had no desire to wed. At eighteen she went into opera, acting as well as singing her roles, unlike more stationary divas. Then she lost her singing voice. She took to the dramatic stage—due to her plain looks, romantic parts were out—and broke through, with cheering audiences and glowing reviews, as Lady Macbeth in 1835. In 1837 she joined the Park Theatre, then New York's most prestigious company, bowing as Patrick in *The Poor Soldier*. But four years later she was stuck mostly in secondary roles.

She quit and moved to London, where she became a star on her debut, which one reviewer claimed surpassed anything seen there since the talent of Edmund Kean thirty years before. Besides Lady Macbeth, Cushman essayed Cardinal Wolsey in Shakespeare's *Henry VIII* and Hamlet in Edwin Booth's borrowed tights. When she returned to the United States after five years, her British stardom made her a welcomed celebrity, and she went from triumph to triumph. Cushmania peaked in 1852 when she gave her farewell performances and moved to Rome.

Though rich, she continued acting in Europe. At her final performance, shortly before she died from cancer in 1876, a tribute was bestowed upon America's greatest actress, with William Cullen Bryant presenting her with a laurel wreath. Cushman's passing garnered headlines around the world. Half a century later, she was the first member of her profession to be inducted into the Theatrical Hall of Fame. She was the first American actor to be as highly regarded as an English actor. She eschewed the usual histrionics and ad-libbing of the era for *felt* and disciplined acting. Cushman was initially thought eccentric because she insisted upon play rehearsals. She may also have been the first to institutionalize curtain calls.

P.S. Like some twentieth-century actresses, Charlotte Cushman wore men's clothes offstage. In the 1800s this caused tremendous comment. Yet she didn't camouflage her nature by presenting men to the public as "beaux." The press played down her relationships, various of which Elizabeth Barrett Browning termed "female marriages." Yes, Virginia, America's first star was a lesbian.

Q: *Was Agnes de Mille's dream ballet in* Oklahoma! *(1943) the first?*
A: From its Freudian influence and how much has been written about it, one would think so, but it wasn't. George Balanchine used a dream ballet in 1936 in *On Your Toes.* There was one in the 1937 *Babes in Arms* and in 1938 in *I Married an Angel,* whose title ran afoul of censors objecting to the idea of fornication with a heavenly being. *Pal Joey* (1940) and *Lady in the Dark* (1941) also featured dream ballets, but thanks to *Oklahoma!*'s impact they became a staple into the 1960s. (Their waning popularity paralleled Freud's.)

As realism crept in, as exemplified by shows like *Pal Joey* and *Cabaret,* audiences were less willing to accept different actors playing the same characters, i.e., Laurey and Curly and a Dream Laurey and Dream Curly.

Q: *Which musical conventions are now extinct?*
A: Besides dream ballets, the scene "in one": a scene played in front of a traveler curtain while behind it the scenery is changed. Technology obviated the need, and today's audiences are used to watching a set change or move before their eyes. Also, musicals feature less dancing today. Television has shortened attention spans, but also, the more realistic the musical, the less dance fits in. Dancing in contemporary musicals typically requires an aggressive and/or erotic edge, else it seems hopelessly old-fashioned.

Q: *Don't good reviews help a theatrical career?*
A: Theatrical success is more dependent on good notices than is success in the movies. But consistently good reviews can indicate boredom or being taken for granted. Peggy Wood, best remembered as Mother Abbess in the film version of *The Sound of Music* (she "sang"—dubbed—"Climb Every Mountain"), enjoyed "a wonderful career on the stage," working with the greats and doing important plays. She noted, "I was very lucky and even renowned for my good reviews. I never really got a terrible one." But Wood never became a stage star. Sometimes controversy, or at least variety, helps.

Q: *Do all theatrical producers yearn for hits and hope to avoid flops?*
A: In today's more complicated fiscal arena, it's not so simple. Mega-musical producer Cameron Mackintosh—openly gay yet Britain's highest-paid subject—admits that during a premiere's intermission, "I retreat to the bar and pray that it will be a mega-disaster so I can pull it off straight away. The worst thing to have in the theater is a near success." Macintosh produced *Cats, Les Misérables, The Phantom of the Opera,* and *Miss Saigon,* but also, for example, *Moby Dick,* which sank almost without a trace.

Q: *Has an actress ever beaten up a producer?*
A: The aptly named June Havoc, the former Dainty June and Mama Rose's real-life daughter, did when the 1944 musical *Sadie Thompson* closed prematurely. The closing notice went up on New Year's Eve. She recalled: "[A.P. Waxman] was a little man; everyone loathed him. On closing night, he called the cast out onto the stage. I did not come out of my dressing room. Then the little man made the mistake of coming to my room.

"I don't know what it triggered in me, but he started toward me and I closed the door, locked it, and let him have it. I beat him unmercifully. I was taken to the hospital. . . . They gave me a sedative, and when I came to, people from the company were sitting there waiting—they were taking shifts. They had *all* wanted to beat him up."

Q: *What was the most scandalous thing Tallulah Bankhead ever did?*
A: The "Alabama Foghorn" was outrageous, outspoken, exhibitionistic (a flasher even in her sixties), and almost-openly bisexual in *those* days. Her biographies read like glamorous soap opera. Probably Tallulah's most then-shocking public gesture was deciding not to wear stockings on stage in 1919 during a particularly hot New York summer night. Producer Lee Shubert begged her not to so affront "public decency," but she did, receiving hisses, mostly from women.

Through the 1920s Bankhead was an ongoing hit in London. When stage veteran Mrs. Patrick Campbell (her actual billing) was asked the source of Tallu's West End success, she declared, "She's always skating on thin ice—and the British public wants to be there when it breaks."

Q: *Who were the Shuberts?*
A: Brothers Sam, Lee, and Jacob were Lithuanian immigrants to Syracuse, New York. Sam died prematurely in 1905. Lee and "Jake" (or J.J.) helped break the power of the Theatrical Syndicate or Trust, which had almost monopolized show business in the US. The Shuberts' theater empire became the largest ever. The brothers' business savvy and their penchant for real estate gave them

unrivaled theatrical power. Predictably, they put the bottom line before art and were eventually referred to as a near-monopoly.

Lee was a big fan of Sarah Bernhardt—whose 1906 American tour he sponsored—not only for her talent but for her business acumen. Years later, he would often recount, "English she couldn't talk. English she couldn't pronounce. But, boy, could she count in English!"

Q: *How was the stranglehold of the infamous Trust broken?*
A: In 1895 six powerful businessmen joined forces to seize control of the American stage, not just in New York. Their Theatrical Syndicate all but took over the supply-and-demand ends of show biz by booking nearly all the acts and players and by owning or controlling almost all the theaters. By eliminating competition the Syndicate could fix prices. As growing urban populations' demand for live entertainment increased, the sextet's greed did too, and ticket prices went up while performers' salaries and production costs were slashed.

The Trust intimidated star after star into signing with it. One lone actress-manager consistently stood against them: Minnie Maddern Fiske (1865–1932). For twelve years the star toured under adverse conditions, sometimes acting in a tent. Yet people flocked to see her. She chose controversial plays and performed in a boldly naturalistic style. Fiske made plays by Ibsen acceptable and successful in the US, even when dealing with a volatile topic like divorce in *A Doll's House.*

The energetic and progressive Fiske opposed bullfighting and clubbing seals to death for their fur, and almost single-handedly rescued the snowy egret from extinction after its feathers became popular on women's hats. She shamed society ladies into giving up egret feathers, and within one season the fashion for them died. The publicity resulted in laws to ensure the birds' protection.

Fiske's allies against the Trust were impresario David Belasco and the brothers Shubert, who quietly bought up individual theaters as they became available (sometimes using other names). The embryonic Shubert empire was shaky and heavily mortgaged; to enable the brothers to retain their theater network, Minnie Maddern Fiske agreed to use her drawing power on tour in their mutual war on the syndicate. Ironically, the woman later nicknamed the Trust-Buster would live to see the Shuberts become almost as monopolistic on Broadway as the Trust had been.

Finally, a telegram from Manhattan was sent to Fiske while she was performing in Cincinnati, offering her the use of any Trust theater she cared to occupy, and on independent terms. The monopoly was broken, marking the moral highpoint of a shining forty-five-year career that earned Fiske the significant title of "First Lady of the American Theater."

Q: *Did a musical ever have its premiere in the Yukon?*
A: The 1964 Broadway flop *Foxy*, starring veteran ham Bert Lahr (the Cowardly Lion in *The Wizard of Oz*), did open and play seven whole weeks in the remote, frozen Yukon. Why? *Foxy*, inspired by Ben Jonson's *Volpone* (1616), was set in that area, and Canada was pushing tourism to the Yukon, so it co-produced and opened the show. Canadian-born star Beatrice Lillie was chosen to show up and introduce *Foxy* on opening night in far-off Dawson City.

Playing in the middle of nowhere, with a skimpy population and few tourists even on weekends, the musical saw mostly empty houses. Fading star Lahr was at loggerheads with much of the cast and crew. He mugged and ad-libbed madly, trying to completely dominate the show. When it reached New York Lahr won critical raves and a Tony Award, but few younger audience members—he was celebrating his fiftieth year in show business. *Foxy* was his Broadway swansong.

As for playing the frozen north, Lahr declared, "*You kon* have it, buster!"

Q: *Was Mitch "Man of La Mancha" Leigh a one-hit wonder?*
A: Most Broadway composers used to have several hit songs, but Leigh had "The Impossible Dream." Period. However, he'd previously worked in advertising where he had created another hit "song": "Nobody doesn't like Sara Lee."

Q: *Why is Broadway gayer than Hollywood?*
A: Because the stage is more of an actor's medium, and it's from a distance. The camera specializes in outer personality, gestures, stereotypes, and reaching mass audiences versus a more sophisticated and tolerant urban audience. As to why so many performers are gay, Sir Ian McKellen (a Tony winner) explains, "We learn to start acting, to start passing, as children and teens, as soon as we realize we're different."

Why are so many gays creative and artistic? Novelist-playwright Truman Capote believed, "We channel our creative instincts into our surroundings and the world itself, not just into reproducing. We want to make the world more attractive and kinder, more wonderful. . . . Theatre's the best and easiest place to pretend."

Q: *What proportion of Broadway is gay?*
A: Who can say for certain? But theatre columnist and author Mark Steyn offers, "On the basis of my own unscientific research, I would say that, of the longest-running shows of the 1940s, some two-thirds had a homosexual contribution in the writing/staging/producing department. By the 1960s, the proportion of long-runners with a major homosexual contribution was up to about ninety percent."

Leonard Bernstein once apprised a friend, "To be a successful composer of musicals, you either have to be Jewish or gay. And I'm both."

Q: *Did someone ever commit suicide to ruin a theatrical premiere?*
A: The playwright Congreve wrote, "Hell hath no fury like a woman scorned." Rachel Roberts's dramatic promise was subsumed by her marriage to superstar Rex Harrison. After he left her (he had six wives, and mistress-actress Carole Landis's suicide in 1948 nearly cost him his Hollywood career), Roberts's life went downhill. She yearned for a remarriage; friends said she'd been more in love with Harrison's Portofino villa than with the testy actor himself. But Rex refused, and the already suicide-prone actress planned to kill herself in time to spoil his much-heralded return to Hollywood in a revival of *My Fair Lady.*

That production took in the largest amount of money for a single week of any show until that time: $409,884, at the 2,699-seat Pantages Theatre in January 1981. Rachel had intended to grab the newspaper headlines for herself and in so doing remind the town and industry of the Landis suicide. But her Hispanic gardener didn't show up to discover her body on the appointed day, and the LA coroner, despite Roberts's precautions, didn't at first believe it was suicide. After all, she was in her fifties, and British.

Q: *Was Irving Berlin the greatest-ever Broadway composer?*
A: He was one of the all-time greats, and one of few, like Cole Porter, who wrote both words and music. As a pianist, he wasn't good and played only in one key, F sharp. Nor did he actually *write* his music; he dictated tunes to an assistant. He'd become a composer via misunderstanding: when asked to deliver a *lyric*, the Russian (born Israel Balin) thought he also had to compose the melody.

Berlin lived long enough—1888–1989—to become a legend in his own time, but early on wasn't that universally esteemed. When Berlin, a Jew, married Ellin Mackay, she was expelled from the Social Register, whose editor sniffed, "Irving Berlin has no place in society." Berlin's wife's eighteen-year-old sister lived with a Nazi diplomat and undiplomatically showed off her charm bracelet with a diamond swastika to her brother-in-law.

Berlin, who wound up agnostic, composed America's most widely played secular yuletide song, "White Christmas," and the most popular Easter song, "Easter Parade." He also created "God Bless America," whose royalties go to the officially homophobic Boy Scouts of America (the British-founded group's UK branch is not anti-gay).

Q: *Who made the most money from a play in the shortest time?*
A: Noel Coward claimed to have dashed off *Private Lives* (1930) in a few days. Anne Nichols wrote *Abie's Irish Rose* (1922) in three days (in her twen-

ties). The "sentimental comedy" supporting religious tolerance (a Jewish-Irish couple) broke Broadway's record for longest-running play and held it for fourteen years, though for three years producers had declined it. Nichols eventually used her own house for collateral to help finance her play. Though she's barely remembered today, the *New York Times* recorded in 1962 that *Abie's Irish Rose* "brought its author spectacular fame and fortune, earning her more money than any single play has ever earned a writer."

Q: *When did music become more than mere entertainment on Broadway?*
A: One of the benchmarks was December 27, 1927, in *Show Boat*, by Jerome Kern and Oscar Hammerstein II, when the first-night Manhattan audience got a shock that made several gasp: the curtain rose on a chorus of sweating black stevedores loading cotton while singing, "Niggers all work on the Mississippi. Niggers all work while the white folks play. . . ." The two Jewish artists confronted theatergoers with an aspect of American life that they'd preferred not to think about, let alone paid to learn more about. The musical, which dealt with interracial love and became an instant, often-revived classic, was based on the novel by best-seller Edna Ferber (*So Big, Giant*).

Q: *On a lighter note, what about musicals and swimming pools?*
A: Though *Miss Saigon* boasted an actual helicopter, it wasn't until 1952, in *Wish You Were Here*, that a swimming pool was put onstage in a musical. Alas, most critics found it shallow. Conversely, the first musical to take place *in* a swimming pool—at Yale—was the Burt Shevelove–Stephen Sondheim adaptation of *The Frogs*, an ancient Greek classic which most critics found too deep.

P.S. The first musical to feature electric light was *Evangeline*, in 1888, with personal supervision by Thomas Edison.

Q: *Who was the unluckiest American stage performer ever?*
A: It had to be Laura Keene, a renowned actress with her own company. Her biggest hit was *Our American Cousin*, of which a benefit for her one-thousandth performance as Florence Trenchard would take place on April 14, 1865, in Washington, D.C. The event would include the farewell performance of "clown consummate" Harry Hawkes as Asa Trenchard. Since the recently ended Civil War, theaters had reopened, and this gala occasion would find President Lincoln and his wife, Mary, in attendance.

The comedy was heartily and gratefully received. Laughter erupted after Asa bawled, "Well, I guess I know enough to turn you inside out, old gal—you sockdologizing old man trap!" At that moment, the door behind the presidential theater box opened while the guard assigned to the Chief Executive was in the bar drinking whiskies. Disgruntled actor and Southern fanatic John

Wilkes Booth aimed a .44 derringer at Abraham Lincoln's head and fired once at point-blank range. Booth then jumped down to the stage, shocking the actors into petrification while much of the audience wondered if this were a planned entertainment. Despite a leg injured in the dramatic leap, Booth got away—for the time being.

Lincoln's assassination ruined the career of Laura Keene, one of the first American women to head an acting company. She and her company were punished via guilt by association. John's brother Edwin was forced into temporary retirement. Theaters across the country were closed, and hundreds of actors lost their livelihoods, as preachers and newspapers denounced the entire profession as heading for hell. As recently as the 1960s when actor Ronald Reagan ran for California governor, his rival proclaimed that, "An actor killed Lincoln."

After Lincoln died, before dawn, Laura Keene and her fellow actors were arrested for conspiracy. Although Edwin Booth later made a comeback, Keene tired of fighting the taint of Lincoln's assassination. Her fortunes dwindled in her remaining eight years, and she briefly found work as a lecturer, dying of consumption in 1873 at fifty-four. One of Keene's theatrical innovations had been spending significantly on advertising. J.H. Stoddard, a popular actor of the era, deemed her "the greatest stage manager I have ever known." In 1867 she was one of the first American managers to encourage native talent by offering the then-considerable sum of $1,000 for the best play written by an American.

P.S. John Wilkes Booth's violent action hurt numerous individuals outside of the theater, as well. One was a Dr. Mudd, at whose home the fleeing assassin stopped to have his broken leg set. Mudd had no idea who Booth was or what he'd done. But after the episode came to light, the doctor was imprisoned for life, his sentence eventually commuted because of his services at the jail during an epidemic. The innocent physician's predicament gave rise to the popular expression, "Your name is Mudd."

Q: *Who is or was the most sexual personality on Broadway?*
A: Some may have matched director-choreographer Bob Fosse in quantity, but no one probably surpassed him. Richard Adler, composer of *Damn Yankees*, stated, "There is nobody who knows anything about Fosse who doesn't know about his sex life. He made it very public; he just didn't care. How he portrayed himself in [the film] *All That Jazz* is playing down what he was really like. This man was sexually insatiable!"

Q: *Was* Carrie *the musical really as bad as they still say?*
A: On a superficial level, *Carrie* resembled a more recent teen-centered movie-into-musical, *Hairspray*. Of course, the latter doesn't have a blood-spattered heroine or a religious-fanatic mother whom she offs by fadeout.

Carrie's unlikely source was Stephen King's 1974 novel, made into a hit film in 1976. Betty Buckley, the movie's kindly gym teacher, enacted Carrie's monster mom in the Broadway musical twelve years later.

Carrie was the most expensive flop in Broadway history, losing $8 million for its British and West German investors. First performed in England, it originally starred Barbara Cook, who had the insight or luck to bolt the production pre-Broadway. (Reviews were terrible, and a stage accident reportedly almost decapitated her.) Cook had been attracted by the music. The Broadway reviews, even worse than the British ones, focused more on the plot and dramatics than the score or the elaborate staging.

The show aimed too (non-) squarely at the MTV crowd rather than average theatergoers, and didn't have time to find its audience, nor for word-of-mouth to spread. *Carrie* played less than a week—reserve funds to keep it running had already been eaten up. Theater historian Ken Mandelbaum observed *Carrie's* jarring mix of "often breathtaking sequences and some of the most appalling and ridiculous scenes ever seen in a musical. It alternately scaled the heights and hit rock bottom . . . and unlike so many flops, was not dull for a second."

Q: *When was Broadway's golden era?*
A: The 1920s was the Great White Way's most exciting, pioneering, and booming period. America's participation and victory in "the Great War" (World War I) provided energy and optimism. Prosperity had reached the masses, and there was a building boom. Over seventy-six "legit" theaters were in operation, with more coming. During the hot and humid summers Broadway all but closed down, except for girl-and-comedy revues like Florenz Ziegfeld's *Follies*. Yet in 1927 alone, there were 268 openings. Tickets ranged from fifty cents to five dollars, and a show was a hit if it passed one hundred performances—producers and investors had a one-in-three chance of success. Plays and musicals didn't have much to fear from movies, which were still silent.

But Broadway differed from other U.S. theatrical venues due to being part of Manhattan Island's expensive real estate. From way back, theaters have had to compete with other sorts of land use. Thus Broadway was and is primarily a commercial theater. Its acknowledged goal is profits first, art second.

Regarding art, it was in the '20s that plays and musicals moved into the modern era. Stage realism and naturalism in acting developed rapidly, partly thanks to the enormous impact of the visiting Moscow Art Theatre. Stanislavski, the "Method," Russian actors who remained in America to coach, and American disciples like Lee Strasberg would influence Broadway (and also Hollywood) acting for decades to come, and still do.

By Any Other Name

- The record-breaking hit *Abie's Irish Rose* was presented in Los Angeles, pre-Broadway, as *Marriage in Triplicate*.

- Joseph Kesselring's comedy hit *Arsenic and Old Lace* was earlier titled *Bodies in Our Cellar* and was a thriller before producers Howard Lindsay and Russel [sic] Crouse helped give it a lighter touch.

- After terrible reviews greeted Nunnally Johnson's Broadway play *The World Is Full of Girls*, he reportedly sent a telegram to producer Jed Harris: "Change title immediately to *Oklahoma!*" Except that "Girls" opened some nine months earlier!

- *Oklahoma!* would likely have been a smash hit whatever its title, but it began as *Away We Go!* (after the square-dance call, not Jackie Gleason's catch phrase); based on a non-musical poetically titled *Green Grow the Lilacs*—not a hit—"experts" believed it was doomed because it featured a murder and was the maiden effort of the new team of Rodgers and Hammerstein. The latter had experienced a string of failures, but collaborating with Rodgers completely changed lyricist Hammerstein's luck.

- The title *Who's Afraid of Virginia Woolf?* was a graffito found in a Greenwich Village men's room by playwright Edward Albee; he did seek widower Leonard Woolf's permission to use the late writer's name. (Early on, producer Richard Barr overheard one playgoer telling another after the show, "Well, I loved it. But why did they call the wolf Virginia?")

- *The Seagull* features a stuffed seagull perched on a bookcase, per the playwright's stage directions; Noel Coward, no fan of Chekhov and particularly not of *The Seagull*, once said, "I hate plays that have a stuffed bird sitting on the bookcase screaming, 'I'm the title, I'm the title, I'm the title!'"

- "My *last* show was *Everybody Loves Me* (1956). I shouldn't have set myself up like that. Hardly anybody loved it. That was *the end*." —producer MAX GORDON in 1970 (he produced *Born Yesterday* in 1946 and had four concurrent hits during the 1933–34 season)

Fatal Thespians

EVERYONE KNOWS ACTOR JOHN WILKES BOOTH assassinated Abraham Lincoln in 1865 in Ford's Theatre in Washington, D.C. For many years he was the only actor to have murdered somebody in a theater. The only actor to have been murdered just outside a theater was William Terriss, popularly known as Breezy Bill, a hero of melodramas. He was killed in 1897 outside the stage door of London's Adelphi Theatre by a small-part actor with an imagined grievance against the star.

Terriss's friend, the even more popular Henry Irving—the first actor to be knighted, in 1895—bitterly and accurately predicted, "Terriss was an actor—his murderer will not be executed." Justice for actors in those days was unlikely, if at all.

No actress has ever killed in a theatre. However, not long after women were allowed to perform onstage—Shakespeare's female roles were, of course, written to be enacted by males—two British actresses did get down and dirty. Elizabeth Barry (1658–1713) and Peg Woffington (1714–1760) each non-fatally stabbed a rival actress.

Another fatal fellow was Irish actor Charles Macklin, born in 1700 or earlier. He died in 1797 and last performed in 1789. Apparently peaceful at home, he was quite cantankerous at work. He once caused a "violent disturbance" just by appearing on stage, and another time indirectly caused a riot via his friends' aggressive support. When another actor once borrowed a wig of Macklin's without permission, he poked the offender in the eye with his cane, which penetrated to the brain and killed the colleague.

3

THE MERM

Ethel Merman was probably the biggest star Broadway ever produced. Also the loudest, renowned for her bold, brassy voice more than for her looks or acting—she sometimes made a bargain with a costar that she wouldn't react to his lines if he wouldn't react to hers. A native New Yorker, she was born Ethel Zimmerman (1908–1984), an only child who enjoyed singing and as a young adult became an almost overnight success. Ethel went from a stenographer who sang at private parties and nightclubs to a Broadway star in the Gershwins' *Girl Crazy* in 1930 with maximum confidence.

She reportedly never had to audition, didn't have to rise through the ranks, and was never "one of the kids" in the chorus, facts which ingrained in her a sense of predestined stardom and privilege. Seemingly nerveless, Merman once said, "Why should I worry? I'm good. If I wasn't, I'd be an audience, not a star."

Her low tolerance for "excessive" rehearsal, she explained, was on account of "whenever I open my mouth to sing, it comes out swell." "The Merm," as she was often called—sometimes affectionately, sometimes derisively—definitely knew her own worth. In later years, when a TV talk show host commented that Broadway had been very good to her, she shot back, "Yeah, and I've been very good to Broadway!"

There were two frequent misconceptions about Merman. One, that she was Jewish. In fact, the lifelong Episcopalian Republican was at times vocally anti-Semitic—also homophobic, misogynistic, penny-pinchingly cheap, greedy (she demanded extra tickets to her shows, which she then "scalped" for considerable profit), and cheerfully vulgar, even obscene.

Two, that she was lesbian. After all, she was nearly as butch as actor Ernest Borgnine, her fourth, final, and least-loved husband. "All men are cheatin' bastards," she concluded upon quickly divorcing him. In fact, the Merm was heterosexual, or at least predominantly so. She may have had an affair with obsessive admirer Jacqueline Susann, who after Ethel abruptly terminated their relationship took revenge by closely patterning Broadway villainess Helen Lawson after her in her number-one best-selling novel *The Valley of the Dolls*.

As early as *Anything Goes* (1934), Merman had refused to sing Cole Porter's "Kate the Great" because of its sapphic and clergical references. Due probably to his jittery homosexuality (which unlike, say, Noel Coward, Cole camouflaged with a wife), Porter readily dropped disputed songs. "Merman wasn't just the star of almost everything she was in, outside of Hollywood," said actor Keith Prentice, "she was a tyro and a tyrant used to getting her way." Playwrights, producers, and writers knew that she would put up with only so many dialogue changes while rehearsing a new show; she thereafter became what she called "Miss Birdseye," for as far as she was concerned, the show was "frozen." Since she was most always a hit and a money-spinner, associates put up with her habits.

"What she didn't have was tact," explained Prentice, who appeared in *Gypsy* but became known as the handsomest of *The Boys in the Band*. "Merman could be humorous, she could even compromise, but diplomacy she did not have. . . . To be fair, she was a perfectionist. She worked damn hard and expected others to. But she did turn off so many people with that confrontational manner. . . . It didn't scarcely matter. She didn't have to refine herself or mend her ways, as it didn't really hurt her career."

Nonetheless, the lack of like from many of her peers and the theatre establishment meant that a theater was never named after her, as with Helen Hayes, Lunt and Fontanne, female impersonator Julian Eltinge (after whom an American battleship was also named), and even critic Brooks Atkinson. Elaine Stritch was quoted in the book *It Happened on Broadway*, "She made a lot of enemies because she wanted to get it right. She was a selfish old broad. Still, it's a sin that they haven't named a theater for her."

"DESPITE IT ALL—and the fans didn't know the half of it in those days," believed record and revue producer Ben Bagley, "fans couldn't help admiring and relishing Ethel Merman. Belting out a song or just owning the stage, no one could touch her." Strangely, in one of her two memoirs she asserted that her voice was inimitable. On the contrary, hers became one of the most imitated—by women and men, then and now—of singing voices. "Merman was so wrapped up in herself," said Bagley, "she couldn't be a good judge or objective about herself. . . . She knew she wasn't overly cultured, very educated, but she thought she was a reasonable, regular person."

Besides her at times scalding tongue, the Merm was very competitive, blunt, and childishly crude. After viewing the unique, not-yet-a-star Carol Channing in *Gentlemen Prefer Blondes* (1949), Ethel mirthfully informed her, "You walked like you hadda pee." Carol was dumbfounded: "That was her complete summary of my portrayal of Anita Loos's monumental character Lorelei Lee." In her memoirs, Channing repeatedly professed a fan's adoration of Merman, who was apparently oblivious to her own impact on others, particularly her often unintentional humor. She would often ask Carol, "What the hell are ya laughin' at?"

Long after, when Channing was a hit in *Hello, Dolly!*, she fell out of Merman's good graces. At one public function, Carol said, "Hello, Ethel," to no response. Columnist Radie Harris asked, "Don't you answer Carol when she says hello?"

"Carol who?" said Merman, while Channing thought, "Maybe she doesn't like hit shows that she isn't in?"

"Did you see *Hello, Dolly!*, Ethel?" asked Radie.

"Yeah, I turned that show down," which was the first Carol heard of it. (Jerry Herman had written it for Merman, who wasn't interested in working anymore.)

Another time, Carol was invited to Sardi's restaurant to help hang someone's caricature in front of the press and photographers. She and Ethel were to do the joint honors. But the Merm declined. "Nope, no picture. Not wit' Carol."

Many years after that, the two would work together in Los Angeles on a *Love Boat* episode. They re-met in a limousine en route to the studio. Channing found that Merman now bore a striking resemblance to silent-movie star Harry Langdon. Silent, however, she was not. In the backseat, she yelled, "Hi, Carol!" then enthused, "I had the strangest airplane trip out here. A passenger was bleeding from the rectum."

Carol pondered, "Now that's the first thing she's said to me since 1964," and wondered why Ethel was suddenly so chatty after such a long estrangement. Explanation was ventured by Mary Martin: that Merman's eventually fatal brain tumor had been growing for nobody knew how long. However, Channing thought Ethel's behavior had never really changed at all.

In any case, Merman had taken it upon herself to diagnose the bloody passenger. "What the hell are ya laughin' at? I'm a *good* nurse," she informed Channing. "I volunteered to serve at Roosevelt Hospital for every Thursday."

Carol would write, "Now I ask you, if you were strung up in Roosevelt

Hospital, wouldn't you dread Thursdays? I mean, this woman walks into your room . . . and screams, 'Ah'm your nurse! Roll over.' Wouldn't you? Dread Thursdays?"

While filming the *Love Boat* episode, Ethel's jowls were alleviated by hidden rubber bands that pulled her lower face up and gave her a perpetual—until they were released—smile, which made her less intimidating to coworkers. One day, Merman was installed under a large, heavy hair dryer in order to give her extra curls. (Flouncy hairdos and dresses helped mitigate her innate manliness.) A few minutes later, Ethel barked, "Hey, I'm burnin' up. Come here, you bitch. Get me outta here." But since she was still smiling, attention wasn't immediately paid. The upshot was that Merman's ears got singed and were red and swollen for about a week.

Channing noticed that Ethel's once "brilliant, electric mind" couldn't comprehend script changes—for example, two additional lines. Nor could she remember that Channing's character's name was Sylvia. "'Hey! Cybill! Sophie! Shirley! Come here, ya dumb cunt!' And I would come . . . just like any of us would once we experienced her onstage."

In 1983 Merman suffered a massive stroke. Tests revealed a malignant brain tumor, and ten months later she died. Friendly rival Mary Martin stated publicly, "I *had* to be glad that she was gone, because Merman without performing or without sound would never make Merman happy." She'd deteriorated fast and terribly, cruelly frustrated by her immobility and a limited ability to communicate—also by the cortisone that swelled her face and the chemotherapy that cost her her hair. Carol Channing recalled, "I went from Ethel's [room] straight to my lawyer to make out a living will. No one should suffer like Ethel did."

AWAY FROM THE LIMELIGHT, Merman's life had often been anything but a bed of roses. Her only daughter died from a drug overdose that Merman insisted was not a suicide. Her only son's wife, actress Barbara Colby—best remembered as the prostitute Mary meets in prison in *The Mary Tyler Moore Show*—was mysteriously shot to death. And Robert Levitt, Merman's third husband, with whom she had two children, killed himself after eventually remarrying.

Merman asked friends if she wasn't a terrible mother. While her children were growing up, she strongly favored Robert over Ethel Jr. (Yet how many mothers name their daughter Junior?) Toward the end of her life, when Merman had to fly to Rio de Janeiro, she telephoned Robert to ask if he'd like to fly down with her. Perhaps unwilling to endure a long flight together, he replied instead that he'd be glad to *meet* her there. "How do you raise a son so he understands?," she asked. Mother and son had many ups and downs, but were reconciled when Ethel's terminal illness was discovered.

Career had long come first and had delayed her getting married, which she did for the first time (in 1940) after breaking off with a married family man. For thirty years Merman was the queen of Broadway, ending on a high note with the popular and critical success of *Gypsy* (1959). Her Broadway career, which she intermittently resumed, ended in 1970 when she took over the lead in *Hello, Dolly!*, to carry that production to its 2,844th performance, and the "longest-running Broadway musical" title (held for nine months, before *Fiddler on the Roof* surpassed it). Merman made her first film in 1930 and her last in 1980, yet she never made many and never became a movie star. She was too large, too *much* for that close-up medium.

"Ethel was never a beauty," said Ben Bagley, "and had neither the vulnerability required of a lead actress nor the acting gift required for dramas and romances."

Merman's self-absorption and dedication to her work were legendary—to the point that her character's line in *Gypsy*, "Sure, I know there's a war on. I read *Variety*," was often attributed to her. Via her long string of musicals, the Merm introduced more musical standards, hits, and now-classics than probably any other American singer, starting with "I Got Rhythm" in 1930.

Unwavering belief in her performing style was another Merman trait. In 1956 she was rehearsing *Happy Hunting* with Argentine heartthrob Fernando Lamas, who shortly interrupted to ask, over her head, if the actress was going to be reading her lines to the audience while he read his lines to her? Offended, the star asserted, "Mr. Lamas, I want you to know that I have been playing scenes this way for twenty-five years on Broadway."

The macho foreigner replied, "That doesn't mean you're right. That just means you're old." Another feud had begun. The hit musical included an inevitable kiss between its unsimpatico costars. Lamas eventually did the unthinkable and unprofessional when after The Kiss he walked to the footlights and wiped his mouth with the back of his hand. The incident became news, and Mike Wallace asked him about it on TV. Lamas described kissing Merman as "somewhere between kissing your uncle and a Sherman tank."

The infuriated star filed a protest with Actors' Equity, which reprimanded the Latin lover.

For *Gypsy*, Ethel's male lead was the non-singing Jack Klugman, pre-TV stardom. During his audition he'd feared having to compete with the big Merman sound during their duet, "Small World." Director Jerome Robbins begged Ethel to for once lower the volume, which she did. "She sang so softly, so un-Mermanly," offered composer Jule Styne, "that her voice cracked." She normally sang at full throttle, whether in rehearsal or in performance. Once, after rehearsing "Before the Parade Passes By" in the producer's office for a TV special, she received applause from an office two doors away.

(Due to the fact that she could carry a show on her own and also because she made each show her own, male stars were generally unwilling to costar with her. Her male leads, who weren't so much her costars as her characters' love interests, were typically lesser-known, faded, or foreign actors, who also had to be macho enough not to be overpowered by her.)

Although she lived well into the age of microphones, Ethel Merman declined to soften, lower, or alter her singing style. She advised one pro-mike producer who said, "You don't have to belt," "That's not what I'm all about. What I do is me. That's what I am."

DESPITE HER NATURAL COMPETITIVENESS, Merman sometimes encouraged young performers, usually male ones. She comforted an actor-dancer in *Gypsy* who was nervous before opening, "Honey, if they could do what you do, they'd be up here."

However, with females of all ages there was an invariable one-upmanship. For instance, at the home of some friends, the family grouped for a photo with "Aunt" Ethel, who often doted on their son. But when their little daughter Trudy stood in front of Merman, the star tartly ordered, "Back up, honey. Nobody upstages your Aunt Ethel."

Give-and-take came hard to Merman. Despite her wealth, she was notorious for giving cheap gifts for birthdays and Christmas. And though occasionally she agreed to perform for charity, she expected first-class treatment all the way. In 1977 she and Mary Martin headlined a benefit for the Theatre and Music Collection of the Museum of the City of New York.

Both had starred in *Hello, Dolly!* and were to wear the famous down-the-staircase red gown. When the producer suggested borrowing the gowns from the David Merrick office, Merman told her, "Are you kidding? You're asking Mary and me to wear secondhand outfits? We're stars. You'll have to make new costumes." In spite of the plea that expenses were being kept to a minimum, Ethel got her way, with $2,500 added to the charity's budget.

Then the producer explained that to get to rehearsals, "The museum has a taxi service that will be at your disposal." Merman cried, "A taxi service! Whaddya think we are, a couple of chorus girls? Get us limos." The limousines upped the budget by a further $2,200.

The ornery Ethel, who told friends Carol Channing was "a vulgar publicity seeker," also opined that "Dolly was a foolproof part. Look how many gals have done it. Even Betty Grable!"—who had parlayed her Broadway success in Cole Porter's 1939 musical *DuBarry Was a Lady* into screen superstardom. Despite having declined to leave the States to play *Gypsy* in London, Merman was furious when Angela Lansbury played Mama Rose there, to huge box office and critical acclaim. Lansbury said, "Ethel figured

Rose was her private property, and I had no right to play the role. She told people that. . . . Also, I got the Tony [for the role—in 1974, for *Gypsy*'s first Broadway revival] and she didn't, although she richly deserved it."

Merman was more legitimately aggrieved when asked to play a recurring role on Jack Klugman's TV series *The Odd Couple*. She'd ordered her agent to "get me some of that dough they're throwing around at all those second-rate actors out there" in Los Angeles, where she did appear on *Batman* as villainess Lola Lasagna. Ethel was enraged and stung when she learned, "They want me to play Jack Klugman's aunt?! Goddamnit, he was my leading man in *Gypsy*! Why the hell should I play his aunt? It's insulting." The producers reconsidered and said she could play Klugman's older sister. "Absolutely not!" she replied.

Ethel's coarseness was well known, and though she voted and even campaigned for conservative candidates who made an issue of their "moral values," she reveled in public shockers. According to biographer Bob Thomas, at one "rather formal reception in a palatial Manhattan residence," Merman was going up a double staircase while actor-director José Ferrer was going down on the other side. "Hey, Joe!" she suddenly yelled. "Did you hear the one about the Polack who was so dumb he thought Fuck-ing and Suck-king were a couple of Chinese cities?" The embarrassed Oscar winner answered, "No, I hadn't, Ethel," and walked on.

She was also partial to risqué greeting cards that dealt an unexpected shock. Like one that read, "Help bring love to the world . . ." on the front and on the inside "Fuck someone today." "She collected dirty jokes and nasty stories," said friend and associate Benay Venuta. "At parties, she was known for telling them . . . [and] trying to make the hostess blush. . . . Ethel was received in several of New York's finest homes—usually *once*.

"Back in '72, a mutual acquaintance was at a restaurant party with her. After Ethel exhausted her fund of bodily function jokes, she let someone else talk. So this guy mentions that he'll be voting for [George] McGovern in the upcoming elections. Ethel was aghast, and couldn't or wouldn't keep it to herself. In her book, McGovern's a 'Commie,' so she starts talking up Richard Nixon, actually calling him 'a fine and noble man.' Most people already knew not to bring up politics in front of her."

MERMAN DECRIED MOST OF THE CHANGES sweeping America in the 1960s and '70s, and many or most of the younger stars. Modern trends and new Broadway plays usually appalled her, but it also hurt that fewer youngsters knew who she was, or who she'd been. Gone were the days when Cole Porter had announced, "I'd rather write for Ethel Merman than anyone else in the world." Though formerly she'd disapproved of people doing Ethel Merman impressions, toward the end of her life she was glad, even grateful, to hear them.

"There's practically no great singers today," she explained in a 1970 inter-view syndicated in Australia. "You gotta have style and real personality for 'em to imitate you." About female movie stars, she somewhat hypocritically offered, "Half of 'em are tramps. Nobody acts like a lady anymore." About Jane Fonda she specifically said, "No one wants to hear an actress's opinion about politics!" Regarding a young female rock singer, she summed up Grace Slick as "gimmicky but good" (not explaining what the gimmick was), then allowed that she didn't "get" Janis Joplin (who died later that year):

"That girl has problems. . . . Bein' heard ain't one of 'em; like me, she gives an audience their money's worth. But when I sing, everything's comin' up roses. When she sings, it's a primal scream, for heaven's sake!"

Though she took up touring in concerts, Merman became an exile from Broadway. She refused to consider supporting roles, except on the screen, which came calling even less often than before. To a younger generation she became known as the aggressive lady with the booming voice and the very imitable vibrato. "As she got older," noted conductor Les Brown, "Ethel's voice remained strong. Yet when she held a note, there was now a vibrato, and it just seemed to get worse, until it became the easiest thing in the world to 'do' Ethel Merman just by singing loud and energetically, with an exaggerated, almost comical vibrato." For many who'd never heard her in her prime, Merman's voice sounded "funny," and they questioned her vocal reputation.

Ironically, when she recorded a 1979 album of her hits set to a disco beat, the vibrato was temporarily gone, but *The Ethel Merman Disco Album* came out at the end of the disco era and appealed to neither her older nor her younger fans, including most gay ones. "I heard nearly every copy that sold, sold to gay men," said Ben Bagley, "not that many copies sold at all."

Though not as personally well liked as some other Broadway icons, Ethel Merman shone brighter over the Great White Way than most anyone else. Her career coincided with its years of glory and universal appeal, a time when a Broadway star could be a national star without aid of other media, and when many of the nation's hit songs came from Broadway shows.

. "Talent and charisma made Broadway stars," said stage actor George Rose. "Not the cosmetic, shallow appeal of Hollywood, but real, in-person qualities. It takes real stamina and natural magnetism to keep an audience captivated and to make them return. When she got on the stage and performed, Ethel Merman crushed any traces of boredom or restlessness. . . . People might get bored or impatient at a Merman musical, but only when she wasn't on. When she was, she captured all eyes and ears.

"She grabbed your attention and never let go till after the curtain calls. And *she* decided when the curtain finally fell. . . . Nobody else could consis-tently pull in crowds even to mediocre musicals. Merman was in good ones, bad ones, great ones, and so-so ones. Regardless, you went to see *her*. Crude or loud, funny, boisterous, she had the true magnetism, that star quality. Ethel Merman just lit up Broadway." In her heyday, she *was* Broadway.

Merm und Drang

"Ethel could see right through people, usually. She could tell if someone wanted to use or exploit her. Except with some of her husbands. . . . After she saw the movie *All About Eve*, she kept asking how come a sharp dame like Bette Davis hadn't seen right through that conniving little Eve?"—friend and co-worker BENAY VENUTA

"The motion picture was *It's a Mad, Mad, Mad, Mad World*—correct me if I'm a 'Mad' short. I was the token Englishman; Miss Merman—which I'd imagined was a male mermaid—was the token leading lady. She was merely the most foul-mouthed and loud-mouthed female I have ever had the shock and displeasure of working with."—TERRY-THOMAS (Stanley Kramer's 1963 comedy hit also costarred Edie Adams and Dorothy Provine)

"Ethel's a good egg. I got to see her shy and vulnerable side when she came to see me about *Gypsy*. I think her bluster was a façade. . . . She was very eager to please, and always loved applause, always sought that."—GYPSY ROSE LEE

"A bitch. When Ann Sothern got the screen version of *Panama Hattie*, I hear Ethel Merman wrote her a poisonous letter. . . . A lesbian? Not a bit of it! She loathed women."—ARTHUR TREACHER, who appeared in the 1940 stage musical *Panama Hattie*

"She liked being one of the boys, but she did wish to be treated like a lady. A great gal. Great voice. On a clear day you could probably hear Merman on Catalina [Island]."—BING CROSBY

"Ethel played my wife in *There's No Business Like Show Business*. (The film costarred Marilyn Monroe.) Now, if you don't think playing Ethel Merman's husband is acting, let me tell you. . . . She was about six or seven years older than me, but the emotional, temperamental difference was wider than that. . . . A very challenging assignment."—DAN DAILEY

"Playing a love scene with her [in the film of *Call Me Madam*] was like acting opposite a refrigerator. I felt I was selling a product, with rather chilly resistance from the product."—GEORGE SANDERS

"She treated her supporting cast like dirt. That's not what I call the spirit of show business. So when she sings that song and gets to the line about 'There's no people like show people,' I just have to laugh, or try to."
—BETTY GRABLE, who before her screen superstardom worked with Merman onstage

"If you talked to her, it took a lot of courage. And if she answered you, it was always like answering the group—she would include everyone. It was always like she was being interviewed. She never said anything about my performance, but she would give me a few taps on the shoulder before I was ready to go on—and that was acceptance."—SAL VITELLA, who was in the touring company of *Call Me Madam*

"I remember once, onstage, we were in the middle of the 'Mr. Goldstone' scene, and a couple of stagehands were listening to a ball game on the radio and you could hear it all onstage. And suddenly Merman said, 'Excuse me.' And she goes off through the set and yells, '*Shut the fuck up!*' Then she comes back onstage and finishes the scene. She wasn't about to put up with that."—MERLE LOUISE, who played Dainty June in *Gypsy*

"When she found out I'd offered her role [as a madam in *The Art of Love*] to Mae West first, Ethel stopped talking to me. She said she wouldn't consider being in any more of my pictures. I sent word that I hadn't considered her for any more of my pictures. To paraphrase Dorothy Parker, Merman ran the spectrum of emotions from A to B—or should I say from A to Me."—producer ROSS HUNTER

"Working with her [on screen], I learned she's a big mouth, and I refer not solely to her singing. I'd really rather not discuss her."—movie star RAY MILLAND

"She was not a top-drawer actress . . . but she wasn't given the chance until *Gypsy*. Singing and strutting is what she did best. In *Gypsy* she got to show some range, at long last. It could have been the start of a new . . . era for her. But then she decided to retire."—*Gypsy* director-choreographer JEROME ROBBINS

"I do not at this time recollect anything of printable value about working with her."—ALICE FAYE, leading lady of *Alexander's Ragtime Band*, a 1938 film whose title song was one of Merman's hits

"I think the movies we made together were good for Ethel Merman's screen career, but she was better for her Broadway career, if you catch my drift."—EDDIE CANTOR

"We were both in *Girl Crazy*, [but] she stood out. She had a clarion voice and a heck of a song ["I Got Rhythm"]. I went to Hollywood soon after, and I guess Ethel made the most of her talent on Broadway."—GINGER ROGERS

"She was tough, but in a way she had to be. She could look at a row of balcony lights in a dress rehearsal and tell you the third one on the right should be pink and not yellow—and the guy would say, 'Oh, shit, you're right!' A lot of women in the theater couldn't do that." (Nor a lot of men.)—stage and TV star JERRY ORBACH, who worked with Merman in the Lincoln Center revival of *Annie Get Your Gun*

"What a commotion that woman liked to make! Center of attention or nothing. What nowadays they call a drama queen. Which is funny, because she always struck me as rather a drag-queen type, even when she was younger. . . . She tried to irritate me by using a Spanish accent when we did a movie at Fox [*Happy Landing*, 1938]. A regular bigot! She never got to me, because I'm just as American as I am Cuban. Hell, I went to high school in New Jersey!"—CESAR ROMERO

"I think that like most eccentric people, Miss Merman thought all the people around her were strange. She strived to give the impression of being terribly well adjusted, but I'm sure psychotherapy could have helped her." —VIVIAN VANCE (the *I Love Lucy* costar, who worked extensively onstage before turning to TV, was a strong advocate of psychiatry)

"She played Dolly Levi—Dolly lost. It was pure showbiz, purely commercial. She wasn't Dolly up there, she was Ethel Merman in Dolly clothes. . . . The audiences came, of course; they came to see the Ethel Merman version. But it wasn't *Hello, Dolly!* anymore; it was *her* show. . . . Channing or Streisand, they were part of a cast, trying to act out a character. But with Ethel Merman—and not just her fault, with the *audience*, she was such an institution—the rest of us felt like just her chorus boys or her chorus line."—DANNY LOCKIN, who costarred as Barnaby Tucker in both the stage and film versions

"The explosion in Forty-Fourth Street last evening was nothing to be alarmed by. It was merely Ethel Merman returning to the New York theater." —BROOKS ATKINSON's typical welcome-back-Ethel review in the *New York Times*, on December 7, 1956

"Ethel Merman was New York's musical version of the Statue of Liberty. She was that big, that famous, that awesome—really a case of they don't make them that way anymore."—MICHAEL BENNETT

"A monument is what the Merm was, while she was on the stage. You don't judge or measure a monument in moral or relative terms. There was nobody else like her. Back then, already people knew and appreciated that fact."—stage star BURGESS MEREDITH, who costarred with Merman in an episode of TV's *Batman*

4

TENNESSEE WILLIAMS

"A Southern genital-man."
—what ungentlemanly critic GEORGE JEAN NATHAN called Tennessee
Williams

For quite a long run, Tennessee Williams (1911–1983) was America's fore-most playwright. He ruled over Broadway in the 1950s and via film versions of his plays became a household name. A "Tennessee Williams play" was a theatrical genre of its own, and during the repressed post-war era audiences flocked to see and be titillated by his very "adult" plays. "He leaves comedy to the jokers and kids," said Bette Davis, who did his *The Night of the Iguana* on Broadway. "Tennessee delivers the dramatic goods, and he *really* understands women."

Tennessee (born Tom) was the first major playwright widely known to be "that way," and for that reason, several myths sprang up about him and his work, some of them still flourishing. One centers on one of his most famous charac-ters, Blanche DuBois in *A Streetcar Named Desire*. She is but one of Williams's mature, glamorous, on-her-own women, often drawn to crude younger hunks. Like various of Tennessee's characters, she's somewhat neurotic; however, some critics labeled Blanche neurotic simply because she fancied handsome young men—others equated the attraction with veiled homoeroticism.

A popular theory held that Blanche was originally intended as a male character. Such thinking imagined that a gay writer's female creations cannot be genuine—as opposed to heterosexual men's females?—and are actually camouflaged males. A related myth held that Blanche is really Tennessee, or what he'd like to be. That myth took a while to gel, for the immediate "scandal" produced by *Streetcar* was that a man, Stanley Kowalski, was the object of desire and that the lust came from a woman, Blanche.

As with the outspokenly sexual Mae West (frequently rumored to be a man; she wasn't), such an inversion of tradition disturbed the status quo and somehow made questionable the femaleness of the woman who lusted. Immemorial custom had it that the pursuer be masculine, the lusted-after feminine. Tennessee Williams broke this rule with his 1947 hit play. Years later, when a friend opined that there was as much Blanche as Stanley in Tennessee, the media seized on—only—the first half of the statement as an "explanation" for her staring at Stanley's bared torso with undisguised lust.

Though many or most of Williams's plays are partly autobiographical, especially his early success *The Glass Menagerie*, in which he didn't bother to re-work Tom as "straight," *Streetcar's* Blanche is *not* Tennessee. Rather, to quite a degree she's inspired by his older sister, Rose. Rose had definitely been the model for his *Menagerie* sister, Laura, and his mother, Edwina, the basis for the play's mother, Amanda. *The Glass Menagerie* is almost cheerfully minus a father, absent because he "fell in love with long distance." Unfortunately for Tennessee, Cornelius Williams, a loutish alcoholic, was very much in residence off the stage.

In the preface to his collected short stories, Tennessee, who seldom alluded to his younger brother, Dakin, in his work or publicity, wrote of his father: "He always enters the house as though he were entering it with the intention of tearing it down from inside." Except when returning after midnight, drunk.

Rose eventually let it be known that her father had made drunken sexual advances toward her. Cornelius denied it, while Edwina was mortified by any such talk in her household. In order to prevent Rose's repeating the deeply disturbing accusation, Edwina arranged for her daughter to undergo one of the first lobotomies. The prudish matriarch, who later turned Cornelius out after he was hospitalized for a drunken binge, said she wouldn't be able to live with her husband if she had to believe such a wicked thing about him.

The lobotomy in effect erased Rose as an individual. She was no longer a worry to her parents, especially after being put away. However, Rose's fate became a deep and lifelong source of regret for her devoted brother, who gradually turned against their puritanical mother and came to sympathize with his father. The lobotomy provided a seed for Tennessee's short play, *Suddenly, Last Summer*, in which a puritanical woman tries to lobotomize a niece who correctly insinuates that her late cousin Sebastian was homosexual.

THE INAPPROPRIATE HETEROSEXUAL BEHAVIOR attributed to Cornelius Williams echoes and is magnified in the rape of Blanche DuBois by brother-in-law Stanley Kowalski in *A Streetcar Named Desire*. The tendency to over-identify Blanche with her creator overlooks the play's very real theme of violence against women. Edwina is partly reflected in Blanche's sister, Stella, who following her husband's rape of Blanche allows her to be taken off to be put away (and perhaps lobotomized). Stella wonders, "I don't know if I did the right thing." Blanche famously informs the men in white that she has "always depended on the kindness of strangers." Strangers who, as in real life, are sometimes less emotionally fatal than family members. (A recent study gives the chances of an American female being sexually abused before age eighteen as one in four, usually by a family member.)

Stella tellingly declares, "I couldn't believe her story and go on living with Stanley," to which Eunice, a traditionalist friend, advises, "Don't ever believe it. Life has got to go on."

Ironically, the sexual violence in *A Streetcar Named Desire* and its screen version was mitigated by the casting in both of the enormously attractive Marlon Brando, who was also too young for the role, which Williams had envisioned as closer in age to his father. Brando glamorized Kowalski (note the *k* sound, as in "Cornelius"), making him more commercially appealing. He inadvertently made the rape scene seem less an act of evil than a possibly secret fantasy—not so secret on the part of some heterosexual women and some gay men. Tennessee felt that Marlon's youthful beauty "humanizes the character of Stanley in that it becomes the brutality or callousness of youth rather than a vicious older man."

To his surprise, Marlon was identified with Stanley by Tennessee Williams: "Tennessee has made a fixed association between me and Kowalski. I mean, we're friends and he knows that as a person I am just the opposite of Kowalski, who was everything I'm against—totally insensitive, crude, cruel. But still, Tennessee's image of me is confused with the fact that I played that part. So I don't know if he could write for me in a different color range."

If *Streetcar* does have a character based on Williams, it would be Blanche's late homosexual husband, Allan (note the double *l*'s in both names), a sensitive soul and a poet. Tennessee Williams always considered himself a poet at heart and often aired his belief that like his role model, gay poet Hart Crane, he would die young. Deeply personal poems are embedded in various of Tennessee's plays. But as with the murdered Sebastian Venable in *Suddenly, Last Summer*, the suicidal Allan doesn't actually appear in Williams's play. Gay characters in his early plays were typically spoken of, rather than fleshed out, and were, of course, stereotyped.

The playwright usually readily agreed to censorship of movies of his work and practiced self-censorship in his plays, reasoning that a watered-down message reaching a wide audience was better than an undiluted one reaching very few—"though generally I try to leave messages to Western Union, you know."

The myth is that America's first semi-openly gay playwright (eventually openly gay) was: (a) pro-gay and thus "biased" toward gay characters, (b) "obsessed" with injecting homosexuality into his plays, and (c) was far ahead of his time in so doing. Williams was prescient in delineating psychosexual— occasionally including homosexual—themes and motivations in his avant-garde plays. However, his treatment of non-heterosexual characters and themes was very much of its era; similarly in his less self-censored short stories. Tennessee's gays are stereotypical, hated, and self-hating.

His Baron de Charlus in *Camino Real* (1953) contemplates a sexual inter-lude comprising "an iron bed with no mattress and a considerable length of stout knotted rope." Too often, Tennessee's homosexuals don't enjoy sex, or they require it in S/M fashion. The Baron requires "Chains this evening, metal chains, I've been very bad, I have a lot to atone for."

Death prematurely takes too many of Williams's gay characters, who fre-quently instigate their own demises. Ergo, even while the playwright was "dar-ing" in even broaching how the other tenth purportedly lives—and loves—or that it even existed, he habitually placated authorities, critics, and average the-atergoers by depicting and terminating his gay characters in the traditionally approved way. Williams's plays are *not* brimming with gays and lesbians. Time and again, a gay theatergoer's reaction to encountering one of Tennessee's gay characters—they almost never come in pairs—turns quickly from pleasure or validation to embarrassment or anger at the artist's heavy-handed and disap-pointing methods.

In any case, the myth that the playwright's female characters were dis-guised men or based on himself doesn't hold water. A great many were partly based on his mother or sister. His women, older or younger, often embody the iniquitous and cruel circumstances inflicted by men and by women who uphold patriarchy's double standard. If Williams "pleads," it's less for his fellow gays than for the young and the old Roses—blossoms trapped and crushed by a society not of their own devising.

It was this early feminism, as much as his incorporating even a whiff of lavender, that drew the establishment's ire. Any man who underlined women's problems would have been suspect, a "traitor" to male-heterosexual hegemo-ny. As Tennessee's sexual and affectional orientation became known, yet not openly written about, critical indignation grew. "Fetid swamp" was *Time* reviewer Louis Kronenberger's phrase of preference for describing the play-wright's output and "obsessions." Since Tennessee's plays often dealt with neu-roses, he was himself labeled neurotic by detractors neurotically obsessed with keeping homosexual men in their "place."

Under the aegis of far-right religious zealot Henry Luce, *Time* magazine for three decades spearheaded the anti–Tennessee Williams charge, invariably assigning his plays negative reviews. In the early 1950s *Time* had gone so far as to label Williams a "pervert" in print. Shy, relatively new to the limelight, and vulnerable, he didn't sue, and the media made him a habitual target. *Time* and other reactionary periodicals' ongoing theme regarding Tennessee Williams's plays was, "This is what our nation is coming to." When the 1959 film of *Suddenly, Last Summer*, starring Elizabeth Taylor, Montgomery Clift, and Katharine Hepburn became a hit, *Time* critic Richard Schickel monopolistically bemoaned, "Why do we have to have all of this homosexuality in our movies?"

The *New York Times* was anti-Tennessee too, and by the late '60s when he was in steep commercial decline, it became universally "in" to bash him. Henry Luce's *Life* magazine took out a full-page ad in the *Times* to sell issues by criticizing Williams.

When Tennessee had included passing homosexuality in his early works, there had been nervous indignation, but his newer plays, with their undisguised and unmarried gay characters, elicited ever-greater media contempt and vituperation. Instead of allowing that the playwright was, like most mature artists, moving in new, less dollar-oriented directions toward a more specific, personal truth, critics dismissed his latest plays out of hand and declared that he was "past it" and his output no longer worthwhile.

Several of his later, "smaller" plays have been posthumously acclaimed and withstood the test of time, but Williams, after people stopped flocking to his plays, was no longer in fashion. After he stopped writing for wider audiences and his runs grew shorter, vengeful detractors could and did make a difference. Word of mouth, from fewer mouths, counted for less than biased reviewers' judgments, regardless of a given play's merits. Then too, people were no longer so easily shocked—thanks to Tennessee, among others—and a "shocking" theme no longer automatically brought in the crowds.

The mostly hostile critical reaction to Williams's plays was ironic in that his treatment of gay characters didn't evolve much. As late as the 1972 *Small Craft Warnings* he had a character ruing the alleged fact that "There's a coarseness, a deadening coarseness, in the experience of most homosexuals"—never mind that homophobia is both coarse and deadening. Among the worst anti-gay influences working upon the impressionable playwright had been a homophobic psychiatrist to whom he'd trustingly, or masochistically, submitted his troubled psyche. Like many gay men of his era, Tennessee didn't have sex with somebody else until late—his late twenties—and when his shrink ordered him to stop having sex and even give up Frank Merlo, his devoted partner of fourteen years, he did. After Merlo died young of cancer, Williams was remorseful for the rest of his life.

Williams reportedly came to regret some of the anti-gay screen changes to which he'd so readily, and profitably, agreed, as in *The Night of the Iguana*

(1964), featuring extra lines—not by Tennessee—ordered by director John Huston which made the lesbian character Miss Fellowes seem more villainous and pathetic. Just as well that by the mid '60s celluloid adaptations of Williams's work were no longer guaranteed hits and finally petered out.

Gore Vidal, who remained friends with Tennessee—but not with fellow gay novelist Truman Capote; they had an amity-shattering argument in Tennessee's home—observed that although Tennessee "survived witch doctors and envenomed press, they wore him out in the end."

By his late sixties Williams was admitting, "I don't feel a day over eighty. Not most of the time." Success or no, he continued writing, which he considered his lifeline. The only time he'd been, as he put it, "scared scriptless," was when he'd been hired by Hollywood to write heterosexual love dramas. When a British reporter inquired of the gay playwright about loneliness and whether he regretted being "childless"—or child-free—Tennessee responded, "Well, my children are my plays . . . they are my posterity. And unlike the other kind of offspring, they support me rather lavishly in my old age."

Tennessee Williams's body of work is arguably the greatest left behind by any American playwright. But he learned the hard way that personal truth costs. During the painful 1970s he pointed out, "In writing classes, they say, 'Write about what you know.' What they don't say is, 'Write about what you know *unless* we disapprove of who you are and what you know.'"

The Life of William Inge: No Picnic

"WILLIAM INGE WAS THE EXTREME EXAMPLE of a playwright who killed himself for lack of continuing success," said Tennessee Williams. "I think that unlike most homosexual playwrights, he felt too little of and about himself. . . . Without success and the sustenance of acclaim, he chose to end his residency."

William Inge (1913–1973) put the Midwest on the Broadway map, dramatically speaking. Before him, many Midwestern characters were happy and/or rural, often musical, and frequently shallow. Angst was not part of the scene. Inge's themes were loneliness, frustration, loss, and despair. His characters craved love, and he was to the Midwest what mentor and, briefly, lover Tennessee Williams was to the South. In the 1950s Inge enjoyed four consecutive Broadway hits: *Come Back, Little Sheba, Picnic, Bus Stop*, and *The Dark at the Top of the Stairs*.

Picnic won him a Pulitzer Prize, and he later earned an original-screenplay Academy Award for *Splendor in the Grass*, a 1961 movie. (The shy ex-instructor had declined to go to the ceremonies in Los Angeles until the studio stopped insisting he attend with a female starlet.) The statuette was Inge's last glittering piece of professional success.

A deeply closeted man who apparently never lived with and never had a longtime partner, Inge didn't introduce gay characters into his work until late in his career. His Jewish youth who kills himself because of anti-Semitism in *Dark* has often been called a stand-in for a homosexual character. Once Inge did include gays, all too often they were stereotypes, and he did not abandon his habit of endorsing majority mores and relationships, only.

Inge had begun as an actor but due partly to parental desires (he was a fifth and final child) focused on teaching. He was an occasional radio news announcer and scriptwriter; also an art, music, book, and drama critic for the *St. Louis Star-Times*. (St. Louis was Tennessee Williams's hometown.) A college-level English teacher, Inge grew to hate the profession—although he returned to it temporarily, post-Broadway—and pinned his hopes on a successful play to remove him from it and the Midwest.

(One of Inge's students, in a dramatics class, was fellow Kansan Vivian Vance, who soon left for what she hoped was Broadway stardom. After middling stage success, she finally achieved national recognition on television in *I Love Lucy*.)

In 1944, when he met the two-years-older but much more successful Tennessee Williams, William Inge resolved to become a playwright. (Tennessee, visiting St. Louis, accepted Inge's invitation to visit his apartment, where their intense affair began.) After a positive Theatre Guild tryout in Westport, Connecticut, *Come Back, Little Sheba*, Inge's second play, opened on Broadway in 1950. It won praise and prizes for him and star Shirley Booth, who repeated the role on screen and took home an Oscar for it. *Picnic* proved Inge was no flash in the pan, as did *Bus Stop*; the movie versions of his plays made him more wealthy and famous. But after *The Dark at the Top of the Stairs* came a critical backlash. "It amazes me how violent they get when a play is not a hit," Inge said. "They act as though it were a personal affront to them that such a presentation should be made."

The onslaught was spearheaded by *New Republic* critic Robert Brustein, who wrote a poisonous article, widely publicized, in *Harper's*, titled "The Men-Taming Women of William Inge." The young non-playwright slashed *Dark* and all Inge's earlier work, which he assessed as mediocre. Brustein's "charge" of aggressive female characters who tame or put men down in Inge's plays was the unimaginative but attention-getting tactic of more than one jealous and homophobic reviewer. It was also incorrect insofar as Inge's women are heavily dependent on their male counterparts, and it applied more accurately to many females in the musicals of heterosexuals Richard Rodgers and Oscar Hammerstein—think of Mrs. Anna, Fraulein Maria, Nellie Forbush, and others who put pompous men in their place.

Unfortunately, Inge was devastated by Brustein's malice and allowed it to interfere with his work. In any event, by the late '50s change was in more than the air, and many observers felt Inge was increasingly old-fashioned, others that he'd gotten away from the midwestern themes and milieux that had been his forte. His fifth Broadway play, *A Loss of Roses*, opened in 1959 and was his first flop. Movie rights had sold for a fortune, but the resultant *The Stripper* with Joanne Woodward was a bomb. All Inge's subsequent plays failed, and he grew disgusted with Hollywood when his work on the film *Bus Riley's Back in Town* (1965) was considerably altered to expand Ann-Margret's purr-esence. Novels were a last resort, but both sold embarrassingly. After becoming more and more reclusive in the Hollywood Hills, the writer reached rock bottom and chose carbon monoxide poisoning while seated in his Mercedes, weeks after turning sixty.

Shirley Booth, who'd withdrawn from *A Loss of Roses* before it opened, felt, "That play wasn't terribly well written, and it wasn't well rewritten. . . . The previous ones were better, but what happened shocked him: at the first sign of a weak play, the ill-wishers who'd been holding their tongues suddenly all let loose . . . they opened fire on Mr. Inge."

His friend James Leo Herlihy, whose novel *All Fall Down* Inge adapted for the screen, offered, "Bill was fragile, though he'd come up the hard way. . . . Success softened him. He got too used to it, and it lowered his defenses. He let that nasty Brustein character pierce him to the core." Inge later admitted that the critic "represented all the things I feared," including the intimation that the playwright's great success had been a fluke. Herlihy, best known for his novel *Midnight Cowboy*, stated, "Bill had a melancholy streak, as you could guess from his work. But to my mind, that helped his plays. He tapped into something people hadn't yet articulated about small-town America.

"Bill did care too much what others thought. Then, when other people's esteem went away, it seemed to leave him with nothing." Less than a year before his death, William Inge looked back to 1959, to the catastrophe of *A Loss of Roses*, the play he'd believed was his best yet: "I lost my audience, and I haven't been able to get it back."

Inge's sister, with whom he lived and who found his body, lamented, "Sometimes, just the fear of writer's block froze him up. And I don't think he even had any writer's block. . . . Writing was his life. He had no other interests."

5

EVERYONE'S A CRITIC

"A bad idea gone wrong."—WALTER KERR on the 1965 musical *Kelly*, which closed on opening night

"Good Fielding. No hit."—KYLE CRICHTON on a play version of Henry Fielding's classic novel *Tom Jones*

"It contains a number of those tunes one goes *into* the theater humming." —KENNETH TYNAN on a derivative musical

"A titanic letdown."—the NEW YORK DAILY NEWS on the hit musical *Titanic*, which won five 1997 Tony Awards, including Best Musical

"With lyrics like these, hop a raft."—the BERGEN RECORD on *Titanic*

"The real *Titanic* sank five days into its maiden voyage 85 years ago. . . . The show may not run much longer."—the SCOTTISH DAILY RECORD

"Tripe."—London's SUNDAY TIMES on the popular and critical hit *Amadeus* (1979)

"I don't believe in astrology. The only stars I can blame for my failures are those that walk about the stage."—SIR NOEL COWARD

". . . British actors remain more experienced, more dextrous, more poetic than their American colleagues."—theatre historian ETHAN MORDDEN

"Jones sounded like a one-stringed double bass with a faintly Calypso accent, and rolled about like a huge barrel set in motion by a homunculus within."—JOHN SIMON on James Earl Jones as a tribune in Shakespeare's *Coriolanus* (1965)

". . . she's about as Latin as a New England boiled dinner."—DOUGLAS WATT in the *New York Daily News* on Jane Alexander in *Goodbye, Fidel* (1980)

"Nor will I say that *Portofino* is the worst musical ever produced, because I've only been seeing musicals since 1919."—WALTER KERR in the *New York Herald Tribune* in 1958

"*Our Town* is not only disappointing but hopelessly slow . . . [a] disjointed, bittersweet affair of smalltown New Hampshire life."—VARIETY in 1938; Thornton Wilder's play ran "only" 336 performances, but won the Pulitzer Prize for drama

"Go to the Martin Beck Theatre and watch Katharine Hepburn run the gamut of emotion from A to B."—DOROTHY PARKER on rising star Hepburn in *The Lake* in 1933

". . . this Broadway adaptation of the film classic—and really, is there a more frightening phrase in all of showbiz? . . . "—TIME OUT NEW YORK magazine (June 2002)

"Lord Alfred Douglas having an exciting melodramatic cup of tea with Beverley Nichols."—GEORGE JEAN NATHAN's homophobic dismissal of John Gielgud's 1930 Hamlet, otherwise critically acclaimed (Douglas was Oscar Wilde's lover; Nichols was a famous 20th-century male writer)

"No smash hit, no blockbuster."—VARIETY on *Fiddler on the Roof*, which opened in Detroit in 1964; it opened later that year in New York, won the Best Musical Tony, and broke all attendance records

"Tony winner Tom Bosley of *Fiorello!* attained his niche on TV. But now he's gone from *Happy Days* to Sappy Nights."—*Movieline* magazine editor ED MARGULIES on Bosley's return to Broadway in *Beauty and the Beast*

"The thing about Maggie Smith, who is a great performer, is that she never allows you to forget that she is performing."—fellow thespian JEREMY BRETT

"Fallen archness."—FRANKLIN PIERCE ADAMS on Helen Hayes as Cleopatra(!) in Shaw's *Caesar and Cleopatra* in 1925

"Mr. Ferrer likes pauses. He pauses at the slightest provocation. He pauses at the beginning, in the middle and at the end of every line."—WALTER

KERR on José Ferrer's *Cyrano de Bergerac* (1947), the film version of which won him a Best Actor Oscar

"It is as long as *Parsifal* and not as funny."—SIR NOEL COWARD, after the 1960 Toronto tryout of *Camelot*, which scuttlebutt said hastened the death of director-producer Moss Hart and prompted the retirement of composer Frederick Loewe

"The most serious musical comedy I ever saw . . . Maurice Evans [Sam's father on *Bewitched*] plays a crusading minister who wants to eliminate the production numbers."—WALTER KERR, *Herald Tribune*, on *Tenderloin*

"A largely marvelous Leonard Bernstein score that drags Alan Jay Lerner's book and lyrics behind it like an unwanted relative . . . of all the patched-up musicals that have limped into New York, this is the most pitifully pieced together one I have ever seen."—MARTIN GOTTFRIED, *New York Post*, on *1600 Pennsylvania Avenue*

"'Tis pity she's a bore."—playwright BOB RANDALL on Madonna in *Speed-the-Plow* (punning the title *'Tis Pity She's a Whore*)

"Guido Nadzo is nadzo guido."—playwright GEORGE S. KAUFMAN critiquing actor Guido Nadzo

"You've heard of people living in a fools' paradise. Well, Leonora has a duplex there."—KAUFMAN on Leonora Corbett in the 1946 play *Park Avenue*

"[Director] Terry Hands saw this slight story of an adolescent girl seeking peer group acceptance [*Carrie*, the 1988 musical] as a Greek tragedy. To this end, he staged the show not in a recognizable high school but on a bare monochrome set enclosed by sterile, all white, high-tech walls: 'The Black and White Menstrual Show.' . . . *Carrie* the musical should have been *Grease*, not Greece."—author MARK STEYN

"Dreadfully lacking in box office appeal."—VARIETY in 1930 on Marc Connelly's *Green Pastures*, a "race" (black) story which won a Pulitzer Prize in 1931, ran for 557 performances before touring for four years, then returning to Broadway in 1935, closing with its 1,653rd performance; it grossed a then-remarkable $3 million-plus, partly because its black cast was underpaid

"*Strange Interlude* will probably interest a comparatively small public. It is solid gray in tone, slow-paced and repetitious in performance, and forbidding in length."—*New York Daily News* critic BURNS MANTLE in 1928; Eugene

O'Neill's long and strange play became his biggest success, also one of the Theatre Guild's most profitable productions

". . . her very Whoopi-ness dilutes our sense of Rainey's dark subterranean pain and knowledge. And with her uninformed singing voice, Goldberg fails to become what she must: the spiritual centerpiece for the music."—ENTERTAINMENT WEEKLY on a 2003 revival of *Ma Rainey's Black Bottom*

"For those of you who missed it the first time, this is your golden opportunity: you can miss it again."—MICHAEL BILLINGTON on a 1981 revival of the musical *Godspell*

"The best play I ever slept through."—an OSCAR WILDE critique

"Well, for Crichton out loud."—WALTER WINCHELL, bored with James Barrie's play *The Admirable Crichton*

"I saw it at a disadvantage—the curtain was up."—WALTER WINCHELL (also ascribed to GROUCHO MARX)

"It was one of those plays in which all the actors unfortunately enunciated very clearly."—ROBERT BENCHLEY

"The scenery was beautiful, but the actors got in front of it."—ALEXANDER WOOLLCOTT

"There's less here than meets the eye."—TALLULAH BANKHEAD

"The audience came out whistling the set."—ANONYMOUS CRITIC on Irving Berlin's 1949 *Miss Liberty* and its less than memorable songs

"Irving Berlin's score is musically not exciting—of the real songs, only one or two are tuneful."—*PM* critic LEWIS KRONENBERGER on the 1946 Broadway opening of *Annie Get Your Gun*, the biggest success of Berlin's stage career. Among its "real songs": "There's No Business Like Show Business," "They Say It's Wonderful," "Anything You Can Do, I Can Do Better," "Doin' What Comes Naturally," "You Can't Get a Man With a Gun," and "I'm an Indian Too"

"Me No Leica."—WALTER KERR on *I Am a Camera* (1954)

"*Hook 'n Ladder* is the sort of play that gives failures a bad name."—WALTER KERR in the 1950s

"This is the kind of show that gives pornography a dirty name."—CLIVE BARNES on *Oh! Calcutta!* (written by a fellow critic)

"A Month in the Wrong Country."—SIR NOEL COWARD on a US production of Chekhov's *The Cherry Orchard*, set in the Deep South

"Oh, to be in England, now that April's here."—BROOKS ATKINSON assessing a British actress by the first name of April who was performing on Broadway

"I love Nathan Lane's comedy performances. It's such a funny one."—WAYNE WARGA of *Entertainment Tonight*

"There was scattered laughter in the rear of the theatre, leading to the belief that somebody was telling jokes back there."—GEORGE S. KAUFMAN on an unfunny comedy

"Odets, where is thy sting?"—ROBERT GARLAND on *Clash by Night*, by the formerly fierce Clifford Odets

"It isn't the sort of entertainment folks buy in the theater. Nor ever have bought, within my memory. There is no emotional satisfaction to be had from sheer ugliness."—BURNS MANTLE on *Tobacco Road* (1933), which, hillbilly or not, yielded 3,182 performances

"*Zorba* is one of the ugliest, most life-denying pieces of evil shit ever perpetrated as a Broadway musical, not least because it pretends to be beautiful and life-affirming."—theater historian ETHAN MORDDEN, appalled by the 1968 show's selfish title character

"She says she wants to explore character on the stage. She means, of course, her own."—producer LELAND HAYWARD on Ethel Merman

"Not while I'm alive!"—GEORGE S. KAUFMAN's reply when a mutual acquaintance opined that producer Jed Harris was his own worst enemy

"I'll send you a bill for the suit."—critic JOHN SIMON to actress Sylvia Miles after she dumped a plate of food on him due to a bad review
Her reply: "Good. It'll be dry-cleaned probably for the first time."

"If you were to ask me what *Uncle Vanya* is about, I would say about as much as I can take."—ROBERT GARLAND in *Journal American* in 1946

"The play opened at 8:40 sharp and closed at 10:40 dull."—HEYWOOD BROUN on a Broadway comedy

"The Messrs. Shubert seem to forget that the female knee is a joint and not an evening's entertainment."—PERCY HAMMOND on girlie shows built around the then-shocking knee and popular in the 1920s; in another review he noted, "I find that I have knocked everything but the chorus girls' knees, and there nature anticipated me"

"Miss Streisand's contortions and shifting inflections while singing might be less jarring if she wore sunglasses—might one suggest a musical set in southern California?—due to her strabismus, or semi crossed-eye condition."—WYATT COOPER on *Funny Girl*'s star

"[Mrs. Warren] is a generous role for womanly and impassioned actresses, and many performers have essayed it. I can think of four, however, who have not: Totie Fields, W.C. Fields, Tutankhamen's mummy, and a trained monkey. Not until now, that is; Miss Gordon's performance combines elements of all four."—JOHN SIMON on Ruth Gordon in Shaw's *Mrs. Warren's Profession* at Lincoln Center; he accused producer Joe Papp of (mis)casting her solely because of her Oscar-winning turn in the hit movie *Rosemary's Baby* (1968)

"The most insipid, ridiculous play I ever saw in my life."—SAMUEL PEPYS, British author and public official, on William Shakespeare's comedy *A Midsummer Night's Dream* in 1662; however, Pepys disliked another play even more: *Romeo and Juliet*, "a play of itself the worst I ever heard in my life."

Anti Critics

"No man can be criticized but by a man greater than he. Do not, then, read the reviews."—RALPH WALDO EMERSON in 1842

"I really stopped caring what critics said when I was in a play by Maxwell Anderson, very famous guy at the time. *Truckline Café* (1946). Not the best play, not the worst. Pretty good—good enough. The reviews were atrocious. That's when I figured out it wasn't a serious thing. It was just a game. And nobody was immune."—MARLON BRANDO

"I say I'm going to read [reviews] later, and then I don't. I guess I've read a few, and then friends call and leave them on your machine. I've heard them that way. And occasionally you get the gist of them from the way people act after opening—smiling or in a slump. At the time that they're relevant, you really can't read them, because good or bad, you have to continue with what you're doing. And then, afterwards, it's like, who cares?" —STOCKARD CHANNING (*Six Degrees of Separation*)

"Most reviewers of the theater are Communists, trust me."—conservative playwright GEORGE KELLY, Grace's uncle

"There are a couple of critics I would gladly off, if I could get away with it. I won't name them. Not because of legal reasons, [but] just in case."—BOB FOSSE, who admitted, "My friends know that to me happiness is when I am merely miserable and not suicidal."

"Are all reviewers in the States so juvenile? They dote on puns and bad jokes. More than once, they've actually written, 'She played the part *Baddeley*'" —Englishwoman HERMIONE BADDELEY

"I attended a charming little musical in Beverly Hills that I'd seen Off-Broadway, and both times some critics complained that the cast 'played to the audience.' Who *else* would they play to? You could tell the actors were relishing their roles and lines and the songs . . . and audiences loved that show, critics be damned."—production designer RICHARD SYLBERT (the musical was *Ruthless!*)

"A reviewer once described me as 'a delicious ear in a field of corn.' I deluded myself into thinking the key word was 'delicious,' that it was a compliment. The key word was 'corn.'"—MARIE "MY FRIEND IRMA" WILSON, who in the early '60s toured as Lorelei Lee in *Gentlemen Prefer Blondes*

"Someone has to write about, and describe, plays. But how did it devolve into Broadway critics having the power to close shows down?"—CAROL BURNETT

"I realized how pretentious critics can be when *Cats* came along and several of them tried to discern or invent different levels of meaning or significance and symbolism in the show. Others wrote with such conviction about the wonderful or the terrible performances in *Cats*—either way, how could they *tell?*"—MADELINE KAHN (*The Sisters Rosenzweig*)

"Critics are snobs who only want to write about stars. It's not about credit where credit is due. That's why they deliberately ignored Joe Cino, who helped revitalize Off-Broadway—more than a few of its hits came out of his coffeehouse. By day he was a typist, just to pay the overhead on his productions. He called it Off-Off-Broadway, and he deserves so much credit, but he didn't get it, nor money or any glory. . . . When he died in 1967, a suicide, the critics still thought he wasn't a Name and wouldn't praise him."—the *Village Voice* columnist ARTHUR BELL

"It is the arrogance of certain critics to believe that their job lies less in assessing an art than in guiding or even bullying it. But art can properly appear only as the product of the free artist."—theater historian ETHAN MORDDEN

"On Broadway, the critics attend previews rather than the official opening night, write their reviews in advance and have them ready for the first editions—which usually means the notices arrive when the [post-premiere] party's in full swing and, if they're unfavourable, clear the room quicker than a nuclear warning. . . . In London, happily, first-night reviews are still reviews of the first night . . . there are no brutal critical dissections to cast a pall over the [party]. The critics, like the hangovers, belong to the morning after."—THE STORY OF MISS SAIGON (1991 book)

"Jule Styne, *Gypsy's* composer, implored [writer] Arthur Laurents to remove a joke about the Vatican because critic Walter Kerr was Catholic. He wouldn't. And Laurents wouldn't let Kerr leave till he'd seen all of the show. Kerr had naively thought that since Gypsy Rose Lee was a stripper, the show would end with a strip tease, which he didn't want to see in front of his wife. But this was an Ethel Merman musical, and it ended with Merman's biggest number.

"It came out swell. Kerr's review was a love letter. He called *Gypsy* 'The best damn musical I've seen in years.' *Damn*, mind you!"—pop culture historian MARTIN GREIF

"I doubt most New Yorkers are Catholics. Yet they seem willing to let their theatre critics make up their minds for them . . . reading the notices as if they were papal edicts and infallible, when mostly they deliver a lot of bull."—RICHARD BURTON (*Hamlet, Camelot*) in 1968

"I resent critics who use their excess weight to try and damage a production. And those who get too personal and can harm an actor. . . . My attitude is, generally, that of a famous Frenchman who wrote a letter back to a nasty critic while sitting in the loo. He said that he had the bad review in front of him, but that soon it would be behind him."—RICHARD KILEY (*Man of La Mancha*)

". . . critics don't write for their readers. They write for each other, or for what they are sure is a personal following of superior intellect."—producer DAVID MERRICK

"You have to stand up for yourself from the very beginning of your career. The playwright doesn't have to make changes, and the playwright would be wise not to. I never went into the theatre to be an employee. If you refuse to be owned and refuse to be an employee, they'll probably start to revile you . . . [It] makes them angrier and angrier, because they can't cripple you."—EDWARD ALBEE on his past treatment by critics

"A newspaperman whose sweetheart ran away with an actor."—columnist and sometime critic WALTER WINCHELL'S definition of a drama critic. (On his tradition of praising the first play he saw in any given season, he said, "Who am I to stone the first cast?")

"Criticism is prejudice made plausible."—writer H.L. MENCKEN

6

MONSTER MAMA

How surprising is it that the real-life Mama Rose of *Gypsy* was lesbian? Her grandson Erik Lee Preminger publicly acknowledged it. Rose Hovick's performer daughters "Gypsy" Rose Lee and June Havoc didn't admit it as readily. In Lee's eponymous memoir, which bears minimal resemblance to the Broadway musical, Rose's sexuality was camouflaged by her marital past; the 1959 musical added "Herbie" (Jack Klugman) as Rose's fictitious love interest. Gypsy Rose Lee told writer Arthur Laurents that she wished she'd invented Herbie herself.

Lee penned *Gypsy* as a "monument" to herself and, hopefully once it was musicalized or filmed, a path toward permanent solvency. The glory, not the facts, concerned her. When Laurents asked how she'd gotten the nickname "Gypsy," she replied, "Oh, honey, I've given fourteen or fifteen versions. Yours will be as good as mine." Like daughter, like mother, for Rose had never let the truth stand between June—the younger and more talented of her daughters—and success. For one of Dainty June's finales, Rose showcased her in a gown flocked with rhinestones which she claimed in a program note was worth a then-whopping $1,000. Rose had had to be dissuaded from adding that three seamstresses went blind while making the garment.

The musical's credit read, "Suggested by the memoirs of Gypsy Rose Lee." In the Broadway version, after Louise blossoms into a relatively demure stripper and strikes out on her own, it's suggested that Mama (never referred to as "Mama Rose") could open an acting school for kids, to keep occupied. She rejects the idea indignantly. In reality, Rose Hovick wound up running a lesbian boarding house and brothel. This was revealed in June Havoc's second autobiography, *More Havoc*, published in 1980, by which time The Topic could finally be broached (her first book, *Early Havoc*, in 1959, was a sisterly attempt to grab back some of the limelight from Gypsy, whose memoirs had angered June less than the resultant hit musical).

June's mother had informed her, "Sex is dirty because men are dirty." As for her lesbian tenants, Rose warned, "Don't you dare feel superior to those girls. At least they have the good sense to know they can't get pregnant with spit!"

The 1984 book *Gypsy and Me* was by Erik Lee Preminger, the out-of-wedlock son of Lee (1914–1970) and director Otto Preminger, whom he strongly resembled and who eventually acknowledged his son. Erik noted that his surrogate father had been a gay man who lived with Gypsy and son during the boy's formative years. He was more candid about the non-heterosexuals in his background during gay-press interviews in 1993 while publicizing the TV remake of *Gypsy* that starred Bette Midler.

"Boyd Bennett was there to make sure that I grew up thoughtful and considerate of others. He told me, 'Your mother is arrogant and grand. But you're not going to act like the son of a diva if I can help it.' I couldn't have learned the lessons I learned if I'd been raised by a straight man." Among other things, Erik was taught to value women for more than their looks. "I think Red Buttons was [Gypsy's] only straight friend. Mother would have been happier if I had been gay. She wouldn't have had as much trouble with me."

Ironic that although most of the musical's creators were gay, it had no lesbian or gay content, then or in revivals. In his 2000 memoirs Arthur Laurents recalled that one impetus for *Gypsy* had been gay or bisexual writer Liz Smith showing up at a party with a girlfriend named Selma Lynch who confessed that her first lover had been Gypsy Rose Lee's mother. Laurents wondered if Gypsy herself, like many strippers and hookers, was bisexual, possibly lesbian? He added that June Havoc had written about lesbian cocktail parties that Gypsy and Rose gave for their friends, who had to pay admission.

LAURENTS AND OTHERS have described Rose as not just the quintessential stage mother but a "monster" trying to live out her dreams through her daughters. "I was born too soon and started too late," the fictional Rose asseverates. As played by Ethel Merman, Rosalind Russell, Angela Lansbury, Tyne Daly, Bette Midler, Bernadette Peters, and others, Rose is an egomaniacal dynamo. An unusually strong female character for a musical, she is judged more severely by theatre critics and audiences than many similarly domineering male characters in straight plays.

Merman, who originated the role, had long awaited a musical that offered a real dramatic challenge. When *Gypsy* was published, Ethel read it and told

Gypsy Rose Lee at a cocktail party, "I want to do it. I'm going to do it. And I'll shoot anyone else who gets the part." After the show became a reality and a smash hit, Lee advised reporters, "I told Ethel to drink lots of milk and stay healthy. She's going to be my annuity." Merman, while relishing the starring role of Gypsy's mother, tried to distance herself from the harsher aspects of Rose's personality. Herself a domineering mother, she announced, "Rose and me, we got hardly anything in common, 'cept for love of show business."

In any case, the real Rose Hovick was considerably tougher than the Lee, Laurents, or Merman versions, and the relationships and incidents presented on stage varied markedly from the truth. For instance, the break with rebellious daughter June (born in 1916) wasn't as final as in *Gypsy*. Yet the scene after June up and weds a boy named Bobby from their act was more dramatic in real life. Where the fictionalized Rose resigned herself to the loss of her thirteen-year-old daughter and chief breadwinner, the real Rose went straight to the law and demanded of a police lieutenant, "You aren't going to let him abduct my baby, are you?"

The cop, who spent the day investigating the case, answered, "Marriage isn't the electric chair." With the boy present, he assured Mrs. Hovick that her new in-law was of good family and long-range intentions. He ordered, "Shake hands, please." In *Early Havoc*, June described what came next. "Mother moved toward Bobby; her eyes glistened. He extended his hand, but just then Mother produced a small automatic. . . . Ten inches away from Bobby's chest, she pulled the trigger—once . . . twice."

Rose carried a gun in her car for nighttime traveling protection but knew nothing of guns. The safety catch had locked the action and kept her from becoming a murderess—in which case *Gypsy* might not have been written, or if it had, would probably not have been musicalized (in those pre-*Chicago* days).

"One of the cops grabbed Mother and the gun. She wrested herself free, and then she piled on Bobby—fists, knees, fingernails, and teeth. It took the whole night staff to pull her off." Mrs. Hovick was detained until Bobby could depart the police station without further harm. When Bobby returned to June he was "battered but undaunted." The flustered police lieutenant advised June before she and Bobby left by train for their new life together, "Write to your poor mother at once and she will forgive and understand because she loves you so."

JUNE REMINISCED THAT "MOTHER" (not "Mama" in her case) had a marvelous vocal range, with "musical" low tones, and speech that could send "chills up your spine with its loveliness." But "Her fury was like the booming of a cannon. She could be heard halfway down the block." Rose's father had kept his daughter from pursuing her own showbiz dream. Though eventually a rebel, like most girls she was initially compliant. Likewise *her* mother, of whom June wrote:

"She had married Grandpa when she was fifteen. . . . She hadn't really wanted to marry Grandpa. She hadn't wanted to have any children at all, but careers were seldom for women in those days."

June, who summoned up the courage to strike out on her own personally and professionally, was the first woman in her family for generations, perhaps ever, to attain her goal. She disclosed after establishing herself that "I never went to school a day in my life." Feminine education was a not a priority during that era, and June's grandmother suffered for her near illiteracy when her husband asked her to sign a paper and she did, not knowing it was a divorce paper that would sever her 48-year marriage.

Grandpa, whose alter ego in *Gypsy* won't give Rose eighty-eight cents to pursue her dream when she requests "eighty-eight bucks," intended to marry a neighbor woman, much to the fury of his ex-wife and daughter Rose. But while driving home one day from a picnic the couple, not yet wed, was hit by a train at an intersection and killed. Who knew the dour "Papa" in *Gypsy* had such a dramatic ending?

Rose typically overdramatized after catching June and her coworker Bobby kissing one day. The youth said he'd thought June was "at least sixteen." Rose insisted June was thirteen; she kept multiple birth certificates, two of which made her younger daughter out to be twenty-one for when it was useful. Rose slapped Bobby hard, then fired him. In the dressing room, she slapped her daughter twice, then hit her on the back of the neck with her fist. "We had never come to blows before," wrote June.

When June protested, Rose screamed, "Who do you think you are? You're nothing. I can't even get the audience to accept you any more. Out there on the stage, you're *nothing*. And now you try to break my heart. I'm not hitting you—I'm spanking you!"

When June ordered her out of her dressing room, her mother yelled, "Your dressing room?" Then she struck her daughter with a hand mirror. After it shattered and the stage manager shouted, "Fifteen minutes, first act, Mrs. Hovick," Rose fell into a chair and sobbed, "What have I ever done to deserve this?" Referring to the shards of mirror on the floor, Rose said, "This is your seven years of bad luck, not mine."

June Havoc's professional breakthrough was on Broadway in *Pal Joey*. Despite her blonde beauty and partly because of her aloofness, she failed to become a star in a long string of films during the 1940s. She had her own TV series, *Willy*, but returned to the stage time and again. Her most disappointing comeback was the flop movie *Can't Stop the Music* (1980) as the mother of Steve Guttenberg's character, who co-founds a heterosexualized version of

The Village People. (Gays and straights alike hated the disco film, directed by stage star turned TV star Nancy Walker.)

In her second autobiography, June recalled memories she'd never shared with her mother. They included "the uncles," men Rose had "liked temporarily" who "had put my hand inside their trousers; who cuddled alongside me in bed, rubbing a huge penis against me. Nothing had come of any of this. Just my five-year-old disgust."

Gypsy the musical sugar-coated men, show business, the girls' lives, and, of course, Rose. Missing from the stage version was any reference to the real-life episode of a tenant of Rose's who was desperately unhappy with her life and prospects. Rose later explained to June: "I said, 'Why not just check out if you're that unhappy?' And there was the gun, and—well, I think she knew what she was doing." Rose insisted, "I didn't do a thing. She took the shotgun out of my hand, put the nozzle in her mouth, stepped on the trigger, and pow! I didn't actually offer the gun, don't you see? I just had it, that's all."

June remembered that "Mother's mouth hardened in contempt. 'I've never been able to stomach a poor loser.'" Mrs. Hovick's big concern, after burning the young woman's tell-all diary, was the future of her own older daughter, Gypsy—"with your sister trying so hard to be a Hollywood star, and that fool girl blowing the whole top of her head off." The studio helped squelch any major publicity.

ANOTHER HUSHED-UP, MORE LEGENDARY EPISODE was the one in which Rose Hovick allegedly killed a man. *Gypsy* fleetingly and comically alludes to it in the scene where a landlord invades the rooms of Rose and her troupe. Not only is she guilty of cooking, she's housing too many people and harboring pets. Rose at first denies all, then abruptly switches tracks and pushes the man into her bedroom where she tears at her clothes, disshevels her hair, then opens the door and claims he tried to attack (rape) her.

"Oh, my babies!" she wails, soon on the verbal attack and warning fellow boarders against those "dangerous middle-aged men!"

In real life, Rose apparently pushed such a man—a hotel manager who'd threatened eviction because she had five boys sleeping in a room rented to one daughter—out a window to his death. Her defense was self-defense and motherhood. Of all the glaring events in Rose Hovick's colorful, unstoppable life, this was the one most shrouded in mystery and the least explored. Her daughters, otherwise bold and provocative, understandably shied away from this chapter.

Additionally, the real Mama seems to have favored whichever daughter was riding higher at the time. As *Gypsy* the musical shows, Louise got short shrift while her more talented and personable little blonde sister was charming audiences. But it was Gypsy Rose Lee who became more famous via her then-risqué specialty, which eventually led to acting and authoring (including a novel). Her autobiography created a rift between the sisters, whom Rose had encouraged to compete with one another.

In *More Havoc*, published after her big sister's death from cancer, June declared that the musical *Gypsy* "meant more than anything or anyone in the world" to Louise, who believed, "It doesn't have to be factual, it only has to be big, exciting and—and a smash!"

June demanded, "What about me? It's all untrue, and it makes me a heavy . . . a whining kid who grabs and runs."

Gypsy embraced her sister, offering, "We all know it's a fable. It's going to be billed like that—a fable. Please let me have my monument."

Thus, primarily for legal reasons, *Gypsy* is officially "a musical fable." A financial settlement was made with Havoc regarding her depiction in the musical. She'd already requested certain changes, so many in fact that the producers were going to rename June "Claire." In the end, she opted to be included via her own name rather than be left out in the cold. Gypsy's son, Erik, felt that his Aunt June let it slide "almost as a gift, sister to sister."

Rose had long since become closer to Louise/Gypsy. Still cantankerous and suspicious, ever the injured party in her own mind, Rose was nonetheless proud of her elder daughter's determination and success; less so—sometimes throwing it up in her face—of June's determination and lesser success (besides acting, she wrote two plays and directed). June described her mother's deathbed scene in 1954, with both daughters at her bedside, the elder one closer and thus nearer to reproach.

"I know you," Rose accused Louise. "Greedy, selfish! You want me to die. I'm the only one knows all about you . . . so, die. . . ." As she moved closer to Louise, Rose's long suede grouch bag (used for storing money) that she wore strung around her waist was revealed through her nightgown, which burst open. Gypsy warned, "You'll fall!" and grabbed for her mother.

Rose yelled, "*No!*" interpreting the grab in mercenary terms. "You can't have anything back! Just because I'm letting go—it's mine! My house, my jewelry. . . ." She swayed, and Gypsy took hold of her. It turned into something of a slow-motion wrestling match, with mother pinning daughter down and offering a parting curse: that Louise would never lose the memory of her mother holding her ever so tightly and wishing she could take her "all the way down with me!"

Gypsy's face showed no emotion. Rose let her go, and regained her strength. On her feet and stunned into silence, Louise heard their mother swear that this was not the end, that all the rest of their lives, her daughters would know and feel her presence. Rose dared Louise to tell her "classy friends" how funny Rose was, how much less intelligent—but to remember that when Louise got her own "private kick in the ass," it would be a "present" from her late but undeparted mother.

Gypsy waited until Rose's breath came evenly, then left the room. Outside, June held Gypsy's hands while she insisted to her protesting sister, "Oh, yes, June, [those things] will happen. Just like she promised. She'll never let me go. Not ever."

As they prepared to depart, June asked, "Why only you? Why not me?"

Louise replied that June had "failed" Rose by not being exciting enough to reflect their mother's dream self. The non-stripper, unlike her sister, hadn't featured in the tabloids, caused sensations, or been arrested. "How many times has she enjoyed a ride in a police car with you?" Louise asked. As the musical made clear, Rose was molded and enthralled by colorful, jazzy vaudeville, not the legitimate stage toward which her younger daughter aspired and left her for.

According to insiders, at the end of her life Gypsy Rose Lee was convinced that she was dying of cancer, prematurely (1914–1970) and long before her younger sister (still alive at this writing), because of her mother's dying curse.

7

MUSICAL TONY: NO AWARD

Like most movie stars of his generation, Anthony Perkins (1932–1992) initially set his sights on the stage. It was particularly apt for the only child of Osgood Perkins, a minor movie actor but a stage star despite his mousey, pinched features. Tony made an inauspicious screen debut in a 1953 adaptation of Ruth Gordon's *The Actress*, for which he'd been discovered and "mentored" by gay A-list film and former stage director George Cukor.

Perkins, who felt he was too "special" for movie leads—boney, awkward, and shy—then stayed off screen until 1956. Meanwhile he returned to the stage, where in 1954 he got his big break in *Tea and Sympathy*, the Broadway hit in which he replaced John Kerr (who later did the film version with non-relative Deborah Kerr). The then-daring play had homosexual undertones; through much of it Tony's character's sexuality is in question and under fire. In the manner of the 1947 film *Gentleman's Agreement*, ostensibly about anti-Semitism, *Tea*'s ultimate message was, Don't treat somebody "different" badly, because they might turn out to be "normal."

After returning to Hollywood and contracting with Paramount, Perkins's relationship with star Tab Hunter was masked by studio publicists with "double dates" involving female starlets. However, Tony's real home remained in New York, where he felt freer socially and sexually. Even after becoming a movie star he harbored hopes of being bicoastal and alternating stage and screen work. In 1957 he starred on Broadway to considerable acclaim in *Look*

Homeward, Angel. His next goal was to sing onstage. Director George Roy Hill, later a prominent Hollywood director, was Tony's choice to guide him in what would be each man's first and final musical: *Greenwillow* (1960).

It featured a slight plot set in an imaginary village on the banks of the Meander River, with Perkins as young wanderer Gideon Briggs. The slight novel on which it was based had frustrated celebrated composer Frank Loesser, who'd determined to transform it into his own *Brigadoon*. He eventually sought outside help; screenwriter Lesser Samuels coauthored the musical's book. *Greenwillow* thus earned the nickname the Evil of Two Lessers.

Perkins had a pleasant enough singing voice, but a Broadway musical was a stretch for a teenybopper idol who'd recorded various songs for swooning, uncritical fans. While preparing for his Broadway musical debut, Tony was making *Psycho*, the film which would begin and end his superstardom, forever stereotyping him as a lethal oddball. On the *Psycho* set director Alfred Hitchcock opined to screenwriter Joseph Stefano that Perkins was "excessively shy around women," and so spared him having to appear in the notorious shower scene with Janet Leigh. The gentlemanly Hitch felt it "just wouldn't be very nice" to subject Tony to the intimate and brutal scene with a supposedly nude motel guest. A double was hired to hack Marion Crane to death while Norman Bates's alter ego was taking musical training in Manhattan.

In *Psycho*'s revelation scene, in which Norman appears in drag dressed as his own late mother, Perkins was supposed to "scream as loud as I could" when John Gavin grabs him and saves the life of Marion's sister, Lila (Vera Miles). However, Tony was committed to his singing lessons, and told *The Hollywood Reporter*, "I asked if I could pretend to be screaming—to save my voice—and they could dub in screams later. Hitchcock liked the silent screams so much he never added the sound."

Unfortunately for the earnest star, Frank Loesser wasn't as accommodating or tolerant as the English Hitchcock, who once admitted that except for his (mousey and bespectacled, also very talented) wife, Alma, he might have lived homosexually. Loesser, difficult to begin with, was "a screamer," according to George Roy Hill. Loesser had wanted an established theater director like Moss Hart (himself rumored to be a closeted nonheterosexual), but Tony, then relatively uncloseted, felt more comfortable and trusting with Hill, who after *Greenwillow* went to Hollywood for keeps.

Record producer Ben Bagley, for whom Tony sang on six albums, stated that the reportedly homophobic Loesser deliberately gave Perkins notes too high for him to sing, and also insisted that Perkins was never loud enough. Tony's most demanding song was the showstopping, semi-operatic "Never Will I Marry," the sole song from *Greenwillow* to live on, due to recordings of it by Judy Garland, Barbra Streisand, and Linda Ronstadt. The song refers to the curse endured by male members of the Briggs clan, each fated to be a wanderer, visiting his hometown only to help "plant" a baby, but never able to settle down in one place with one partner. The curse can only be broken when a male Briggs chooses not to marry and not to beget another wandering generation. Gideon makes that same choice. (Notice that male singers refrained from recording this masculine but anti-marital song.)

"Never Will I Marry" had the most high notes of any of Perkins's songs. Despite the vocal training and extensive rehearsals Tony undertook, several insiders felt his voice wasn't up to carrying a musical. Frank Loesser was particularly exasperated because his last two shows, *Guys and Dolls* and *The Most Happy Fella*, had been big hits, and he sensed that *Greenwillow* might be anything but. Perkins was almost neurotically dissatisfied with the recordings he'd made, and one reason he agreed to do *Greenwillow* was to prove to himself that "my voice was better than it sounded on those records."

Though he tried to increase his volume, he had to be miked while singing—today a commonplace, then a rarity. Partly to camouflage his vocal deficiencies, Tony over-gesticulated madly during "Never Will I Marry." He may have been unaware of how bizarre it looked. Perkins biographer Charles Winecoff wrote that "Loesser silently, maybe even maliciously, failed to correct" the broad gestures that were also incorrect. Cast member Maggie Trask recalled, "When it came to lines like, 'Wide my world, narrow my bed,' Tony would throw his arms open on 'narrow my bed'—which was just the opposite. Maybe he was being funny? I never figured it out."

Actor-dancer-singer Don Atkinson remembered that Perkins would "hyper-extend his arms back with stiffened elbow" while singing. "He looked so strange, because he was big and had a huge arm span. I told him to at least bend his arms a bit at the elbow."

Lee Cass, who played a villager, offered, "Everybody sang well except Tony Perkins. I heard him sing ["Never Will I Marry"] later . . . and it was even worse than I remembered it." She was referring to a 1985 PBS-TV special, *Best of Broadway*, in which Perkins, visibly stiff and nervous and already cadaverous (though pre-AIDS), reprised the song "with excruciating difficulty," yet no doubt proud to remind viewers of a past when he'd starred on Broadway instead of playing endless kooks and killers, increasingly in a supporting capacity.

In 1960 audiences and most critics disparaged Perkins's voice, but he had his defenders. One was pal Stephen Sondheim, who felt Tony's peculiar vocal style was right for his characterization. "One of the things that makes 'Never Will I Marry' so brilliant is the crack of his voice when he reaches the tenth."

George Roy Hill adjudged Tony's singing "remarkably good. It didn't have the timbre of a real Broadway voice, but it didn't have the hard edge. It had a quality of its own." Alas, that quality was too specialized or offbeat for the time, and poor word of mouth hurt *Greenwillow* at the box office. Advance ticket sales were enough to keep the show running for thirteen weeks, mainly on the strength of Loesser's name. The lure of a movie star lead was nowhere near what the producers had imagined. Things might have been quite different had the phenomenally successful *Psycho* already been released.

To Loesser's chagrin, even pre-sold theater parties didn't help fill the theater weeknights. The show's musical director Abba Bogin noted that on Friday nights "You could graze sheep in the theater—there was nobody there!" Though he tried his best to hide it, Tony Perkins's embarrassment was acute, and colleagues were embarrassed for him. One, *South Pacific's* Ray Walston, went to see *Greenwillow* but left before the second act. He didn't know that his presence and his premature departure had been reported to Perkins, who soon after ran into Walston in a Manhattan pharmacy:

"I'd never realized how tall he was, despite the fact that I'd made a film with him. Maybe it was because he was angry. He looked at me and said, 'Why didn't you come backstage? Even if you didn't like the fucking thing, why didn't you come backstage and at least say hello?!' And I couldn't answer him, just stood there looking into those brown eyes. He got what he had ordered, walked out the door, and that was it."

Later on, Tony tried to paint the experience as an uplifting one. "When I played in *Greenwillow*, we'd get terrible houses—only a handful of people on some nights. I always liked that . . . I always felt if there were five or ten people out there, I could give each one my individual attention."

Despite its closing after ninety-five performances, *Greenwillow* yielded Perkins a Tony nomination. Ray Walston recalled, "It just floored me. But once in a while a Hollywood notable gets handed a nomination merely for lending his gilt-edged presence to the Great White Way." (Jackie Gleason won the award that year.) Tony Perkins conclusively learned that his Broadway presence was not gilt-edged when he returned in 1962 to make his comedy stage bow in the satire *Harold*. (Celebrated playwright George S. Kaufman once quipped that satire is what closes on a Saturday night.)

Harold folded after twenty-six performances, losing its investors nearly all their money. In the future, Perkins virtually ignored *Harold* in conversation and interviews, yet continued to rhapsodize over *Greenwillow*. Ray Walston, a (Rexford Drive, Beverly Hills) neighbor of this author, confided, "Tony was too androgynous to be a commercial stage lead. Filmmakers and cameras have their tricks and subterfuges, but out on that stage, it's all you. On the stage, you are exposed. "Tony once said his fondest ambition was to become a beloved musical comedy star. He wanted to be a singing as well as acting talent. In other words, to outdo his father."

In 1989, three years before Perkins's death, Susan Loesser, Frank's daughter, requested an interview with Tony about *Greenwillow* for her upcoming biography of her father. By then less inclined to play the stellar game of glorifying one's failures, Tony declined, informing friends that his "most miserable days" had been working with Frank Loesser. Which, considering the downhill years after *Psycho*, was saying something.

P.S. Anthony Perkins had married at forty, partly to change his image and to become a father. Though the relationship was said to be a loving one, he continued having casual sex on the side and eventually died of AIDS. Widow Berry Berenson (Marisa's sister) died nine years later, in 2001, when her airplane flight, guided by Muslim terrorists, slammed into Manhattan's World Trade Center on 9/11.

Tuning Tommy Out

DANCER, ACTOR, CHOREOGRAPHER, AND DIRECTOR Tommy Tune is the only individual to have won Tonys in four different categories and to win the same two Tony Awards two years in a row. Yet he couldn't land a movie career to speak of—he had passing roles in *The Boyfriend* and *Hello, Dolly!* and costarred in a European film. Here's why:

On "New Year's Eve, nineteen-seventy-something," Tune attended a Josephine Baker concert at the Palace Theatre in New York. Professionally, he was riding high with a long run at the Uris Theatre in *Seesaw*, playing one of the first openly gay major characters in a mainstream Broadway musical comedy. Hollywood had recently come calling; a team of producers who'd expanded their scope from theater to an Oscar-winning film musical had developed a musical screenplay tailored for Tommy Tune, future star. His contract included a clause providing for a trailer dressing room tall enough for the dancer with the heron's legs to be able to *stand* while changing into his wardrobe.

At the Baker concert, the older diva was vainly requesting people from the mostly elderly audience to come up and "Dance weez me, we make beeg deescotheque on Palace stage deez very New Year's Eve," as she cooed in her semi-genuine French accent. Tommy recalled, "Not an old soul was stirring in that nostalgic crowd." She pleaded, "Come on, come on!" until Tune took pity and joined her on the stage. Josephine didn't know who he was, but many in the audience did, and applauded. The two danced, and he finally returned to his seat somewhat embarrassed and thrilled.

Until the next day, when he read a newspaper account of the gala evening. Just before the curtain had gone up, Tommy explained, "a tall, heavily perfumed black man in a turban and white caftan—it could have been Geoffrey Holder, but it wasn't—passed up and down the aisle flamboyantly passing out bouquets of red roses with the whispered command, 'These are for Josephine. Throw them on the stage for her. Let's cover her in roses.'"

In the newspaper, a venomous critic who according to Tune used "cruel, disheartening, washed-up descriptions," wrote dismissively about the tall man in the turban and caftan, a "sashaying, sentimental camp follower." Tommy Tune was mentioned by name in the same paragraph, so that the impression given was that the dancer-actor was "a flamboyant drag queen come to pay homage to his gay icon," as he later described it.

Sure enough, "the big boys in the Hollywood studios [sic]" picked up the item and called the producing team, who called Tommy, demanding, "What in the hell did you think you were doing last night? You've caused a big problem for us out there with the guys in California. I mean they kept it quiet about Cary Grant but he wasn't ever dancing around in drag onstage with Josephine Baker!"

Despite his insistence that he wasn't the tall man in the article and had not appeared in drag, but had simply gone onstage to help a faltering star out, the damage was done. "It doesn't sound like that in the paper!" Tommy was told, for heterosexual publicity—the truth be damned—is crucial for movie stars, or potential ones. The movie deal dissolved, not immediately, but "by subtle lessening degrees, and then one day it was invisible, like it had never happened." The picture never got made, as it had been so specifically tailored to Tune, plus musicals were by then a financial risk.

"And I never became a movie star," Tommy wrote in his 1997 memoirs, in which he finally came out. He prefaced the story with "I have no regrets," which, in light of his subsequent Broadway career, could well be true. Besides, how many 6' 6 ½" movie stars have there ever been?

8

FIVE OF BROADWAY'S MOST INNOVATIVE MUSICALS

Pal Joey (1940)

IN 1952, RICHARD RODGERS called *Pal Joey* the first musical in "long pants," that is, the first grown-up musical. Rodgers and Hart's sophisticated show centered on an opportunist named Joey who loves himself first and last and who falls in lust, not love. He's also a man kept by an older woman: Vera, an ex stripper. The musical eschewed lovey-dovey, moon-in-June romanticism for realism, even promiscuity. For instance, the now-classic song "Bewitched, Bothered and Bewildered" had to have some of its lyrics—sung by Vera about her stud muffin—altered before it could go on radio to become a national hit.

Ahead of its time, *Pal Joey* was not a hit. Twelve years later when it was revived, things had changed enough that it was successful and acclaimed. However, and of course, the 1957 film version subverted much of *Pal Joey's* innovative quality. Two successful stage revivals in 1961 and '63 starred Bob Fosse in the title role.

After *Pal Joey*, Richard Rodgers wished to musicalize Lynn Riggs' unsuccessful 1931 play *Green Grow the Lilacs*. But Lorenz Hart, an urbane gay man—Jewish, like Rodgers—driven to alcoholism by a mixture of homophobia and misery over his extreme shortness, wasn't interested in the rural project that would become *Oklahoma!* and which opened months before his premature death.

★★★★★

Oklahoma! (1943)

THE FIRST COLLABORATION of Rodgers and Hammerstein boasted songs that furthered the plot and helped explain the characters. Although the popular impression is that *Oklahoma!* is a light, all-American tunefest centering on a 1906 picnic, the show is also about a virgin's sexual fears and fantasies (at times the same thing) and about attempted rape and murder. Its primary theme is responsibility and the need to establish a community, e.g., cowboy Curly's becoming a farmer and a husband to Laurey, and territory folk's uniting to become a state (one of the last two to join the continental US).

Agnes de Mille's choreography also broke new ground. The dances were integrated into the plot, and her influential Dream Ballet revealed as much about Laurey as Laurey's words did. *Oklahoma!* forewent the tradition of using female anatomy, specifically legs, to lure heterosexual male customers. Its costumes weren't glamorous, the conversation wasn't cosmopolitan, and the curtain rose on elderly Aunt Eller churning butter. Yet the unorthodox musical became the longest-running show to date, with 2,212 performances, in an era when runs didn't reach 1,000 performances—the next-longest-running show was the 1919 musical *Irene*, with 670 performances.

Oklahoma! also offered insight into and sympathy for its villain. The songs "Pore Jud" and "Lonely Room" disclose that what Jud really wants is a woman who will love him and not be afraid of him. When Rodgers and Hammerstein agreed to team, Oscar Hammerstein II asked Richard Rodgers if he could pen the lyrics first (Larry Hart had fit his words to Rodgers' music). Because the pair was aiming for significantly expressive lyrics that were as important as the melodies, Rodgers willingly reversed the usual work process of composing music first.

★★★★★

Cabaret (1966)

THIS MUSICAL, BASED ON STORIES by Christopher Isherwood, didn't just have a dark character—a Joey or Jud—but was itself dark, set in an early-'30s Berlin irrevocably turning Nazi. (*Cabaret* followed *Flora, the Red Menace*, the Broadway debut of John Kander, Fred Ebb, and Liza Minnelli; that 1965 flop featured communists in Depression-era U.S.A.) Two non-German lead characters served as audience surrogates in the grim worlds of the Kit Kat Klub and the boarding house where Sally Bowles works and lives, respectively. An Englishwoman dreaming of fame, she falls in love with visiting American writer Cliff. (In the movie, Sally is American—Liza Minnelli—and Brian is English; based on Isherwood himself, Chris was closetedly gay in the stories, hetero in 1966, and bisexual in the 1972 film.)

The main German character is the Kit Kat's emcee—Joel Grey onstage in 1966, in the movie and in the 1987 Broadway revival. He presides over what could be called the musical within a musical, for *Cabaret* is both a musical play and a revue. Many of its songs are performed in the context of performances at the Klub. Like *Mame* the musicalization of a straight play, *Cabaret* was adapted from the 1951 *I Am a Camera*. Unlike prior musicals, *Cabaret* emphasized darkness, using it to tell a story of a time and place. Darkness was embodied by the breakup of the affair of Sally and Cliff, and his departure from Berlin; the seediness of the Emcee (not bisexualized until the UK–derived 1998 Broadway revival); the desperate lives of its characters; burgeoning anti-Semitism; and the eschewing of happy endings that would have betrayed historical truth.

In the manner of Greek drama, *Cabaret* challenged audiences to rethink their initial assumptions. Critical reception at the time was downbeat, puzzled, or indignant. Yet the original production ran 1,165 performances. It bears noting that only *successful* innovative musicals attain the longevity and impact to become major influences.

★★★★★

Hair (1968)

MANY OR MOST MUSICALS BARELY, if at all, reflect their times. But in the late 1960s, *Hair* integrated pop-rock music, the hippie counterculture, sexual liberation, drugs, and the Vietnam war in a nonlinear presentation that would echo in shows like *Company, Follies,* and *A Chorus Line. Hair* had less of a story than a theme: peace, love, and equality. The strand of plot concerned whether Claude would be sent to fight in Vietnam.

With book and lyrics by Gerome Ragni and James Rado and music by Galt MacDermot, the psychedelic, impressionist musical ignored almost every rule in the book. It offered non-rhyming lyrics, various songs that didn't end but rather slowed down or segued into the next number, four-letter words, nudity, sexual content, an integrated and sometimes gender-bending cast, and a unit set. The title, of course, referred to the hirsute symbol of individualism that so threatened the Establishment; beards and hair below the collar were enough to keep males out of restaurants, clubs, schools, and elsewhere.

Although *Hair* featured no big names, it launched the careers of Diane Keaton, Tim Curry, Melba Moore, Donna Summer, Peter Gallagher, Nell Carter, Joe Mantegna, Meat Loaf, Ben Vereen, Cliff DeYoung, and others.

Even those who never saw the show heard the omnipresent hit songs that fueled the 1,750 performances that made *Hair* the fourth-longest-running musical of the '60s. Most famous were "The Age of Aquarius" and "Let the Sun Shine In." The latter, which concluded the "tribal-rock musical," isn't a cheerful Broadway ditty, but a call to action that urged audiences to give up dark resignation for the light of activism and change.

Less well-known but more-provocative songs included "Sodomy"—The *New York Times* marveled that *Hair* didn't frown upon homosexuality— "Colored Spade," about racism; and "Black Boys/White Boys," in which women sing about preferring men of the opposite race—the *Times* commented that *Hair* approved "enthusiastically of miscegenation." The latter song was innovative in that the singers objectified males the same way men had always done with "girls," and daring in that several US states at the time had laws against interracial marriage.

Even if to a large extent *Hair* preached to the converted—the *Times* admitted that the show wouldn't please "adherents of Governor Reagan"—its revolutionary format and crowd-pleasing topicality shattered the conventions of what a musical should be. Its success impressed upon producers that new musicals could and perhaps ought to present the voice of today rather than the day before yesterday.

★★★★★

Rent (1996)

JONATHAN LARSON, a fan and student of Broadway musicals past and present, used Puccini's opera *La Bohème* as inspiration for his portrait of survival and illness in New York's East Village. Larson spotlighted homelessness, struggling artists, and AIDS—an unprecedented four main characters in *Rent* have AIDS. Although the title refers also to payment for lodging, Larson's preferred meaning was *torn*, as in between conflicting feelings, as in split relationships, as in torn by pain.

Ironically, Larson's own life was rent apart before his epochal show opened. After seven years of *Rent* workshops and rewrites, the 35-year-old felt unwell. One hospital diagnosed flu, another food poisoning. The night before the preview, after a final dress rehearsal, Larson returned home, began to make tea, collapsed, and died of an aortic aneurism. The artistic team headed by director Michael Greif had to decide which remaining changes Larson would have made.

Extravagantly endorsed by the media and audiences, *Rent* soared. The *La Bohème* connection elicited much publicity; however, *Rent* wasn't really an update, though it focused on artists and illness—AIDS instead of tuberculosis. Where Puccini romanticized death, Larson glorified survival. *La Bohème* was tragic, *Rent* joyous. A few critics complained that *Rent* was a-cynical and too direct, rejecting Sondheim's by then widespread "frosty intellectualism." Yet its spirit grabbed spectators even in the absence of any real set, of costumes, of superficial glamour or a chandelier or helicopter. *Rent* does include a substantial diversity of heteros, gays and lesbians, blacks, Hispanics, transvestites, and junkies, though its two lead characters are male, white, and heterosexual. More mysteriously, why do two unimpoverished roommates decide not to pay rent this year or next, as if it's a noble act?

Almost entirely sung, *Rent* often gives the impression of nonactors on a stage revealing their own life stories. It connects with the times and viewers in a way few musicals ever have. Larson had written that in a troubled world, "We can all learn how to survive from those who stare death squarely in the face every day." He sought to present and bond the human community on stage, using genuine rock music, albeit more '70s than '90s. Larson believed his musical style was Broadway's future, and declared in 1992 that his masterwork "exalts Otherness, glorifying artists and counterculture as necessary to healthy civilization." His exuberant and enormously successful legacy has expanded musical horizons and continues to inspire theatre artists seeking to reconcile individuality with community and difference with tolerance.

★★★★★

Low *Rent*

STAGESTRUCK IS THE DEEPLY IRONIC TITLE of novelist and playwright Sarah Schulman's non-fiction book about Jonathan Larson's alleged plagiarism of her 1990 novel *People in Trouble* for his musical *Rent* (1996).

By his own admission and that of colleagues, Larson was poor at plot and narrative. *Rent*'s story owed a lot to *La Bohème* and, apparently, to characters and storylines from Schulman's novel, the first about East Village artists struggling with AIDS and homelessness. *Rent* includes several parallels and similar or identical details. It turned out that Larson knew the novel, which Schulman's reps shopped around extensively for a prospective rock opera (one team of composers that declined Schulman's story instead did one about a gay man, Harvey Milk), and had allegedly told an associate he was "using" it for *Rent* (but made no effort to contact its author).

Schulman's novel was lesbian centered. Larson made *Rent* male- and heterosexual-centered. "*Rent* acknowledges that lesbians exist," explained Schulman, "therefore it claims to be tolerant. The fact that it repeatedly inscribes lesbian relationships as unstable, bickering, and emotionally pathological is the required conceit." Schulman added that the brilliant composer-lyricist—not known for the depth of his characters—"claims that heterosexuals are the heroic center of the AIDS crisis" and that *Rent* "clearly depicts a world in which heterosexual love is true love.

"Homosexual love exists but is inherently secondary in that it is either doomed or shallow or both." Schulman accused Larson and other artists, and the corporate interests behind them, of routinely co-opting the work of women and minorities to lend a fashionable and profitable aura of diversity and authenticity to their own work/product.

When Schulman sought to publicize her plagiarized situation, she found herself blocked at every level. *Rent* was a huge hit, the media was championing it—"*Rent*," she observed, "gives New Yorkers a comfortable image of themselves. . . . 'AIDS is so sad, but straight love is real love, what a relief.'"—and almost no one wished to oppose *Rent* or the accelerating financial interests driving it. A *Wall Street Journal* article about Larson's estate added up the sales, licensing, merchandising, and other *Rent* deals "now worth one billion dollars."

"In the middle of the night" Schulman "suddenly realized that if Larson had done the right thing and taken out an option on my novel, even at the rock-bottom rate of 2.5 percent, my share would now be $25 million."

Meanwhile, Lynn Thompson, *Rent*'s dramaturg, had sued his estate for a fairer share than the $2,000 she'd originally been paid—closer to $40 million. She declared that she'd written nine percent of the song lyrics and forty-eight percent of the libretto. Although the judge acknowledged Thompson's contributions as considerable, she lost the case, which further discouraged Sarah Schulman from legal action. She'd been warned time and again to drop the issue—The *New York Times* wouldn't touch it; an article finally appeared in *New York* magazine on January 13, 1997—or else it might harm, even destroy her career.

In *Stagestruck* she clarified that, contrary to the movies, justice is not readily available to those who can't afford it (the lesbian activist-writer sometimes had to purchase food on a credit card and couldn't afford tickets to most Broadway plays) or who challenge institutionalized white-heterosexual-male privilege.

In her 1998 book, published by Duke University Press, Schulman moved on from her low *Rent* experience to larger questions of how lesbian and gay people, as well as people with AIDS, are misrepresented and commodified in American culture. She argues convincingly that had *Rent* not been presented by a white heterosexual male, with "straights" as the focus of AIDS, struggle, and poverty, it would never have been welcomed with such open—and rewarding—arms.

P.S. The 2005 film version of *Rent*, like that of the similarly heralded and innovative stage musical *A Chorus Line*, was a resounding critical and financial flop.

9

LUCY ON BROADWAY

In 1960 Lucille Ball was at a crossroads. Approaching fifty and in the process of divorcing Desi Arnaz, her husband of nineteen years, she believed she was through in television. "I will never do another TV series. It couldn't top *I Love Lucy*, and I'd be foolish to try. In this business, you have to know when to get off." (Of course, she would go on to do three more TV series and umpteen television specials.)

For a change of scene and pace, she chose to star in a Broadway show. A musical—never mind that she couldn't sing. Her misadventure in *Wildcat* illustrates the high esteem in which even the biggest stars then held the Great White Way and the fact that extreme success in another medium may interfere with qualitative success in the theater.

While completing filming on a "mature comedy" with Bob Hope titled *The Facts of Life*—about adultery—Ball told the press, "The Broadway stage has always been my first love. I never made it, and I want to prove something to myself. Years ago, before I came to Hollywood, I was a showgirl. But just before a new revue or musical would start, I'd always get fired. I was shy and had no personality—I don't blame them.

"*Wildcat* is a story about a female [oil] wildcatter in 1912. It's sort of a tomboy sort of role. She wants to link up with the top male wildcatter in the territory and spends the show chasing him."

Desilu announced it would invest $360,000 in *Wildcat*, holding original cast album rights and planning a TV "spectacular" around it called *Lucy Goes to Broadway*. Ball publicly admitted, "I'm terrified of the musical end of it. But

I have some good people who know I'm not a singer and will write accordingly. I'll be doing a lot of cavorting around while I'm singing—and maybe that will keep people from paying too much attention to the quality of my voice." Ironically, she would end her lengthy film career with a flop musical, *Mame* (1974), for which she was deemed too old and her singing voice roundly criticized.

The star explained that she would "stay with (*Wildcat*) a year and a half. . . . I'd like to devote about five years to Broadway." The musical's libretto was by N. Richard Nash, who'd written the hit *The Rainmaker*. Michael Kidd would choreograph and direct, both men co-producing. Lyricist Carolyn Leigh and composer Cy Coleman teamed for their first Broadway show—unfortunately their score would yield only one hit: the rousing "Hey, Look Me Over."

Nash had created his heroine, Wildcat or "Wildy" Jackson, as a twenty-seven-year-old, yet Lucy saw the part as ideal for herself. She no doubt wished to continue playing onstage the leading roles that her age increasingly precluded before the camera. Nash opined, "If it had been a straight play, the difference in ages between her and the rest of the cast would not have been so pronounced, but she was a generation away from them and had never been truly trained as a dancer or singer." One chorus member was future TV star Valerie "Rhoda" Harper.

Outwardly, Ball was gung ho on *Wildcat* and starting a new lease on life and work. Nash observed, however, "She desperately wanted to get away from Hollywood and get away from [Desi]. So for her, this musical was a period of major escape. . . . She was deeply, deeply unhappy."

Leaving California behind, Lucy moved to the Big Apple with five vanloads of possessions; her mother, DeDe; her two children; two maids; the children's nurse; a driver; a limousine; and a regular automobile. Lucy's new home was the new luxury highrise the Imperial House at 69th Street and Lexington Avenue. Publicity surrounding her relocation was widespread, as were the public expressions of hope—spearheaded by columnist Walter Winchell—that America's favorite couple would reconcile.

Besides being psychically wounded, Ball was still physically bruised from an accident incurred while making *The Facts of Life*. Preparing to step into a rowboat, she'd caught her foot and fallen nine feet, gashing her leg and hitting her face hard enough to become unconscious for several minutes. The egg-sized bump on her forehead healed; but when she went into rehearsals for *Wildcat* she still bore facial scars that had to be covered with special makeup.

The pressure of the musical, in which the star was the focus of every scene, helped relax her mind. It was an era when divorce made many people, women especially, feel ashamed of the public knowledge that they'd failed at marriage. Lucy later confessed to having been very depressed and ". . . very

ashamed. Very embarrassed." As usual, she immersed herself in her work, atten-
tive to every detail though not yet—Broadway was after all new territory for
her—the "control freak" boss she became on subsequent TV series (see this
author's *Celebrity Feuds!*).

Wildcat opened in Philadelphia on October 29, 1960. Local critics were
generally loving, and *Variety* pronounced the show "Surefire for Broadway,"
adding, "Miss Ball sings acceptably and dances with spirit." But Desi Arnaz was
on hand, still playing mentor to the older and more successful Lucille Ball. He
strongly felt that Wildcat should behave more like Lucy Ricardo: childlike
and lovable. For instance, like Lucy, Wildy should not be disreputable; if she was
greedy and at times conniving, it would be only because she wanted to take
care of her crippled younger sister.

The aging Ball had already proclaimed her desire to put Lucy Ricardo
behind her, and Nash's lines could not, legally, be altered without his consent.
However, "We saw the show was not coming together as hoped," Nash said; it
was his first musical. Also, Lucille's confidence enacting a new character on the
stage was shaky. Her prior experience had been in a touring company of
Elmer Rice's *Dream Girl* in 1948, when her movie career was mostly washed
up. Although Ball resisted Arnaz's suggestion that "Hey, Look Me Over" be
sung at the musical's beginning, ending, and twice in between, she started
Lucy-fying her lines and performances, to which Nash hardly objected, since
audiences ate it up.

For example, when an actor came onstage in a nightgown and Wee Willie
cap, the same getup that always got a laugh for William Frawley on *I Love Lucy*,
Ball as Wildcat quipped, "Say, you know a fellow named Fred Mertz?" From a
formally theatrical point of view, worse was yet to come, particularly after the
New York opening on December 16. Critics liked Lucy but not the show.
They derided it as a *tame* cat, and its plot similarities to *Annie Get Your Gun* and
The Rainmaker (which Nash would later musicalize as *110 in the Shade*) only
pointed up the inferiority of *Wildcat*'s storytelling and music. Nonetheless,
people swarmed to see the fabulous redhead—wearing a long fall and blue
jeans—in person.

World-Telegram critic Frank Aston stated, "The ovation greeting the frisky
lady threatened to reach into next month. And all evening affection ran so high
that the last words and notes of specialties were drowned in applause."

Thus, Lucy Ricardo gradually took over. When Lucille Ball muffed her
lines, she would halt the show, point out her mistake, then start again, capti-
vating most audience members while breaking a cardinal rule of the theater. If
her children attended the show, she called them up on stage to join her. When
an animal relieved itself during a performance, Lucy joked that her contract

called for her to clean up after it, and with a broom and dustpan she did so. When she entered, she salaamed.

She mugged and gladly admitted to it in chatty press interviews. (During *I Love Lucy* she'd been forbidden to do TV talk shows by her husband and co-producer, who didn't want the public to learn the big difference between Lucy and Lucille.) A "third act" at curtain call found Ball talking to the audience, dancing, and doing a lively encore of "Hey, Look Me Over."

Tickets sold out, word of mouth was great regarding the star turn, and the massive divorce publicity made Ball the most spotlighted celebrity in the country. "She was desperate for laughs, and so she would ad-lib on stage," explained Nash. "Sometimes her laughs came off, sometimes they didn't. She would ask me to write laugh lines for her; I was not a gag man by any means. She wanted gags right at the beginning of the show."

Desi Arnaz eventually called the playwright to ask if he could send out two *I Love Lucy* writers to add material? Nash acquiesced, but the new material didn't work. "Michael [Kidd] and I went backstage [afterward] and said, 'It's a different medium, Lucy.' . . . She took all the lines out instantly. That was a bad shock for her. In television, those lines had worked."

The relentless Broadway schedule took its toll, as Lucille lost weight—in time, twenty-two pounds. On February 7, 1961, exhausted, she suspended the musical for two weeks' vacation. The star's latest guide and motivator was the 1937 book *The Art of Selfishness* by David Seabury. On her bathroom mirror she would post a message to herself: "Is this good for Lucy?" The question helped determine her day's activities and reactions. Where she'd recently considered getting back with Desi for the children's sake, she now decided that the bad times which were sure to recur—including his drinking, womanizing and gambling—would not be worth it.

SOON AFTER SHE RETURNED to the show, Ball announced that it would close temporarily in late May. Broadway producer Ronald Lee, in the *Wildcat* chorus at the time, recalled, "We became a joke. It was the only show that played two out of every three weeks. We never really could get angry with her, because we knew she was sick." General manager Joe Harris offered, "She did have trouble doing the Broadway routine. She was only 49, so it surprised me that she wasn't strong. We used to have oxygen on the side. She was out of breath doing the show." (Lucy was a chronic smoker.)

Among her ills, she suffered from painful bursitis which one night delayed the curtain for half an hour until a doctor gave her a painkilling shot. Lucille's loud, untrained singing put such a strain on her vocal chords that she developed nodes; their removal left her *I Love Lucy* voice deeper and gravelly, as evidenced in her later TV work. In late April she collapsed on stage, her fall cushioned by an actress whose wrist was then broken. Upon returning from spring break with her children, Ball was in a bad mood and declared that she'd thoroughly disliked visiting Jamaica.

The star knew she was in a losing show, even if it did turn a profit whenever she appeared in it eight times a week. She was already tired of the pace, the material, and the un-TV-like repetition. Before *Wildcat* opened, she'd assumed it might run for years but had contractually limited her participation to a year and a half because "Five years would be too much in *one* show. How long can you have a ball saying the same things and dancing the same steps?" If she'd waited a few years, Lucy might have taken on a bona fide, long-running hit like *Hello, Dolly!* (Sure, she couldn't sing, but could Carol Channing?)

Perhaps the negative emotions of impending divorce, nearing fifty, and not really conquering Broadway except in superficially crowd-pleasing terms led to her rash of physical problems during *Wildcat*. These included "an unshakeable virus," a fractured finger and an injured back. May 24, 1961, was Lucille's 171st performance. She was too drained to continue for the time being. By early June, just after her divorce became final, she was down to ninety-five pounds and her doctor insisted she leave the show. She agreed but said she would return in August and perform through January.

But she never did. Her understudy, Betty Jane Watson, took over for the rest of that May week, but after Lucy's departure the box office plummeted and Desilu had to refund $165,000 in tickets. Among the actresses approached to replace Lucy in *Wildcat* were Ginger Rogers, Gwen Verdon, and Mitzi Gaynor—all of whom declined to try to fill her enormously popular shoes.

Meanwhile, the musicians' union demanded that its members be paid during the layoff. Desi Arnaz refused to pay the salaries and the theater's rental while Ball was away. So *Wildcat* shut down for good and the redhead's theatrical career was over, though she later considered a straight play based on James Kirkwood's semi-autobiographical novel *There Must Be a Pony*. (Lucy would have been directed by the mercurial Joshua Logan, with whom Bette Davis clashed on the aborted musical *Miss Moffat*.) However, even without singing and dancing, Lucy remained wary of the stage, and post-*Wildcat* was ready to move to Europe and return to California only for the occasional film role.

"Lucy felt her Broadway experience was a big disappointment," noted Gary Morton, the trumpeter-turned-comedian whom she wed in November 1961. "Not from a financial standpoint, but the material wasn't worthy of her. . . . If she'd done *Mame* on Broadway, she'd have been ten times as popular in it as Angela Lansbury."

Director Michael Kidd believed, "She could have been a major Broadway star, but Lucy came to it too late. It wasn't just the wrong choice of vehicles; by then she'd become, totally, a television person."

10

THE PROBLEM WITH MUSICALS

"You ask what happened to musicals? Hell, what happened to music?"
—Sean Connery, former *South Pacific* chorus boy in London

"What happened to the good-time musical? I'll tell you: its promises couldn't
be kept."—theater historian Ethan Mordden

"The problem with musicals isn't usually the music or even bad lyrics. It's the
awkward or unbelievable transitions from speaking to singing, and back
again. That's why I like *Tommy* and *Evita*. They're seamless . . . and don't
cheat your belief, like so many older musicals."—Steve Reeves, the
movies' Hercules, who appeared in Carol Channing's 1955 Broadway flop
The Vamp

"What's wrong with musicals now is all the gifted men who've died of
AIDS—who would otherwise be here today creating great theater."
—Madeline Kahn

"We've lost a whole generation of stage talent, especially to AIDS, and it will
take a generation or more until that void is filled."—celebrity photographer Herb Ritts, who died of AIDS

"Like the French or Viennese operetta, the Broadway musical, as we know it,
is virtually dead. The guts were knocked out of it when Lennon and
McCartney chose not to write a musical. Why should they have done a
show that closed in Philadelphia when they could do ten pop concerts
and make a fortune?"—drama critic Clive Barnes

"The one thing the theatre can't do is be in the vanguard of popular music. I don't think it's a coincidence that Andrew's greatest successes have always been great soaring ballads, timeless in their quality. The most obviously pop score, *Starlight Express*, was the only one that threw up no real hits."
—CAMERON MACKINTOSH, who has produced several Andrew Lloyd Webber musicals

"Sometime in the 1970s the American musical's golden era ended when rising costs and decreasing talents allowed the producers to take over. . . . Most of the new material is mediocre, and most of the 'new' shows are the old ones because they have brand-name recognition."—stage composer and TV actor ALBERT HAGUE in 1992

"These days the problem with Broadway musicals is television. *Ads*, of all things! There's so little to *Pippin* (1972), and without Bob Fosse's inventiveness, even less than that. But now it's been running about three years, thanks to this new gimmick of TV ads for musicals that actually lures suckers in. What next?"—ROSE MARIE (*The Dick Van Dyke Show*) . . . *Pippin* ran almost five years

"I was [billed] *Kay Ballard* when I starred in *Molly* [1973] because a numerologist told me one less letter in my name would bring more success. *Wrong!!*"—KAYE BALLARD, whose turn as radio and TV star Molly Goldberg was not a hit

"In the sung-through musical . . . the narrative function has been taken away from the playwright and given to the songwriter. You listen to a song in a completely different way than you listen to a scene. Auden makes the point that rhyme makes any statement acceptable, gives it authority. . . . Song is not sufficient to establish character; it cannot carry the burden of psychology and situation. You need prose and plot."—JOHN LAHR, critic, writer, and son of Bert

"Most American musicals were still stuck in the '60s or before, by the 1980s. Then the British musicals came along. . . . The sung-through imports are an ingenious updating of the European art form of opera. Yet these new musicals are original, not rehashes, and are marketed brilliantly."—DUSTY SPRINGFIELD in New York

"The Brits redefined the musical . . . turned it into a spectacle, an event, with the visuals as important as the music. Musicals were no longer quaint or dated, but cutting edge, with more bang for your buck."—agent and nightclub owner ROBERT HUSSONG

"Maybe one day we'll write [a musical with dialogue]. But if they're going to talk, it's got to be for a good reason. What I don't like at all is when you don't know why they've started singing or why they've started talking; they can say the same thing talking or singing, it doesn't seem to make any difference. . . . The best example of that kind of show is *A Chorus Line*—there are good reasons for when they sing and when they talk."—ALAIN BOUBLIL, co-creator of *Les Misérables*

"There's all this complaining now about 'sung-through' musicals. Many people say they have no book, it's just songs. But they *do* have books. It's just that the words are sung, instead. Why the terrible fuss? The *result* is everything . . . I think much of this is just xenophobia, because the English and the French have pioneered these musicals and have been so successful with them. In essence, most Americans would prefer to have a monopoly on success."—French actor-director JEANNE MOREAU in 2003

"I think it was Richard Rodgers who, when asked which came first, the music or the lyrics, said, 'The contract.' Was that the beginning of the great decline? I'm kidding—sort of."—lyricist CAROLYN LEIGH (*Peter Pan, Little Me*)

"You have two stages in the declining creativity of Broadway musicals. First, turning nonmusical movies into musicals, which hardly ever works; *My Fair Lady*'s the big exception, yet they keep doing it, madly panning for gold. And second, not even that—*revivals*."—costume maker LEE BREWSTER (*The Birdcage*, etc.)

"In a play, it's about the relationship between characters. In a musical, it's about the relationship between performer and audience—that can never have the same depth. Particularly when special effects take the place of talent and charisma."—playwright WILLIAM INGE

"Superman has always been a hit, right? Our show had everything: Hal Prince directed, music by Charles Strouse [*Bye Bye Birdie; Applause; Annie*], and on TV *Batman* was so popular it was airing twice a week . . . and *I* was in it. It crashed to earth, dead as a dodo."—JACK CASSIDY on *It's a Bird . . . It's a Plane . . . It's Superman* (1966)

"When we took out the music, for starters, it flew. . . ."—DAVID NEWMAN, who with Robert Benton wrote *It's a Bird . . .* and then the 1978 hit movie *Superman* (starring Christopher Reeve)

"Musicals derive from professional musical people. Stars, including singers, aren't necessarily musical experts, and many a meddling star has interfered with the progress of a stage musical."—producer ROBERT FRYER (*Mame*, *Chicago*)

"From her first performance . . . Streisand stopped the show with her 'Miss Marmelstein' number. The number was foolproof. The only time it didn't stop the show was well into the run, when she begged the musical director, Lehman Engel, to let her do it her own way. She took liberties with the rhythm, and the song got applause but by no means did it stop the show. Streisand immediately went back to doing it the way it was written."—critic and author HOWARD KISSEL on *I Can Get It for You Wholesale*

"The problem with most musicals is that the spectator is often impatient. If it's a good musical, he's waiting for the next song. Or else he's waiting for the song to end."—playwright BOB RANDALL (*6 Rms Riv Vu*)

"Nobody sings!"—composer RUDOLPH FRIML, explaining why he walked out on *My Fair Lady*

"People expect more from a musical. If a play doesn't meet their expectations, they sometimes question their own taste. It may have been symbolic or avant-garde, perhaps something escaped them? But with a musical, no such excuses. So you have to try much harder."—playwright MAXWELL ANDERSON, who did two musicals (book and lyrics), both with Kurt Weill: *Knickerbocker Holiday* and *Lost in the Stars*

"It's better than what most 106-year-old writers are doing."—GEORGE ABBOTT in 1993 (Broadway's centenary), when asked about his update of his 1955 hit musical *Damn Yankees*

"Most of the fellows on Broadway these days are playing at being producer; they sack the assistant choreographer because it's the sort of thing a producer does."—British columnist MARK STEYN

"We all wanted to do something again after *West Side Story* [but] Lenny was hipped on it being important. He kept saying, 'It's gotta be important.' And it just seemed such a truism but I said to him, 'If it's good, it'll be important.'"—writer ARTHUR LAURENTS on composer Leonard Bernstein, whose last major musical was *West Side Story*

"Now, scenery is bigger and stars are smaller. The chandelier in *Phantom* and the staircase in *Sunset Boulevard* should get billing."—BEATRICE ARTHUR

"The day we closed *The Fig Leaves Are Falling* [1969], the matinee was sold out. After I sang 'All My Laughter,' the audience made me do an encore—they kept on clapping, they wouldn't let the scene go on till I'd sung it again . . . to show how much they loved my song and the show. It was wonderful, I'll never forget it. But too late. Once people heard we were closing, then everybody flocked to see it."—DOROTHY LOUDON (*Annie*)

"I wish we'd get back to more human values in musicals—caring about what happens to people. I think people want to get involved. They want to laugh, but they also want to cry. I guess it's not fashionable. I'm afraid audiences today don't accept the idea of characters bursting into song the way they used to."—BARBARA COOK

"It's more business now than it is show. All of that tradition is gone. Everyone just wants to know how much money they're going to make. That's why I decided to get out of musical comedy and just be an actor."—ANITA GILLETTE (*Carnival*)

"If you're a singer with a big voice, it works against you now. They mike everybody. So a big voice has to be toned way down. Do you know, Ethel Merman wouldn't have a chance today."—CAROL CHANNING

"People aren't as disciplined as they used to be. Dancers are not trained in period styles. They don't even get ballet. They come out of the 'sidewalk' school of ballet, where they learn things like how to roll around on your navel. There's no technique to back it up."—PATTI KARR (performer, *Pippin, Seesaw*)

"The inability to sing rarely keeps a name performer out of a musical, whether in Los Angeles, New York, London, or your local dinner theatre. Sometimes, though, an imperfect voice conveys the character perfectly, whereas a magnificent voice is all wrong. Carol Channing in *Hello, Dolly!* illustrates the first premise, Kiri Te Kanawa on a recording of *West Side Story* the second."—entertainment writer SAM STAGGS

"They used to have so many big musicals about big, real-life people. Like *Gypsy* was. . . . [Artist] Keith Haring was a good friend of mine, and I'm glad they've done a 'musical installation' about him (*Radiant Baby*). I don't know what it's like yet, but special people with special lives should have more musicals made about them."—MADONNA in 2003

"I was twenty, I looked forty, I got the job."—ELAINE STRITCH on her qualifications for understudying Ethel Merman in *Call Me Madam*

"Ethel Merman sang loud. You appreciated it, all the more if you were way in the back. . . . In *Rent*, the cast keeps coming downstage to sing in your face, trying to force your emotion. I don't appreciate that."—KATHLEEN FREEMAN, 2001 Tony nominee for *The Big Monty*

"It's *Hairspray* meets *Rent* . . . I always think, Go big or go home."—ROSIE O'DONNELL, producer and sole investor in the $10 million Boy George musical *Taboo* (2003) (about two male Londoners in the '80s, and criticized for its $100-a-seat prices)

"Broadway producers and directors today are featuring music by the inept to be enjoyed by the untutored."—record and revue producer BEN BAGLEY, in the '80s

"As recently as the '70s or '80s, you still had a fairly large assortment of people making musicals. Today it's just a handful, so no wonder musicals tend to look, sound, and feel the same."—CHER

"An idea can be ahead of its time, as happened with *Kwamina* [1961]. It was a love story with me and a black man, and so . . . we couldn't even touch. Regardless, enough Americans became incensed that I couldn't open my mail after receiving death threats and used toilet paper. Once, in Boston, [leading man] Terry Carter had a gold bangle he slid up my arm—and when he went past my elbow, I heard people in the audience gasp, and several walked out. But I'm still very proud I did that show," which played thirty-two performances on Broadway—British singer-actress SALLY ANN HOWES, best known for the film *Chitty Chitty Bang Bang*

"Amazing, some of the things that get staged. . . . At first, people went to see the new Jule Styne musical, his first in a while. That's how it was advertised, and people expected another *Gypsy* or *Funny Girl*. . . . But *One Night Stand* [1980] was about a composer who invites an audience to hear his songs before he commits suicide in front of them. Any surprise that it closed after eight previews? The real surprise is how it got on." —LEONARD BERNSTEIN

"I hear *The Lion King* is better than the movie. That's a switch, if true. But I'm not enticed, because that movie is one of the most anti-gay, as well as sexist—just analyze it, it's pretty clear, with the gay villain and stereotypes. . . . Theatre still has homophobia, both in too many depictions and too many real-life closetings."—Grammy-nominated conductor PHILIP BRETT

"A rose by any other name. . . . A musical, if it's crappy, is crappy by any other title. I remember when the Uris Theatre was to open [in 1974] and Mr. Jimmy Nederlander booked in an awful musical. The title was *Up*. How would that look on the marquee: *Up* Uris. So they renamed it *Via*

Galactica, and it was still awfully crappy."—actor CHRISTOPHER HEWETT (*The Unsinkable Molly Brown*)

"When my partner Norman Lear told me there was a new hit musical in London called *Cats*, and we should bring it to Broadway, my first thought was, oh, no, not a show about Joel Grey's father!"—producer STUART OSTROW (Joel's father, Mickey Katz, was a successful comedian who sometimes worked with his son)

"I could write better lyrics than some of the Broadway pro's. Music's another matter, but lyrics . . . for *Bye, Bye, Birdie*, this fella [Lee Adams] did the words to a rather putrid song called 'Spanish Rose.' The words were embarrassing even then [in 1960]. If I said them now, I could probably be sued. I didn't personally object to the discrimination so much as the rotten lyrics."—PAUL LYNDE, who costarred in the Broadway and film version (which dropped the song)

"It's better than Hollywood, but I think even in the theatre they could benefit from more imaginative casting. I was Conrad Birdie when I toured in *Bye, Bye, Birdie*, and there was this grumbling along the way; I overheard a lot of it: Who is this Latin guy playing an Elvis type? And Elvis wasn't even yet sacred then. But I couldn't have been Birdie on Broadway, let alone Hollywood. Back then, they probably wouldn't have cast a Hispanic as Ritchie Valens—who was born Valenzuela."—actor RAUL JULIA

"I applauded Bea Arthur's first starring role in a musical. . . . But even with songs, it's not easy to make a castrating mother that lovable, and the ladies in musicals, like the ladies on TV, have to be lovable."—GARY MORTON, husband and business partner of Lucille Ball, who starred with Arthur in the film *Mame*, on Arthur's post-*Mame* Broadway flop *A Mother's Kisses*

"Who kills a show? The fate of a musical can be affected by anything as arbitrary as the wrong choice of theatre, or an inexperienced producer, or the competition from across the street."—authors DENNIS McGOVERN and DEBORAH GRACE WINER in *Sing Out, Louise!*

"The trouble with lots of break-through musicals, before they get a chance, is the naysayers who reject all but the tried and true, no matter how tired and through. Happily, they don't always have the last word. For instance William Paley, head of CBS, which used to invest heavily in musicals. He was a closet Jew who insisted *Fiddler on the Roof* was 'too Jewish' . . . [and] passed it up. No vision there, and not a lot of pride either."—choreographer BILLY WILSON

"What can happen is a musical becomes over-identified with one performer. This hurts in the long run. Have you seen *Funny Girl* revived since Miss Streisand, my favorite octopus, left the show and Broadway forever to do the movie of it?"—*Funny Girl's* Broadway director GARSON KANIN

"They don't learn, do they? Does the greed blind them? Here we are, four years into the so-called New Millennium, and it happens again: they made a dud musical out of *Saturday Night Fever*, so what do they do? Another mediocre [John] Travolta movie gets the Broadway-melody treatment: *Urban Cowboy*. Get set for a cheesy musical of every movie that made money in the last 30 or 40 years."—MICHAEL JETER (*Grand Hotel*, based on the 1932 classic that won the Best Picture Oscar)

"Very few people would presume to think they could write a drama on the order of Tennessee Williams or Arthur Miller. Yet I'm frequently, and confidently too, advised by people like my mail man and a delivery boy I know that they're working on a terrific new musical."—stage and screen star GEORGE C. SCOTT

"With the obvious exceptions of *Hair* and *Tommy*, when Broadway tries to speak in the voice of genuine rock and roll, the show is almost always a flop. The reason is that in rock the most important element is the beat. The melody, the chords, and the lyrics are often very repetitive, and they all serve the beat—the emotion and energy matter, not the intellectual content. But in theater music, the lyrics are the most important element. The lyrics not only have to be heard and understood, they also have to tell the story, to advance plot and character . . . to convey a lot of information in very few words; repetition is a luxury modern theater composers and lyricists can't afford."—SCOTT MILLER, author, playwright, and artistic director of New Line Theatre in St. Louis

"The problem with musicals now is the same as the problem with plays: size. Economics now favor only the big. Fluff with a corporation behind it will thrive, but something small, that takes time to find an audience, to build word of mouth, that does not have millions to spend on TV advertising, scarcely has a chance . . . it takes business away from the smaller, more experimental, more daring, or simply better show."—GREGORY HINES (*Jelly's Last Jam*)

"On Broadway, the most significant development of the '90s has been the emergence of Disney as legit producer with *Beauty and the Beast*. The audience goes into the Palace Theatre for no other reason than to see the movie reproduced as exactly as possible. It's worked so well that Disney is now planning to do the same all over the world with the rest of its catalogue: legitimate theater as merchandizing."—MARK STEYN

"It is such a pity when a musically, comedically, entirely talented star from another medium or country fails to land in a successful show. Patricia Routledge and I did a musical, *Darling of the Day* [1968], in which she was superlative. The critics all thought so too. Yet somehow it became the most expensive show ever to go down on Broadway. It broke my heart—for Patricia's sake, my sake, the show's sake, and the audiences' sake."—VINCENT PRICE (Englishwoman Patricia Routledge was very positively reviewed in four musical flops that ran a combined 38 performances on Broadway; she achieved international fame in the TV Britcom *Keeping Up Appearances* as Hyacinth Bucket—pronounced "bouquet")

"Some people find musicals too long. Especially husbands. . . . Today, everyone remembers *Camelot* with fondness and even reverence. At the time, though, this was not so. The production's expense and its running time were often and adversely remarked on in print and in person."—RODDY MCDOWALL, who costarred in *Camelot* (1960) on Broadway but not on screen

"Someone like Ray Bolger, very much of a star in musical comedy, would never think of missing a performance. A lot of today's young people will miss a performance if they're breaking in a new pair of shoes."—KAYE BALLARD, stage (*The Golden Apple*), screen (*The Ritz*) and TV (*The Mothers-in-Law*) actress

"It's not easy to get shows on. There aren't many of us doing them now. Michael Bennett is dead. Bob Fosse is dead. Joe Layton is dead. Gower Champion is dead. The director-choreographer is dead. And the writers are all in California making lots of money on sitcoms and movies."—TOMMY TUNE

"Three things you can say about [Susan] Stroman's success. She's earned it. As a woman, she'll probably survive longer than a man counterpart. . . . And since's she not a gay man, her career won't be cut short by AIDS."—IRENE WORTH, who won three Tonys for her performances in plays by Tennessee Williams, Edward Albee, and Neil Simon

"The Broadway musical will never die. But it's slowly bleeding to death."—NANETTE FABRAY (*Let's Face It*)

"I blame it all on the guitar. With pianos, you made music. What else could you do? With guitars, which became the 'in' thing with all the kids, they went into telling stories—mostly ones that nobody else would want to hear. It was part of the new narcissism: kids in love with the sound of, not music, but their own voices. And if I were young, I might be too."—GEORGE BURNS

"*Miss Saigon*? I miss speaking, period. I have a decent singing voice, but after three Webber musicals, I'd like the chance to *talk*, to say lines. . . . I mean, suppose actors like Robert De Niro and Anthony Hopkins or Meryl Streep were hired only to sing. They'd never make it! Well, Streep could . . . women are more comfortable singing, and maybe do it better. They always had more women stars in musicals, you know. Now, with singing-only shows, dramatically speaking, it's gotten out of hand." —ANONYMOUS MID-TWENTIES ACTOR

"Now that you have musicals lasting longer than ever . . . longer than our pets live, to me it means I can wait that much longer to see a given show that doesn't immediately attract me. I just keep postponing it indefinitely." —MARY TYLER MOORE (Broadway's *Breakfast at Tiffany's*)

"I have a practical proposal, in view of how Broadway has changed. To be honest, and more descriptive, let's switch the word order and call it *business show*. We'll get used to the sound of it; we've already gotten used to the reality of it."—theatrical executive DWIGHT FRYE JR. (whose father played Renfield in the film *Dracula*)

"What happened to musicals is too many dancers are getting into it not for love of the dance, but to become choreographers, and from there choreographer-directors. It's veered from an artistic choice to a career move."—GWEN VERDON (*Chicago*)

"The only things wrong with musicals today [the 1960s] is they cost too much to produce and therefore to see, and they need to reinstate the dance as the core of musical theatre. We need to encourage dancing on every level . . . (because) when you're dancing, you can't do drugs and you can't make war."—*Oklahoma!* choreographer AGNES DE MILLE

"I mistrust people who categorically hate musicals. Musicals aren't supposed to be realistic. Is fiction always realistic? . . . There have always been good musicals and bad musicals—always will be. [There are] musicals for every taste. So just stay home and watch your evening news! Enjoy all the dismal reality, and leave the musicals to people who can still dream." —KATHARINE HEPBURN (*Coco*)

I Hate Musicals!

"Anything that is too stupid to be spoken is sung."—VOLTAIRE

"Remember that song [from *Paint Your Wagon*] where it says, 'Hell is in hello'? Well, for me, hell is in *Hello, Dolly!* revivals."—MICHAEL JETER (*Grand Hotel* Tony winner)

"I heard this foul rumor that Ray Stark, who produced *The Way We Were*, asked Arthur Laurents, who wrote the movie, to turn it into a Broadway musical starring Kathie Lee Gifford. I couldn't believe it, would not believe it. But years later I read it in Laurents's own book. Talk about horror."—EILEEN HECKART, who received a Tony for lifetime achievement in the theater

"I really oughtn't to say so, but outside of a few superior ones, I'm not much for musicals. They can get very boring. I personally prefer a thumping good mystery or some old-fashioned English music hall. *That's* entertainment!"—ROBERT COOTE of *My Fair Lady* (Col. Pickering) and *Camelot* (King Pellinore)

"I hate doing anything musical in the States. They reserve the position that Englishmen have no right to sing on, off or anywhere near Broadway."—British movie actor LAURENCE HARVEY, who performed in *Camelot* in London in 1964

"Am I the only one who thinks music should be heard and not seen? I love all types of music, but most musicals . . . they're so trying! As if designed for childish adults or romantically deprived housewives. Or even masochistic gay men so they can tell their friends about all the musicals they've sat through. Not me. When it comes to musicals, give my regrets to Broadway!"—SAM JAFFE, talent agent and producer of *Born Free*, whose title song won an Academy Award

"The last scene of *Carousel* is an impertinence. I refuse to be lectured by a musical comedy scriptwriter on the education of children, the nature of the good life, and the contribution of the American small town to the salvation of souls."—ERIC BENTLEY, drama critic of *The New Republic*

"I have a wonderful singing voice, vastly underused. . . . One would think the perfect venue for me would be the musical stage. In fact, I loathe musicals. . . . Too many songs in far too many tedious musicals have absolutely nothing to do with the plot, such as it is."—GEORGE SANDERS, Oscar winner for *All*

About Eve who starred in *Sherry!*, a 1967 flop musicalization of *The Man Who Came to Dinner*

"Recently I caught a Susan Hayward movie on TV: *I'll Cry Tomorrow.* I wish someone would do a musical titled *I'll Sing Tomorrow*, and keep their word."—WILLIAM HICKEY, stage (*Small Craft Warnings*) and screen (*Prizzi's Honor*) actor

"Dumb lyrics, you always had—some. They were more than compensated for by great music . . . a melody that you left the theater humming. What's unforgivable in a musical is music without melody or that's altogether unmemorable. Or is closer to noise than music!"—SUSAN STRASBERG (*The Diary of Anne Frank*)

"We unrealistically romanticize musicals, whether Broadway or Hollywood. We remember the special song or two, or the terrific film clip. Thing is, those are just minutes from a movie or show—most of which, when you sit through the whole thing, is dull or silly. The plots are better now. They are. But the music's worse."—film critic GENE SISKEL

"I find that those musicals which have entertained me and held my interest were the ones that would also have been interesting without songs. Like *Cabaret*. There's a story there. A setting, an era, a moral, and a central relationship. Without music, it would be fine. With music, great. But strip most musicals of their music, and you have . . . startlingly little."—JACK GILFORD of Broadway's *Cabaret*

"Broadway doesn't grow stars for musicals any more. They just bring in some movie star for the box office who doesn't sing too good. 'Cause the ones who do sing good are either dead, retired, lost their voices [Julie Andrews?] or they're talented kids without names or individual personalities."—BUDDY HACKETT, who did one Broadway musical (*I Had a Ball*, 1964)

" . . . now, you go to the theatre, and forgive me, but what you see is a great makeup job; you have to listen to lip-synching and prerecorded music. I resent that. The Phantom is onstage for 20 minutes, and a lot of that is prerecorded. That's not Broadway."—actor PATRICK JUDE (*Marlowe, Jesus Christ Superstar*)

"They booted Milli Vanilli out of the music business for lip-synching after they won a Grammy. But now Broadway does the same thing! You all pay so much money and, like, it's supposed to be theatre and live and all, but . . . it's more like a fraud."—JANET JACKSON (Milli Vanilli had not themselves recorded what they lip-synched)

"I don't mind avant-garde material, like in *Urinetown*. A musical doesn't have to be fantasy . . . or *Brigadoon*. But I sorely miss the sheer beauty you typically found in musicals, either in the impossibly romantic love story, or the leading lady, or the incredible music—Lerner and Loewe, Rodgers and Hammerstein, etc. *Something* in a musical should be wondrous and beautiful, should transport you. . . . Musicals aren't supposed to be completely down to earth."—KIM HUNTER (*A Streetcar Named Desire*)

"You didn't just go to see musicals. Sometimes you went despite that. You went to see great musical stars—performers that were larger and more exciting than everyday life or your neighbors."—stage director JOSE QUINTERO (*Long Day's Journey into Night*)

"I hate musicals that think dance is expendable, . . . that it's unquestionably better to have two actors sing at each other. Dance is what musicals were originally about, and why musicals came into being."—legendary choreographer JACK COLE

"These two enormous, too-big hits, *The Phantom of the Opera* and *Les Misérables*, they actually have no dancing in them! How could it be, someone forgot? They have much music, yes, but are they really musicals?" —ballet dancer NATALIA MAKAROVA

"The increasing corporate influence detracts in small ways from the experience of theatergoing. Shows are much larger, more difficult to manage, especially in the old facilities. Amenities are lost; the public is not treated as well."—JOSEPH TRAINA, house manager of the Belasco Theatre

"What's moving in today's bloated musicals isn't the music or performances, but the rotating sets."—ROBIN WILLIAMS

"What I hate about employment in these mega-musicals is they make unheard-of profits for a few billionaires and corporations, but not being personality driven, they can recast with no effect on the box office. The show's the thing—good, lousy, or indifferent. And most of us in it are more interchangeable than ever, just cogs in a wheel. The producers and owners have more power and control than ever. Performers have less than ever; we're units now, not members of a theatrical ensemble or family. The atmosphere gets colder and colder."—ANONYMOUS "THIRTYISH" ACTOR

Drat! The *Cats*

THE LONGEST-RUNNING MUSICAL until *Phantom of the Opera* surpassed it in 2006, *Cats* may also be the most dogmatically disliked musical ever. For every fan, there's at least one detractor, including many who've never seen it. "I identified with every cat on that stage," purred Rosie O'Donnell, while Dennis Miller barked, "Sitting through *Cats* is as pleasant as listening to two of them fighting or mating at three in the morning."

Some purr-tinent "Cats" facts and quotes:

- Widow Valerie Eliot gave composer Andrew Lloyd Webber an unpublished eight-line fragment about Grizabella the Glamour Cat that T.S. had omitted from his *Old Possum's Book of Practical Cats* as being too grim for children.

- Eliot had declined Walt Disney's request to turn his cat poems into an animated feature; the poet insisted his felines were "hard-scrabble alleycats, not cute little anthropomorphs."

- *Cats'* title was never translated into another language; the musical has been translated into ten languages.

- During *Cats'* run at New York's Winter Garden Theatre, maintenance workers removed 237 pounds of chewing gum from underneath theatre seats.

- *Cats* opened in London's West End on May 11, 1981; on January 21, 1996, its 6,141st performance made it London's longest-running musical ever; in April, '99, the production's gross box office topped the equivalent of $184 million.

- *Cats* opened on Broadway October 7, 1982, playing until September 10, 2000 (in 1997 it became Broadway's longest-running musical), for a total of 7,485 performances and a gross of over $400 million. (American ticket prices were higher.)

- Over 150 singers have recorded the song "Memory" (Barry Manilow—*meow*—publicly disparaged Barbra Streisand's less Muzak-y rendition); the Broadway cast recording sold over two million copies.

- 59,705 condoms were employed to protect singing cast members' body mikes from makeup and perspiration.

- Some of the show's more memorable cat names included Bombalurina, Rum Tum Tugger, Rumpleteazer, Skimbleshanks the Railway Cat, Macavity the Mystery Cat, Jennyanydots the Gumbie Cat, and Etcetera.

"You'd think *Cats* was the very first of its kind. It isn't. In the 1950s Eartha Kitt and I did a Broadway musical, *Shinbone Alley*, about Archy the cockroach and Mehitabel the alleycat—very famous characters, and much loved. . . . We had good music, plenty of dance, and there were cats. . . . Many people liked it, and those who have compared it with *Cats* prefer our show. However, expensive musicals will pretend they're the first of their kind." —stage (*The Gay Divorce* and film (*Top Hat*) actor ERIK RHODES

"I hated *Cats* from when I first heard about jellicle cats and pollicle dogs and the words were treated like some secret or sacrosanct language. Then I find out all it meant was T.S. Eliot as a child misunderstood a relative who was saying 'dear little cats' and 'poor little dogs.' Too, too pretentious for words."—UK stage and TV (Sherlock Holmes) actor JEREMY BRETT

"I hate it when they turn animals into humans, with the sexist, mostly male voices. . . . The cats in *Cats* look so weird. I love cats, but not *Cats*. When it finally shuts down, I'll probably celebrate."—NELL CARTER (*Ain't Misbehavin'*)

"I haven't seen *Cats*. I resent that they have to tear theatres apart for these shows. I wonder if the Winter Garden will ever be the same. I hope they have to return the theatre to pristine condition after it closes. If it ever closes."—BARNARD HUGHES (*Da*)

"I hate to go to the theatre anymore. . . . How can *Cats* still be running? It's terrible. And the microphones. My God, people are miked all over—I can't believe it!"—MARIA KARNILOVA (*Fiddler on the Roof*)

"If you're paying $60, you want a lot for your money. And whether you approve or not, *Cats* at least gives you a lot of cats."—composer CHARLES STROUSE (*Annie*)

"You could throw away every song except 'Memory' and it wouldn't make any difference."—composer JULE STYNE (*Bells Are Ringing*)

"Most musicals get advertised with a line from a good review or something that makes sense. *Cats* just ignored the critics' opinions—like, no wonder—and used its own line: 'Now and Forever.' Which to me sounds more like a threat."—actress ROSEANNE BARR (*The Wizard of Oz* at Madison Square Garden)

"The logo-slogan 'Now and Forever' on the *Cats* poster proved to be prophetic [though] one critic said [the show] made him feel like something was peeing on his leg for two hours."—producer STUART OSTROW (*M. Butterfly*)

P.S. The Off-Broadway *The Fantasticks* (1960) outlasted the "Now and Forever" *Cats*.

11

HELLMAN ON WHEELS

In 1934, veteran author, Communist Party member, and alcoholic Dashiell Hammett yielded up his final work, *The Thin Man*. The same year, Lillian Hellman, whom he had met in 1930 and would live with until his death in 1961, debuted her first work, the play *The Children's Hour*. Coincidence? "Like a vampire, Lillian took and took from Dash," said MGM executive David Lewis. "She really only decided to become a writer, to be serious about it, after meeting him."

Others also suspected that more than a little of *The Children's Hour*, or at least its structure, was by way of Hammett, who mentored Hellman in her writing. What was unsuspected at the time was that despite her claim, the play was not an original story. Hellman borrowed much of it from a real-life case in 19th-century Edinburgh, Scotland, concerning two schoolteachers who committed no impropriety but were simply and accurately revealed as lesbian. Such was the bigotry of the place and era that contemporary newspapers wouldn't even mention what the two longtime companions were "accused" of, unlike the subsequent Oscar Wilde case in London.

In 1983, the scholarly book *Scotch Verdict* brought the facts of the case to light, much to the chagrin of Lillian Hellman, who made no official comment. What she did create, besides updating the story and making one of the women heterosexual with a fiancé, was the play's stereotypically unhappy ending. "To her everlasting shame," stated author and psychologist Dr. Evelyn Hooker, "Hellman invented a viciously moralistic and pandering finale in which the actual lesbian of the two rumored lesbians is so consumed with self-hatred that she hangs herself." That ending is repeated in revivals and, more widely, in the 1961 movie version, often on television due to its starring trio of Audrey Hepburn, Shirley MacLaine as Martha, and James Garner.

"That ending has vilified women's feelings for each other," wrote Dr. Hooker, "and horrified and haunted generations of lesbians, particularly young, impressionable ones. It is a cruel and needless ending," also untruthful, for in real life the two women did not lose their case, and nobody committed suicide. Unfortunately, the notoriety which accrued to the two victims—rather than to their homophobic victimizers—broke up the female pair.

Although in her play Hellman sternly disapproved of "gossip" about some-body's being homosexual—whether true or not—in real life she blithely jus-tified her means by her personal ends. An example, cited in William Wright's *Lillian Hellman*, was her fury when a reporter printed that the director of her 1963 play *My Mother, My Father and Me* had been fired and Hellman was directing in his place. She telephoned the paper in a huff and without denying the story, demanded a retraction. The writer refused, knowing the story was true. Hellman said she'd soon see about that.

The following weekend the reporter visited some gay bars in Manhattan. On Monday the playwright, who'd obviously hired a private detective (shades of Sam Spade!), phoned the journalist to declare that if he didn't print the retraction she'd inform his boss where he'd been over the weekend. Because the newspaperman was openly gay, the alleged social activist's threat fell flat.

"The great independent thinker, right? Sorry—image, not reality. Lilly was very much of the period she grew up in," noted director Mary Hunter Wolf. "Directing was once upon a time thought a very masculine undertaking, sup-posedly the death of individual femininity. . . . Hollywood's two lady directors of note were Dorothy Arzner, an acknowledged Sapphic (tape-interviewed in this author's *Hollywood Lesbians*), and Ida Lupino, who was forever insisting she didn't *direct* men, she just made suggestions.

"It was slightly better on Broadway. . . . Today it seems ridiculous, all the fuss so many of us made. The ladies really did protest too much." Wolf direct-ed the rumored-to-be sapphic Mary Martin in the well-loved *Peter Pan*.

LILLIAN HELLMAN'S MAKEUP contained more than a bit of self-hate, her outward confidence and aggression notwithstanding. She didn't identify with or activate for feminist or gay issues, rather choosing the more socially accept-able cause of black civil rights. "Lillian gives the impression of not caring whom she offends," explained playwright Leonard Spigelgass. "But believe me, she chooses her enemies carefully, and ultimately she does crave public acceptance and admiration."

Eventually the best-known American woman of letters, and before that the leading US female playwright of her day, Hellman wrote plays that generally haven't held up well and even in her heyday paled next to those of her leading contemporaries. "She had incredible luck," opined Spigelgass. "Besides [having] a live-in, honest-to-goodness real writer in the form of Dash Hammett, she had a first play that became a hit due to prurient interest. It wasn't a gay play per se, so it wasn't shut down, and its anti-gay touches, certainly that tragic denouement, reassured the status quo who liked to think they were attending a really daring play."

Spigelgass continued: "[Hellman's] *The Little Foxes* was a hit insofar as it was a tour de force for Tallulah Bankhead, a big star at the time." It was also a screen triumph for Bette Davis. "When it gets revived, it's because it's a whale of a part for a showy, big-name actress," as with Elizabeth Taylor in 1981. Hellman did a far less popular sequel (sans Tallulah) to *The Little Foxes*, whose theme was anti-capitalist; and her anti-fascist *Watch on the Rhine* was admirable at the time—and became another film with Bette Davis—but is seldom revived because it's so dated.

Hellman more than once tried to achieve success and big bucks (despite her Marxist credo) at screenwriting, with generally poor results. Her eagerly awaited original screenplay for *The Chase* (1965) was a major flop in spite of stars like Marlon Brando, Jane Fonda, and Robert Redford.

"The question of how much if any of Lillian's output was written or rewritten by Hammett will always remain open," said film producer David Lewis. "I personally suspect he had a minimal involvement, or else her plays would be better . . . more subtle and better characterized."

Despite being the country's ace female playwright, Hellman's literary and cultural reputation ultimately rested on her four books of memoirs, which came later in life. Those too would become suspect, closer inspection leading to a crumbling of the reputation. "Hellman claimed *The Children's Hour* was her own invention," Lewis pointed out. "It was not. She claimed her celebrated books were chronicles of fact. They were not. They were significantly of her own invention, for self-aggrandizement."

Scoundrel Time, about the post–World War II political witch hunts, was deemed an instant classic in 1976. It recounted Hellman's principled stand against the House Un-American Activities Committee in 1952. She famously snorted, "I cannot and will not cut my conscience to fit this year's fashions." However, Lillian's reputation for defying those who would have her name names was based more on what she later claimed she'd done and said than on the facts.

Understandably, she'd been terrified, for she and Hammett were actual communists—not that that was illegal—unlike a majority of the mostly Jewish and/or gay (sometimes both, like former communist Jerome Robbins) witnesses summoned by the Republican leadership. Hellman had desperately sought not to have to appear before HUAC, and wrote a letter "full of trembling and cringing," said Leonard Bernstein, who worked with Lillian on *Candide*. "It surprised me, when I finally read it. This was not the proud, defiant, and arrogant missive that she described but no wonder did not reproduce in full" in *Scoundrel Time* and that even abased her Jewish heritage. "She might have imagined she could pacify or fool HUAC . . . that no one had guessed she was Jewish."

HELLMAN'S INDIGNATION SEEMED TO GROW with the years. She took to saying she was a playwright and memoirist, not a historian. "I always wonder if I'm telling the truth," she admitted. "Very tricky business, the business of oneself, plus memory, plus what you think you can do plus what has moved you, sometimes without your knowing it."

Though she was rightly celebrated for defying HUAC, she wasn't the only one to do so, though she derived the most from it, nurturing her own legend, or myth, and making herself seem a lone dissenter. She wrote that her heroic resistance to the inquisitors was interrupted by a voice in the press gallery, clearly and loudly stating, "Thank God somebody finally had the guts to do it." That voice was not heard by anyone else present, including her attorney Joseph Rauh. Hellman insisted that she'd been determined to tell HUAC the truth about herself, come what may. Yet in the first draft of her letter to the committee she declared that she'd been a Communist Party member from 1938 to 1940, the years of the Hitler-Stalin pact, though in *Scoundrel Time* and to the committee she claimed she hadn't been—a lie revealed only after the draft's discovery in 1988.

Eric Bentley's Off-Broadway play *Are You Now or Have You Ever Been?* (the committee demanded if witnesses were or had ever been "a member of the Communist Party?") featured Hellman's HUAC appearance as a dramatic highlight, with actresses Colleen Dewhurst, Tammy Grimes, Peggy Cass, and Liza Minnelli re-enacting the scene of a brave, contemptuous "Lilly" declining to cut her conscience.

Although Hellman abhorred Hitler, she idolized Joseph Stalin, defending the murderer of millions—including a disproportionate number of Jews—to the end of her days. She wasn't merely a Marxist, but an apologist for Soviet dictatorship—as Tallulah Bankhead dumbfoundedly discovered (more anon). In his book *The Scoundrel in the Looking Glass*, philosopher Sidney Hook summarized Stalin's evils, including the invasion of Finland, the invasion of Poland and murder of the Polish officer corps in the Katyn forest, the subjugation of the Baltic states, the Moscow purges, the suppression of Hungary's would-be

1956 revolution, the murder of Trotsky, etcetera, and concluded that most of Hellman's readers would never guess that she was "once one of the most vigorous public defenders of [Stalin's crimes] which even Khruschev did not hesitate to call crimes."

Indeed, many literati already impressed by Hellman the playwright were prone to canonize the lone post-Hammett literary lioness who'd fought so many dragons and survived, head unbent. Jules Feiffer felt, "I don't believe it was ever a matter of choice with her to play it safe or not. . . . She honestly knew of no other way to behave." John Hersey believed her the personification of rage against injustice of all sorts, and William Styron was "in awe of this woman . . . a mother, a sister and a friend and in a strange way a lover of us all."

Hellmann was no friend to Dashiell Hammett's offspring, from whom she, in charge of his literary legacy, withheld royalties. "When the literary powers decided to enshrine the non-marital union of Miss Hellman, who was already married, and Mr. Hammett," declared playwright George Kelly, "they chose to leave out his booze and apathy and her mercenary ambition and all the hypocrisies and politics." It wasn't printed at the time that the pair were far from inseparable or sexually faithful.

HELLMAN'S 1973 MEMOIR *Pentimento* led to her widest audience yet via the highly praised 1977 film *Julia*, starring Jane Fonda as Lillian and Vanessa Redgrave as her purported pal Julia (wags nicknamed the movie "Reds in Bed"). The picture's emotional centerpiece is the attempt by brave, freedom-loving Hellman, who risks her life—for once acknowledging being Jewish—to smuggle $50,000 into Hitler's Germany for the activist Julia and her underground colleagues to use to smuggle Jews and others out of the fascist fatherland. Questions about Hellman's account of events were mushrooming. When put on the spot, she allowed, "Everybody's memory is tricky, and mine's a little trickier than most, I guess."

In 1983, the year before Hellman's death, a retired physician named Muriel Gardiner published *Code Name Mary*, an autobiography. It was the same story as the Julia chapter in Lillian's *Pentimento*. However, Gardiner's version was verifiable through Austrian records and witnesses. In 1978 Gardiner had written to Hellman, intensely curious about *Julia* and its resemblance to her own life. She wondered why she had never heard of another young female American doing work for the Austrian resistance while she, Gardiner, was there, starting as a medical student in Vienna in the mid-1930s. Hellman never responded to Gardiner, and later denied even receiving her letter.

Though Hellman and Gardiner—the real "Julia"—had never met, both were clients of the famous Austrian lawyer and raconteur Karl Schwabacher. Carol Brightman, a biographer of Hellman foe Mary McCarthy (no relation to

the Republican senator), theorized that Schwabacher "may well have entertained his clients" with tales of Gardiner's derring-do, later appropriated by the
memory-free—and sometimes conscience-free—Lillian Hellman. Gardiner
was on the verge of suing Hellman when the latter died.

By that time Lillian had famously sued writer and critic Mary McCarthy.
"That goddamned *name*," she'd cried, "it comes back to haunt me!" (For a
fuller description of Hellman's contentious relationships with McCarthy and
Bankhead, see this author's *Celebrity Feuds!*) It had happened that Hellman, no
longer easily able to read, tuned in to Dick Cavett's television talk show in
January 1980. At 74, suffering from glaucoma, chronic bronchitis, and emphy-
sema, she was limited to bed and a wheelchair. Her usual rage was com-
pounded by the ravages of old age and decades of unfiltered Camel cigarettes.
"Goddamn my eyes," Lillian swore to a friend, "and my pacemaker and goddamn my arteries."

Cavett's guest was Mary McCarthy (sister to actor Kevin, one of
Montgomery Clift's closest friends). Mary had met the six-years-older and
much-more-successful Hellman only twice and had seldom reviewed her
plays, which she considered dull, contrived, and unworthy of attention (partly
out of jealousy?). Perhaps that was as well for Hellman, since McCarthy—a
failed playwright—was known for her jaundiced views: for example, Tennessee
Williams's *A Streetcar Named Desire* "reeks of literary ambition as the apartment
reeks of cheap perfume," and *The Iceman Cometh*'s Eugene O'Neill is "probably the only man in the world who is still laughing at the Iceman joke or pondering its implications." McCarthy, who finally hit it big as a novelist with *The
Group*, was known for her at times foolish flipness, which more than once
landed her in trouble, for instance in 1944 when she'd said she felt sorry for
Hitler 'cause the poor guy just wanted to be loved.

Pressed by Dick Cavett to put down a name writer, McCarthy repeated
on air a bit of libel from *Paris Metro* that Hellman was probably aware of but
hadn't sued over. (Few people read the scholarly periodical.) McCarthy averred
that Lillian was "dishonest." "How so?" asked Cavett. Replied McCarthy, "I said
once in some interview that every word she writes is a lie, including *and* and
the."

Hellman could hardly believe her ears, and immediately after phoned several people. One was Cavett, who offered her the chance to appear and rebut
McCarthy's slander. Hellman declined. Two weeks later she sued, a choice that
many literati deplored because they felt McCarthy, as a critic, was entitled to air
her opinion, regardless. An astonished McCarthy claimed not to remember
what she'd said on the Cavett show, though by then it had been reprinted several times, also reiterated on TV, at cocktail parties, etc. People chose up sides,
and issues of free speech were invoked. While many observers felt McCarthy

had gone too far, they also believed Hellman's lawsuit, if decided in her favor, would limit the rights of critics and journalists.

Lillian let it be known she would drop her suit if McCarthy would publicly apologize. This the younger woman resolutely refused to do. "*Liar* I said, and *liar* I meant," she gloated two years later. During the lengthy legal process, some tidbits spilled out as Hellman's autobiographical writings were culled for inaccuracies or inconsistencies, and anti-Hellmanites made their voices heard. An elderly Hungarian claimed that Lillian had stolen *The Little Foxes* from her late playwright husband, whose agent had submitted a play to Hellman's friend and producer Herman Shumlin. And then there was *Code Name Mary.* . . .

Finally, in 1984, in an eighteen-page opinion, Judge Harold Baer Jr. denied McCarthy's motion to dismiss the suit on First Amendment grounds. He declared that her statement about Hellman "seems to fall on the actionable side of the line—outside what has come to be known as the marketplace of ideas." Most resoundingly, Judge Baer asseverated that Hellman was somehow not a public figure—as Lillian had disingenuously contended—and was thus entitled to greater protections than, say, actors or politicians, whose work is for the most part performed in public.

McCarthy was astounded, and much of the cultural community saw it as a blow to free expression and a move toward increased censorship. An appeal was launched by McCarthy and PBS-TV. But before the appeal could be tried, Lillian Hellman died at 78. McCarthy was immensely relieved, then quickly cocky: "There's no satisfaction in having an enemy die—you have to beat them." Asked years afterward if she would have done the same thing again, Mary said, "If someone had told me, 'Don't say anything about Lillian Hellman because she'll sue you,' it wouldn't have stopped me. It might have spurred me on. I didn't want her to die. I wanted her to lose in court. I wanted her around for that."

THE FIRST PERSON TO STATE IN PRINT that Lillian Hellman had deliberately lied was Tallulah Bankhead, star of Hellman's play *The Little Foxes* (1934). The accusation, in her 1952 memoirs, was written off as a flamboyant actress's theatrics, possibly motivated by greed for publicity. Not until the 1980s would the late stage star be vindicated. The original episode, which devolved into a lifelong feud, began about a year into the run of *The Little Foxes* (1939).

In 1939, Russia, under Stalin, invaded its tiny neighbor Finland. Later in the year, after Tallulah and the play's cast informed the press they would be doing a benefit performance to aid Finland, they were stunned to learn that Hellman and producer Herman Shumlin had declined to give permission. Hellman declared that it wasn't America's fight and she didn't want to encourage warlike sentiments. Bankhead apprised reporters, "I've adopted Spanish

Loyalist orphans and sent money to China, causes for which both Mr. Shumlin and Miss Hellman were strenuous proponents. . . . Why should [they] suddenly become so insular?"

Insiders knew that Lillian was hiding her real motive: a fanatical devotion to Soviet Russia. She countered her star by proclaiming, "I don't believe in that fine, lovable little Republic of Finland that everyone gets so weepy about. I've been there and it looks like a pro-Nazi little Republic to me." It was a slap in the face of freedom-loving Finland, which was as anti-Hitler as its Scandinavian neighbors. The comment marked Hellman's moral low point, and at the time only her collaborator Shumlin knew that Lillian almost certainly had never been to Finland, though she would continue to paint it in fascistic colors.

Hellman and Bankhead became mortal enemies. Tallulah didn't like being crossed when she knew she was in the right. Lillian didn't like being questioned and was used to getting her way minus the glare of publicity that a Broadway superstar brought to bear. Hellman made several enemies via the incident. Up until then, the extent of her adherence to Marxism had not been widely known. The feud, conducted in the press, made her hardline views famous—and reviled.

Just as the incident was dying down, Hellman made things worse. Feeling a need for further vindication, she lied that the real reason she'd turned down Tallulah's benefit was that when the Spanish government had fallen to Franco and his Fascists, Hellman and Shumlin had requested the actress to do a benefit for the Loyalists who were fleeing to neighboring France. Tallulah and company, the playwright said, had refused! The star was outraged by the lie— but in almost any ruckus pitting an outspoken, theatrical actress against a male producer and a serious, plain, and grim female playwright, the actress was usually discounted out of hand.

In her autobiography, Tallulah wrote, "The charge that I had refused to play a benefit for Loyalist Spain was a brazen invention. Neither Shumlin nor Miss Hellmann ever asked me to do any such thing. Nor did anyone else." Bankhead would have used stronger language but feared legal reprisal— Hellman spoke loudly and carried a big lawyer. After *The Little Foxes*, the two women never talked again. They continued to speak ill of each other, but Hellman created a more scathing portrait of Bankhead than vice versa, both via inclination and the fact that she wrote about Tallulah posthumously.

After Hellman's death, cultural commentator Hilton Kramer labeled her a "shameless liar" and sweepingly stated that "the 'memoirs' that brought her wealth, fame, and honors of every sort are now shown to have been a fraud."

"The tough thing about discussing or dissecting Lillian," said Leonard Spigelgass, "is discerning the motives of those deconstructing her. She doesn't merit complete dismantling. Are her detractors objective in listing every faux pas and contradiction? Or are they reactionaries eager to exploit her flaws to promote their own intolerant agenda?"

Tallulah's costar and intimate friend Patsy Kelly noted, "Back before the whole McCarthy mess, you wouldn't have imagined Lillian Hellman would become so very admired, outside of on Broadway. It took that backtracking Congress we got after Roosevelt to make Hellman look like a victim. . . . If she'd been a smarter cookie, she'd have stayed on Tallu's good side and Tallu would maybe've made hits out of her [subsequent] plays. But Hellman couldn't stand feminine competition, or any gal who took a chunk of her limelight and her reputation.

"Tallulah was practically the only woman star she ever had in any of her ole plays."

It was after ex-witch-hunter Richard Nixon's Watergate downfall that Hellman's fame and admiration reached their peak. "Creating her memoirs was a master stroke," said David Lewis. "But a thing you need to remember about Hellman is that once public opinion shifted in her favor, what really made her look good [were] her enemies. Lillian the monster had to be compared to worse monsters like McCarthy, Nixon, and Roy Cohn to come out smelling like a rose. She really was damn lucky . . . great timing."

Time and her books elevated playwright Lillian Hellman from a Broadway figure to a national icon and supposed role model. But more time and one too many lies, plus her unquenchable egotism, tumbled down the carefully constructed edifice of her brave and daring, freedom-loving persona in her final years and after. Ironically, after her assorted memoirs were largely discredited, it was Hellman's plays—largely undistinguished but mostly untarnished—that formed the backbone of her remaining reputation.

George Kelly—All in the Family

GEORGE KELLY IS AN EXAMPLE of a playwright who achieved big but quite brief and specific success. Better remembered today as Grace Kelly's gay but very closeted and deeply conservative uncle (1887–1974), he had three hit plays between 1922 and '25: *The Torch-Bearers*, *The Show-Off*, and *Craig's Wife*. The latter is the most widely known due to its third screen version, *Harriet Craig* (1950), which starred Joan Crawford in an eerily self-parodying performance. (Daughter Christina said she had virtually played herself, clean-freak and all.)

In the mid-1930s Kelly experienced a successful run with his previously unproduced 1929 play *Reflected Glory*, because it starred Tallulah Bankhead, playing an actress married more to the stage than to any man. Kelly's fourth play, *Daisy Mayme*, without a star to carry it, had flopped in 1926. A critic said it had too much manner and too little matter. Kelly plays typically featured three types: freeloaders, silly women, and haughty women.

Craig's Wife concerns a woman who cherishes her house more than her husband. Rosalind Russell, who starred in the 1936 movie version directed by Dorothy Arzner, later offered, "I had little to play. She's written as an iceberg. . . . The story's main point is the horror of a woman trying to rule the home." Kelly, of course, advocated a patriarchal dictatorship, not a marriage of equals. In his play the ending is sad: the woman is abandoned by hubby and everyone else, left frightfully alone in a big house (hers to keep). In the significantly revamped Crawford version, the ending is happier: Harriet, never much of a people person, is left with the meticulous mansion she craved for herself all along.

Kelly began as an actor and worked in vaudeville. He wrote sketches. Older brother Walter was a successful monologist—also a bigot who refused to share the stage with a black act. Even after he took up writing plays, the younger brother admittedly attended the theater very seldom, movies virtually not at all, and he never owned a television set.

After his fourth and subsequent plays failed on Broadway, George blamed it on "the New York Jews" and moved to Hollywood in 1931 to work at conservative MGM. (Even post-Watergate, he was staunchly pro-Nixon.) George Kelly, who destroyed all his personal papers before he died, later turned to directing revivals of his plays once he decided he couldn't and wouldn't compete with the Broadway-bound "filth" written by the likes of Eugene O'Neill, Tennessee Williams, etc.

Between 1946 and his 1974 death in Pennsylvania, where he had been born, Kelly yielded no more plays. Today his output reads mostly as stilted and repetitive. He tended to write situations more than active scenes, and has been cited for an excessive amount of stage directions and attention to sets, especially portieres. Actor Alfred Lunt once opined to critic Alexander Woollcott, "Mr. Kelly's characters could talk you to death before intermission."

By the 1950s the publicity-shy "bachelor" was a near recluse, living out West because he loved the sun, hated "frigid weather and frigid women"—the latter featured often in his plays. He did speak to a few reporters in praise of political witch-hunter Joseph McCarthy and penned a teleplay for Broadway star Shirley Booth. By then he'd long since given up writing for the movies. His sole screen credit was a 1935 Wallace Beery vehicle titled *Old Hutch*. Kelly's failure at screenwriting he attributed to "those Hollywood Jews."

P.S. George Kelly, successful so long ago, has for the most part only rated a chapter or subchapter in books about his family or niece. Predictably, academic studies of him and his work have denied or elided his gayness. A 1977 book, *Those Philadelphia Kellys —With a Touch of Grace*, admitted his homosexuality, focusing on his primary or perhaps only same-sex relationship and how most of the Kelly clan treated his "companion" shabbily, if at all. A 1999 volume of *Three Plays by George Kelly*, a co-publication of the Princess Grace Foundation—USA, included an introductory essay by a retired academic who not only denied the increasingly available evidence but misrepresented it: referring to the material in *Those Philadelphia Kellys* as "speculation," he reduced the evidence to a mere friendly "gesture" that George Kelly had made toward a young (nine years younger) hotel employee whom he met in New York City. What the Foundation-sponsored retiree from reality didn't declare was the fact that George's "gesture" was to live almost inseparably with the ex-bellhop for possibly as long as fifty-five years—a longer union than hardly any other Kelly ever experienced.

12

THESPING

"You know, Thespis is the god of acting. But he was a real person. And that's what we of the stage are—we're all too human, yet at our histrionic peak, and in what we give to audiences, we sometimes achieve divinity."
—JOHN BARRYMORE

"Actors are like other people, only more so."—Broadway producer CHERYL CRAWFORD on the desire for masks

"Actors on camera are shadows, at best two-dimensional. In theatre, actors are flesh . . . alive . . . in the round. The performance is being created and lived out before you. It's the next thing to life, but more thrilling."—YUL BRYNNER (*The King and I*)

"I love the live performance of the theatre, of building a character and taking her from the beginning to the end of the play. Theatre is so full and rich. I feel so *high* when I come off stage, and you get that immediate response [from the audience]."—singer-actress LAINIE KAZAN

"And then there's something I very seldom talk about. Within all of us we have a secret place filled with sulfuric acid and bile and the most horrible thoughts. . . . And that's what you often have to call on, and it's hard to do. Because you don't want anybody to know about it. Nobody in the cast has to know about this, and even the audience doesn't know about it. But you know. And it's hard."—film and stage actor CHARLES DURNING

"Acting is the most minor of gifts and not a very high-class way to earn a living. After all, Shirley Temple could do it at the age of four."—KATHARINE HEPBURN

"Acting is the expression of a neurotic impulse. It's a bum's life. The principal benefit acting has afforded me is the money to pay for my psychoanalysis."—MARLON BRANDO

"Only actors and prostitutes have to perform nightly. Without extra inspiration, it can get pretty mechanical."—SARAH JESSICA PARKER, Broadway and *Sex and the City* star

"Doing [HELLO, DOLLY!] on Broadway was the biggest thrill. At first it felt like a command performance . . . I finally got used to the idea that New York audiences are not royalty—but it took time!"—PHYLLIS DILLER

"On Broadway, you act just as you would act in any play. The only extra ingredient is glamour."—MATTHEW BRODERICK (*The Producers*)

"The difference between stage acting and acting for the camera isn't talking louder. It's making what you say on the stage seem more important."—EILEEN HECKART

"'My boy,' she said to me, 'act in your pauses.' At those moments, you are a creator, not a servant of playwrights."—SIR CEDRIC HARDWICKE, recalling stage legend Ellen Terry's advice

"A strong bit of advice which I received long ago and have never forgotten on or off the stage: In acting, never underline. Anything one underlines is bad art."—SIR MICHAEL REDGRAVE

"I recall a Broadway actor giving me belated advice about Shakespeare. 'Don't bother,' he said. 'If you're not playing a king, you never get to sit down.'"—SIR NIGEL HAWTHORNE, Tony-winner for *Shadowlands*

"Shakespeare died when he was 52. If *I* had, I'd never have been in *The Matchmaker* or met Mia [Farrow, her *Rosemary's Baby* costar] or been on the Joey Bishop Show or flown 67 times across the country or won an Oscar or eaten papaya or been robbed of all my jewelry or seen *M*A*S*H* or *Where's Poppa?* or Don Rickles."—writer-actress RUTH GORDON

"Come on, man, do you want the sad face, the glad face, the fast face, or the slow face?"—JASON ROBARDS JR. to a director

"It's like cramming, don't you know. Only with more heart and passion involved."—CAROL CHANNING, on staying up all night re-reading every line before opening a show

"Theatre actors have the luxury of being fanatics. You can, for several hours, become a character, live and breathe it. As Miss Channing does. We repeat nightly, we do it in sequence, and if lucky we do it month after month. . . . When you're not in a hit, you don't wish to be an actor every minute of the day; when you are, you do. The true Broadway actor dreams of dying in harness."—DAVID BURNS, Carol Channing's leading man in *Hello, Dolly!*, who suffered a heart attack while performing in Kander and Ebb's *70, Girls, 70* (1971) and died soon after

"Actors. . . . The most modest of them . . . matches the conceit of the solitary pretty girl on a slow ship."—writer H.L. MENCKEN

"It is best in the theatre to act with confidence no matter how little right you have to it."—playwright LILLIAN HELLMAN

"In the theatre lying is looked upon as an occupational disease."—TALLULAH BANKHEAD

"Temperament is something that is an integral part of the artist. Not temper, temperament. There is a vast difference."—BETTE DAVIS in *The Lonely Life*

"The next actor may be the completion of your best scene. I *run* to actors."
—Tony winner TED ROSS (the Cowardly Lion in *The Wiz*)

"I have to laugh when certain politicians and preachers say actors are 'too liberal.' Actors deal with art and emotions. We see all sides of life. We come from everywhere and we mix with others and we accept. We work with and are indebted to a large percentage of gays and Jews. So what are we supposed to do? Regress and become narrow again, intolerant and bigoted?"—stage and screen actor DAVID DUKES, responding to a comment by then–Speaker of the House Newt Gingrich

"I don't much care for bad actors. I don't understand them and could never make a friend of one. I adore good actors, who are the sensitive sort of people one would like for friends."—DAME EDITH EVANS

"People think actors are smarter than comedians, but we write our own material. Actors don't. If they did, they'd be playwrights. . . . A daughter of a friend of mine was considering it. She said, 'I have half a mind to go into acting.' I told her, 'Honey, that's one of the requirements.' Fortunately, she chose veterinary medicine."—BUDDY HACKETT

"I always wanted to play Juliet. Somehow. It took me a long time to accept what was obvious to everyone else, and myself really—that physically I could never play her. It took even longer for me to accept that if I continued to act, it would not be in drama—my strong preference—but in comedy, to which I inevitably became accustomed with time."—DAME MARGARET RUTHERFORD

"In a Broadway musical, you act *up*. Even if you don't smile, you constantly seem capable [of it]. In a drama, you sound big but keep still—let the audience zero in on you. . . . In a comedy, play it straight and be very, very alert to your fellow players. React with your eyes, not your body."—BOB HOPE in the 1980s (in the 1930s he left the stage for Hollywood)

"Left eyebrow raised, right eyebrow raised."—non-theater UK actor ROGER MOORE on his technique

"Acting is merely the art of keeping a large group of people from coughing."—SIR RALPH RICHARDSON

"I remember reading that Sir Laurence Olivier was asked what part of the body was most effective for acting on the stage and on camera. He said, for the stage, the arms, and for the screen, the eyes. I've never forgotten that."—LUCILLE BALL

"On the stage, an actress needs bigger hair and more eye makeup. That's half the battle."—MARISSA JARET WINOKUR (*Hairspray*)

"Bright colors and big features help [on stage]. . . . Bernadette Peters conquered Broadway with her Kewpie-doll look, and Carol Channing also has big, startled features—that helped too."—makeup expert WAY BANDY

"[What the character should look like] is never me! I never get that out of my head. I can think back on every role I've done and picture who should have played it instead."—ROBERT SEAN LEONARD (*The Invention of Love*, *Arcadia*)

"When I'm hired for anything new, I usually get the feeling the director or producer is soon going to take me aside and inform me that he's sorry but it's not working out. This happens in the medium I'm most associated with, television, it happens in film, and it certainly has happened on the stage."—MARY TYLER MOORE

"I've had a lot of terrible moments. Once I was doing *The Master Builder* . . . and Sam Waterston and I were involved in this very passionate [scene] . . . and in the middle of it, I farted. The audience didn't hear it but he did. Our eyes just locked, and I didn't even say my next line. It just stopped me dead."—CYNTHIA NIXON

"You know, if I were an acting teacher, I would have young actors learn ballroom dancing as opposed to tap or modern or ballet, because that's all solo. In ballroom, you have to consider the other person. I'd have men dance with women and with men, and vice-versa. I'd have men lead, and I'd have women lead. And the purpose would be to get used to depending on someone else. Many actors act alone because they don't know how to interact."—CHARLES DURNING

"The youngest generation of actors now, the ones that hardly know what the stage is, are so into themselves, they'd prefer a monologue to a scene for two. I am not kidding. It's about stardom, bucks, and instant glory—and to hell with craft, paying your dues, with other people. In fact, all *other people* mean to most aspiring young actors—excuse me, *stars*—is a word: *networking*"—Tony winner RODDY McDOWALL

"I taught acting for 45 years. I don't teach it anymore, because they don't want to learn. They want six weeks, then their own showcase, then [TV producer] Aaron Spelling."—actor-director CHARLES NELSON REILLY (*Skyscraper, Hello, Dolly!*)

"There's no better incentive to learning to do something well than criticism from somebody you admire tremendously—if it's well-intended. . . . I dreamed of someday being half as good on the stage as my idol John Gielgud. . . . I was new, I knew that I wasn't very good at all, and after one excruciating rehearsal I asked if I'd been fired, and he said no, not really. Rather, he suggested I go away, then return in a week, 'after you get someone to teach you how to act.'"—SIR ALEC GUINNESS

"People think I'm powerful and intimidating. It's due entirely to the roles they've seen me perform. I don't mind. I'm not an actress who particularly sought to be loved by total strangers. . . . Long ago I realized that the only time I'm in control is when I am acting."—DAME JUDITH ANDERSON, star of stage (*Medea*) and screen (Mrs. Danvers in *Rebecca*)

"When an audience remains indifferent, you either seek frantically to convert them, which can result in overacting, or you feel the coldest contempt for them, which may inspire you to act brilliantly, at least for yourself and your fellow thespians."—CLIFF GORMAN (*The Boys in the Band*)

"On stage, an actor is entirely responsible for his performance. With a camera, there are shortcuts galore and a lot of the final performance is in the hands of the director, cinematographer, and editor."—ALBERT HAGUE, who won a Tony for the score of *Redhead* (1959) and acted on TV in *Fame*

"Some actors are too conscious of audiences . . . more into approval, I guess. Overall, an audience should be ignored, unless you're doing comedy; then, their laughter can really feed you. In drama, you ignore them."—Tony and Emmy winner MICHAEL JETER

"You have to guide [audiences], rather like children. They must be kept interested, but when they become too eager they must be taken in hand and made more patient."—GLENDA JACKSON, actress turned member of Parliament

"Audiences? No, the plural is impossible. Whether it be in Butte, Montana, or Broadway, it's an audience. The same great hulking monster with 4,000 eyes and 40,000 teeth."—JOHN BARRYMORE in 1906

"Coughing in the theatre is not a respiratory ailment. It's a criticism."—ALAN JAY LERNER in his memoirs

"It doesn't take much talent to wear a pair of shoes with three heels to it!" —KATHARINE HEPBURN during a rehearsal for *The West Side Waltz* to a talkative spectator

"Let's play horse. I'll be the front end and you just be yourself."—JACK WALDRON to a heckler

"Remember, you are speaking of the man I love!"—FRANK FAY to a drunk who came up onstage and told him he stank

"There's only one animal that throws a scent."—FRANK TINNEY to a customer who threw a penny at him while performing

"Please, lady, would you like it if I came over where you lived and turned off your red light?"—JACK WHITE to a female heckler

"Won't someone please get the poor girl a lawyer?"—visitor PETER USTINOV, after watching acting coach Lee Strasberg criticize and harangue Geraldine Page for an hour

"I had an acting coach who would yell at me every time she thought I was acting. She got me very confused. 'Don't act, just *be!*' I think she got used to or enjoyed yelling at me. Then I got very despondent. I even pondered giving up acting. But somehow or other I made a smart move, a crucial one: I instead gave *her* up."—ANITA MORRIS (*Nine*)

"The theatre is a powerful sexual stimulant, but when its power is not misused it is a powerful awakener of other ideas."—stage director SIR TYRONE GUTHRIE

"Acting is like sex. You should do it, not talk about it."—Oscar winner JOANNE WOODWARD, who prefers stage to screen

"I was at an interview the other day in Los Angeles, and this guy came up to me and said, in front of a lot of people who were sitting around, 'Oh, I saw your Hamlet. . . .' And I was quite pleased, and everyone looked up from their newspapers, and I thought, well, good, now they know I've played Hamlet. And then he completed the sentence:'. . . the night your codpiece fell off.' That's the worst."—ROGER REES, Tony winner for *Nicholas Nickleby*

"If actors need to brag now and then to hold up their self-esteem, let them. It is a very de-nuding profession, and of little respect. Up until not so long ago, the Church routinely excommunicated dead actors. Many were dumped into unmarked lime pits. . . . In Voltaire's *Candide*, when he goes to the theatre he asks how actresses are treated in France. 'Adored when they are beautiful, and thrown into the gutter when they are dead.'" —French stage and screen star JEAN MARAIS

"What actors need more than anything else is persistence. Just hanging in there. Looks and talent get judged and misjudged by all sorts of people and fads and biases. You must hang around until your chances present themselves. You can't play if you're not at the table."—BARNARD HUGHES (*Da*)

"When opportunity knocks, you better be prepared, honey. It don't knock often, and you better have taken enough lessons, polished your product, and be ready to show up responsible and on time!"—NELL CARTER (*Ain't Misbehavin'*)

"For a lot of actors, being in therapy is the flip side of getting up and nightly baring your insides to strangers. Therapy is trying to get your insides back, but in better order. That is, unless your therapist screws you up—a lot of them need therapists too."—ELLIOTT GOULD (*I Can Get It for You Wholesale*)

"Acting can't be taught, but I think experiences can be shared. And you can advise to a certain degree. But as Sandy Meisner says, 'The bottom line is talent.'"—actor-teacher VICTOR GARBER (*Deathtrap*, *Sweeney Todd*)

"Most people cannot believe I've done Shakespeare. . . . People tend to forget that no matter what an actor is famous for, he is or was an actor first and wanted to play diverse parts. I've done accents from German to English to hillbilly, but it's the casting people that ultimately decide how to categorize you—and how to limit you."—JIM VARNEY, best known as Ernest P. Worrell ("know-whut-I-mean-Vern?")

"Sometimes your image of yourself doesn't jibe with what others see. I never was Minnie Pearl, though I did soon grow to love her. Also I grew to love laughter. . . . With a middle name of Ophelia and my love for the legitimate stage, my original big-time goal was Broadway. I was going to be a dramatic actress. I thought Minnie was just a comedy character part, but after I introduced her at the Grand Ole Opry, she sort of took over my career, if not my life."—SARAH OPHELIA COLLEY

"An audience's laughter is easily obtained, and the comedian often mistakes it for affection or approval."—NANCY MARCHAND, star of stage and of TV's *The Sopranos*

"To me it's funny, I mean unusual, that so many people find it *funny* when a married couple play two characters who court and reject each other and argue and make up, then argue even more heatedly. But it's because we're married and as married people go through all that off the stage that we can play it so well."—JESSICA TANDY, who costarred with Hume Cronyn in *The Gin Game* (1977)

"Young lady, if you want reality, go out into the street and observe a fist fight. This is theatre and the theatre is not reality. Shall we press on?"—director TYRONE GUTHRIE to an actress questioning the reality of a scene

"The special effects, the pyrotechnics, all the money they were pouring into these things. I had to learn everything all over again, which is one of the things that makes acting so exciting."—TOM BOSLEY (TV's *Happy Days*), who after twenty-four years returned to Broadway in 1995, as Belle's father in *Beauty and the Beast*

"[Theatre] is not a profession in which people, generally speaking, grow old gracefully. In part because it's so marginal. It's all sort of by the seat of your pants and the economics of it are so shaky. There is no tenure and there are no pensions. You can be sixty and still facing a life of insecurity after having done a life of good work."—playwright TONY KUSHNER (*Angels in America*), a 2006 Oscar nominee for screenwriting

"A short run on Broadway has happened to everyone, even the biggest stars. Which hardly makes it any less humiliating."—CAROL BURNETT

"The question actors most often get asked is how they can bear saying the same things over and over again, night after night. But God knows the answer to that is, 'Don't we all anyway—might as well get paid for it.'" —writer ELAINE DUNDY

"Drama [is] what literature does at night."—critic GEORGE JEAN NATHAN

"I write plays to find out why I'm writing them."—EDWARD ALBEE (*The Goat, Or Who Is Sylvia?*)

"The one-man show evolved in Britain long ago, contrary to current Broadway thought or assumption. It had to come about, because actors were limited as to where, not only what, they could perform. Only two theatres in London were licensed by the crown—plays couldn't take place anywhere else. So an enterprising actor would put on a solo performance at the theatre in the daytime—when they didn't have plays—or at a private club, and invite friends, and that way he—and I do mean *he*, only—could get around the Licensing Act."—PAULINE COLLINS, who won several awards for her performance in the one-woman show *Shirley Valentine* (its film version earned her a Best Actress Oscar nomination)

"The intensity of a role is magnified in a one-person show. . . . For *Lillian* [Hellman], I underwent deep loneliness . . . even morning sickness. It had to do with being the only actor . . . it had to do with Lillian being a very difficult person, somebody I resisted letting inhabit me, but of course had to."—ZOE CALDWELL

"It's hard when you're out there all by yourself. They think that's what an actress loves. What I love is to be with an ensemble, to work with other actors. But listen, I'm not knocking being out there alone. It's just a hell of a lot of responsibility. You'd better keep moving, I'll tell you that. Because it's not easy to entertain an audience solely, talking about yourself for two-and-a-half hours."—ELAINE STRITCH, whose *At Liberty* won a Tony in 2002

"I heartily recommend a bit of honesty and eccentricity to keep one fresh in a stale part. It also keeps an audience from taking one for granted if one isn't born with the form divine."—SIR RALPH RICHARDSON, who once stopped a show cold by suddenly peering into the audience and asking, "Is there a doctor in the house?" and then questioning the man, "Doctor, isn't this play awful?"

"I don't try going on the stage because it's hard to find the part for me that's right, and if it's a drama I don't think I can keep it from being comedy."
—performer turned politician (redundant?) ARNOLD SCHWARZENEGGER

"One can play comedy; two are required for melodrama; but a tragedy demands three."—writer ELBERT HUBBARD

"A farce or a comedy is best played; a tragedy is best read at home."
—ABRAHAM LINCOLN in 1863 after a performance of *The Merchant of Venice* starring Edwin Booth; two years later, while attending a comedy performance, he was assassinated by Booth's younger brother

"The pleasure and thrill of acting on Broadway is mitigated by having to perform chiefly for the critics. At the outset, they have to approve your show or it may not last, which is outrageous, really. Once you're running, then you can enjoy the acting, because then it's for the audience, as it should be."—FAYE DUNAWAY (*Hogan's Goat*, Off-Broadwy)

"Every once in a while I inadvertently curse Mrs. Dorothy Brando, who got me into this. She was active in the Omaha Community Playhouse. . . . I'd come home to visit from college. Mrs. Brando telephoned one day. They'd lost their male lead . . . she said I'd be perfect for it. I was flabbergasted. I reminded her I couldn't act . . . [but] the notion of it, and the glamour, seduced me. I wound up doing three years at the Playhouse, and I did act opposite Mrs. Brando [who] was very good indeed. If she'd had more ambition or if she hadn't had kids, she could have made it on Broadway."—HENRY FONDA (Brando's daughter Jocelyn and son Marlon became professional actors)

"Milton Berle was not a hit on Broadway. He thought he was funny, which is death for a comic actor. Theatregoers like to *discover* you're funny, not be told about it. By contrast, Berle was a hit on television . . . on the other hand, in those days you had only two or three channels, and none were twenty-four hours."—CHRISTOPHER HEWETT, stage (*My Fair Lady*), film (*The Producers*) and TV (*Mr. Belvedere*) actor

"I was friends with a very amusing American actor who went to play one of his comedy hits in Melbourne, known as the most English and reserved of Australian cities. He was astonished and disheartened by how little mirth his performance elicited. Until afterwards, when several members of the audience informed him that the play and he in it had been so hilarious that they'd had trouble in not laughing."—RICHARD BURTON

"In spite of her imposing manner on stage, the great Edith Evans was a shy person. Even though she'd love to have become a Broadway institution as well, the fact is she was shy of American audiences—found us rather frighteningly aggressive. She once told me, 'They will clap so loudly, won't they?'"—VINCENT PRICE, who in later years returned to the stage to portray Oscar Wilde

"If we have a deficiency, it is definitely in vocal training. The English stress that. They can always 'do' us, but for us it's more difficult. When it isn't impossible. I did an entire picture where my character thought he was Sherlock Holmes (*They Might be Giants*, 1971). It was damned hard, and I did not sustain [the accent] consistently."—GEORGE C. SCOTT

"First wipe your nose and check your fly."—SIR ALEC GUINNESS, on preparing as an actor

"I go over and over the script [to prepare]. But actually, I think about the hair. I say, 'What kind of hair does this guy have? Is it long, short, curly, straight, combed, parted on one side or in the middle, smooth or jagged?' And when I find the hair . . . that starts the basis of my character. . . . Once the hair comes in, everything else falls into place."—SAB SHIMONO (*Mame, Pacific Overtures*)

"It's often smart to approach a comedic part from a dramatic point of view, and approach a dramatic role from a comedic point of view. It's surprising how often this works so well."—STOCKARD CHANNING (*Six Degrees of Separation*)

"It's wonderful to have talent. It's far more wonderful to develop it." —ANGELA LANSBURY

"I would never do another play. What if it's a hit? Long runs bore me." —BARBRA STREISAND in 1987

"During a long run, you lecture yourself this way: 'So what if you don't want to go on tonight; remember the days you used to walk the street and say, "My arm, my leg, you can have it, if only I could be up there."'"— COLLEEN DEWHURST

"You hear them denigrated so often, but an acting school or class is better than nothing. *Much!* Acting requires other people. . . . Writing you can learn on your own, but not acting. . . . Acting is more than one person, and with conflict necessary."—EDWARD JAMES OLMOS

"[In the 1940s] for my audition at the American Academy of Dramatic Art in New York, I wrote my own material, not knowing that everyone normally did well-known scenes. Mine was a depressing sketch about a woman whose furniture was laughing at her. When they accepted me, I thought it was so marvelous—not realizing at the time that they would have accepted a tree if it had applied."—COLLEEN DEWHURST

"The low down on acting is you're a puppet . . . constantly waiting and wishing to get hired, which after you are, you're used as a puppet to fulfill the writer's and director's visions. Actresses object to this much less than actors do."—REID SHELTON (*Annie*'s Daddy Warbucks)

"I enjoyed the theatre but I found, in my limited experience, that moviemaking was full of sharks. The ethical level is higher in politics."—theater star HELEN GAHAGAN, who made one film and later became a congresswoman

"Every actor has a natural animosity toward every other actor, present or absent, living or dead."—former film star LOUISE BROOKS

"The theatre community is very supportive. I've always felt comfortable and accepted there. . . . There's less jockeying for position and behind-the-scenes goings-on than in Los Angeles."—CAROL BURNETT

"After I left acting [after marrying Ted Turner], I felt relieved at not having to compete so relentlessly, and empowerment at not having to speak someone else's lines."—JANE FONDA

"To become an actor, you have to be one."—novelist HAROLD ROBBINS

"If you're friendly and not a big gossip, your fellow actors will like you. Unless you're a success. That's unforgivable."—JAMES EARL JONES

"A young actress working with Greta Garbo noticed that before each take, Garbo would get alone and do some sort of preparation. After a take, the young actress nervously approached the star . . . [and] asked . . . was it sense memory, inner monologue, affective memory? Garbo looked at her and said, 'No, darling. I'm imagining my face sixty feet by forty feet.' . . . It's why many stage actors don't work in films."—JEREMY WHELAN, actor and author of *Instant Acting*

"In the theatre, the actor of less than classical good looks is sheltered by the distance between audience and stage and the often unrealistic stage makeup. For older or physically flawed actors, theatre is more tolerant and nurturing than working before a camera."—actor-dancer BARTON MUMAW (*My Fair Lady*)

"An actor can remember his briefest notice well into senescence and long after he has forgotten his phone number and where he lives."—JEAN KERR, playwright and critic's wife

"If you think you'll be boring onstage, you will be. Attitude counts . . . just allow the magic of the theatre, which has been weaving its spell since at least the ancient Greeks, to work for you. But if you do play a boring character, *you* must not be bored. It takes animation, it takes an active interior life while onstage, to play even a bore."—RICHARD KILEY (*Man of La Mancha*)

"I have the greatest admiration for actors who sing on a stage where there is no mechanism to make them sound perfect. There can't be anything more exposing than to perform in a stage musical. How do they do it?" —PETER O'TOOLE

"When you've done movie musicals, even the ones I did with Astaire and Rogers, Broadway tends to label you a lightweight. So you get lightweight roles. But this should help; people take Broadway musicals pretty seriously. If they're hits."—ERIK RHODES, a Broadway replacement in *A Funny Thing Happened on the Way to the Forum* who then toured with the hit show

"Theatre's less money crazed than movies and less ratings dominated than TV. And there is much less of a caste system in theatre, where supporting actors are also vital and everybody has to be on their toes to give forth a good play."—actor and acting coach JEFF COREY

"In theatre one can play with a role. One actually can have a good time while being professional . . . experiment while building and improving. I never have been comfortable in film. It's dead serious, all business and pressure, with intermittent visits from horrible men in suits and sunglasses. It's like working in a straitjacket."—SIR JOHN GIELGUD, who won a supporting Oscar for *Arthur*

"In my drawing room I can bring out the essence of an actor with a few strokes. Most actors do the same thing, using broad strokes to present essential character traits, then filling in when necessary. On the stage, they have more time to do this, though obviously the featured [supporting] players are given less time, and so those strokes have to be even broader, more caricaturish."—master caricaturist AL HIRSCHFELD, after whom Broadway's Martin Beck Theatre was renamed in the 100th anniversary of his birth in June 2003

"We were trained to project. We sang with those big voices, no microphones. There was an energy in hearing that. Now we are totally in the charge of that man who dials your voice up and down. Many singers don't have the volume, and many dancers don't have the extensive training. They're more athletic and aerobic, but there's a loss of artistry and discipline."—LEE ROY REAMS (*Applause, 42nd Street*)

"What we say [on stage], how we walk, how we sit—these are just the facts. But the soul of the character is when you sing and dance it. Suddenly, the dream of you is what you become—you-without-flaws emerges, the essence of the person."—CAROL CHANNING

"It's much easier to make the transition from singer to actress than from dancer to actress because people think of dancers as being mute. I can't tell you how often I've heard people say, 'Oh, she can't open her mouth. She can't talk.' I must have been saying *something* up there on the stage for all those years. . . . I'm still waiting to be considered an actress."—GWEN VERDON

"Getting ready for a musical is like preparing for an athletic event. You have to go into training. I think doing Shakespeare is simpler. [In musicals] you have to get your voice, your body, and the whole thing together. You can't be a reprobate and do musicals. . . . You can't stay up late or smoke or go out partying."—CHRIS SARANDON, *The Light in the Piazza*

"Musicals are very tiring. The effect is cumulative. . . . The minute I stopped playing *Applause*—which ended in London and had taken five years of my life—my body fell apart. Because that daily discipline was over."—LAUREN BACALL

"Trying out any show is always a nightmare. I had three understudies in *West Side Story*, and you were always under the gun of being replaced. You have to be running at 200% all the time."—CAROL LAWRENCE

"I have had the dubious yet fascinating experience of reading my own published obituary. Accidentally, ten years ago. I had very mixed emotions. . . . I will say that had I been a different sort of public figure, such as a politician, such an egregious error would not have occurred. They would have taken more care to check. But it can readily happen to an actor; we're mere entertainers."—actor-playwright EMLYN WILLIAMS

"Back in the 1970s I did a revival of *Charley's Aunt*, and I learned something . . . about drag. Actors can surprise ourselves about how easy it is to get into something, or used to it. Actors discover aspects, new things, sometimes shocking, about themselves . . . not just drag. . . . Being an actor, you get to explore the most exciting—and the most frightening—subject of all: yourself."—RAUL JULIA

"When you eat food on the stage, it has to be soft. If it's hard and you choke, you can't say the playwright's lines. When I was in *The Matchmaker* I had quite a bit of eating to do, and we used soft, ripe pears that could be sculpted to look like chicken and veg . . . [and] in *Ethan Frome* our meat stew and gravy was made out of bananas and prune juice. The glamour and good taste of acting are of course overrated."—actress, playwright, and author RUTH GORDON

"It's absolutely out of the question. I could *never* impersonate a woman who had such a peculiar notion of hospitality."—DAME EDITH EVANS on why she would not play Lady Macbeth

"[The doctor] sprayed my throat with a solution laced with cocaine. It stimulated my larynx, relieved strain on my vocal chords, and reduced my chances of becoming mute during a performance. At [the pharmacy] where I presented the prescription, I was given a bottle of pale little lozenges, labeled 'Cocaine and Menthol.'"—TALLULAH BANKHEAD on how she coped with laryngitis

"Applause is as the actor's very breath, giving life to a performance."—actress SARAH SIDDONS in the late 1700s

"As for me, I find that I act best when my heart is warm and my head is cool."—19th-century American actor JOSEPH JEFFERSON III, when asked whether he agreed with Constant Coquelin [the originator of Cyrano de Bergerac] that actors should feel nothing, or with Henry Irving that actors should seem to feel what they're declaiming

"Saying 'the Method' is silly and limiting. It's like saying 'the American way.' There's more than just one."—dancer-actor GREGG BURGE (*A Chorus Line*)

"I wish I knew what that means. Me, I just act."—MONTGOMERY CLIFT, asked about the Method in 1959

"Method acting's an abomination. The chief lesson actors from these so-called modern schools learn is complete egotism. They are taught to relate everything to self. . . . Marlon Brando has been known to place rubber stoppers in his ears so he cannot hear the words spoken by other players!"—BORIS KARLOFF, stage and horror-film star

"The best method of acting is *often*. In acting too, practice makes perfect." —RENEE TAYLOR (*An Evening with Golda Meir*)

"Actors are like athletes. They must work or they atrophy pretty quickly." —LEN CARIOU (*Sweeney Todd*)

"Go for the performance that feels good, feels right. Compare this with the audience's reaction and the opinions of your honest colleagues. Be aware of what you do and don't do and how you vary. Be self-critical, but not self-destructive. Be aware of how good you sometimes are, and open to how much better you have yet to become."—stage legend EVA LE GALLIENNE

"My pet peeve is the nervous or overeager audience member who laughs too loud and too often and irks the hell out of me."—JASON MILLER, playwright and actor (*The Exorcist*)

"Some younger actors laugh, but I still do it. I put red dots in the corner of my eyes so when someone is looking at you from way up in the balcony it doesn't look as if I have just one eye. That and false eyelashes are a big help to an actress."—GERALDINE PAGE

"In movies it's another story, but on the stage it is such an asset to have big eyes. . . . Actresses also have the advantage of being able to create a bigger mouth. But I mostly did that for compensation; I was very sensitive about my exophthalmic eyes, which no one poked fun at until I left the theatre for movies. Apart from body language, the eyes and mouth are almost entirely what you express emotion with."—BETTE DAVIS

"I'll admit, esthetically speaking, my nose isn't a complete disaster. But dramatically, it lacks punch."—ORSON WELLES, who often used putty

"The camera can come in and pick up little things that happen on your face, and you'd never see it in the theatre. There's a different physical reality on stage . . . [where] you are the transmitter . . . the mechanical means by which the message is sent out—rather than a camera picking it up. You use your whole physical self."—MADELINE KAHN

"Lots of Hollywood actors don't like to rehearse . . . think it's just repeating or draining themselves. Wrong. It's improving and fortifying. In pictures, they don't always want it right, they want it by five o'clock."—JOHN GARFIELD, one of the first film stars to get it in his contract that he be allowed to return annually to Broadway

"So many kids now are scared off of theatre by the memorization. It's so many more lines than TV, movies, or in commercials! But all the lines do fall into place; that's what rehearsal does for you. So what I tell kids is to look at some of the intellectually challenged movie stars who've been on Broadway. Okay, Stallone hasn't to my knowledge, or Schwarzenegger. But so many have, and if they can do it, so can you!"—stage and TV actress LYNNE THIGPEN

"The cinema is little more than a fad. It's canned drama. What audiences really want to see is flesh and blood on the stage."—film icon CHARLIE CHAPLIN circa 1916

"I wouldn't become an actor again if I could change. I'm too bright for a career that runs out. I thought I'd spend my life telling good stories to an intelligent public. I must have been out of my fucking mind."—Canadian actress KATE NELLIGAN, who left England for Hollywood

"My only regret in the theatre is that I could never sit out front and watch me."—stage-and-screen star JOHN BARRYMORE

"We are born at the rise of the curtain and we die with its fall, and every night in the presence of our patrons we write our new creation, and every night it is blotted out forever; and of what use is it to say to audience or to critic, 'Ah, but you should have seen me last Tuesday'?"—Irish theatre legend MICHEAL [SIC] MACLIAMMOIR

"I don't know. I'm just beginning to get the hang of it."—SIR RALPH RICHARDSON at eighty-three, when asked what acting was all about

"You really only begin to act when you leave off trying."—DAME EDITH EVANS

"I have an affinity for acting, but that doesn't alter the terror. Do you realize what happens to us actors on opening night? It's almost a disease. I did a play with Helen Hayes, and we were waiting to make our entrance, when I looked at her and she looked like I looked: absolutely waxen. I leaned over and whispered, 'Still, Miss Hayes?' And she looked up at me and replied, 'Gets worse every year.' . . . As your reputation grows, other people can blow a line—but not the star."—JONATHAN HARRIS (TV's *Lost in Space*)

"I remember once in a rehearsal of something or other, I asked [Dame] Sybil Thorndike—whom I knew all my working life—'Sybil, when will it get easier?' She looked at me as if I were a half-wit and said, 'It will only get worse, my darling. Naught for your comfort, my darling, naught for your comfort.' Do you know, it *does* get worse? Cruelly, nature takes confidence away instead of giving it!"—DAME WENDY HILLER, stage, screen, and TV star

"The camera magnifies Hollywood actors. Theatre actors must magnify themselves."—*Rent* composer-lyricist JONATHAN LARSON

"Acting is an art. It's a responsibility. It's a privilege."—playwright TERRENCE MCNALLY

The Producers

"Every individual has a given number of heartbeats, and I don't propose to waste any of mine apologizing."—contentious producer JED HARRIS

"The Broadway theatre could be greatly improved by the subtraction of most of its actors."—producer ALEXANDER H. COHEN

"Psychiatrists are where simpleton actors go to feel they're complex."—producer DAVID MERRICK

"He must have been a marvelous shot."—playwright-actor-director SIR NOEL COWARD upon hearing that a not very intelligent producer had shot himself in the brain

"The real power struggle isn't between actors and anyone else. Actors know how interchangeable they are, unless they're stars, and even then. The real friction is between producers and directors, because they're the ones sharing the power."—producer ROBERT FRYER (*Mame, Chicago*)

"Most producers lie—that's the word—somewhere between affluent accountants and artistic poseurs. They have the taste of auctioneers and the souls of playground bullies. If theatre were properly funded, we could do away with them entirely."—critic WYATT COOPER (a husband of Gloria Vanderbilt)

"He loves to kill. He derives joy from the kill. He is power hungry and lusts to destroy. [He's] not a critic—a dictator, a savage dog."—DAVID MERRICK on critic Frank Rich

"At British awards ceremonies, unlike the Broadway Tonys, only the authors get to collect the Best Play and Best Musical trophies; the producers are kept firmly offstage, as if not deemed to be part of the 'creative team.'"—theater columnist MARK STEYN

"The most hated people on Broadway are producers. Selfish tyrants like David Merrick and, before him, Jed Harris. . . . Jerome Robbins is right up there, but when you have artistic vision, versus mere money and power, it balances things toward the tyrannical director. Robbins was no nicer than Merrick or Harris, but producers themselves don't produce any art." —*West Side Story* and film costume designer IRENE SHARAFF

"Commerce owns theatre much more than it used to. The costs are preposterous, [and] it makes cowards out of producers. . . . It just means that as the ticket prices go up, it drives the audiences that you want out of the theatre."—playwright EDWARD ALBEE

"There used to be one or two names over the title: Feuer and Martin, David Merrick, Alex Cohen—a producer whose voice counted for something, whose taste meant something. Now you have 15 names."—theater historian FOSTER HIRSCH

"In most cases, the producer is very aloof . . . and distant from the process of making a show. . . . I think producing is to Broadway shows what a sperm donor is to the child that he'll never know but helps enable."—RAUL JULIA (*Nine*)

The Directors

"Your audience gives you everything you need. . . . There is no director who can direct you like an audience."—FANNY BRICE

"Comes down to it, the director's a traffic cop. If he doesn't ramble on too long, you listen politely. Then you do what made you famous, what the audience pays to see. Nobody pays to see a director."—BERT LAHR, a bigger star on stage than screen (the Cowardly Lion in *The Wizard of Oz*), and a notable scene-stealer

"The advantage of working with film actors is that the director, editor, and producer can smooth or balance the actor's performance. Actors on a stage can improvise, ad lib, overact, play tricks, and upstage their fellows. That, I contend, is why the stage is called the actor's medium."—GEORGE S. KAUFMAN, who got to direct only one film, *The Senator Was Indiscreet*, which archconservatives objected to even before the famous playwright was blacklisted in Hollywood

"Edward Albee as a director is a very good playwright."—BARRY NELSON, directed by Albee in his non-hit *Seascape* (1975), which costarred Deborah Kerr and Frank Langella

"As a Broadway director, Alfred Lunt is a fine Broadway actor."—attributed to MEL FERRER, who costarred with wife Audrey Hepburn in the Lunt-helmed *Ondine* (1954)

". . . we had an English director. I can't ever remember the name of anyone of which I think so very little. We would have understood each other better if he were Chinese."—CAROL CHANNING on Lindsay Anderson, director of the Broadway-bound *Legends!* (his films included *This Sporting Life* and *The Whales of August*)

"I want a [director with] a vision that's like a force running through everything. [Otherwise], well, my sister told me once, when she was in third grade, her whole class went into the city. When they came up from the subway, the teacher—for a moment—didn't know where she was. My sister saw that look, and suddenly was terrified. She lost all faith. And that's horrible when it happens with a director, and it can happen in an instant. If they have an unshakeable vision, it won't happen."—stage and film actor ROBERT SEAN LEONARD

"Good actors don't need much directing or babying. Occasionally I trot out a sound piece of advice for certain uncertain actors: Try to imagine the audience in their underwear."—director-choreographer JOE LAYTON (*Barnum, George M!*)

"In so many cases, the director is a person fond of the theatre but not good-looking or special enough to be an actor, and with a secret lust for power. If he wasn't fond of theatre, he might become a policeman."—MADELINE KAHN

"One reason I prefer the stage is that presence and talent will out. Onstage, the spectator's eye goes where it belongs. But in TV and movies, it's all camera choices. The *director* chooses what you focus on. Your eye is *directed*, and you get only part of the scene or picture. When you think about it, that's a very unnatural way to view something."—HUGH JACKMAN (*The Boy from Oz*)

13

J.R.

When choreographer-director Jerome Robbins was given a 70th-birthday party in October 1988, one of the celebrants was designer and longtime friend Oliver Smith. Soon after, back at work, the older but no wiser Robbins disagreed with Smith over the color of a backdrop and chose to ridicule his work onstage in front of a cast of people. Smith announced, "I do not have to take this anymore. From now on, you speak to me through my agent or the Shuberts." Another Robbins friendship undone.

He was tough on friends and frequently impossible to those he worked with. Former soloist Mel Tomlinson of the New York City Ballet famously declared, "If I go to hell, I will not be afraid of the devil. Because I have worked with Jerome Robbins."

When Robbins made a comeback with *Jerome Robbins' Broadway* in 1989, many people were rooting against him. Even some of the cast, whom he'd drilled as mercilessly as usual. Charlotte d'Amboise recalled the opening-night applause, during which she cried, "because it was such a relief. Now, I thought, I can leave now, it's done. It felt like closing night. And some people did give their notice that day. You were so sick of the material, I can't tell you." She added that Robbins "got his reviews and he got the show that he wanted."

But even with six Tony Awards, including Best Musical and Best Director for Robbins (he later claimed to have forgotten to thank his co-director), and despite advance sales of $8 million and a new-high ticket price of $55, the show lost money—about $2 million. Robbins blamed the producers for the box-office failure that he felt reflected directly on him. Gerald Schoenfeld, chairman of the Shubert Organization, explained that the show was very difficult to market, including the poster, which couldn't convey much information about the production because Robbins insisted his name be so big on it. Later, when the show didn't do as well as he'd believed it would, he blamed the Shubert people for the "lousy poster." "I said," explained Schoenfeld, "'You wanted your name that way and you approved it.' He said, 'Not at all, I didn't care what you did with my name.' He would alter the past to suit the occasion."

Concurrent with his eponymous show, Robbins was represented on Broadway by a hit revival of *Gypsy*; there was also a new national tour of *Fiddler on the Roof*. His combined weekly royalties thus came to $48,000. Yet it was the poor business at "his" show that preoccupied him. "Jerry had to have a bone of contention to gnaw on," offered Gwen Verdon. "He'd hit the top of his profession, always excepting his failed Hollywood ambitions, but still he had to have something to gnaw on." An example was a pending project during meetings for which he spent more time defensively insisting that he hadn't *really* been fired from the film of *West Side Story* (he shared a co-directing Oscar with veteran director Robert Wise) than he did discussing the project at hand.

"Jerry could be prickly. If he was in a good mood," half-joked fellow director-choreographer Joe Layton. "When he wasn't on the offensive, he was on the defensive."

In later years, his Broadway triumphs behind him, Robbins returned to the more-comfortable, less-public world of the ballet. Weeks after *Jerome Robbins' Broadway* opened, he announced a leave of absence from the New York City Ballet that extended into, for the most part, a retirement. But he eschewed rumors of failing health—although his hearing was going—and apprised *Newsweek*, "George Balanchine, Bob Fosse, Antony Tudor, Freddy Ashton, Gower Champion, Michael Bennett—that's a lot [to lose] in five years . . . It makes one think a little." Robbins was virtually the last of Broadway's choreographic giants.

HE'D HAVE MUCH TO THINK OVER, and gnaw on. What gnawed at him most, besides the movie noncareer, was the persistence of his reputation as a heartless informer during the McCarthy witch hunts. "Jerry wanted to work in Hollywood," said revue producer Ben Bagley, "wanted to leap from ballet into the movies, with theatre as a stepping stone. . . . After he got to Hollywood by doing what he did, most doors remained shut to him. They wanted *established* directors who'd informed, like Elia Kazan and Edward Dmytryk, and heterosexual theatre people, like Jose Ferrer.

"They didn't want demanding gay types who were hard to work with and hard to keep within a budget."

For the rest of his life, Robbins (born Rabinowitz) would often try to justify his actions, short of a private or public apology. His excuses included everything but naked ambition. He referred often to being Jewish; the inquisitors were mostly right-wing Christians. (The witch hunts commenced soon after Republicans took control of Congress in 1947, even though being a Communist Party member was never illegal in the US.) Robbins stated that his upbringing had instilled in him the fear that Jews could have everything taken away from them at a moment's notice. Yet he was far from the only Jew in jeopardy; though it ostensibly targeted Marxism, a hugely disproportionate number of the Red-baiting's victims were Jewish and/or homosexual.

Robbins almost never referred to his greater fear that as a gay man he would be socially and professionally destroyed if he didn't cooperate with Congress's House Un-American Activities Committee—in any sort of witch hunt, gay men are typically and historically the most vulnerable targets. However, as someone working in ballet and the theater, Robbins would have been much less vulnerable to the blacklists that infested the film and television industries. It was his big-screen goal that prompted him to inform avidly, even if in apparent terror. Whether the brevity of his Tinseltown career made him regret turning tail is generally unknown.

But his blithe arrogance on the topic gained him more enemies and soured many co-workers. Years after his 1953 turn before HUAC, Robbins breezily informed *Gypsy* associate Arthur Laurents, "I suppose I won't know for years whether I did the right thing." Laurents, also Jewish but openly gay, answered back, "Oh, I can tell you right now. You were a shit."

To Laurents's surprise, Robbins, in *his* surprise over Laurents's bluntness, began to cry: "Jerry expected the loyalty from me that he himself hadn't given friends."

Ironically, by most accounts Robbins hadn't been a committed Marxist to begin with. Biographer Greg Lawrence characterized his initial involvement as "a flirtation that served his choreographic ambitions." One motivation was a favorable review of the gifted young ballet choreographer by a leftist female critic. A relatively late bloomer, Robbins switched from modern dance to ballet, also eventually discovering or admitting to himself that he was a more talented "dance director" (as choreographers were often called) than dancer.

JEROME ROBBINS (1918–1998) had his young but ambitious imagination fired by George Balanchine's request, prior to the 1936 Broadway opening of *On Your Toes*, to have his billing amended from the usual "Dances by . . ." to the newfangled "Choreography by . . ." Use of the Greek word lent new stature and classicism to the men arranging onstage dances. However, the new term was widely ridiculed. Irving Berlin, for one, penned a lyric about the chaps who'd done taps no longer merely tapping: now, "They're doing *choreography!*"

Twenty-one years later, Robbins won extra notoriety when his vanity-credit demand, "Entire production conceived, choreographed, and directed by Jerome Robbins," for *West Side Story* was granted—though he did not conceive the production. The innovative, dance-heavy musical was a career highlight for Robbins, who'd broken through when his ballet *Fancy Free* evolved into the 1944 hit musical *On the Town*, which he choreographed.

Another triumph was *Gypsy* (1959), which boasted the last stage role created by the legendary Ethel Merman, who nonetheless toured for the first time with it. The steamrolling star experienced no problems with Robbins. The friction occurred elsewhere. When Robbins, typically more interested in dance numbers than songs, tried to cut the touching and revealing "Little Lamb," he was furiously overruled by composer Jule Styne. After lyricist Stephen Sondheim devised the song titled "Everything's Coming Up Roses," the uncomprehending Robbins demanded, "Everything's coming up Rose's *what?*"

"The man knew dance," said Ben Bagley. "Actors and singing were something apart. He habitually wanted to cut songs in favor of more dancing, whether it suited the show or not. . . . He did treat dancers badly, but he didn't really relate to nondancers."

In 1991 Ron Rifkin explained, "I just finished working on a workshop piece with Jerome Robbins. . . . He will say to somebody, 'This is what I want you to do. Put your left hand in this position, put your right hand in that position,' and the dancer does it. So he would say to me as an actor, 'I want you to do this.' And I told him that I couldn't work that way. No actor can."

A pre-fame Charles Durning also experienced Robbins's non-technique with actors. Durning appeared in *Fiddler on the Roof* on the road but not on Broadway because his "character got cut the week before the opening in New York." Durning was impressed by star Zero Mostel's versatility. "Jerry would say, 'It's not right, Zero.' And Zero would change it. 'That's not right.' He'd change it. 'That's not right.' And Zero would change it every time and give him something completely different and that fast. Now, I can't work that way. That's genius.

"Zero said to me later, 'He really doesn't know what he's looking for, but when he sees it he knows what it is.'"

An anonymous *Jerome Robbins's Broadway* performer was quoted, "Jerry doesn't approach emotion as an actor, a director, or, necessarily, as a human being. Emotion scares him. He seems to prefer the formality and logic of dance."

Numerous associates remarked over the years how difficult it was to get close to or know Robbins. Some believed his coolness and tantrums were meant to keep people at bay. But his consistent behavioral extremes suggest a deep sadistic streak. Several *West Side Story* cast members have gone on record about Robbins's cruelty toward also-gay male lead Larry Kert (who much later died of AIDS). Robbins habitually needled and ridiculed Kert in front of the company, even calling him "fag"—and Kert took it. John Carradine of *A Funny Thing Happened on the Way to the Forum* (1962) affirmed, "Talent or no, the guy couldn't rein himself in. He'd let go, explode, indulge in childish and embarrassing excess. It was a big bore."

Some observers felt that Robbins was furious with life itself. The fact that he often treated gay men the worst of all indicates that he may have punished others for what he most hated in himself. Joe Layton theorized, "He's always wanted so much to belong, to fit in and succeed. . . . To a greater degree than most of us have, he's internalized the homophobia we're all forced to grow up with."

Though most dancers and actors were eager to be in a Jerome Robbins production, many dreaded it, and many or most came to dislike or hate the man. One of the most famous stories about how extremely he alienated his associates recalls the time he was [again] berating an assembled cast that saw him edging backwards toward the edge of the stage. Nobody said a word to prevent his falling into the orchestra pit, which he did.

ON THE OCCASIONALLY MASOCHISTIC SIDE of the coin, Robbins endured sweet revenge as well as abuse from Zero Mostel after he agreed to take over and doctor—*sans* credit, for director George Abbott—*Forum*, starring Mostel and Jack Gilford, both victims of the McCarthy blacklists. The friends had been wary when Robbins was approached. Zero was asked if he would mind working with Robbins. He gave in, explaining, "We of the Left do not blacklist." Gilford, whose wife, Madeline Lee, was *named* by Robbins, was inclined to quit the show until she advised, "Why should you blacklist yourself?" (Mostel and Gilford appeared in the 1966 movie version too.)

Mostel also worked with Robbins in *Fiddler on the Roof* (1964), which Robbins officially directed and choreographed. Initially considered "too Jewish" for mainstream appeal, *Fiddler* went on to surpass *My Fair Lady* and *Hello, Dolly!* as Broadway's longest-running musical, a record it held until *Grease* surpassed it in December 1979. Though Mostel willingly took direction from Robbins, the actor did his best to make his boss's life hell. The large, boisterous Zero made scenes, referred often to Robbins's informer status, and openly called him "the Jewish fag," which Robbins for the most part tolerated. Cast member Leonard Frey said, "Maybe he felt he had it coming . . . or even deserved it. . . . After the fiasco of his *West Side Story* dismissal, Jerry must have sensed that being gay would permanently hold his career back. Only, instead of that activating him against prejudice, he just became sort of a gay passivist."

Choreographer-turned-movie-director Herbert Ross, who'd married a ballerina for cover, offered, "The dislike many individuals feel for Mr. Robbins isn't necessarily from politics. Not everyone gave a damn about that. . . . He stayed [contractually] single, and after years in the spotlight his sexuality became known. . . . A lot of individuals have no use for him personally," for instance the homophobic Richard Rodgers. (Robbins choreographed Rodgers and Hammerstein's *The King and I*, 1951.)

When Robbins wasn't hired to choreograph, never mind direct, the highly anticipated film of *Fiddler on the Roof*, theater denizens deemed it a mixture of homophobia and political payback as well as natural reaction to Robbins's abrasiveness and blithe disregard for cinematic schedules and budgets. "Jerry went into [the movie of] *West Side Story* strong," said Joe Layton, who also didn't succeed at a Hollywood career, but was far easier to work with than his colleague. "He got them to make him co-director with Robert Wise, who soon after did *The Sound of Music*.

"But then there were clashes. There was hand-wringing. When studio executives saw the rushes, the sight of youths in tight trousers doing ballet steps on the streets of New York terrified them. It was a whole lotta dance, and it was about Hispanics, with an unknown male lead [Richard Beymer] . . . a big gamble. No one knew it would be a hit and win two Oscars for Jerry, who got fired rather early on but still shared credit with Wise, who easily directed most of it."

Even though *West Side Story* also took the Best Picture Academy Award, the episode dampened Robbins's hopes for future screen projects—he would never get another. Gay VIPs shunned him too. One who "avoided him professionally and socially was Herb Ross," said Layton. "You know, after his wife died he wound up marrying Jackie Onassis's kid sister, and at the wedding Jackie was heard to ask another guest if the groom was gay." The closet cases who eschewed Robbins's services and company did so for varied motives of camouflage, jealousy, politics, or self-hate.

In any case, Robbins was more comfortable, he told friends, in the less-oppressive worlds of ballet and theater, where he was less shunned and judged (except politically) and could dictate, even tyrannize, with less resistance or repercussions. Gwen Verdon once observed, "Dancers will take abuse more readily than any other group of performers except trained dogs." Isobel [sic] Lennart, who wrote *Funny Girl*'s book, observed, "Dance used to be far more identified with homosexual men. On Broadway, male dancing could be art. In Hollywood, [it was] a necessary evil, something to be disguised. Jerry should never have left New York at all."

ROBBINS WAS THE ORIGINAL DIRECTOR for the Barbra Streisand stage vehicle *Funny Girl* (1964), but departed after a dispute. He was briefly succeeded by Bob Fosse, then Garson Kanin, who left after Robbins was lured back (the eventual credits read "Directed by" Kanin and "Supervised by" Robbins). As with Merman, Robbins was awed by his leading lady, whom he didn't attempt to bully. Unlike Merman, Streisand, then in the beginnings of her career, was somewhat "scared" of Robbins, or at least his reputation.

"It's funny, because Jerry's intimidated by strong personalities and anyone who stands up to him," said Ben Bagley, who shared a lover with Robbins (not concurrently). "Like most bullies, he's also a coward." Stars like Merman and Streisand could appreciate a director who also choreographed their movements and showcased their strengths. "Divas love him, humans hate him. The age of stage divas is past, but Jerry continues a dance diva himself."

The controversial Robbins was a frequent magnet for criticism of director-choreographers. Broadway's leading dance star, Gwen Verdon—*Damn Yankees* co-star Ray Walston called her "a nice diva"—defended Robbins: "The choreographers were a lot more interested in the book scenes than the book directors were in the numbers. When the orchestra started up, George Abbott used to go out and play golf. Yet the directors were happy to take all the credit.

"Even today, people don't realize what a choreographer does. In *Phantom* in the scene with the four opera singers, there's no dancing at all. But it's still staged by [choreographer] Gillian Lynne, not Hal Prince. That's why, in the '50s, Bob [Fosse], Jerry Robbins, and Michael Kidd figured that, as they were doing so much of it anyway, why not do it all?"

As for Robbins, Verdon allowed, "You wouldn't, perhaps, want to spend time in his home, but you did know that time spent together professionally would, after all was said and done, yield something special and be a growth experience." Verdon, who trained under gay dance tyrant and virtuoso Jack Cole, was a believer that that which doesn't kill you makes you strong.

Eventually Robbins wished to prove himself as a director of plays. His first nonmusical, in 1962, was the at times grotesque comedy *Oh, Dad, Poor Dad, Mamma's Hung You in the Closet and I'm Feelin' So Sad*. The title character is a corpse carted around by a rich widow in her travels with their demented son, who meets a girl . . . who gets killed. Although *Dad* did surprisingly well in New York—it had flopped in London and would flop as a Rosalind Russell movie—it left Jerome Robbins dissatisfied. He preferred material onto which he could impose his vision and his dance contributions. He hadn't been very pleased with the relatively dance-free *Gypsy*, as opposed to the dance-laden *West Side Story*.

Following *Dad*, there were assorted canceled and aborted Broadway plays and musicals. Robbins never found another *West Side Story* to put his stamp on. Thus, before the 1970s he was back in the world of ballet, where he mostly remained. "Jerry wasn't great at selecting material," stated producer Robert Fryer. "He knew what a gamble Broadway was—more and more, with higher production costs. He got less bankable with time as the golden years faded. . . . Like most of us, he hates growing older, not that it's mellow-ing him. . . . In the ballet demi-monde he's a law unto himself; he can shape or create works that don't cost a fortune, and—and this counts heavily with him—he doesn't have to deal with words, spoken or sung."

Although Jerome Robbins lived to seventy-nine and did not end up for-gotten or a has-been, his tragedy was not learning from his mistakes, profes-sionally and personally. Unlike a number of choreographer-directors who died in harness—except for his eponymous retrospective show—Robbins left Broadway behind, and vice versa.

"I kept hearing from mutual friends or colleagues," said actress Dody Goodman, who'd worked with Robbins, "that at the end, he was still apt to turn on you. I mean as a professional *or* just a friend. He kept, he reserved that power for himself—the power to misuse people or dispose of them, and to continue on doing it."

Robbins enjoyed a long and distinguished career. Via American Ballet Theatre and the New York City Ballet, he became a leading American chore-ographer, and his work on Broadway shows like *On the Town,, The King and I, Peter Pan, West Side Story, Gypsy, Fiddler on the Roof, Funny Girl*, etcetera, earned him five Tony awards. Even the screen career that fizzled produced two Oscars. Yet mention his name and twinned with recognition of his accomplishments is the almost invariably negative reaction to him as a person. TV star Eddie Albert, who worked with the choreographer in 1949, averred in the same breath: "Robbins was rude, a little shit," and, "Jerry Robbins was a marvelous artist."

The legend of the man's often vile personality and misdeeds grew as large as or larger than his dance oeuvre. "Nobody today, praise the gods, could get away with what he did to so many people," concluded *On the Town's* co-lyricist and -book writer Adolph Green. "Then, it detracted from what he achieved. Today, and in the future, it will detract more. . . . Artistic temperament is often excused, or it's accommodated. Everyone is bound to have flaws in their character. With Jerome Robbins, the flaws became the character."

Jerome Robbins

"Attila the Hitler"—what one ASSISTANT to Jerome Robbins called him, according to biographer Greg Lawrence (*Dance with Demons*)

"I let him come in my dressing room, but I'll tell you something, I never shook his hand."—ZERO MOSTEL

"As a person, Robbins was a rat fink. He was a rat and he finked. If he hadn't gone into the dance, he'd have been a rat catcher, on the theory that it takes one to know one."—actor EDDIE ALBERT (TV's *Green Acres*), whose Mexican wife, Margo, was blacklisted

"He was usually nice to children. But adults were all fair game, potential victims. You explain it to me."—stage and TV (*Rhoda*) actress NANCY WALKER

"At a party in New York in 1975 he came on to me. In a very cold, condescending way. That's not why I dislike him—and I did say no, by the way. . . . He's one of those people I hate to admit is gay. And since he tried so hard and so long to hide it, maybe we don't have to count him as gay."—musician turned journalist LANCE LOUD

"Jerry Robbins claimed not to be in any way inclined toward fascism. That may have been true. But he played right into their hands, and he couldn't hide the eagerness—the selfish eagerness—with which he did so."—lyricist NANCY HAMILTON (*One for the Money*)

"I don't think anyone on Broadway was ever so admired and so hated, simultaneously."—playwright BOB RANDALL (*6 Rms Riv Vu*)

"He did not treat [dancer-choreographer] Carol Haney very well at all. I thought it was awful the way he treated her . . . and she was very sick. He tended to take people who were weakened and get at their weak points."—*Funny Girl* stage manager TOM STONE; Haney was fired after Robbins came aboard but retained her choreography credit

"Bea Arthur was ready to quit. Bea was brilliant [as the matchmaker], but Jerry wanted the focus on Tevye and his wife, Golde. So he kept cutting [Bea's role] down. . . . I was so angry in Washington, D.C.—we were playing the National—and I stormed out of the theatre. There's a long alley by the side . . . Bea was sitting there smoking a cigarette. I came out and I said, 'Bea, I'm going to rip his cock and balls off and shove 'em down his throat.'

"And Bea looked at me, she took a puff of her cigarette, and she said, 'What cock? What balls?' And then took another puff. I never forgot that; the timing was superb, naturally."—*Fiddler on the Roof* dancer CHUCK RULE

"Naturally, Robbins adored the ballet, and who knew better than he what dedicated, disciplined, and strong athletes they are? So it irked the hell out of him when bigoted ignoramuses like [New York City Mayor Fiorello] La Guardia publicly said [in the 1940s] that he loathed male ballet dancers. Robbins came out publicly against that statement, defending the ballet and [saying] in Europe it was a beloved and historic art form. . . . After Robbins capitulated to the bigots in 1953, it killed him that these were the very men who would most hate ballet, especially male dancers."—*Dance* magazine editor-in-chief WILLIAM COMO

"Jerome Robbins's father was against his becoming a dancer and tried to stop it. Jerry hated his father. But then he went and transferred that hatred to a goodly percentage of the people in show business."—DODY GOODMAN, who worked with Robbins in *Wonderful Town* (1953)

"He has his own way of doing things . . . I don't judge, and I don't get involved if I don't have to. I'm the boss, but I trust his judgment. . . . The great thing is, he takes care of every detail of the dancing. He loves all that stuff." —GEORGE ABBOTT, who directed several of the musicals that Robbins choreographed

". . . after a certain point he just can't do it anymore. And then he turns. And it was really true. He was trying so hard to be nice [to people he liked], and then he just lost it. And he did that with so many people . . . pretty much with almost everybody in the office. . . . I think it was like being in an abusive relationship if you stayed with him. You became like a victim of domestic violence, because that's what it was like in the office. I know that he could be really difficult elsewhere, but I think there are more people who have nice things to say about him in the theatre than people that worked with him administratively. Because the [theatrical] end product was so amazing."—former assistant SARA CORRI

"He would push me to do more, but never mock me or make fun of me as he did with the chorus. Boy, if they couldn't do it, he would chew them up one side, down the other. I would walk away in horror at this person—I'm looking at Jekyll and Hyde."—star NANETTE FABRAY of the 1947 hit *High Button Shoes*

"(*Miss Liberty*, 1949) was in trouble, and of course that meant trouble for Robbins. He was shouting at everyone. I didn't have much dancing [in it . . . but] I was in the middle of one of my routines, and he shouted at me. So I stopped and walked over to him and said very quietly, 'If you do that again, I'm going to throw you up on the fucking balcony.' I didn't have any trouble with him after that."—EDDIE ALBERT

"What Jerry loved to do was create friction between his dancers. Not just competition. He'd go so far as to tell one dancer something nasty that another dancer had supposedly said about him. . . . He was a malicious child with an adult's talent."—CAROLYN LEIGH, co-lyricist of *Peter Pan* (1954)

"It's been said, and I fully agree, that Jerome Robbins was not evil because he informed but, rather, that he informed because he was evil."—BEATRICE ARTHUR

"Unlike many who were hauled up before HUAC (the Republican Congress's House Un-American Activities Committee), Jerry had actually joined the Communist Party. Which it was legal to do. . . . As an actual party member and as a homosexual man without wife and no kids, he was extremely vulnerable. What he did was wrong, but HUAC was wrong to begin with, and the times were horrendous. Honestly now, how many communists, or former communists, who were Jewish *and* gay would have spat in HUAC's slimy face? If you didn't cooperate, they merely put a stop to you. The real horror, after America had fought European fascists [in WWII], was that the domestic ones could now put a stop to you."—stage star HERSCHEL BERNARDI (*Fiddler on the Roof*)

"There was a period when [Robbins] wanted to become an actor. An impetus for that was the relation to a genuine movie star, Edward G. Robinson. He was born Emanuel Goldenberg and was a relative of Robbins's uncle Benjamin Goldenberg. What turned Jerry off acting, I don't know. Unless it was his father's ridicule."—stage producer ROBERT FRYER (*Wonderful Town, Chicago*)

"The genesis of Robbins's ballet *Fancy Free* (1944), which opened so many doors to him, was a painting titled *Sailor Trilogy* by the gay artist Paul Cadmus. It got banned in Washington due to some minor gay content or innuendo, but it really captured Robbins's imagination. Of course *Fancy Free* became totally heterosexual in theme."—CHRISTOPHER ISHERWOOD

"Montgomery Clift and Jerome Robbins had an affair. After, it became a friendship. . . . It was Monty who first suggested, when they did line readings together from *Romeo and Juliet*, that somebody should do a modern-day production of the play as a musical and use gangs instead of warring families. Robbins seized the idea, and later he claimed the 'conceived by' credit for *West Side Story* (1957). But it was not his idea, he wasn't creative that way. . . . The friendship came to a halt when Robbins testified; Monty lost any respect or admiration he'd had for Jerry."—Montgomery Clift biographer ROBERT LAGUARDIA

"Jerry wanted everything so thoroughly, so quickly, that every fiber of your being had to be at his command. . . . He was brutal, he would humiliate us, always in front of the entire company. . . . Instead of saying, 'You're just not warm enough in this scene,' or, 'I don't believe you,' he would say, 'You're the most talentless idiot I've ever met in my life, why can't you *get* this?' It was like being cut in two."—CAROL LAWRENCE (*West Side Story*)

"One time his lawyer calls me. She says, 'Megan, we're filing a lawsuit against you and a police report.' I start laughing and say, 'What for?' And they were totally serious. . . . She said, 'You've stolen the doggie raincoats, the Persian rug, and the vacuum cleaners.' So I had to pay somebody to go out to his house out in the Hamptons and get these things out of the house and bring them back so that I wouldn't be prosecuted. Doggie raincoats. And I had two days in the office of him screaming at me because he thought I had stolen them. And the rug was rolled up in his bedroom closet in Manhattan."—former assistant MEGAN RADDANT (as for the pet raincoats and vacuum cleaners, they'd been misplaced by a maid)

"Nobody working or contemplating working with Jerry doesn't know to expect wounds. It goes with that particular, very talented territory."
—LEONARD BERNSTEIN

"You know in those interviews where they ask if someone couldn't have done what they did, what would they have been? If there were one person show business would have rejected that would have become a serial killer, that person would be Jerome Robbins. And then his neighbors would say on the evening news, 'Well, we did hear shrieking and ranting next door, but whenever we saw him he was such a shy, quiet, nice-seeming little guy.'"—JACK GILFORD (*A Funny Thing Happened on the Way to the Forum*)

"I was in this flop comedy play, *The Office*, and the famous Jerome Robbins directed. I don't think we even made it out of previews. A member of the crew said to me, 'Well, the bad news is we've folded. But there's good news.' 'What's that?' I inquired. 'No more walking around Jerry Robbins's eggshells.'"—JACK WESTON

"[Robbins] is stingy with compliments and approval. Some people just are. What made it kind of rotten is once he realized you want his approval, then you're sure not to get it."—fellow choreographer MICHAEL BENNETT (*A Chorus Line*)

"It's never been gone into in depth, but several people who knew him well say he had a horrendous childhood . . . terrible things were done to him. The ironic tragedy is that, like Eugene O'Neill, who turned around and did to his kids what his father did to him, Robbins nurtured the negative experiences and memories and became a machine of exceptional negativity. He was *so* un-Zen!"—*A Chorus Line* dancer GREGG BURGE

"Jerry worked for the Paris Opera for a time. . . . If it weren't for the language, he might have moved there. He loved that in France he was more esteemed than Balanchine was, where in the United States it was the reverse. And that had to do with greater French tolerance of homosexuality. . . . One time, the subject came up of all the awful Jerry Lewis movies on American TV. Robbins didn't like them either, but refused to criticize Lewis. I later heard it was because the French liked Lewis and Lewis's first name was *Jerry*. Everything always boiled down to Jerry Robbins."—LEONARD FREY (*Fiddler on the Roof*)

"First, Robbins wanted to direct [the 1993 TV movie of *Gypsy*]. When it became clear that would not happen, he told the producers he wanted to co-direct with me. I idolized his work, but no way. . . . He tried to have telephone relationships with me and Bette [Midler], but we wouldn't call him back. So he abused the producers with really venomous phone calls and threats—things that could have been reported to the police and probably would have been if he hadn't been Jerome Robbins."—director EMILE ARDOLINO

"I think that all the people who worked with him became the equivalent of abused children."—*Gypsy* telefilm executive co-producer CRAIG ZADAN

"He seriously considered writing his memoirs. But how could he? The witch hunts, his behavior, all the enemies, the Hollywood episode . . . He couldn't, he would not deal with that. He gave it up. In its place he wanted to do an autobiographical ballet or theatre piece about his troubled relationship with his father. So in 1991 he devised what was called *The Jew Piece*, then *Robbins by Rabinowitz*, then *The Poppa Piece*, but it was all too frank and disturbing and personal, and finally he dropped it completely."
—record and revue producer BEN BAGLEY (an ex-lover of Montgomery Clift)

"When it came time to do what became *Jerome Robbins' Broadway* with all these dance numbers from his past shows, it was very peculiar and yet impressive in that Robbins didn't remember the staging of many of his own numbers, and they had to recruit half of Broadway's surviving VIPs to help to remember and recreate them."—JACK KLUGMAN (*Gypsy*)

"When he was hospitalized for a slipped disc or had open-heart surgery, yes, there were more than a few people in New York City who got together for lunch or drinks, to celebrate."—Broadway costume designer MILES WHITE (*Oklahoma!*, *Bye Bye Birdie*)

"Our friendship got breached over a political issue. . . . There was a black girl in *The King and I* ballet [in *Jerome Robbins' Broadway*, 1989] . . . and it bothered him that of all the dancers' arms that were showing, hers were black, and would she mind whitening up. She wept and ran out of the room. I saw the union representative go after her. . . . So I went to Jerry and I said, 'Jerry, go to that girl and apologize to her—now!' Well, we got into it, big time. Major accusations. He did go and he did make the apology. But boy, that was it."—GROVER DALE, co-director of the retrospective show

"If Jerry hadn't had a social conscience, he'd have felt much less defensive about being a cooperative witness. It's just that career always, always was number one."—*Gypsy* composer JULE STYNE

"I have to say, Michael Bennett's a sweetheart next to Jerry Robbins. But who isn't? It's a matter of degree, and Michael can still give me the willies. At least Michael has a smile that he sometimes means."—TUCKER SMITH, who played "Ice" in *West Side Story*

"Yes, dear, of course I've heard the rumor. Who hasn't? But I've never gotten around to asking my son, Larry, about it."—MARY MARTIN, on whether the *Dallas* villain played by Larry Hagman was really named J.R. after Jerome Robbins

The Most Hated Man on Broadway

WHEN IT COMES TO THE TITLE of Broadway's most-hated individual, there's no contest. Producer-director Jed Harris (1900–1979) proudly asserted, "If there is one word in the English language I hate, it's the word cooperation." After postwar play production costs ballooned and he had to yield his complete control, Harris became extremely unhappy. No co-producers or limited partnerships for him. He directed but did not produce Arthur Miller's epochal *The Crucible* in 1953, which was the usual grim experience for all involved, but this time also for Harris.

He refused to continue directing for other people, no matter how esteemed or successful the play. Ego was all, even though Harris often claimed that he loved the theater but had no interest at all in "show biz." By the '50s he'd alienated almost everyone whose path he'd crossed. Associates and relatives alike dropped him. "Friends, he never had," said playwright George S. Kaufman, who wouldn't speak to him for forty years. When a mutual acquaintance declared that Jed Harris was his own worst enemy, Kaufman famously responded, "Not while I'm alive!" Kaufman noted, "Some people have a talent for friendship. Harris has a talent for making enemies."

Ironically, Harris's hatefulness made him all the more famous. Laurence Olivier based the look and mannerisms of his Richard III, captured on film, upon Harris. The Englishman and his then-more-famous wife Jill Esmond experienced Harris while costarring on Broadway in 1933 in the gay-themed *The Green Bay Tree*. The gleefully homophobic producer-director alluded more than once to that closeted pair's bisexuality. Playwright Ben Hecht penned a nasty *roman à clef* about his former colleague, and Walt Disney's Big Bad Wolf was also based on Jed Harris, who claimed he was the first theatrical personality to make *Time* magazine's cover, in 1928.

In 1926, Harris had shot to fame via the huge hit *Broadway*. He also had hit plays with *The Royal Family*, *The Front Page*, and *Coquette* (it starred Lillian Gish, who actually showed up at Harris's memorial service; the 1929 film version won Mary Pickford her Oscar). Between 1930 and 1947 Harris was active in ten theatrical seasons, directing and producing such hits as *A Doll's House*, *Our Town*, and *The Heiress*. But despite the successes, fewer and fewer people were willing to work with him.

"He was a bully," said stage actress Beatrice Straight, later best known for her brief but Oscar-winning turn as William Holden's cuckolded wife in *Network*. "He made a contest of everything. Nothing could be on the level . . . [and] he always tried to position things so that one person, preferably him, won and the other lost. Life was entirely adversarial for him."

Harris's brilliant early career was doomed. He himself predicted that he would part prematurely with success. Biographer Martin Gottfried offered, "Arrogance, egoism, cruelty, and Machiavellianism kept his talent from being spent, and that was his greatest tragedy."

Finally, Harris not only fell from the Broadway scene, he landed into poverty. He sometimes borrowed, then refused to pay—and other times outright stole—from his few friends, whose hospitality he typically abused, especially women's, since they generally put up with more from him.

Not long before his death, Harris was tapped to appear on Dick Cavett's TV talk show. The stage-struck host, who repeatedly called his guest a legend, had him on for an unprecedented five nights—they aired posthumously. Many people were surprised to learn that Jed Harris had still been alive. Actor-director Jose Ferrer explained, "Jed was embarrassed by his financial status, yet he didn't let on. He kept a low profile and traveled the country. Whenever he met up with people he knew, he acted as if they should feel honored that he'd turned up."

The Cavett show performance was unforgettable. Harris characterized himself as a patient if not a tolerant man: "Well, most people in the theater are idiots, fools of one kind or another." He spoke of actress Ruth Gordon, whom he said lacked beauty but had made a go of *A Doll's House* via her talent. Harris had fathered a son named Jones via the unlovely Gordon. He admitted, "I don't like my children better than anybody else's." Cavett reverently asked if he kept in touch with his son?

"As rarely as possible. I don't particularly like him." The man added that the child's birth was something Ruth Gordon "did willfully. It was part of being an actress, having an illegitimate child by a famous director. It had nothing to do with me."

Harris was paid $500 for his TV guest spot. After cashing the check, he pretended not to have received it and demanded that another be sent, right away.

Harris's New York City memorial service, in May 1980, was attended by his ten-year-old granddaughter, even though he'd never bothered to meet her. Jones Harris showed up. Jed Harris's two living ex-wives did not; one had scissored all his photos out of her albums. His younger brother didn't attend. Nor did most of his relatives or associates, New York–based or otherwise. The granddaughter came with her great-aunt. Her mother, Harris's daughter, didn't go, explaining later, "I don't believe there is a person walking the face of the Earth who would have a good word to say for my father."

That included the senior nurse at the hospital where he died: "He was in the worst possible condition you could be in and still be alive." His congestive heart failure was exacerbated by severe complications. Blistered and oozing, he was rude and defiant to the end, and his bed curtains were drawn for the sake of the staff. The nurse added, "If you're going to do what I do, you can't be superstitious or religious. But if there's anything to the idea of being punished in the way you die for the way you lived your life, I'll tell you this: the only other patient we ever had who suffered the way Mr. Harris did was Giuseppe Gambino. You know, the Mafia don."

The same year he died, Harris published "a unique memoir of the theatre" titled *A Dance on the High Wire*. It told little of the Jed Harris story. Jose Ferrer felt, "It's mostly hyperbole, with a rather jarring mix of fiction and self-promotion. . . . Jed didn't leave out the hurtful things in order not to hurt. He simply left out what didn't matter to him. He'd have been quite willing to admit that he told his own son, 'You're nothing, and you always will be nothing.' Jed would have just shrugged as if to say, 'I said it, so what?'"

The "unique memoir" naturally contained photos of its subject, but not one of his parents, purported loves, offspring, colleagues, or any other human being beside Jed Harris.

14

WHO'S AFRAID OF THE PLAY'S THE THING?

"**S**hockingly often, the producer is an enemy of the stage," ventured producer Richard Barr (*Who's Afraid of Virginia Woolf?*, *Sweeney Todd*). That he didn't become a household name as Broadway producers go was likely due to his integrity and focusing on the play. Broadway historian Andrew B. Harris noted, "Barr was one of those extraordinary producers who felt that the playwright, not the star or the director, was of central importance in the theatre."

Frederick Combs, costar of Mart Crowley's *The Boys in the Band*, produced by Barr (see Chapter 16, "The Curse of *The Boys in the Band*"), said, "A producer, or showman, like David Merrick was first and foremost for himself . . . with or without taste or interest in productions of social significance and quality. Richard's for the actor, for the theatre, and the play comes first."

Perhaps because he was gay, Barr (1917–1989) was strongly pro-underdog. Though he knew Broadway was chiefly money oriented, he believed theater should have a higher calling than just profits. "Light comedies and run-of-the-mill musicals have their place," he felt, "and I even enjoy them now and then, but that's not what I want to do for a—for want of a better word—living. I have to be loving what I do for a living."

Barr, who'd trained as a director, developed a professional relationship with playwright William Inge, who sought to present his native Midwest in a more realistic, enlightening way. But by the mid-1950s, Broadway's financial demands often quashed pioneering, experimental, or "radical" material. More and more playwrights were affected and inhibited. Inge broke through with *Picnic* but advised Barr, "I have a major hit on Broadway. I am going to be very rich. And I am miserably unhappy."

Inge, who eventually committed suicide after his gilt-edged run of hit plays ended, was depressed that director Joshua Logan had joined with management to demand that Inge rewrite *Picnic*'s final act as "less sad and less frightening"—else no production. For the sake of a wider audience, the playwright reluctantly gave in. He felt betrayed by Logan, whom he knew to be gay though very deeply closeted. Revue producer Ben Bagley has stated, "Logan was dedicated to the buck and snaring the biggest audience going.

"Of course," Bagley said, "he featured beefcake when he got the opportunity, clothing it in diaphanous heterosexuality," a famous example being the mostly topless sailors in *South Pacific* singing "There Is Nothing Like a Dame." Broadway gays were basically divided into the Logans, often very commercially successful and usually with-wife, and the Barrs, Inges, and—soon to come—Albees.

Appalled by what was expected of and extracted from William Inge, Richard Barr aimed his energies at Off-Broadway, where the financial stakes were lower and a playwright-supportive theater was still possible. In 1960, at forty-two, Barr broke through as a producer after optioning newcomer Edward Albee's one-acter *The Zoo Story* and presenting it Off-Broadway. (It had premiered the year before in Berlin—deemed too offbeat and intense for United States audiences.) The ultimately acclaimed work didn't proceed without problems, partly because of television, which co-opted so many theatrical performers. Actor George Maharis, *Zoo Story*'s Jerry, found out he couldn't be on stage for long, as a TV pilot he'd filmed, *Route 66*, had been picked up. (He later left the hit series for a movie career that fizzled, then eventually became *Playgirl*'s first celebrity nude, well-enough endowed to prompt TV host Johnny Carson to note that when he'd viewed the centerfold in which Maharis posed next to a horse, Carson felt sorry for the horse.)

During rehearsals there were clashes between Maharis and director Milton Katselas. Producer Barr sided with his star. Sal Mineo, who later rehearsed *P.S. Your Cat Is Dead!* with Katselas in Los Angeles, declared, "Milton is a star in his own mind. Some directors are failed actors, some are would-be stars. A lot of them, out here, become temperamental and egotistic. I like Milt, but . . . let's just say that beside himself is one of his favorite positions."

Barr requested that Katselas exit the production, but playwright Albee objected. A compromise ensued whereby Katselas received directorial credit in the program although Barr took over final rehearsals, using his early directorial skills.

RICHARD BARR'S COMPANY, Theatre 1960, was able to reach wider audiences via Albee's *Who's Afraid of Virginia Woolf?* in 1962. The adopted grandson of vaudeville impresario E.F. Albee, Edward (born in 1928) grew estranged from his ultra-conservative adoptive parents. His latter success, *Three Tall Women*, was based on his severely bigoted mother. Edward arrived on the theater scene when its Big Three playwrights, Tennessee Williams, William Inge, and heterosexual Arthur Miller were on the decline. Few could have predicted Albee would inherit their dramatic crown.

Controversy dogged and stimulated *Virginia Woolf's* success, for Albee, an avowed student of Williams's work, realized that "bad" but effective box-office publicity often adhered to plays featuring overtly sexual female characters. "The straight men, as they choose to call themselves, give [audiences] women who are sex objects and seldom women with sexual objectives of their own," Tennessee once wrote. Albee commenced *Woolf* with the character of Martha, then added husband George and built a plot.

Much of the play revolves around Martha's pursuit of an affair with a younger man. In the early 1960s, that led to several critics' accusations that this was a thinly disguised story of a gay marriage, a homosexual play in heterosexual clothing. Some said Martha, in light of her foul language and promiscuity, must be a man in drag. Katharine Hepburn, averse to controversial projects since playing a very convincing "youth" in the 1935 film flop *Sylvia Scarlett*, declined to play Martha when offered the role, disingenuously claiming she wasn't good enough.

George was offered to Henry Fonda, whose agent returned the "shocking" script unread without informing his client, who relished theater work and was seeking an image-busting challenge. When he later found out, Fonda was livid. He spoke with Albee about eventually working together. Albee hoped Fonda would be able to play Charlie in *Seascape*, but Fonda was committed to a film and was thus unavailable. Bette Davis, much more challenge-prone than Hepburn, recalled that she'd longed to play Martha on stage or screen and had pursued the role. However, she only became interested once *Woolf* proved a hit. Said Richard Barr, "Miss Davis wasn't particularly theatrically oriented. Unlike Tennessee Williams's, Edward Albee's name wasn't yet big enough for her to expend her talents on." Davis did appear on Broadway in Williams's *The Night of the Iguana*.

Richard Barr and company had sought backers for *Virginia Woolf* among numerous producing organizations and theaters, in vain. They found the material too abrasive and coarse, even though its roster of four-letter words was briefer than publicity would later have it. Fabled impresario Billy Rose, best known for his "girlie" shows, came to Barr's unexpected rescue.

In 1958, Rose had bought the National Theatre on Forty-First Street and had it given his name. He was thus able to claim all manner of expenses to the

Internal Revenue Service. But once in a while a legitimate hit show was needed to offset the losses, real and alleged. "Rose was a slice away from being an out-and-out con man," explained Barr, who'd hesitantly presented Rose with Albee's script. True to form, Rose didn't read it, but relied on the recommendation of an educated young man employed in his office.

Rose did read the title, and liked it. He also believed if this oddball work were marketed as a "dirty" play, it might become the hit he now needed. Rose thought the title very funny—although he was unfamiliar with the daunting bisexual authoress. Unfortunately, the tune to *Who's Afraid of the Big Bad Wolf?* could not be used in the play because its lyricist, Ann Ronell, was still alive and demanded big bucks for its usage, primarily because Walt Disney had paid her peanuts when it was used in his *Three Little Pigs* cartoon. Co-producer Clinton Wilder later substituted the melody of the nursery rhyme "Here We Go 'Round the Mulberry Bush" for use with the play's "title song," which is sung in the play.

Although numerous stars were approached, it became apparent that no big names would be appearing in *Who's Afraid of Virginia Woolf?* At this point, Richard Barr proposed a publicity stunt: *two* productions of the play, one on Broadway and one Off-, both opening the same night. This, partly to point up the double standard by which serious, "controversial," or gay-themed plays were dismissed, even shunted aside by Broadway. The parsimonious Rose vetoed the idea.

Martha eventually devolved upon the highly respected and very selective but not necessarily box-office actress Uta Hagen, today revered in memory as a great acting teacher. She'd been away from Broadway for six years, and had succeeded Jessica Tandy as Blanche DuBois in *A Streetcar Named Desire*. George was Canadian actor Arthur Hill, who'd appeared on Broadway in *Look Homeward, Angel* and *All the Way Home*. A pre-blonde Melinda Dillon played Honey and Nick was George Grizzard; Richard Barr had declined contender George Segal, who was Jewish, as "too ethnic," but in the celebrated screen version Segal was Oscar-nominated along with his three castmates—Elizabeth Taylor and Sandy Dennis won, he and Richard Burton didn't.

Virginia Woolf did not try out out of town. It was controversial enough for more sophisticated New York, where it opened Off-Broadway on October 13, 1962, at a cost of $75,000. The play would return at least thirty times its cost to investors, who included Edward Albee—Barr and his partner had decided to make the playwright another partner in their company, with twenty-five percent of weekly operating profits rather than the ten percent he would have gotten via the Dramatists Guild's Minimum Basic Contract.

"Albee will be all right," Richard said of Edward's fiscal prospects after the play had been running a few weeks.

It was the cementing of a beautiful professional friendship. Wealth and a parade of prizes would be the frosting on Albee's literary cake. He explained, "I write for me. For the audience of me. If other people come along for the ride then it's great."

Barr wondered, "Why not take a journey with an interesting, intellectual, and unusual human being? Too many theatregoers trust to the opinion of a critic. I think critics are part of the publicity process, for better and typically worse. But if the man who wrote *The Zoo Story* came up with a fresh, rather shocking new full-length play, any discerning theatergoer would want to see that. Plays are rather intimidating things even to a lot of theater lovers. That's why so many trust to the critics, naively because, as it turns out, the critic is also in the business of publicizing himself and pushing his own sociopolitical agenda. . . . It's just a—to me, surprising—fact: audiences, actors initially, and most producers are fearful of plays."

SURE ENOUGH, THE PIONEERING *Who's Afraid of Virginia Woolf?* scared and alienated many people. Critic Robert Coleman of New York's *Mirror* called it "a sick play about sick people," unnecessarily and royally adding, "We loathed it." Veteran critic Walter Kerr in the *New York Herald Tribune* took a fairer approach: "It is a brilliant piece of writing. . . . It need not be liked, but it must be seen." The lengthy and intense media debate over *Woolf*'s morality and crypto-homosexual origins (via Albee, known to be nonheterosexual, later openly so) was great for business.

Billy Rose, in seventh heaven, cackled, "Any playwright who can get that many laughs with that much venom and invents a game like Hump the Hostess is my kind of writer. I've got the hit I was looking for." Under the table, Rose—who refused to lower his theater's rent when the producers moved toward six rather than eight shows a week—made another fortune by selling prime house seats at sky-high prices to ticket brokers. That money wasn't, of course, reported to the IRS. Later Barr revealed, "The money was carried to [Rose] nightly in a suitcase filled with cash by one of his minions after the treasurers and managers had received their split." Rose publicly acknowledged making nearly $3,000,000 (legally) on *Woolf*'s run.

One negative opinion that inadvertently helped the box office was John Chapman's *News* headline on October 21, "For Dirty-Minded Females Only." Audiences naturally became curious about the play that was being so strenuously put down. (Actors invited to view *Woolf* were busily spreading the word about the quality of the acting and writing.) As more people saw *Woolf*, they—and the critical establishment—became aware that it wasn't intended primarily to shock; it was *good*. Newspapers took a second look, and wrote about the phenomena that were *Virginia Woolf* and Edward Albee. Even *The Christian*

Science Monitor, which had dubbed Tennessee Williams "the poet laureate of degradation, decadence, and despair," allowed that Albee's play had substance and influence. The times were clearly though slowly a-changing.

Who's Afraid of Virginia Woolf? established producer Barr and playwright Albee big time and eventually became an American classic. Its film version was instrumental in ending the archconservative censorship code instigated in 1934, although a more subtle, commercially daunting censorship yet continues. The play did not sweep all the available awards, as many had predicted. "The Pulitzer [Prize] was denied to Albee," said Barr. "It was voted, and *Woolf* won it, but it was held back." The expert panel was in effect vetoed by the Trustees of Columbia University who give out the prize. The falling out and public dispute, noted Barr, was as "vitriolic as any of the loud shenanigans in George and Martha's marriage . . . and don't think the use of those two names—as in Washington, the First Couple of our country—didn't infuriate those who noticed the historical allusion" (U.S. novelist and historian Gore Vidal has written that evidence indicates that the child-free father of his country may have been secretly gay, bisexual, or asexual).

In the end, the furor over the Pulitzer denial led to a change in how the prizes were awarded, granting more power to the judges and less to the moneymen and corporate figures cum trustees of the University. Albee went on to win three of them, his first in 1966 for *A Delicate Balance*; some saw it as a belated reward for *Woolf*, but *Balance* stands on its own merits.

Richard Barr added, "*Virginia Woolf* justified my aggressive hunch that a play can entertain, provoke, shock, and illumine . . . [and] that there is an audience for productions based on a strong play rather than on sheer spectacle, star power, or advertising campaigns. . . . It takes an Albee, and the Albees are rare, but I still contend and always will, that the play's the thing." Barr, who went on to a long and colorful theatrical career, died of AIDS in 1989 at 71.

As for Albee, he had his ups and downs before achieving legendary status among American playwrights. He followed *Virginia Woolf*'s success with a non-hit adaptation of crypto-lesbian novelist Carson McCullers's *The Ballad of the Sad Café* (1963), an essentially butch-lesbian tale with an ill-fitting traditionalist ending. His *Tiny Alice* was at times fascinating, but the allegory was vague and frustrating, more so because Albee blithely insisted in the published text that "the play is quite clear." Writer Ethan Mordden called this "something between impishness and a swindle." Albee resurrected the imaginary child from *Virginia Woolf* in *The American Dream*, and later still penned *The Play About the Baby*.

Indeed he does write for himself, yet at his best, when he questions and challenges society-as-usual, he writes for us all.

Who's Afraid of Terrence McNally?

THE REVIEWS THAT GREETED the 1965 Broadway comedy *And Things That Go Bump in the Night* were among or possibly even the worst in theater history. So venomous that many people wondered: was the play really that bad, that unfunny, or possibly that funny? As for young playwright Terrence McNally, some read between the reviews' lines and correctly guessed that he was gay, for vicious reviews often accrue to iconoclastic and/or ambitious nonhetero playwrights.

The "atrocious" play kept going, partly because the "Things" company decided to keep it on at a mere $1.00 per ticket. Lines stretched around the block, and audiences discovered that the play was indeed hilarious and outrageous. It heralded a brilliant new talent who would become a long-running, occasionally controversial Broadway institution—and an openly gay voice. Even with *Ragtime* (1997), which had no gay characters, McNally figured, "I do my bit for the cause if *Ragtime* is a big hit and a good show and people say, 'You know, the book writer's gay.'"

The prolific McNally's output has ranged from *The Kiss of the Spider Woman* and *Love! Valour! Compassion!* to *Master Class*, *A Perfect Ganesh*, *Frankie and Johnny in the Clair de Lune* (a two-character heterosexual romance of sorts), and *The Ritz*, a mainstream hit set in a gay bath house.

McNally succeeded via both talent and persistence. Apart from the anti-reviews for his 1965 breakthrough, when he surfaced in the theater world he was already known as the love of now-openly gay dramatic playwright Edward Albee, with whom he lived for six years. Besides the thinly veiled animosity this created in many critics' reviews of his work, McNally had to contend with early rumors that his plays were influenced or even partly written by the nine-years-older Albee. That is, until the two men's writing styles and personas revealed themselves as almost antipodal. Now who's afraid of things that go bump in the night?

15

⚜

MAMES

The fabulous role of Auntie Mame in the eponymous 1956 Broadway play, based on the previous year's novel by Patrick Dennis, was first incarnated by Rosalind Russell. Unusually, the veteran film and stage star next got to reprise her part in the 1958 hit movie version. Onstage, she was succeeded by Greer Garson, Beatrice Lillie, and Constance Bennett (once Hollywood's top-paid actress). Sylvia Sidney and Eve Arden did national tours of *Auntie Mame*.

The 1966 musical version, *Mame*, made a belated leading lady of Angela Lansbury, who did not get to do the (non-hit) 1974 film version that was Lucille Ball's screen swansong. Lansbury was followed by a veritable parade of stage Mames, from Ann Miller and Celeste Holm to Janis Paige, Jayne Morgan, and, in Las Vegas, Susan Hayward—also, in a 1998 New York benefit perform-ance, Charles Busch (with Peggy Cass returning to enact her unforgettable Agnes Gooch). *Mame* revivals have starred Ginger Rogers, Juliet Prowse, Patrice Munsel, *Laugh-In*'s Joanne Worley, Christine Baranski, and others.

Even before *Auntie Mame* became a smash stage hit, people were asking whom the madcap character was based on. She purportedly derived from Patrick Dennis's own aunt. Supposedly the novel was barely veiled reality, but the bestseller was more than mere veiling—a closet was involved. To begin with, Patrick Dennis was really Edward Everett Tanner III (1921–1976), raised in affluence by his parents, not by an aunt. Tanner's other pseudonym was Virginia Rowans, and in all he penned sixteen frothy, today mostly obscure and out-of-print novels. He enjoyed more bestsellers on the *New York Times* list at one time than anybody else for decades to come.

Did anyone really believe that Mame Dennis, despite the story's obligatory matrimonial wedding, would have a *heterosexual* ward and nephew? Tanner, though madcap and flamboyant, was content to let the world imagine that he was "little Patrick" all grown up. In the conservative 1950s, "Pat" tried hard to hang on to and increase his hard-won super-success. His first two novels had made no impact. Then *Auntie Mame* was rejected by nineteen publishers before seeing the light of print and spending two years on the bestseller lists.

Several women claimed to be the model for Mame Dennis, but once, in non-media company, Pat was asked who Mame *really* was? He smiled knowingly and pointed at himself. In 1958, there was a book sequel, *Around the World with Auntie Mame*. Like its precursor, it was less a novel than a collection of stories featuring Mame. The chief difference between the stage version and the books was that Patrick Dennis, an admittedly light and superficial scribe, kept the relationship and growing bond between aunt and nephew—which is the heart of the play and the musical—in the background. (A gay-straight duo, Jerome Lawrence and Robert E. Lee, transformed the book into a play, and another gay man, Jerry Herman, composed and wrote the lyrics for the sometimes philosophic songs in *Mame*.)

Another of Dennis's books, *Little Me*, made it to Broadway as a 1962 musical with TV star Sid Caesar enacting eight roles (a '90s revival starred the even more versatile Martin Short). Another novel, *Guestward Ho!*, became a CBS sitcom pilot starring Vivian Vance in her attempt to break out from Lucille Ball's shadow and get her own TV series. To her lasting chagrin, the series—short-lived, as it turned out—instead starred the younger and slimmer Joanne Dru, forcing Vance to resume second-banana status opposite her red-headed costar and boss.

By the early 1970s, Patrick Dennis was all written out. His gossamer style had become outdated and his sales were ghostly. He'd long since become an alcoholic, attempted suicide (in 1962), and been confined for eight months to a mental institution (electroshock therapy and all). Finally aware that he could never escape his true sexual and affectional orientation, he left his wife and kids and moved to Mexico for several years. He himself had been abandoned by a male partner who left him for a rich woman and a seemingly hetero lifestyle in Morocco, where that pair wound up alcoholic recluses.

Pat's final transition was his most unusual, like something out of a novel. Always a big spender, though no longer on the bottle—for the most part—he was in need of a job. *Auntie Mame* had made him rich, but the contract he'd signed for subsidiary rights included nothing about a musical comedy adaptation, and so he drew very little income from the huge success of *Mame*, which ran five years on Broadway. To settle the matter, arbitration was sought, but the situation wasn't resolved until after the author's death. He had declined to attend *Mame*'s opening and didn't see it until summer 1967, while visiting New York City.

He wrote his sister: "I found it a crashing bore. Angela Lansbury was just too common for words, which is the one thing Mame cannot be. Celeste Holm should at least be a bit classier." But the supporting actress from *All About Eve* and *Gentlemen's Agreement* (for which she won an Oscar) proved far less popular and acclaimed than Lansbury.

And so, in what he couldn't know would be the last few years of his life, Edward Everett Tanner III became a butler. One of the references given by Edwards Tanner—his new alias—to his first millionaire employer was from Patrick Dennis. "Who is Patrick Dennis?" asked the former ambassador and ex-owner of Brentano's. Pat wrote his son, "Considering that *Auntie Mame* kept that defunct art-supply establishment in the black during both 1955 and '56, I was a little miffed when he [asked]."

The once-famous writer sold most of his belongings and threw himself into his new lifestyle, glorying in a generous salary, privacy, and anonymity, authority over a household staff, and the fact that in between decorating, delegating, etc., he hardly had to spend a cent. He explained, "I am beautifully housed . . . and given anything I want to eat and drink. My laundry is done for me and even the dry cleaner gives a 50 percent discount just because so much work is thrown their way."

As to his new role, "I simply love it. A ham at heart. And when I switch out to serve dinner every evening I feel half actor and half prop man. It's fun. And it's also terribly profitable." Guests would often offer him tips. "Tipping doesn't embarrass me at all, unless it's lower than $50—and it never has been. I simply bow lower, say, 'Modom is too generous,' and tuck it into my jockstrap."

He concluded, "I shall probably [keep doing this] until I drop, as I could never reaccustom myself to paying out money for such fripperies as food, rent, utilities, and telephone bills."

His next employer was an elderly millionairess, for whom he headed up a staff of ten. Finally, he worked for Ray and Joan Kroc, the owners of McDonald's. They were his favorite employers (his least: the Republican dowager). But then came the bad news: like his father and grandfather before him, Tanner contracted pancreatic cancer, a disease often associated with abuse of alcohol and tobacco. He retired of necessity, reunited with his wife and children, and died not long after at age fifty-five.

Although his name, like most of his books, is now all but forgotten, Patrick Dennis was instrumental in the mainstreaming of "camp," or at least a mostly heterosexual version of it. Only in his last novel, *3-D*, published in 1972, did he venture partly out of the closet. His legacy to pop culture is Mame—whether as an aunt, musical, or otherwise, a brilliant and enduring creation and self-reflection.

THOUGH MAME WAS A CHEERFUL, giving, and open-minded spirit, not all of her thespic incarnations were too. The diva temperament sometimes got in the way. Case in point: Ann Miller of MGM and terpsichorean fame, also renowned for her big, black shellacked hairdo. She wasn't the last actress to actively object to a younger, attention-getting actress playing the supposedly shapeless and sexless Agnes Gooch—the amanuensis whose other function is to make Mame Dennis seem younger, thinner, and more graceful by comparison.

In 1969, Ann Miller was the final Broadway Mame. Jerry Herman enthused, "She was very warm and funny and we added a special tap routine for her in 'That's How Young I Feel' that stopped the show. Annie is a good sport and we became quite friendly. We always catch up when we run into each other at opening nights." Miller may have been warm and friendly toward her composer and musical mentor, but not toward one supporting female player.

Laurie Franks had been playing Gooch when Miller arrived in 1969. (Screen rights had sold to Warner Bros. the previous year for $3 million, but no film version could be released before 1971, so as not to compete with the Broadway and national touring productions.) Mame was the first Broadway starring role for "Annie," but upon meeting Ms. Franks she blurted, "She can't play Gooch. Her complexion's too good." Miller determined to get a new Gooch, which didn't happen overnight because Laurie was part of a tightly knit company and had her professional superiors' backing—up to a point.

"[Miller] wasn't really interested in her acting," Franks recalled, "but in getting to the song-and-dance numbers. And she was terrific in those, and they put a tap number in for her, and they were giving her oxygen offstage." Decades earlier, Miller had been clocked as the fastest-tapping dancer alive.

Mame was a challenge for Miller, trying to prove herself in a new medium. However, rather than fall in with the company, she kept aloof and did things her way. Laurie Franks: "We weren't really too pleased with her. In the scene when they were talking about getting me dressed, she would sometimes 'tap dance' with her fingers on the back of my neck." Whether or not Ann was thinking with her fingers, the habit greatly disconcerted Laurie.

Behind the scenes, Miller was trying to banish Franks, which contrasted with Annie's image as a southern-fried, friendly gal who's a lady but can kick off her shoes with the low-down-dest of 'em. In the book *Sing Out, Louise!* (not to be confused with this author's *Sing Out!*), Franks admitted that Miller tried to have her fired when the show moved to the Broadway Theatre. The star declared she would sign her contract if Laurie Franks were dismissed. The producers stated they couldn't do that. Miller responded, "Well, then, I'll go back to LA." So the producers agreed to demote Laurie to playing Cousin Fan, which was fine with la Miller.

"I gave my notice, but I had to stay for two months so they could replace me. It was breaking my heart to be out there onstage playing Cousin Fan. It was really rotten."

MADELINE KAHN GOT A BETTER DEAL than Laurie Franks when she came up against diva Lucille Ball for the 1974 movie of *Mame*. Coral Browne, British costar of the film *Auntie Mame*, recalled, "I heard that Miss Ball was leery of both her female supports," including Bea Arthur, who had already won a Tony for her role of Vera Charles. (Bette Davis had campaigned for the screen role of Mame's best friend, an acclaimed theatrical lush.) Browne, the 1958 Vera, added, "Miss Ball preferred to be the only funny lady in the cast." Yet when *The Hollywood Reporter* intimated that Ball was trying to oust Arthur, Lucy threatened legal action.

"Lucy had no worries about playing Mame," offered producer Robert Fryer. "Most star actresses, by that age, think they *are* Mame. . . . Lucy did worry somewhat about being upstaged." *Mame* would have been Madeline Kahn's second movie. Several critics had written that she almost stole her first one, *What's Up, Doc?*, from Barbra Streisand. Lucille Ball wasn't about to let the talented comedienne, thirty-one years her junior, steal *her* picture.

The star later professed that Kahn couldn't cut it, that she'd waited five weeks for Kahn to create a characterization. "She got them [the producers] for fifty grand," huffed Lucy, "and she knew that all she had to do was play it cool—she would get paid off and go to work immediately on *Blazing Saddles*. She had no intention of giving me Gooch."

Mame director Gene Saks said that Lucy turned on Madeline the first day of rehearsal, criticizing her voice and walk. Kahn stood her ground, which infuriated Ball, who had casting approval and complained to her director and wept in front of her producers. A devastated Kahn was eventually fired, but thanks to her contract, was fully paid. (*Blazing Saddles* was a hit and earned her an Academy Award nomination.)

Stage Gooch Jane Connell, circa fifty but completely lacking in sex appeal and slimness, was hired instead. Said Saks, "She was really too old for the part," especially as Agnes Gooch gets pregnant. But Lucy liked her.

Despite Ball's public disclaimers, she and Bea Arthur didn't get along. Part of the friction was due to Arthur's having become a TV star herself, via *Maude*, which ranked number four in the ratings compared to the long-running *Here's Lucy* at number fifteen. In later years, Arthur remembered *Mame* as one of the worst experiences of her life, while Lucy disparaged Arthur's second hit series, *The Golden Girls*, as being vulgar and near obscene.

Although several Mames had not been inherently musical, the beloved Lucy was in a category by herself. When she began recording "If He Walked into My Life," the ballad that Eydie Gorme had a hit record with, composer Jerry Herman, in the recording booth, tore his earphones off in horror. For her part, Ball dismissed criticism of her voice, saying it was right for the character. "Auntie Mame drank and stayed up all night. Was she supposed to sound like Julie Andrews? Come on!"

Though reviewers carped at Lucy's warbling in *Mame*, she'd have sounded worse if not for Jerry's help. He revealed, "One day, she was trying to sing the line 'Open a new window, open a new door,' but she just couldn't hear that half-tone on *door*. I managed to teach her every other note, but she just couldn't get that half-tone. The poor woman was in agony. So was I."

He finally solved the problem by having her sing the line minus the final word. She was baffled but cooperative. The next day, he played a note on the piano and had Lucy sing only the word 'door,' which she did correctly, with the half-tone. Jerry said thank you, then clipped the note into the track. "I clipped the entire soundtrack together that way." When the film's record album was released, the cover featured only Lucille Ball—no mention of Jerry Herman, who was her vocal coach, the movie's musical supervisor, and the composer-lyricist of every song in *Mame*. Herman threatened lawsuit, and a label was hastily tacked on to every single album. Of course once the movie flopped—more so critically than financially—the album flopped bigger, for it contained Lucy's singing but none of the comedy or classy visuals.

Ironically, Ball had wanted the film to be as close to the Broadway musical as possible (ergo her early insistence that Bea Arthur reprise her stage role). But as Jerry Herman told Warner Bros. after they cast Lucy, "Mame Dennis is not a clown. She is an elegant woman, and when she slides down the banister it's funny *because* she's an elegant woman. It won't be funny when Lucille Ball slides down the banister because she is always doing much more outrageous things than that."

He summarized, "Lucille Ball can't sing and she can't dance. So will you please tell me why you have cast her in my show?" The studio's first choice had been non-singing, non-dancing Elizabeth Taylor, who did star in the film of the Broadway musical *A Little Night Music*, which, no surprise, was a bigger, if lower-profile, flop than *Mame*.

THE CLASSIC AGNES GOOCH was Peggy Cass, whose career highpoint was the movie *Auntie Mame*. In 1984, she looked back, "The story and its message of tolerance was what made *Auntie Mame* so great. . . . The musical has great music, but all the songs kinda detract from the incidents and relationships. The sad thing is that since the musical came along, there went the straight play.

It would be revived today, it could still be a big hit—maybe more than evah—but all they ever revive is the effing musical.

"Today it seems incredible they let Roz Russell do Mame for the movie. It was such a habit to choose somebody else—usually younger—than the person who originated the part on Broadway. . . . For my money, Roz was the best Mame; you liked her at the same time you looked up to her."

Cass acknowledged, "I did hear about that rumpus with Ann Miller. That didn't shock me, 'cause every Mame wants a homely Gooch. They're willing to have Vera be rather grand and nice-looking, but poor Agnes has to be a plain Jane. . . . She's there as sort of a test of Auntie Mame's tolerance, but she also isn't a threat to anyone. Let me tell you, you have to be pretty secure to play someone so insecure, and God forbid you should step on the star's toes!"

When Coral Browne worked with Rosalind Russell she discerned "attitude behind the very professional smile. I've no idea if Miss Russell was at all intimidated by my more extensive stage training, but she soon saw I have as much backbone as she did, and we reached an understanding. In England, actors are all equals, and we have only one Her Majesty.

"Besides, what could I take away from her? No one in the States knew me then, and if you think about it, Vera Charles is a foil to Mame Dennis, more of a parody than a character. A man could play Vera beautifully; in fact, one famous critic said that's what Miss Arthur did, in [Mame, the movie]. . . . People in the 1950s and up until Betty Ford were quite dismayed when a character, a famous theatre actress, was depicted as alcoholic. That enhances Mame Dennis, of course. It also made everyone ask each other who Vera really was, and the consensus was Tallulah Bankhead, who herself would have made a marvelous non-singing Mame."

In Jerry Herman's opinion, the ideal (musical) Mame was Angela Lansbury. She was neither too funny, too madcap, too good a singer, too beautiful, nor too overwhelmingly glamorous. "Miss [Ginger] Rogers tried to swamp her character in rhinestone dazzle and boas," wrote one critic of the actress who in some interviews objected to Mame Dennis's "clearly very liberal politics." When Susan Hayward briefly played Mame, it was said she over-dramatized the role and was too distractingly beautiful.

Herman recalled that when the Oscar-winning redhead "came to my house so I could teach her the score, she took my breath away. With that sweetheart face of hers, she was movie-star gorgeous. You could tell she knew how to wear clothes just by the way she had this cashmere sweater draped casually over her shoulders. I have met many handsome and stylish women in my day; but Susan Hayward and Lana Turner were the most beautiful women I ever saw in my life."

Celeste Holm, by contrast, was a pared-down Mame whose performance lacked much of the warmth she'd exhibited in earlier Broadway shows like

Bloomer Girl and *Oklahoma!* When Susan Hayward had to leave *Mame* (she would die prematurely from a brain tumor), she warned her replacement, Holm, that if she didn't treat the young cast right, Hayward would hear about it and return to "kick [your] ass." Stage star Holm had long since left the theater for Hollywood with hopes of screen stardom. Leading lady Joan Fontaine was quoted, "I once told Celeste Holm, 'You're so lucky not to be a big Hollywood star, not bound to a contract.' Celeste is cool to me to this day."

IN HIS MEMOIRS, JERRY HERMAN declared that his dream Mame would have been Judy Garland. He'd hoped to pay tribute to her by offering her the role of Mame Dennis following Angela Lansbury's departure from the hit show after about a year and a half. But in offering the fast-fading icon the role, he inadvertently caused her pain during a downward spiral that would, in 1969, turn fatal.

When Herman heard via the William Morris agency that Judy Garland was interested in taking over the role, "I just about lost my mind. . . . I was the craziest, the most ardent Judy Garland fan of all time. I still am. I worshipped that woman. It was a passion that went beyond reason. . . . She sang, and it was a religious experience for me."

He admired Judy's underrated acting talent, also her dancing ability, and believed she would be a perfect Mame, making the role her own and the show a bigger hit than ever while staging a definitive and prestigious comeback.

Several meetings took place with Garland, who was charming and "trying very hard to be 'good,' in a professional sense. She believed in her heart that she would be there every night, faithfully." But her private life was chaotic and she was rumored to be drinking. Even Jerry had to admit, "Miss Garland had a reputation for not being reliable." At roughly the same time, after a screen test, costume fittings, and a public announcement that she'd gotten the role, Judy was fired from the movie *The Valley of the Dolls*, replaced by Susan Hayward as Broadway bitch-diva Helen Lawson, based on novelist Jacqueline Susann's ex friend Ethel Merman.

Although Jerry Herman persuaded several *Mame* backers that Garland would be a breathtaking Mame—particularly singing his songs—the final decision was no. "We are very sorry, Jerry," he was informed by the producers, "but we cannot do it. We cannot entrust this show to Miss Garland. We have the backers to consider, and we cannot risk a show that is at its peak and has many more years to go. If it all falls apart because she doesn't show up on opening night, we will have destroyed everything that we all worked so hard to create."

Later, Herman said he replied rashly: "I don't care! Even a bad performance from Judy Garland would be an event. Just to have Judy Garland in this show for *one night* would be magical—historical." He'd spoken with his heart, not his business head. Word got back to Jerry that Judy "was destroyed" when she found out she didn't get the role. She told daughter Liza Minnelli that "her heart was broken, because she knew how *right* she was for it.

"That is something I have had to carry in my own heart through the years," Herman has noted. "This was a woman I truly idolized. I still can't bear to think of how hurt she was because of something I wrote [*Mame*]. It was a very sad experience for me and I have always felt bad about it, because I never wanted to cause that woman pain." The man who brought Mame to musical life felt, then as now, "Judy Garland stood for show business, in all its emotional, theatrical glory. I still hear that sound when I write."

16

✦

THE CURSE OF *THE BOYS IN THE BAND*

About a year after my book *The Lavender Screen* was published in 1993, I received a letter from actor Cliff Gorman in New York City. "I became aware of your book thanks to *Premiere* magazine but did not purchase a copy. The subject matter does not interest me. An actor friend recently mentioned it in a favorable light but then informed me you devote an entire chapter to *The Boys in the Band*. Over the weekend I browsed through a copy in a bookstore. I did not and will not buy it.

"It may interest you to know, although I doubt it, that I've done many other roles, *nonhomosexual*, and that my performance in *The Boys in the Band* was just that . . . I am not a stranger to awards and nominations both on and off the stage, and my career was never limited to that one film you focus on."

What Mr. Gorman, who died at sixty-five and not of AIDS in 2002, hadn't grasped was that *The Lavender Screen* was intended to focus on movies featuring major gay, lesbian, or bisexual characters. Space didn't allow for individual actors' other credits. (In *An Unmarried Woman* he played—equally convincingly—an extremely sexually aggressive heterosexual opposite Jill Clayburgh.) It was Gorman who chose to do Emory in the 1968 Off-Broadway play that ran 1,000 performances and in its screen version. He also chose to play yet another flamingly gay character, a murder victim, in *Justine* (1969). He couldn't have known that the much-anticipated George Cukor picture would turn out to be a costly and critically reviled flop.

A former publicist for Gorman admitted off the record, "He does regret [*The Boys in the Band*]. He's done great work in so numerous things, but most people mainly remember Emory. And some still think you are what you portray." That may be true, but why doesn't that restriction necessarily apply to actors who play wife-beaters, rapists, gay-bashers, and murderers?

It was generally known in the business that Gorman apparently wasn't gay. Just his luck that out of *Boys*' nine-man ensemble, Emory was one of the hardest characters to forget. He had many of the best lines, and Gorman played the funny, amiable, and vulnerable role to perfection. Yet the result was bitter. His letter to me concluded, "I have had to work long and deliberately to move away from that image," as if the issue were the quality of one's work, rather than the overarching problems of stereotyping and homophobia.

Boys' other most indelible character was Leonard Frey's Harold, the birthday boy, a "pock-marked Jewish fairy" of considerable personality and menace. Frey, who'd appeared in *Fiddler on the Roof*, had considerably more post-*Boys* success than Gorman, for a while. For the screen version of *Fiddler* he was Oscar nominated for portraying a husband and father (Tevye's first son-in-law), almost as if the ever-far-from-pro-gay Academy was relieved Frey could play straight—though in fact he was gay.

"When Lenny's nomination was announced, I rang up Cliff, among others," offered Frederick Combs (Donald), who by 1986 was a drama coach in Los Angeles, where I'd just moved. "Mis-ter Gorman was indignant, not happy for Lenny. Very close-mouthed . . . He knew I was gay too, and I always got the vibe that he looked down on us. I didn't call back when Lenny didn't win the award. In fact, I don't think I spoke to Cliff Gorman again."

ROBERT MOORE DIRECTED Mart Crowley's play, which broke ground in that it featured a virtually all-gay set of characters. "The timing was very right," recalled Moore in New York in 1980 while promoting his film *Chapter Two*, by Neil Simon. "It was before, during, and after Stonewall . . . People heard the play was daring, insofar as you had all these outspoken queers on stage. They heard there was lots of laughs and wit, and a party game to boot—the truth game, you know, on the telephone."

Moore was not often willing to discuss *The Boys in the Band*. Maybe one reason was that he didn't get picked to helm the screen version. (Almost invariably, Hollywood prefers heterosexual or "straight-seeming" directors.) Frederick Combs explained, "Bob's being gay was common knowledge. He did try to hide with anti-gay jokes and slurs . . . Bob loved stars and loved acting the star. He wanted to be one, but couldn't." The flamboyant redhead's few acting roles were small and stereotypical. He was Phyllis's gay brother on *The Mary Tyler Moore Show*, later directing episodes of its spin-off *Rhoda*. In Otto

Preminger's offbeat *Tell Me That You Love Me, Junie Moon*, starring a pre-*Cabaret* Liza Minnelli, Moore was a crippled gay man who teams with two other "misfits." (Leonard Frey had a bit gay role in *Junie Moon*.)

In 1980, Moore spoke (on the phone) under the condition that his private life not be broached. Although no longer a performer, he remained in the closet, even though partnered. Moore shed little light on *The Boys in the Band* or his career, and I terminated the session early. Frederick Combs: "Bob's arrogance and queeny manner scared off movie studios. They hired William Friedkin (pre–*The Exorcist*), who might be straight or might be bi . . . He made some ambiguous comments while making *Cruising*," a homophobic film picketed while on location by many gay New Yorkers and coincidentally featuring *Boys*' own Keith Prentice as, what else, a gay murder victim.

Boys' original cast members got to reprise their roles on screen, usually a rarity but not in a time where most Hollywood actors and every star declined to play gay. (Leading or ensemble, gay roles didn't yet yield Oscar nominations or awards.) Studio interest in the hot property cooled after no big name attached itself to the project; Marlon Brando and Rod Steiger had recently enacted gay leads in unsuccessful films (see *The Lavender Screen*'s updated edition). The 1970 movie of *The Boys in the Band*, via National General, not a major distribution company, didn't fare well at the box office—outside a few cities, few people showed up, including gay filmgoers.

As a New York play, *Boys* was a significant hit with homosexual and heterosexual audiences. Despite its grim, almost warning ad line, "*The Boys in the Band* . . . is not a musical," the play and film deeply impressed then-closeted gays. After the 2002 passing of Cliff Gorman, critic Rex Reed wrote, "Sacred memories invade my thoughts of funny man Cliff (*The Boys in the Band*) Gorman," even though the actor was not primarily a comedian.

"Yes, it was a backward and stereotypical play," reflected gay historian Martin Greif, lamenting that its most famous line, via the mainstream media at least, was "You show me a happy homosexual and I'll show you a gay corpse." "But in that era, what a treat just to see gay characters, and central ones at that, and from the pen of a gay man. . . . Obviously, Crowley shouldn't have made that idiotically defensive comment on the order of: There may actually be happy gay people out there, but they're not in *my* play." Greif added, "Remember, *Boys* came out not long after the lifting of the state law which forbade gay and lesbian characters on New York stages."

Robert Moore remembered, "Most people, including gays, came to see the play with an attitude of horrified fascination . . . I think Mart's device of using a birthday party was inspired. It reveals these guys' world and allows them to let it all hang out. It's a party to which the audience is invited, as voyeurs and eavesdroppers."

But *The Boys in the Band* was no party for most of its cast, none of whom went on to stardom. "I think I'm the only actor who embraced the play," said Frederick Combs. "I did it in New York and I did it in London. I can see the upside—being in a hit, being something of a role model or standard bearer—while I can also see, have known, the downside . . . yet I haven't felt trapped and defeated by the curse of *The Boys in the Band*."

Combs described the phases of his experience: the initial thrill of costarring in a pioneering hit play, the movie getting made "with us in it," disappointment that the picture didn't do better even though "It wasn't unexpected. The so-called heartland is not New York—damn it. And then being so identified with the play and the movie, like to the point of, 'You did play yourself, right?' Almost having to apologize for it!"

As more than one cast member pointed out, Middle America never saw the movie—which TV still shuns—but everyone in Hollywood did: casting directors and "anyone with the power to give or deny you a job. . . . Back then, there was real stigma attached to being publicly known as gay, which equated to having played gay," said Combs. "Especially if you weren't a celebrity, someone who'd been photographed on dates with the opposite sex. . . . There was an enduring darkness attached to *The Boys in the Band* once the successful play ended and the unsuccessful movie came out. The tune was like, I told you so and it serves you right for trying to make a movie out of *that*."

FREDERICK COMBS, a once-close friend of *Boys* movie producer-turned-author Dominick Dunne, wrote a play titled *The Children's Mass* which sometime lover Sal Mineo helped produce. Combs appeared on TV's *The Young and the Restless* but found acting jobs in any medium scarcer and scarcer. "It's ironic. On Broadway in 1961 I originated Geoffrey, the gay friend of the pregnant girl in *A Taste of Honey*. That didn't seem to hurt me. Possibly I drank from the same well once too often." The handsome, talented actor was in several New York Shakespeare Festival productions and in Franco Zeffirelli's *The Lady of the Camellias* and was writer-in-residence at the Edward Albee Playwriting Foundation. But in the mid–1970s, Combs moved to LA where he had more of his own plays produced.

He also directed, for instance Harvey Fierstein's *International Stud*. In lieu of acting assignments, Combs worked as a dialogue coach and acting teacher, founding the Los Angeles/Actor's Lab in 1979. He did minor roles in made-for-TV movies and didn't hide his gayness. In the late '70s, he gave a candid interview to gay *In Touch* magazine.

"Do I regret playing Donald in *Boys*?" he repeated my question. "No. Of course not. Not in and of itself. I regret the aftermath."

In 1992, Frederick Combs died of AIDS, at fifty-seven.

KENNETH NELSON CREATED THE ROLE of the Boy in *The Fantasticks* in 1960 and perhaps went further professionally than any other *Boys* cast member. Leonard Frey reminisced, "It was such a beautiful moment . . . Ken singing 'Soon It's Gonna Rain' in *The Fantasticks*. He was *so* much younger then. The stage life can really age and harden you. Me, I was always sort of enveloped in humor, but Ken had leading man potential." In the play and film of *The Boys in the Band,* Nelson had the role closest to being the lead—as Michael, the party host who's a guilt-ridden, alcoholic Catholic.

A talented singer-actor, Nelson had taken over from Anthony Newley in *Stop the World—I Want to Get Off* (1961). "It feels like I've done it all, flops, hits, misses, everything in between," he looked back in British *Photoplay*. "Maybe I should have worked my way west. . . . In movies, they remember you." Nelson's biggest disappointment and final Broadway effort was the much-heralded musical of the popular '50s film *The Teahouse of the August Moon,* retitled *Lovely Ladies, Kind Gentlemen* (1970). He starred as the Okinawan Sakini, enacted on screen by Marlon Brando. Disgusted by the sixteen-performance run of the show, which closed in January 1971, Nelson moved to London where he felt theater was taken more seriously and he wouldn't be typed as Michael nor associated with a big money-losing musical. In the West End he appeared in a revival of *Show Boat.*

Post-*Boys*, he tried to steer clear of gay roles. When a twenty-five-year-anniversary restaging of *The Boys in the Band* was done as a benefit to fight AIDS, Kenneth Nelson was one of two surviving cast members who said thanks but no thanks—the other, of course, being Cliff Gorman. The participants were Laurence Luckinbill (Hank), Peter White (Alan), and Reuben Greene (Bernard).

"Kenneth did have his career hurt by being so prominent in *The Boys in the Band*," stated Combs. "To be honest, though, if Michael hadn't been the biggest role, I'm not sure Ken would have taken it. Among us all, he thought he was the star. *The Fantasticks*, et cetera. He had star attitude." After *Boys* Nelson endured small and shrinking roles on television, as in *Reilly, Ace of Spies, The Trials of Lee Harvey Oswald,* and *Lace II.* He eventually landed the smallest of bit parts in a Pia Zadora vehicle, *The Lonely Lady,* as a fey beautician—a fleeting gay stereotype. His final assignment was in *Tales from the Crypt.* He died in London of AIDS in 1993 at sixty-three.

"I REMEMBER HOW SURPRISED I WAS when I saw [the 1969 movie] *The Magic Christian*," said Frederick Combs, "with Leonard Frey in what amounted to a cameo as a gay vampire. I stayed to read the credits, and for Lenny's character it said 'Laurence Faggot,' right above Laurence Harvey [who played Hamlet], a very unpopular actor according to anything I've heard. At first I thought, 'What a nothing, demeaning role.' And that word, the f-word, it was almost like a slap in the face—to us all—when I read it."

By inclination and via stereotyping, Frey chose a thankless post-*Boys* (the play) gay role. He was likely tempted by *The Magic Christian's* big names (Peter Sellers and Ringo Starr) and big budget. "When you've been part of an ensemble cast and your background's the real work and humility of the theatre," clarified Combs, "you tend to jump at the chance to be in a film. Any film. A little role? Just think of it as 'ensemble' acting. Think how much money you'll get for so little work. You won't know till the thing's released how much or nearly all of you they've left on the cutting room floor."

Leonard Frey did work almost continuously after *Boys* until his death. He'd been on Broadway in *Knock, Knock, The Royal Family*, and earned a Tony nomination for *The National Health*. After, he joined the all-star cast of Ellis Rabb's production of *The Man Who Came to Dinner* (the crypto-gay title role has been essayed by myriad gay actors, from Alec Woollcott and Monty Woolley to Clifton Webb and Nathan Lane).

"Like most actors, Lenny yearned for movie fame, and his Oscar [nomination] only whetted his appetite," said Combs. "Eventually Hollywood must have figured out—I mean, at least three gay roles—that he wasn't straight, and they dropped him, even for secondary roles." Frey had a recurring part in the TV series *Best of the West* and guested on shows like *Murder, She Wrote*. "When he came to England to do *Magic Christian*, which I cowrote," explained Graham Chapman, "he was aloof. Whether he knew or guessed my sexuality, I can't say. But he became even less friendly as time went by." Chapman wouldn't confirm whether he was behind the f-word labeling of Frey's bit role or whether it was aimed at the unpopular and closeted Laurence Harvey. The only deceased member of Monty Python (from cancer), Chapman cowrote and costarred in several films, most notably *The Life of Brian*.

"Lenny could be chilly if he didn't know you," said Combs. "He was shy at first. After the *Fiddler* [nomination], he got very cautious. For a long time he had high hopes, and the grapevine said he wouldn't talk about *The Boys in the Band* or anything gay related." Frey died in New York City of AIDS in 1988 at forty-nine.

"Not many outsiders know that Lenny based his Harold persona on our producer Richard Barr," revealed Combs. Barr, an actor turned prominent stage producer (*Who's Afraid of Virginia Woolf?*, *Sweeney Todd*), had been mentored by Orson Welles and was an apprentice member of the fabled Mercury Theatre. In *Citizen Kane*, it was Barr's character who asked, "Rosebud? What's Rosebud?" Barr died of AIDS in 1989 at age seventy-one.

The youngest cast member of *Boys* to die was Robert La Tourneaux, "Cowboy," the requisite beefcake and "birthday present" for Harold (Leonard

Frey). The movie's initial print ad featured a headshot of Harold in sunglasses, cigarette dangling from his mouth, with the caption "Today is Harold's birthday." To the right, a headshot of La Tourneaux, with a sexy smile and tousled hair, and a kerchief round his neck. That caption read "This is his present." Most American newspapers banned the ad. Had he been heterosexual, or pretended, La Tourneaux, with his Travolta-ish looks and not-too-bright-yet-likeable manner, might have hit it big on the screen.

He'd made his Broadway bow in *Ilya Darling*, the 1967 musical of the hit film *Never On Sunday*. After *The Boys in the Band* he got only one more movie role. "Yeah, *Boys* was a kiss of death for me," he acknowledged. "I went from that to a token part on stage" as Serving Man in director Ellis Rabb's *The Merchant of Venice*. William Como, editor of the crypto-gay New York entertainment magazine *After Dark*," said, "Bobby did an interview for us. Much too frank.

"He named some of his lovers, including Calvin Culver (who starred in an X-rated flick titled *The Boys in the Sand*) and a married bisexual actor who'd been on stage and later got a supporting Academy Award and [was] featured in the never fully explained death at sea of a female movie star with whose bisexual husband he was allegedly having an affair—though of course the media deliberately switched genders and hinted at an affair between the actress and the actor who wasn't her actor husband.

"But we did include Bobby [in the magazine] in '73," added Como. "We felt he was up and coming." However, after signing to costar in Tennessee Williams's *Vieux Carré*, La Tourneaux was fired before the play opened. In 1978 he was quoted in *Quentin Crisp's Book of Quotations*: "Charles Laughton played every kind of part but never a homosexual. People knew he was gay, but his public image [which included a wife] never betrayed his private reality. So he was safe. I wasn't safe."

Eventually the still hunky "Cowboy" did nude photospreads and appeared in the altogether at the Ramrod, a Manhattan male-strip theater. He contracted AIDS and made the tabloids when his landlord tried to evict him for allowing his caregiver to live with him. La Tourneaux sued and won the case, but died soon after, at forty-four in 1986.

The handsomest of *The Boys in the Band*—the play title reportedly inspired by a Judy Garland reference to the band Esther Blodgett sings with in the classic 1954 George Cukor version of *A Star Is Born*—was Keith Prentice. He played Larry, who was partnered with Hank (Laurence Luckinbill, known for his long marriage to Lucille Ball's daughter, Lucie Arnaz). Pre-*Boys*, Prentice was a chorus boy in *Gypsy*, *The Sound of Music*, and Noel Coward's *Sail Away*. He had a bit part in the Rock Hudson–Doris Day film *Send Me No Flowers* and a non-musical role in *Take Her, She's Mine* on Broadway.

Playing gay in *The Boys in the Band* proved a curse for his career too. Prentice worked on TV in soaps like *As the World Turns* and *Dark Shadows*, but Hollywood turned its back on him and he resorted to a tiny—and thankless—role as a gay murder victim to Al Pacino's lethal and supposedly secretly gay cop in the controversial film *Cruising* (1980). "Keith wound up teaching drama at a boys' school in New York City," offered Combs. In 1982 Prentice founded the Theatre Under the Stars in Kettering, Ohio, where he directed summer stock plays. In 1992, about a week after Combs, Keith died at age fifty-two.

Some obituaries listed the cause of death as cancer, some AIDS. In London, Kenneth Nelson, who would die the following year, apprised a columnist, "I don't care what the rags said, it was AIDS. I mean, enough with the shame!"

ONE OF THE LEAST-KNOWN cast members was Reuben Greene, who played Bernard, a quiet, mild gay black man. "I tried staying in touch with Reuben," disclosed Combs, "but either he's still genuinely shy or he wants to keep apart and put that time behind him." Yet Greene did show up at the 1993 charity restaging of *The Boys in the Band*. His other most notable credit is Elaine May's flop movie *Mikey and Nicky* (1976).

Peter White, the unprepossessing blond actor who played Alan (the contractually married party guest who is either the most closeted of them all or the oddball who actually turned out heterosexual), has also remained under the celebrity radar. He appeared in the bisexual-themed play *P.S. Your Cat Is Dead!* by gay James Kirkwood (during LA rehearsals for which Sal Mineo was murdered in his carport by a black robber). On screen, White had a small role as Debbie Reynolds's boyfriend in Albert Brooks's comedy *Mother* (1995). When the concerned son played by Brooks inquires, Mother reassures him that she and White's character aren't intimate or anything; they just have occasional sex.

"There's no question," said Frederick Combs in 1986, "that the one from our play who went furthest professionally was our director," Robert Moore. None of the cast, gay or het, achieved name recognition. Moore, though not a name director, went surprisingly far helming stage star vehicles—typically diva-centered (aha)—for the likes of Carol Channing (*Lorelei*), Lauren Bacall (*Woman of the Year*), and Elizabeth Taylor (*The Little Foxes*, her stage bow as well as her penultimate play). By the early '70s Moore was directing TV movies, including a 1974 NBC version of Tennessee Williams's *Cat on a Hot Tin Roof*, starring Robert Wagner as Brick; his wife, Natalie Wood as Maggie the Cat; and Laurence Olivier as Big Daddy.

More surprisingly, Moore went on to direct such Hollywood films as *Murder by Death* and *The Cheap Detective*, both with glittering all-star casts. "Bob told several friends," said Combs, "that back in the '60s he'd supported

Lauren Bacall in *Cactus Flower* on Broadway, but then [in 1981] he directed her in *Woman of the Year* and that she won her musical Tony for Best Actress mostly thanks to him, since she was a-musical."

Combs laughed. "Bobby was like that. A little fiction, a little selfishness, and lots of laughter and stars in his eyes." Moore died of AIDS in 1984 at fifty-six.

Another *The Boys in the Band* alumnus who died prematurely was W. Robert LaVine, costume designer for the movie version. However, he passed away in 1979, pre-AIDS (officially). Years later, Combs saw a book LaVine wrote, *In a Glamorous Fashion*, published in 1980, sitting on a coffee table at a friend's house. Said Combs: "I examined it and was so unexpectedly pleased to see Robert's name on it. Then I saw he'd died just before it came out, and this was right after the news about Rock Hudson being HIV-positive. It entered my head, for the very first time, 'How many of us are going to reach our deaths way too young?'"

BOYS PRODUCER RICHARD BARR admitted a few years after the film came out, "Our play was possibly the gayest production ever seen on [Broadway]. The majority of men involved in it, actors and nonactors both, were homosexual, and most of those relatively open—that is, within our own theatrical circles. . . . For my part, I think Mart Crowley's gotten a bad rap. He's one of the younger generation of gays who, unlike most older playwrights, is willing to put a gay character or characters front and center.

"Mart's also a realist. He presents a gay world that is true . . . [and] includes stereotypes as well as a diversity of men. He wrote *The Boys in the Band* with warts and all."

Crowley was Natalie Wood's secretary before *Boys* and post-*Boys* co-produced the TV series *Hart to Hart*, starring Robert Wagner and co-owned by Wagner and wife Natalie's RoNa company which also had a wealthy slice of *Charlie's Angels*. (It was a source of ongoing bitterness to Wood's younger sister, Lana—see the chapter on Natalie vs. Lana Wood in this author's *Celebrity Feuds!*—that the stellar couple would hire "outsiders" but not a relative for lucrative positions.)

Crowley did little theatrical writing after *Boys'* success. His 1973 follow-up play, *A Breeze from the Gulf*, with one gay character out of three total, bombed. Frederick Combs felt, "It was inevitable. Audiences were turned off by Mart's story of a strange young man and his parents, while the critics took the opportunity to punish Mart in print for his good fortune with *our* play." (The semi-autobiographical Michael was played by Robert Drivas, probably best known for the Rod Steiger film *The Illustrated Man*, who died at fifty of AIDS.)

No more full-length plays followed, and after *Hart to Hart* Crowley seemed to fade away. He returned in 2002 with a *Boys in the Band* sequel, cleverly titled *The Men from the Boys*.

Thirty years on, it's not a birthday party that reunites the gang at Michael's—the still acerbic host is now on the wagon—but a memorial for Larry. Hank's life partner, it's clarified, did not die of AIDS (ironic, in view of the numerous deaths among the original cast members): "Gay men do die of other things." The cast, of course, was entirely new, and the new characters all young, including a political activist. Crowley was kinder to his characters this time around, and the self-hate much less pronounced.

The Men from the Boys opened in San Francisco to tepid critical and audience response. Intended for fine-tuning en route to Los Angeles and ultimately Broadway, it was dismissed by the *San Francisco Chronicle* as having "no more depth than the average TV sitcom," not to mention the fact that gay characters, once the stuff of tragedy and melodrama, can now be seen nightly on TV. Several observers felt it was much too late for a sequel, which anyway couldn't have a fraction of the impact of *Boys in the Band*, which seldom has been revived over the years due to its datedness.

In 2002, as in 1993 on the twenty-fifth birthday of the play, it was widely noted that *Boys* had attracted major publicity and sizeable audiences because there were so few gay-themed plays of any description in the late '60s—let alone one with numerous gay characters, none of whom was killed off in the end.

Too many reviews of the sequel dwelled on the original's negative points while overlooking its pioneering aspects, such as presenting gay men who weren't monsters, buffoons, or pathetic victims—but who sometimes victimized themselves—and depicting a longtime gay couple, or delivering the play's key line, "If we could just not hate ourselves so much." *The Boys in the Band* shone a sometimes painful but needed spotlight on homophobia and how easily it becomes internalized by its targets. It finally presented a gay community in miniature, men banding together for fun, camaraderie, and solace—solace for their mutual outcast status, not for their inherent and essential nature.

Besides being a landmark play, *Boys* and its legacy have become a symbol, representing the real-life discrimination faced by gay people—certainly including actors—and the challenge posed by AIDS, which has struck the stage world harder than any other cultural or professional sector. Long live the men of *The Boys in the Band*, living and especially deceased, in collective memory and heightened awareness.

17

MISS DAVIS REGRETS: BETTE ON AND OFF BROADWAY

U nlike rival Katharine Hepburn, who bowed on celluloid in 1932, Bette Davis (1908–1989) was not a stage star when she arrived in Hollywood the previous year. Between 1928 and 1930 Bette worked on the stage—not returning until 1952. She'd been rejected by Eva Le Gallienne's theater company, which cited her as insufficiently committed to the thespic art. (Rumor had it that young Ruth Elizabeth Davis wasn't sufficiently attracted to the lesbian Le Gallienne, whose father was a flamboyant poet reminiscent of Oscar Wilde.)

Bette worked briefly in George Cukor's theater company, but he let her go, citing her "lack of team spirit." Although Cukor would become Hollywood's leading director of female stars, he never worked with Davis on the West Coast. As voiced during interviews in this author's *Bette Davis Speaks*, she never forgot—or forgave—the sting of his dismissal. However, a year later, in 1929, Bette secured a place in actress-impresaria Blanche Yurka's Henrik Ibsen tour.

Bette's high point was playing Hedvig in *The Wild Duck*. In 1926 she and her hard-driving but encouraging mother, Ruthie, had attended a Blanche Yurka Company production of *The Wild Duck* in Boston that Davis later credited with inspiring her to become an actress. Peg Entwhistle had acted Hedvig, and in her first autobiography Bette recalled the experience: "I was watching myself. There wasn't an emotion I didn't anticipate or share with her. . . . My heart almost stopped. She looked just like me." She was describing the scene in which Hedvig breaks down after her father has left her. Bette's own father had deserted his wife and two daughters, a major factor in the star's lifelong mistrust of men.

Ironically, and in contrast to Bette Davis, who would become a great Hollywood survivor, Peg Entwhistle would be destroyed in part by her Tinseltown experience, when her stage stardom and acclaim didn't translate into screen opportunity. After considerable effort and disappointment, the large-eyed Peg was given a part in *Thirteen Women* (1932), starring Irene Dunne and Myrna Loy. Before release of the racist melodrama (the villain is a vengeful Eurasian beauty), Entwhistle's small role—one of the thirteen women—was pared down to nearly nothing. Soon after, she earned a place in Hollywood history books by jumping to her death from atop the HOLLYWOOD sign.

As FOR BETTE DAVIS, despite a brilliant comeback in the 1950 classic *All About Eve*, her incipient jowls and a weight gain—not to mention the decade's preference for younger, preferably blonde, actresses—resulted in increasingly small and matronly roles. It was time to look eastward, and in 1952 she decided to star in a revue titled *Two's Company*. On stage, Davis was big box office. Strangely, the revue showcased her less obvious talents as a singer, dancer, and "comedienne," and she did not appear in most of the show's numbers. She did dominate backstage, managing to intimidate choreographer Jerome Robbins, whose accelerating temperament would impact on most of his co-workers, excepting divas like Merman and Streisand and males who bullied him back.

Possibly influenced by Lucille Ball's antics on *I Love Lucy*, Bette in one skit enacted a hillbilly with blacked-out teeth who sawed "at a bull fiddle with a crazy kind of bumpy rhythm," according to director Joshua Logan, whom Robbins flew to an out-of-town tryout in Detroit, with Davis's permission, to view and advise on the revue's eclectic numbers, which weren't jelling into a cohesive entertainment. (Bette Davis, Lucille Ball's favorite actress, was sought by Desilu in the late '50s to guest on its TV show; second choice Tallulah Bankhead did an unforgettable comic guest turn.)

To Logan's amazement, Davis didn't appear at all during the first act he sat through. When he went backstage during intermission, Robbins informed him, "She won't come on. She says her first-act scenes aren't good enough, so she just told the stage manager to cut them tonight."

Logan asked, "But doesn't she have any sympathy for the audience? That they paid to see her?"

Robbins shrugged.

The material was improved, and the commercially successful tour reached New York. However, *Two's Company* ran only ninety performances, several without its star, who claimed she wasn't well enough to appear consistently. Eventually it was announced Davis might have an infected wisdom tooth. Her producers hoped that after the tooth was extracted, she would return full time to the sell-out show. But she never came back, and *Two's Company* closed prematurely, losing most of its initial cost.

Perhaps to cover for her, it was stated that Davis had had an operation on her jaw that necessitated her leaving the show. Joshua Logan later wrote that such was not the case. When his memoirs *Movie Stars, Real People, and Me* were published in 1978, Bette Davis sued for defamation, since he portrayed her as not only volatile but capricious about her work, at least on the stage.

BETTE'S NEXT VENTURE, in 1959, comprised readings of poetry by Carl Sandburg, with her husband (and *All About Eve* costar) Gary Merrill. Although she and Merrill chose to separate during their tour—the stormy marriage involved much mutual drinking and even fisticuffs—Davis never missed a performance, with or without Merrill, who was replaced onstage by Leif Erickson.

In 1961 Bette returned to Broadway in Tennessee Williams's *The Night of the Iguana*, playing the frank and lusty Maxine, a hotel proprietor in love with Patrick O'Neal as a defrocked minister turned travel guide in Mexico (the 1964 screen version starred Richard Burton and Ava Gardner). The manic-depressive Joshua Logan raved about Bette's performance, later recalling that he immediately made plans to have his friends see her in the play. "But before I could arrange it, Bette Davis left the cast. There were rumors that she was sick again; there were other rumors that she wasn't sick at all. Whatever, Bette Davis was no longer in the cast. Cause unknown."

Several observers have said that anyone hiring Bette Davis to star in any stage venture after her erratic history in *Two's Company* and *Iguana* was begging for trouble, since her abrupt departures inevitably hurt the box office. Yet Logan, a leading stage and screen writer-director, chose to cast her—in a musical, yet—as Miss Moffat. The project was based on Davis's semi-classic 1945 film *The Corn Is Green*, but the locale was switched from Wales to the American South and Miss M.'s prize pupil, Morgan Evans, changed from a coal miner to a black field hand. The composer was Albert Hague, who'd scored the stage hits *Redhead* and *Plain and Fancy* plus the TV classic *How the Grinch Stole Christmas*. (Hague later gained fame as Mr. Shorofsky on the TV series *Fame*.)

Emlyn Williams, who'd written the semi-autobiographical *The Corn Is Green* and costarred in the play, was the lyricist and the book's coauthor with Logan. "This will either be another hit on the order of *The Sound of Music*," he predicted, "or a fiasco. Of course it could land somewhere in between, but wouldn't that be dull?"

Miss Moffat had been intended for Mary Martin, a musical star. But after her manager-husband died, she no longer felt like working. Sans songs, the stage role of the dedicated teacher had been shouldered by Sybil Thorndike, Ethel Barrymore, Eva Le Gallienne, and Blanche Yurka. Davis loved the idea of resurrecting a screen triumph during the '70s, when most of her offers were for TV movies.

"Bette didn't realize how difficult theater can be," said Williams, "and she didn't consider the musical challenges as challenges." She'd sung briefly in *What Ever Happened to Baby Jane?* (1962) and other pictures, and insisted she had an excellent singing voice. She also told Logan and Williams that if Rex Harrison could talk-sing his way through a major musical like *My Fair Lady*, so could she.

"Bette kept saying that all the circumstances were now perfect.... She was so excited," noted Williams, "and it was contagious. She said she'd been too young at thirty-six when she did *The Corn Is Green*, and now in her sixties she was just the right age," close to that of Ethel Barrymore, who'd starred in *The Corn Is Green* on Broadway.

Logan planned a forty-four-week cross-country tour, leading up to a Broadway opening for *Miss Moffat* in fall 1975. The highly strung director required constant changes and rewrites, which didn't sit well with the film-trained Davis. The songs reportedly included some gems, but the relocated plot was shaky. During rehearsals, Bette always had a script in hand, "a paper security blanket," said Logan. "It became a game with all of us to try to get it away from her."

Logan had assumed the star was nervous about carrying a musical, and some insiders whispered that the lyrics were inferior to the music. But when the director tried to assuage Bette's supposed fears about musicalizing, she "almost bit my head off."

"Nervous about music? I'm a musician! I understand everything there is to know about music! And I'm very, *very* good at it, so don't say such things." To Logan's regret, Davis decided to flat-out sing her songs rather than talk-sing them.

According to Logan, she soon started to limp, claiming that she'd pinched a nerve in her spine several months back. The doctor whom she visited at Logan's suggestion explained that spinal conditions don't show in X-rays because cartilage doesn't photograph. It would require dye to be injected into her spinal column for a milogram, a painful procedure. Looking back, Logan wrote, "I feel we should have insisted on the milogram, for as it turned out we never really found what was causing her pain."

On stage, Bette began asking other actors to exit or enter more quickly—*to camouflage her own problems?* wondered Logan. Suddenly, her doctors announced she would have to be hospitalized for three to eight weeks. When Logan and Williams visited Davis in hospital, she was asked whether she honestly wanted to continue with the show? Ever the trouper (certainly in public), she proclaimed, "Of course! I love it. I'm passionately in love with it. I must do it," but added that if they couldn't wait for her to recuperate, she'd understand.

Logan and company decided to wait for her and meanwhile to work around her. Three weeks later, she returned for rehearsals for the opening in Philadelphia, arriving on a Sunday. Logan was miffed that, "We did not hear from her until the day was over." Her lawyer showed up and said Miss Davis had slightly injured herself over the weekend. "When, where, and how?" asked Logan.

When she'd gone up to Connecticut to visit her grandson, said the lawyer. "But it was very minor, and she'll be all right tomorrow morning." The show opened a week from that morrow.

Logan later offered in his book, "We were astounded that, sick as the doctors had said she was, she would take the chance of that long automobile ride. Again we realized she was shooting with our dice."

THE SHOW OPENED, an event that drew Bette Davis fanatics from New York and farther afield. The star "got an ovation at the end of the performance that I had never heard before for anyone," recalled Emlyn Williams. "They would have gone on for an hour had she allowed them to." Her performance improved during the first week but sagged notably the second. "She was quite often difficult to hear. She repeated lines in lyrics or left them out entirely. She forgot dialogue she had never forgotten before, then giddily repeated what she had just said."

Rather famously, during one performance Davis stopped the proceedings and addressed the audience, "How can I play this scene? Morgan Evans is supposed to be onstage."

She loudly called, "Morgan Evans, get out here."

Actor Dorian Harewood had minutes to go before his entrance, but ran out onto the stage, looking to Bette Davis for a cue. She then realized her mistake and admitted, "I was wrong. I want you to know that. It wasn't his fault." The audience applauded and cheered. The diva could do no wrong. Bette, as was her wont, elaborated. "It was my own stupid fault, and Dorian had *nothing* to do with it. Go back, Morgan, and we'll start over."

The play was sometimes longer than at other times, up to seventeen minutes, due to Bette's slip-ups. During one scene, after she tripped over her lines leading up to a song, she turned sharply to one of the children onstage. The child, thinking Miss Davis needed help, whispered her line to her. The star snapped, "Don't you tell me my line! I know it! You're a naughty little boy!"

Prior to the Broadway opening, Logan, as was *his* wont, grew increasingly nervous and made further changes in the dialogue—despite almost everyone's advising him that *Miss Moffat* was sure to be a hit. One night he received an ultimatum from Bette's agent and lawyer. "I was to make no changes for a week so that she could get her mind and thoughts organized. Also, we were not allowed even to rehearse the other actors, which was unique in my experience of ultimatums."

Eight days later, Bette resumed rehearsing. Her performance improved, she forgot less material, and she enthused that she looked forward to touring all year, then playing it "at least a year in New York and a year in London," capped by making the—inevitable, she believed—film version.

But the next morning, Joshua Logan was summoned to Bette Davis's hotel suite and escorted into her bedroom, where she lay stiffly in bed. "Has the doctor phoned you?" she asked.

"Doctor? No, Bette. What doctor?"

"The doctor in New York. Hasn't he told you that I can't play it anymore?"

The upshot was, in spite of Logan and company's pleas and threats—"You can't commit this kind of professional suicide"—Davis was leaving the show. Even if she suddenly got well or improved dramatically? "I'm not coming back—ever. I can't. The doctor will tell you I can't." When Logan called the doctor to ask whether Davis was really incapable of playing *Miss Moffat*, he replied, "I wouldn't know without another exam. All I know is that when patients say they can't play a show, I'm powerless as a doctor to tell them to go up on the stage and play it."

After her abrupt departure from *The Night of the Iguana*, Bette had vowed never to work on stage again. This time she publicly insisted she was through with Broadway. "Josh reminded her that she'd lost backers hundreds of thousands of dollars and dozens of actors and crew their jobs in two prior, important productions," said Emlyn Williams. "What I wondered was why, unless Josh savored the drama and placing himself in the spotlight, he'd signed Bette to *Miss Moffat* at all. Any number of more qualified actresses of a certain age would have given their eye teeth to do the part."

Logan, in his book, would question Bette's psychology and whether she was masochistic underneath the tough façade or whether she even liked her own personality. Davis's assistant and paid best friend Vik Greenfield revealed, "She tried never to show her fear. Remember, she was a ram [Aries]—headfirst and thought about it later. But very early I said to myself, 'Bette's never going to make this—she doesn't have the stamina for it anymore.'"

Before opening, Bette confided to her diary her trepidations about the heavy exertion that would be exacted from her. Despite her public bravado, insiders said she was afraid of the show, all the more so since it was a musical. In interviews, she would go on to say the songs had been her favorite part *and* she'd done them beautifully.

Williams pointed out, "She'd really been away too long from the stage to get right back in the swim. She was so hopeful, but it was a bad fit. Two things Bette almost never blames for a failed project are herself or the material. Rarely, she'll say she was wrong for the material. More often, she'll turn to the Hollywood habit of blaming the director." (Williams had already worked with Davis on screen.)

Rather than find a new star, the stunned and appalled Joshua Logan had closed the show. In point of fact, most of its glowing notices had centered on Bette Davis; nostalgia was taking off in the 1970s. The play and its music were less warmly received, and the shift from Wales to the Deep South was not universally welcomed—some felt the concept would have worked better during the 1960s, around the time of the interracially themed film and Kate Hepburn-starrer *Guess Who's Coming to Dinner?* Yet privately, Logan opined to friends, "We were ahead of our time and our movie star was half out of her mind." In 1983 he helmed a revival of *Miss Moffat* that starred Ginger Rogers, a non-friendly rival of Davis. It played two weeks in Indianapolis, of all places, with a mostly non-Equity cast. Then it died, unmourned.

IN 1975, BETTE TOLD INTERVIEWER Rex Reed, "It was a mistake. The audiences stood up cheering and screaming every night, but I knew it wasn't what they wanted. They wanted me to be a bitch, not a middle-aged school teacher." Indeed, when she did return to the stage, as herself in her one-woman show that toured extensively and successfully, Davis played up the bitchiness that audiences had come to expect and relish. After a lengthy yet riveting series of film clips, mostly from the 1930s and '40s, Bette took the stage—her entry line, after the applause died down, was, "What a dump!"—and answered fans' questions in a bold, at times outrageously frank, manner.

In Reed's *New York Daily News* interview, Davis made no secret of her antipathy for Logan. Explaining at length why she'd left *Miss Moffat*, she overlooked her ailing back and fingered her director. Reed wrote that Bette "became enraged when she talked about" the musical and the mercurial Logan, who was furious after reading the piece. He set about refuting each point in his second volume of memoirs, the one over which Bette sued—eventually dropping her suit (as most stars do).

Although *Miss Moffat* played only fifteen performances, it was fully insured, so the half-million-dollar loss was covered. Logan was said to harbor regret over the tremendous box-office advances that had to be refunded. The musical could have been a crowning, toward-the-end-of-a-career triumph for both star and director. Josh Logan died the year before Bette, in 1988, but worked less than she did after *Moffat*. In his controversial book, Logan wrote, "I've written enough about Bette Davis. She's a book I'm trying hard to close." His memoirs ended on that same page.

Lily Moffat did have one more hurrah in store (to date), in a different medium. After offering *Miss Moffat* to Mary Martin and before offering it to Davis, Logan had sent the script to Bette's friendly and aloof rival Katharine Hepburn. She politely but firmly declined, due perhaps to the musical demands (in Kate's sole musical, *Coco*, even she felt that she sounded "like Donald Duck") or Logan's difficult reputation. Or perhaps her lack of familiarity with him. Rather, Hepburn played Miss Moffat in the 1978 telefilm *The Corn Is Green*, directed by old friend George Cukor—their tenth and final collaboration.

Set in Wales, the superior TV movie earned ample acclaim. Davis was said to bitterly regret that the producers, or even former nemesis George Cukor, hadn't approached her first about redoing "her" role. Unlike the 1945 black-and-white version, the color project was shot on location and yielded Hepburn an Emmy nomination. (Davis didn't earn an Oscar nomination for the film.)

In 1982, Emlyn Williams averred, "Bette doesn't mind the assorted actresses who played Moffat on the boards, for those are all vanished memories, unlike picture performances. Now, thanks to the mastery of Hepburn and Cukor, there are two surviving Miss Moffats, and Bette's version must stand constant comparison to Hepburn's."

What Ever Happened to Blanche Yurka?

NEOPHYTE BETTE DAVIS didn't get much chance to shine in the Blanche Yurka Company. Despite eventual assertions that in young Bette her expert eye discerned a future star, Yurka (1887–1974) was by most accounts a self-involved and self-protecting diva. (Or is that redundant?) In 1929 critic Brooks Atkinson called the Czech-born Yurka "an actress of great depth of emotion, blessed with a voice of almost eerie timbre." Like her frame and personality, Blanche's voice was Big.

The veteran stage star had made her belated movie bow in the 1935 version of *A Tale of Two Cities* starring Ronald Colman. She appeared in over twenty films, but her indelible Madame Defarge, the knitting, bloodthirsty French Revolution harridan, became her signature screen role. Yurka's very close Russian lesbian friend, the actress-producer Alla Nazimova (godmother to Nancy Reagan), had been sought for the part but was judged too petite. Five years later, Blanche would seek a role that finally went to Nazimova (whose home became the Garden of Allah hotel). It would be Alla's screen swansong, in *Escape*, one of the first Tinseltown movies to acknowledge the existence of concentration camps—but minus mention of any Jews therein. The character was a woman interned in a death camp due to anti-Nazi activism. Yurka was judged too large for that part.

"I was born too soon and of too ambitious a structure to become a picture star," allowed Yurka, whose ambition had led her during the 1920s to briefly wed a much-younger (possibly gay) actor named Ian Keith. It was printed that "Her career has always come before her private life," something seldom declared of heterosexual actresses. In time, Yurka's image as a tough dame over-shadowed her diminishing Broadway career. In 1940, she starred in *Queen of the Mob*, which she naively believed could have done for her on screen what *Little Caesar* did for Edward G. Robinson. Paramount, however, made numerous cuts and finally released it as a B movie.

While Bette Davis's star rose, the maturing Blanche's fell, although she sol-diered on, "yurking," as she put it, via occasional plays and appearances at women's clubs and colleges where she did programs of readings. In 1969 she starred Off-Broadway in *The Madwoman of Chaillot*. (Katharine Hepburn starred in a flop film version the same year.) But critics roasted the play and theatergoers mostly ignored it, so Yurka published a letter in the *Times* bidding adieu to New York audiences.

The following year she published her autobiomythography, *Bohemian Girl*. (Her parents were Bohemian.) The book disappointed many because it failed to address not only sapphic aspects of the former stage star's private life, but the per-sistent rumor that she had once killed a man and gotten away with it. "When I worked with her, I hadn't heard the rumor," explained Bette Davis. "I heard it much later. But then I kept hearing it, and it did sound plausible. Did she do it? I don't know. Was she capable? *Brother!*" (The last word indicated *yes*.)

It was unrealistic to think Blanche Yurka would discuss the matter, let alone possibly admit to murder in the pages of a book. The topic might have received posthumous book treatment, but after Yurka died in 1974 at age eighty-six even her memorable Madame DeFarge was little remembered (pre-VCR and DVD), and her once-heralded performances as a former stage great were but footprints in shifting sand.

"If she'd been younger," admitted Bette Davis, "she might have had a film career similar to mine. But she was too large for the big screen. I was outsized, but I was *young*—my timing was lucky."

All About Martina

BY CONSENSUS, THE BEST FILM ever made about the theater was the 1950 classic *All About Eve*, which earned a record number of Academy Award nominations and resuscitated Bette Davis's fallen screen career, post-Warners. What was the real story behind the movie's Machiavellian plot, and who were the women behind Eve and stage diva Margo Channing? Tallulah Bankhead often claimed *she* was Margo, and rumor had it that the Margo-Eve relationship was inspired by the bisexual Bankhead and her *Skin of Our Teeth* understudy Lizabeth Scott, whose Hollywood film career was badly damaged by a 1950s "outing."

However, Joseph L. Mankiewicz's literate and witty, albeit sexist, script was based on a short story by Mary Orr titled *The Wisdom of Eve*, published in *Cosmopolitan* magazine in 1946. In 1949 Orr adapted the story into a radio play and changed Margola Cranston's name to the more euphonius Margo Channing. In 1952, there was a one-hour radio version of the movie, with Tallulah as Margo and Mary Orr as Karen Richards (Celeste Holm in the film). There followed a stage version of *The Wisdom of Eve* by Mary Orr and her husband, which steered clear of Mankiewicz's screenplay. (He'd won two *All About Eve* Oscars, one for writing and one for directing.) A 1970 Broadway musical of the movie was titled *Applause* and starred Lauren Bacall as Margo; she was succeeded in the role by Anne Baxter, who'd played Eve in 1950. *Applause* was: "Based on the film *All About Eve* and the original story by Mary Orr."

An actress turned writer, Orr based her story on two real people: Elisabeth Bergner (*née* Ettel), a European stage and screen star better known in the UK than the US, and her twenty-four-years-younger fan Martina Lawrence, born in 1921. Like Eve Harrington, Martina married a man who served during World War II. While he was away, she treated herself on her birthday in 1944 to a performance of *The Two Mrs. Carrolls* at the Booth Theatre in New York, starring Bergner. (The 1947 film version teamed Humphrey Bogart with sapphic stars Barbara Stanwyck and Alexis Smith.)

After the show, Martina—*née* Ruth Hirsch—met the star's husband-manager, Dr. Paul Czinner, who was gay—unlike the movie's Bill Sampson, upon whom the treacherous Eve tried to work her wiles. But, then, Elisabeth Bergner was also gay, or possibly bisexual.

Martina thereafter attended the play several times. As la Bergner had no car to drive her and her partner home (he co-produced her play), Lawrence made herself useful by helping him to hail taxis. "After a month of flagging cabs . . . my reward came. One afternoon after the matinee, Miss Bergner took me home with her."

In time, Martina went to work for Czinner as his secretary. Eventually he asked Lawrence, who claimed to have memorized the leading lady's part, to read a scene with hopefuls auditioning to replace the departing actress who played the first Mrs. Carroll. After a replacement was picked, circumstances conspired to place Martina Lawrence upon the rehearsal stage where she read Bergner's lines opposite the new actress, who would make her debut the following day—while the star's husband watched from the shadows. Afterward, he warmly praised Lawrence on her talent.

That night, when the newcomer asked Martina to replay a scene with her, both Czinner and Elisabeth Bergner viewed the performances. "Several other people were around, on the stage and elsewhere," Martina said. "They were all watching Bergner. Those eyes I had felt fixed on me were hers. Only hers. I'm sure of that."

Miss Bergner was not amused. It didn't help that after Martina's performance, one stagehand yelled to another, "It's that kid that's always hanging around out front. She's just as good as Bergner, and what's more, you can hear her!" The star was known for her small, chirpy voice, and for playing younger than her years and at times overacting. George Bernard Shaw said of her in his *Saint Joan*, "Miss Bergner played Joan as if she were being burned at the stake when the curtain went up instead of when it went down."

Martina later recalled, "Imitation is the highest form of admiration, and that's all I had shown Bergner." But the impersonation threatened the star. "She was so cold! Never before had I felt such a chill. I realized at once that, knowing *the actress* Bergner quite well, Elizabeth the human being was a stranger to me."

Martina Lawrence was banished from the theater, although Bergner allowed her to continue working for her husband. "For several weeks after that terrible night, I waited in the alley [outside the theater] six days a week, before and after every show, six evening performances and two matinees, hoping she would relent and speak to me." Bergner completely ignored her talented admirer. Rather, Martina met Mary Orr, whose husband, Reginald Denham, was directing *The Two Mrs. Carrolls*, and spoke to her about her experience with the diva. Martina became Eve and Elisabeth Margola, and Lawrence's story the basis of *The Wisdom of Eve*.

In the movie classic, Eve becomes a star in New York and then goes to Hollywood. In real life, Martina went to Hollywood to become a star, having co-won an acting competition. But she didn't become a star and didn't remain an actress very long.

An anonymous friend of Lawrence's—a fellow alumna of the Rehearsal Club and an ex-Rockette—volunteered decades after, "Martina later latched on to Renata Tebaldi. I gather she also played Eve Harrington to her, except that this was the world of opera. Good luck finding out about it. . . . Divas don't like to admit they've been had."

18

A CHORUS LINE AND
MICHAEL BENNETT

Right beneath the title *A Chorus Line* comes the line "Conceived, Choreographed and Directed by Michael Bennett." Underneath this come the credits for four co-creators who also received a Pulitzer Prize for what would become Broadway's longest-running American musical: "Book by James Kirkwood and Nicholas Dante," "Music by Marvin Hamlisch," and "Lyrics by Edward Kleban."

Four of the five died prematurely. Heterosexual Marvin Hamlisch, best known for his movie scores, survives. More than most Broadway productions, *A Chorus Line*, or the men behind it, was/were affected by AIDS. (The so-called Curse of *The Boys in the Band* particularly affected cast members, and is a story and chapter in itself.)

"It's difficult to relate to the overall impact of AIDS on show business," record producer Ben Bagley once said. "That's so general, overwhelming. You get a better feel for it if you just look at *one* musical, *A Chorus Line* . . . most of its creative artists and their future contributions lost to AIDS . . . [and bear] in mind that as with Jimmy Kirkwood, AIDS as cause of death is sometimes the unofficial but real one."

Despite his sweeping billing, Michael Bennett (born Michael DiFiglia, with a Jewish mother) did not conceive *A Chorus Line*—which he co-choreographed—the show that made him a multimillionaire and a celebrity in his own right. He married *Chorus Line* performer Donna McKechnie in 1976, but they divorced soon thereafter. She later bemoaned not the end of the marriage, but of their friendship.

The record-breaking success of *A Chorus Line*, which put dancers on the map, as it were, might never have happened but for a little-noted 1973 flop titled *Rachel Lily Rosenbloom (And Don't You Ever Forget It!)*. It starred Paul Jabara, who also did the musical's book, music, and lyrics. A would-be actor who appeared in the non-hit film of *The Day of the Locust*, Jabara's most popular efforts were two Streisand disco tunes he composed. *Rachel Lily Rosenbloom* was produced by publicity-shy stage, music, and film impresario Robert Stigwood, who made John Travolta a movie star. According to actor and Broadway historian Denny Martin Flinn, "Stigwood was thought to have produced the show as something of a favor to Jabara" (who later died of AIDS).

Ron Link was hired to direct the dance- and music-intensive project, but had never directed a Broadway musical before. Denny Flinn observed, "Some of the cast came to believe he had never before *seen* a Broadway musical." Link was eventually fired by the Australian Stigwood, not known as a hands-on producer and as usual holed up in his Caribbean mansion. Director-playwright Tom Eyen, another Broadway musical virgin, was hired to replace the unmissed Link.

Eyen's solution for the looming disaster was to cut several of the dances, which mightily frustrated choreographer Tony Stevens and his assistant, Michon Peacock, as well as about a dozen dancers who'd sweated over the routines for weeks. Then Stevens was fired, in keeping with the Broadway tradition that in problem-plagued musicals choreographers are the first to get the boot—because they're the least to blame. Stevens's replacement was Grover Dale. He added a first-act finale that included a couple of singing "Dykettes" and chorus boys in vine-leaf G-strings who aimed their bare buns at audience members who were dazed or delighted, depending.

Before the show could be savaged by predictable critics, producer Stigwood shut it down. Unusually, he made up the entire loss to *Rachel's* investors from his own pocket. The investors were placated, but not the dancers and choreographers who felt, not for the first time, victimized by inept and/or uncaring directors, producers, and writers. Tony Stevens affirmed, "Most of us—the dancers in the show, the chorus people—knew more about how to put a show together than many of the producers we had worked for."

GROWING UP IN THE MIDWEST, Stevens had aimed to "go to New York, dance on Broadway, and be the Gene Kelly of my generation." In three years he danced in eight shows, then turned to choreography. Michon Peacock came to Manhattan from St. Paul, Minnesota, with similar dreams, and also danced in several non-hits. After *Rachel*, she revealed, "Tom Eyen was very degrading to dancers, and Ron Link was not much better."

A Buddhist, Peacock belonged to the "chanting sect" of Nichiren Shoshu, founded in the thirteenth century C.E. (Other members include Tina Turner, and Patrick Duffy of *Dallas*.) In her bedroom Michon chanted before a small shrine, practicing the sect's philosophy that change occurs from within. She believed it was up to dancers to change their own lot, rather than hoping for better directors and producers. She and Tony got together and talked, then spoke with other dancers, eventually conceiving of a company of dancers who would write, direct, produce, design, and, of course, choreograph their own shows. (From *Rachel*'s chorus, Carole (Kelly) Bishop, Wayne Cilento, and Thomas Walsh would become part of the cast of *A Chorus Line*.)

Peacock and Stevens realized that an influential choreographer, or director-choreographer, would help their first project along. Michael Bennett had begun as a hoofer, then excelled as a d-c. "I chanted for a couple of hours and then called him," Michon explained. "Sure enough, he wanted to see us the next day." They met and decided to "hold a talk session to find out where dancers have come from and gone to, and to create something. . . ." Little did they know.

Michon contacted Bill Thompson, a Buddhist ex-dancer and co-founder of the Nickolaus Exercise Centers. He donated the use of a dance studio. Then the trio started bringing in dancers. At midnight on Saturday, January 18, 1974, the group congregated to dance, talk, and share their experiences. First came exercise and routines. Michon, Tony, and Michael had written down 100 questions for each performer, about everything from real names and astrological signs to childhood backgrounds, life as a dancer, and experiences in New York.

People sat on the floor in a circle, not a line, and everyone spoke in turn. Various dancers had declined to participate, afraid of not being articulate enough or overexposing themselves psychologically. Some had been suspicious of Michael Bennett's involvement and motives. Michon Peacock already had cause to be wary, for she'd been professionally involved with Bennett in *Seesaw*, a 1973 musical he was brought in to revamp. Grover Dale was the original choreographer, but was demoted to working for Bennett, who brought in his close assistant Bob Avian, later the official co-choreographer of *A Chorus Line*.

Michon had been with *Seesaw* from the start, and though lucky to remain with the show, was dismayed by Bennett's firing so many dancers and by the way it was done. He delegated Dale to tap dancers on the shoulder immediately after they returned to the wings from a performance, coolly informing them, "Don't bother coming back tomorrow, you're fired." She and Michael respected but didn't necessarily like each other.

When *Seesaw* ran into financial problems despite the overhaul, Bennett told her, "There's only one thing we haven't tried yet." What, she wondered? "Chanting," he said, for he'd chanted for success, years before. So thirteen people, including *Seesaw* dancer Tommy Tune, gathered in Michon's apartment and for one hour chanted for a financial upturn in their musical. The next day, Mayor John V. Lindsay agreed to a cameo appearance on stage, in place of his "almost lookalike" Ken Howard. He consented to be mugged to music, then picked up by a dancing hooker in the opening scene. Local publicity for the casting stunt was tremendous, including front-page photos of Peacock and other female dancers playing "hooker" with the mayor in the *New York Daily News* and the *Post*. Ticket sales soared, and *Seesaw* was saved.

When he became involved with what would become *A Chorus Line*, Michael Bennett seemed open and acted friendly. Said Nicholas Dante, "He stressed that he was a hoofer, just one of the gang." But though he complimented Peacock on her leadership ability, Bennett gradually took over her and Tony Stevens's dance-themed project. He did not let on how intrigued he was by the material. After a second session with the chorus dancers, the three principals and fledgling writer Nicholas Dante met in Bennett's office. Michael announced his opinion that the material would make an interesting . . . book. Michon and Tony were astounded. They'd had their hearts set on a stage project. Bennett pointed out that he'd signed to direct a Broadway comedy starring Valerie "Rhoda" Harper—*Thieves*, by noted playwright Herb Gardner (*A Thousand Clowns*), from which he and she eventually withdrew, Harper replaced by Marlo "That Girl" Thomas.

GIVEN THE POPULARITY of the playwright and intended star, Bennett didn't want to miss out on a likely hit—*Thieves*. But he also didn't want to relinquish the embryonic project that would become *A Chorus Line*. And so the latter was shelved until the timing was right. Some insiders think he was slow to recognize the material's potential. "It was more about control, really," offered *A Chorus Line* dance captain Alex MacKay, "about getting his hands on a future endeavor which, if it took off, he'd be in total charge of.

"As a former dancer, Michael could hardly fail to find it somewhat interesting, but the passion for telling the stories about individual dancers, getting their reality out to audiences, that came entirely from Tony and Michon. . . . At one point, Michael even voiced his doubts about 'a bunch of gypsies rambling on' about themselves."

After Bennett had left the nascent dance project for *Thieves*, subsequent sessions were poorly attended. Without his presence, most dancers viewed the sessions as closer to psychotherapy than a future work opportunity. "We all tried so hard and we couldn't get past that point," lamented Michon. Thus, after Bennett departed *Thieves*—an ironic title, in view of future events—Michon and Tony met with him and virtually gave away the raw material for *A Chorus Line*. "If you give me the tapes I'll do something," Bennett offered. "I think I can get [producer] Joe Papp interested in doing a workshop. I don't know what it is, but I'll do something with it."

Tony Stevens explained, "It was ours to decide what to do with. . . . We all decided it was better that it had a life. He had the power and the resources, and we did not." The trio making the decision comprised Peacock, Stevens, and Nicholas Dante, the writer who'd been required to type and shape the material; he became the official number two writer after the better-known James Kirkwood was brought aboard. After the three got back to Bennett, he had each sign a brief contract giving him control of all the material. In return, they got one dollar apiece, which was all Michon Peacock and Tony Stevens ever derived from their brainchild.

Tony later said of the highly personal stories, "There was a fear that [the material] would be misused. More than losing a million dollars or whatever, which never really entered our minds at that time, we were afraid somebody was going to get used or hurt. More than anything else, we didn't want that to happen." Michon noted in retrospect, "I think now that Michael knew all along that it was going to be a musical."

The sessions and interviews, with Bennett in full charge and Dante in attendance, continued. The latter typed and did menial work. Formerly a dancer, he'd told about his dramatic and demeaning drag-show years at the first meeting. (As Dante didn't appear in *A Chorus Line*, his story was reassigned to the character Paul San Marco.) "The major reason Michael asked me to write the show was he needed my story and knew he wouldn't get it otherwise." The story, which shocked the other dancers, would be an emotional highpoint of the future musical.

Dante was hired with the proviso that other, more professional writers could be brought in. "For a while," he confessed, "I felt like the little fag dancer that tagged along." Because he was more open about his sexuality, Dante was occasionally the butt of "fag" jokes from Bennett, who was more guarded and coy about his own orientation.

SHREWDLY, MICHAEL took the *Chorus Line* material to Joseph Papp rather than to a commercial Broadway producer. The latter would have demanded high-concept, fiscally promising material that Bennett wasn't all that sure he had. In commercial theater there's success or failure. "Michael was not clairvoyant," said James Kirkwood. "This was very iffy, untried, experimentative material. It could easily have flopped on Broadway, and an uptown flop would have lowered Michael's standing. Like it or not, your artistic standing is tied to your commercial standing."

Via Papp and the Shakespeare Festival, Bennett would be working with a net, could exercise greater control, brook less interference and, if *A Chorus Line* did fail with audiences, chalk it up as a noble, avant-garde experiment. If it did well, it would move on and upward.

To further cover himself, Bennett hired Marvin Hamlisch, recent winner of three Oscars for *The Way We Were* and *The Sting*, to compose the score. An ex-rehearsal pianist for Broadway musicals, Marvin had worked with Michael on *Henry, Sweet Henry*, a 1967 musical derived from the nonmusical 1964 movie *The World of Henry Orient*. *A Chorus Line* would be Hamlich's first Broadway score.

As for the cast, Bennett didn't feel obligated to retain the original dancers. He asked the group to sign legal releases allowing him to use their recorded material and to quote whatever (and however) he wished. Each dancer signed, each received one dollar. When it came time to cast, all the original dancers had to audition—some for the chance to play themselves. Nor were the originals more likely to receive an individual song than a newcomer. The first song written was "Sing!" for Renee Baughman, a Nichiren Buddhist who'd chanted to get her own song.

Original cocreator Tony Stevens was going to appear in *A Chorus Line* as a dancer-actor, but was unexpectedly asked by Bob Fosse to assist him on *Chicago*, which seemed a much more surefire hit. So Tony chose to be the celebrated Fosse's real-life assistant rather than play an assistant to the character Zach. Far from being upset over the defection, Michael Bennett encouraged Tony to strike out. Was it to encourage him to pursue his dream or to be rid of a possibly proprietary (though not legally) originating influence? Denny Martin Flinn, who played Zach and Greg in the international touring company of *A Chorus Line* between 1980 and '82, revealed that Bennett had initially been "gracious" to Tony and Michon, as they had brought the idea and material to him—in return for which each had been paid a token dollar. But once Tony departed, Flinn said, "If Michael felt any twinge of guilt . . . there were no longer any reminders." Michon Peacock had already joined the *Chicago* company.

Michael and his team got on with the business of fashioning *A Chorus Line*, which debuted before a paying audience at the New York Shakespeare Festival on April 14, 1975. In May came the official Off-Broadway opening. Rave reviews ensued, with *The Village Voice* calling it "possibly the most effective Broadway musical since *Gypsy*. . . . *A Chorus Line* is the best commercial musical in years." The paper ironically noted "Bennett's devotion to the myth of Broadway. . . ." In July, *A Chorus Line* opened on Broadway. The rest is theater history, as it went on to become Broadway's longest-running musical until *Cats* superceded it.

Michon Peacock, who with Tony Stevens conceived and launched the idea and material that became *A Chorus Line*, was not only neither devastated nor embittered, but buoyantly philosophical: "To have been able to have been in the right place at the right time to be the instrument for the cause for the whole thing to get moving" was, she believed, "wonderful." For it was a show not just about dancing, but about dancers. Tony was similarly proud to have been involved from the start. "I'm glad for them they're not enraged," reflected Ben Bagley. "I'd have to struggle, really struggle, to have and maintain such a Zen-like calmness and balance."

MANY OF THOSE WHO REMAINED with *A Chorus Line*, although delighted by its reception, grew disenchanted as it became known as Michael Bennett's show. And as it became his golden egg. Once the touring companies opened, he was earning $75,000 a week, not including subsidiary rights. Initially he'd made sounds about sharing the wealth with the company—there seemed to be more than enough for everybody. But when dancers' salaries didn't keep pace with the success of the musical, Bennett backed off the subject or avoided them. The book *What They Did for Love*, by Denny Martin Flinn, told of another performer who "went through [a legal/emotional] ordeal, but the promise of more money was never kept . . . Michael's position was, 'You should have got it in writing.'" Donna McKechnie "did not complain about the experience and has no bitter feelings, [but] from then on she decided to do business only through her agents."

Further resentment occurred when some of the roles grew larger than others as Bennett continued refashioning the material. His sense of showmanship told him some characters had to be "stars," others support. The show's success, of course, gave him greater control over its individual components, and the cast was increasingly dealt with in a heavy-handed, nakedly greedy manner. For instance, out of the blue, a producers' representative called the seventeen cast members together so that each could sign a release for the logo. On signing, each was presented with a balloon with the logo across it: the seventeen dancers in a line. One week later—news to the seventeen—Bloomingdale's debuted towels and other objects displaying the increasingly famous logo featuring the seventeen performers.

The dancers were stunned by the deception and the fact that despite the use of their likenesses, they had no financial participation. Of course because there were seventeen of them, most any one of them was expendable. When several of them said, "We're getting a lawyer," the response of Bennett and management was, "Go ahead, get a lawyer."

The show turned out to be the thing: in spite of its mega-success, *A Chorus Line* did not produce a single bona fide star. (The biggest celebrity it yielded was Michael Bennett.) Today, only a theater buff could name any of the original cast members, most of whom went on to far-lower-profile assignments post–*A Chorus Line*. Only two performers, McKechnie and Priscilla Lopez, achieved a considerable if brief measure of stardom. Though unusual for such a huge hit, the relative anonymity of the cast (on Broadway and in all the show's touring and foreign versions) ties in with the fact that chorus lines are almost invariably just a backdrop for a star—for instance Lauren Bacall in *Applause* or Carol Channing in *Hello, Dolly!* *They* are the many, *she*—it's usually a female star—is the "One" celebrated in *A Chorus Line*'s climactic song of the same name.

A Chorus Line's most famous and popular song was "What I Did for Love." Fittingly, for most dancers, few of whom get a chance at fame (exceptions include Shirley MacLaine and George Chakiris, with males more seldom crossing over), do what they do for love. For love of dance, not for love of money.

Former dancer Michael Bennett's relative camaraderie with fellow hoofers faded with *A Chorus Line*'s success. As it kept burgeoning, he became increasingly territorial. And dictatorial. "The show made him a big-time Broadway player," said Ben Bagley, "and the next step was to become the new Jerome Robbins." He grew impatient with opposition. Example: A photo session with Richard Avedon shooting the cast was planned, but the dancers were given less than the twenty-four-hour notice the union required. Equity deputy Priscilla Lopez informed her colleagues that they did not have to participate if they didn't wish to. Bennett arrived, yanked Priscilla out of the room, and when they returned, he, according to *What They Did for Love*, "lectured the company severely, threatening each of them with the consequences if they didn't appear in the photo shoot."

A year into the show's success, one dancer anonymously revealed, "We all feel like we made the show a success. Or that we helped, individually or collectively. But once it was such a big success, now everyone wants a part of it . . . wants *in*. And those of us who are in gotta watch our step, or we'll be *out*."

The dancers in *A Chorus Line* earned good money at the time, some $650 a week each, more than they'd earned as chorus members in the past. But Bennett was earning dozens of thousands a week, his wages and take continually escalating. The same anonymous dancer disclosed, "He's grown less accessible, no question about it. Conversations? Over. He might lecture or admonish. Socializing or being playful, friendly? It's *Mr.* Bennett now, not Michael. Sometimes he looks pained if you call him Michael."

A CHORUS LINE WAS AFFORDING new opportunities to Bennett, among them that fiscal Valhalla, Hollywood. Yet he had little patience with the show's performers trying to better their own circumstances. When permission was sought to use a photo that would adorn the cover of an André Kostelanetz album—one side of it music from *A Chorus Line*, the other from *Chicago*—each cast member was offered $50. As it had the potential to become a hit album, the $50 was rejected; the performers got together and decided to ask $500 apiece. The offer was withdrawn. According to two cast members, Bennett was contemptuous of both the group's request and their failure to get it fulfilled.

A Chorus Line enriched Hamlisch, Kirkwood, Dante, Kleban, and Bob Avian, but especially Michael Bennett. Hollywood smelled loot and became interested. Who could have guessed it would take ten years to make a flop movie of the smash-hit musical that producer Stuart Ostrow deemed "the first landmark musical since *Hair* in 1968, and possibly the last of the twentieth century"?

Even though Hollywood's attention flattered him, Bennett felt uncomfortable there, in part because it was more homophobic than the stage. Some insiders said after he legally wed he came to realize his sexuality was immutable and that he'd compromised himself in his bid for social and professional acceptance. "Drugs got ahold of Michael, same as with many, maybe most of the *Chorus Line* cast," added James Kirkwood. "That may have played a part in his feeling very disoriented in LA." In any case, Bennett got out of his film deal and returned to the theater.

Tony Stevens eventually danced in Chita Rivera's nightclub act, as did three other *Chorus Line* cast members. Dancing is a profession with a limited shelf life, and many of the show's performers later went into choreography or left the business. Michon Peacock went to work for the New York chapter of Nichiren Shoshu of America. (Another female dancer became a district leader in the organization's Los Angeles headquarters.) Donna McKechnie moved to California but experienced a crippling bout of arthritis, for a while unable to walk. Since recovering, she works consistently onstage, regionally, doing cabaret, etc. Post–*Chorus Line*, Michael Bennett had a relative Broadway failure with *Ballroom*, featuring dancing and an older crowd; it played for 116 performances and received multiple Tony nominations.

He reclaimed success with *Dreamgirls*, based on a Supremes-like black girl group. His next big hope, *Scandal*, was canceled after several workshops due to assorted problems, including sexual subject matter viewed as salacious by some during the Reagan '80s. Ill health caused him to drop out of plans to direct the world premiere of *Chess* in London. Michael moved to Tucson, Arizona, to live out the final year of his life. On July 2, 1987, at age forty-four, he died of AIDS, leaving behind millions of dollars to fight the disease.

Looking back, Michael had informed an interviewer, "I thought I was ready for success. No one is." Insiders said he felt he'd given up too much to become a success, including friendships and some measure of personal and professional integrity. Performer Alex MacKay believed, "In the end, he regretted, I think, the loss of casual intimacy with the extended family of gypsies. With the theatre gang, his success brought him pressure and loneliness."

Performer Denny Martin Flinn reflected two years after Bennett's death, "Only on his own terms could he be generous and supportive. He had desperate, unsatisfied needs to be loved and liked, yet he was incapable of asking for help, or love, and mistrusted those who offered it freely."

James Kirkwood, who died in 1989, felt, "Illness and perspective had their impact on Michael. I think if he could have come back from Arizona, come back to New York, he would have been a better person. I don't think, initially, he quite believed that you can be creative and happy at the same time." Nick Dante concluded, "Michael Bennett bought into the showbiz myth that being an ogre is part of being respected or a successful boss type. He learned too late that it's simply a personality trait, more accurately a deficiency, that does nobody much good in the long run."

Michael Bennett

"He showed us deep truths about ourselves. He made us more aware of *being alive*, to use the words of one of his great collaborators [Sondheim]. The Greeks, I think, call this a catharsis. Michael called it a Broadway musical."—FRANK DiFILIA on his late brother, choreographer-director Michael Bennett

"I never got paid for [additional dialogue for] *A Chorus Line* . . . The only thing that Michael sent me, which was a very weird gift, was a pair of satin pillow cases. . . . But then I remember asking Michael Bennett to help me on a play that I was doing. And he charged me!"—NEIL SIMON

"Michael wanted red costumes for the finale [of *A Chorus Line*]. He had just opened *Follies*, which had a huge red number. Well, I thought red would be a big fiasco."—costume designer THEONI V. ALDREDGE (who went golden)

"Michael was dangerously attracted to flash and big hands, which is not always a good idea. . . . He always wanted to do shows that had some kind of show business reference, and that, I think, was why we never did another one [after *Follies*] together. I would occasionally discuss an idea with him, and he would immediately think of it in a showbiz framework. He was a little too much into showbiz."—STEPHEN SONDHEIM

"I asked for a meeting with Michael. I said, 'I'm not somebody you can just discard like this. I have to find out what the problem is.' But he would not see me. . . . Then the management sued me, because they didn't want to pay me a run-of-the-play salary. . . . There was eventually a settlement . . . I couldn't get a job because of the reputation the firing had given me. It took me years to build my courage, my confidence, and my reputation.

"Years later . . . I ran into Michael when he was drunk and stoned at a disco in New York. He said, 'Lainie, I'm so happy to see you're doing so well' . . . That was the last time I ever saw him . . . I have great respect for his talent. But I didn't respect the way he handled people. . . . He hurt me very much."—LAINIE KAZAN, who was replaced by Michele Lee in *Seesaw* (1973)

"The most incredible moment was on the first day of rehearsal for the [*A Chorus Line*] Gala when Michael did the Cassie dance. It was magic. Seeing him dance the number, you realized that although it was designed for Donna McKechnie's body, there was a lot of Michael Bennett in it. He did it the best."—RICHARD BERG, *A Chorus Line*'s assistant general manager

"What will the critics say about a show about sex whose director is dying of AIDS? Why would anyone want to see a show about sex when its director is dying of AIDS? . . . [But] Michael said to . . . me mid-workshop, 'When my obituary is written, instead of saying 'Michael *A Chorus Line* Bennett,' it will say 'Michael *Scandal* Bennett.' He was so proud of his work on it."—TREVA SILVERMAN, writer of the never-produced *Scandal*

"After Michael Bennett died, it turned out that he left the biggest bequest so far to AIDS . . . some $7 million. Well, first, he'd never have donated anything like that while he was alive, and second, he could well afford it. He totaled up with 25 percent of the show's profits via his Plum Productions; that came to roughly $12.5 million, on top of which his estate was estimated at $25 million. Still and all, I commend him for doing the right thing, which is more than most of the Tinseltown set who die from AIDS ever do."—writer and AIDS activist VITO RUSSO

"Michael Bennett's name is so linked with *A Chorus Line* and, to a far lesser degree, with other musicals. You remember him as a director, and a man who was very ambitious and at times went too far. Especially after *A Chorus Line* happened and changed him, even warped him. But I think it's key to remember that first and foremost he was a dancer, and his first and his last love was the dance."—GREG SIMS, of the Australian cast of *A Chorus Line*

"No matter how much we hated him, we'll always love him."—PAMELA BLAIR, original cast member of *A Chorus Line*

"Michael Bennett may have been the last Broadway genius for musicals. Who knows? Tommy Tune remains—but does he have genius? Is Andrew Lloyd Webber a genius? Is it dying out in America? . . . Will there be a woman genius? Are the gay ones all going to die before 50? What's happening? What does the future hold? Should we be hopeful? But what else can we be?"—MICHAEL JETER (in 1997), who co-starred in Tune's *Grand Hotel* and died of AIDS in 2003 at 52

19

LEGENDS!

James Kirkwood is probably best known as the co-creator of *A Chorus Line* (1975). Solo, he wrote such cult novels as *There Must Be a Pony* and *Some Kind of Hero*, and plays like *P.S. Your Cat Is Dead!* and *Legends!*—which became a legendary debacle starring Mary Martin and Carol Channing. Despite its star power it never got to Broadway but inspired a fabled memoir, *Diary of a Mad Playwright*.

Like many playwrights, Kirkwood began as an actor. But then, his parents were silent-screen stars Lila Lee and James Kirkwood Sr. Jimmy's unstable childhood—he attended eighteen high schools—and his mother's emotional ups and downs were fodder for *There Must Be a Pony*, whose title derived from a parable about a terminally optimistic boy shoveling through a roomful of manure because underneath it all he believes "There must be a pony."

In the 1950s Kirkwood costarred in *Valiant Lady*, Tallulah Bankhead's favorite soap opera. His entrée into New York theatrical circles occurred after he auditioned for a minor Bankhead play, *Welcome, Darlings*, but wound up instead as the aging diva's caddy. Although he successfully segued into writing he didn't abandon acting, and later had small parts in *Mommie Dearest*, *Oh, God, Book II*, and other films. "I did the Hollywood bit, but never got many jobs out there. Just not forbidding enough, I guess." Kirkwood performed in clubs and on Broadway with partner Lee Goodman, and did summer stock. "I love performing, putting on masks," he said in 1986 during the *Legends!* tour, three years before his death.

Kirkwood's path crossed that of *A Chorus Line* collaborator Michael Bennett in 1974, while he was working on a play of his novel *P.S. Your Cat Is Dead!*, which the closeted Bennett found "too daring" for his taste. (It involved a bisexual cat burglar.) The reaction irked Kirkwood, but they worked together, mostly smoothly, on *A Chorus Line*, which opened on Broadway a month after *P.S.* The latter closed after sixteen performances; the former broke records and made the writer a millionaire.

"Tallulah really encouraged me to write," Kirkwood recalled, "and when I did, it gave me such a release. . . . Such creativity . . . as an actor you cannot create alone."

Legends! was intended as Kirkwood's solo entry into the Broadway bigtime. In view of its diva quotient, gay-audience appeal, and general theatergoers' desire to ogle faded-but-once-major stars in the flesh, *Legends!* could have run for years, with a succession of senior actresses eventually replacing Mary Martin and Carol Channing in the same way—but twice over—that Channing had been succeeded in *Hello, Dolly!* by a parade that included Ginger Rogers, Ethel Merman, Pearl Bailey and, of course, Mary Martin and Carol Channing (who returned to the role, and then kept returning).

However, the *Legends!* production seemed almost cursed. The backstage intrigue, back-stabbing, and plain bad luck far surpassed that of the average Broadway show-in-the-making. There were clashes with producers, one of whom regularly threw his considerable overweight around. Another producer died, still another had AIDS. At one point *Legends!* was sans a director. It was constantly being rewritten, including by its stars, who couldn't abide the performance of a supporting player (Roxie Roker of TV's *The Jeffersons*), who enjoyed the staunch backing of a particular producer.

Most reviews were poor to dreadful, often pitting one star against the other. Channing and Martin were already quite competitive, Mary less openly so. Carol's husband-manager was usually pushy and meddlesome, frequently clashing with Kirkwood and the producers. At seventy-three Mary Martin tended to tire easily and, worse, couldn't always remember her lines. As during the second act of a performance in Dallas, where *Legends!* broke the box-office record for the Majestic Theatre. Kirkwood explained that Mary's "ear bug cut out and she was not able to get her lines from Keith. I cannot describe what a muddle ensued."

In the second act, Martin would say lines from the first act, while Channing, wild-eyed, attempted to get the show back on track. Mary, typically averse to derogatory lines, would sometimes utter the start of one insult and complete it with the end of another, so that it didn't make sense, fracturing the play and frustrating the "mad playwright."

Why, at her age, would Mary Martin take on a dialogue-heavy nonmusical play totally dominated by two active, highly competitive diva characters?

Several factors played a part. Mary was getting few offers, let alone for large parts. Her singing voice and the energy required for a musical were much diminished, but she wanted to take advantage of the reflected limelight from her son, Larry *Dallas* Hagman (via her first, heterosexual husband), and her friend and former supporting actress, First Lady Nancy Reagan. *Legends!*, as Martin must have realized, was perhaps her last chance at a big stage vehicle. She loved the title, and in interviews would coyly allow, "Well, yes, I guess we *are* legends." Jimmy had tailored it for two real-life divas, later noting, "Female stars eventually love to play icons."

CAROL'S REACTION to Mary's trouble retaining dialogue was mixed. She would wonder aloud what was happening to her dear costar, then privately urge Kirkwood and the producers, "Can't we try and get Julie Andrews?" to replace her. (Channing had supported Andrews in the 1967 hit movie *Thoroughly Modern Millie*, for which Channing garnered an Oscar nomination and which became the revamped 2002 Tony-winning Best Musical.) Carol got in the habit of correcting Mary onstage in front of the audience, which Martin resented but complained about privately to Kirkwood, not to Channing, whose spouse-manager Charles Lowe served as her buffer and official complainant.

The contractual pair were both devoted to Carol's stardom. Her sole child, a son named Channing, was via a prior husband. Lowe was once asked, "Do you ever sleep with Carol?" He replied, "Why? Would it be good for her career?" In front of others, he invariably called her Miss Channing. In 1998, after over four decades of matrimony, the professional pair moved to divorce. Channing then publicly reported that they'd only ever slept together two times.

The disingenuous Carol informed Jimmy Kirkwood that she'd told her costar that a backstage visitor had said he'd had to view *Legends!* twice because he couldn't hear most of Mary's lines, and added the "pace was so slow." Kirkwood asked why on Earth Carol had told Mary that.

"Well, it was the truth, that's what he said."

"I know, but you know Mary—you didn't have to tell her that."

"Yes, I did. What would you want me to do—lie?" she said, her eyes no doubt as big as saucers. (Channing wore mink eyelashes and habitually streaked red lipstick across her nose to give the impression, from a distance, that it was upturned.)

On another occasion, the tall and often overpowering Channing apprised Jimmy that she'd visited Martin's dressing room and informed her that Kirkwood said Carol terrified her. Channing said Martin denied her fear of her costar, though Martin supposedly seemed "rattled." Jimmy was aghast, and told Channing of course Mary would be afraid of her. "But I went right in and told her," affirmed the second-billed star.

Martin increasingly felt she was being railroaded by the younger, taller, louder, very be-husbanded Channing. (Mary's second husband, who'd been gay and was *her* manager, was deceased.) The image-conscious Martin also objected to the more risqué lines and situations in *Legends!* She'd had to be persuaded to agree to do a speech revealing that her character had undergone a mastectomy. Mary would arbitrarily decide not to utter a line she felt compromised her G-rated image. One night during a performance, she skipped her final line to an exiting cop whom both divas were supposed to insult.

For months, Martin had been telling the policeman character, "And when your next child is born and people ask if it's a boy or a girl, I hope you have to hesitate about an hour before answering."

When Kirkwood reminded her later that night at a party that she'd forgotten the line, she said she hadn't. Rather, she wouldn't be saying the line anymore. Jimmy said the line had always earned a hearty laugh. Mary believed that the audience hated the line because it meant she was hoping the policeman's wife gave birth to a two-headed child.

Kirkwood assured her it didn't mean that. The line's gender ambiguity had completely escaped her. Regardless, Mary Martin concluded that whatever it meant, she would no longer say it, and Kirkwood had the choice of either writing a new line for her or else she would skip it "and let my last line to him be the one before that."

By THE TIME *LEGENDS!* HIT Chicago's Shubert Theatre in October 1986, Charles Lowe was openly at war with the weighty producer, who was also prone to change Kirkwood's dialogue. Although business in the bigger cities was fine to excellent due to fans of Mary, Carol, and camp—which their pairing certainly was—Martin was increasingly restive and tired. When she expressed her intention to leave the show pre-Broadway, James Kirkwood was amazed and angered, though of course he had to treat the Broadway veteran with kid gloves.

Mary was no doubt wary of her Broadway swansong being in a critically reviled effort—fluff that probably wouldn't have had a chance minus two Names—which she had to share with another (overbearing, faster-tongued, and faster-moving) woman. Besides, Mary's health was on the decline, though details were kept strictly confidential.

For decades, Martin's stage shows had been vehicles, and she likely didn't wish her final one to be half a vehicle which her hammy costar-rival was apt to easily steal. "In her way, Mary was two-faced," said record and revue producer Ben Bagley, who dealt with but didn't work with her. "That is, if she didn't like something, either she'd smile or avoid it. If she hated it, she'd send a third party to tell the authority in charge. She was stubborn. You could not push her around. Yet she hated confrontations and always wanted to seem Miss Congeniality."

Charles Lowe eventually also got in the habit, after a Mary Martin memory crisis, of urging, "Get Julie Andrews," who almost certainly would not have been available. Mary must have heard about Carol and Charles's repeated treacherous comment, which may have been the last straw. "Mary wasn't used to sharing a show," stated *Legends!* director Lindsay Anderson, "and I don't think she'd ever had to compete so hard in a show, on the stage and off."

A friend of Jimmy's connected with *Sugar Babies* had spoken with its leading lady, Ann Miller, who'd caught *Legends!* in Los Angeles. She loved the play and was eager to costar with Carol. "The only thing wrong was Mary. I know the character of Leatrice should be sweet, but only up to a point. What you need up on that stage is two cunts, and with me and Carol you'd have a couple."

When Kirkwood contacted Miller, she alluded to Mary Martin's failing memory, then pointed out that she and Channing had worked together on a *Love Boat* episode and "got along just fine. Now, I know she's not all *that* easy to work with. Carol swallowed up little Mary on that stage, but I'll tell you something right now—Carol's not going to swallow up little Annie."

She added, "If I play Leatrice, you gotta write me a few more bitchy lines, because I can say 'em!" Miller was ready to hop on the next plane and commence rehearsing.

Meanwhile, with Mary ready to fly the coop, Carol became more vocal about her belief that nobody had wanted her for *Legends!* in the first place. She may have been hurt by what she perceived as greater respect for a woman generally considered more of a talent, and more of a legend, than she. Part of the extra deference had to do with Martin's age and her more ladylike, at times aloof demeanor. Ben Bagley opined, "Carol was deep down rather honored to be working with Mary Martin. And remember, Mary made Carol look younger than she was." The Martin replacement, if there was one, wouldn't likely be as old as Mary and would probably be more openly competitive and feisty.

Jimmy Kirkwood was cautiously hopeful when he entered Carol's dressing room—she was "putting on her clown makeup, which was enough to paint a wall with"—in order to mention Ann Miller's name as a possible replacement for Mary. "Carol, who had just finished slashing that red streak across her nose, laughed and said, 'Oh, I like Ann, but really—she's a joke.'

"I barely held off an instant of anger and cracking, 'Turn around and check your mirror, sweetheart!,'" said Kirkwood.

Channing, also long unused to sharing a stage, was more ambitious than her ditzy image would suggest. When she'd lost the movie version of *Hello,*

Dolly! to Barbra Streisand—who campaigned for the part along with her female agent, later declaring she'd been *offered* the role, *quelle surprise*—it was the second public super-blow of Channing's stage career, for in the '50s she had lost the film of *Gentlemen Prefer Blondes*, the show that made her a star, to Marilyn Monroe. Though she seemed to take the loss with a grinning grain of salt, years later on TV, she announced, "I've enjoyed wonderful health. The only time I got sick was when I watched Barbra Streisand in *Hello, Dolly!* on an airplane."

"AT THE OUTSET, I think [Martin and Channing] hoped to be chums," said Lindsay Anderson. "Sort of 'us old broads against the world.' It wasn't destined to last. It's too situationally difficult for stars of the same gender to work together and be friends." But if the thrill of working together in the much-publicized, eagerly anticipated play wore off quickly, its stars were loath to publicly indicate they were anything but dear chums. Ironically, *Legends!* was loosely based on the Davis-Crawford feud in *What Ever Happened to Baby Jane?* The two aging stage stars had probably hoped *Legends!* would do for their careers what *Baby Jane* had done for the faded celluloid superstars.

Kirkwood admitted his play was about "two feuding actresses, legends in their time, who were somewhat over the hill, down at heels, [and] had made one film together that was a box-office hit but represented personal hell during the making." *Legends!* became somewhat of a personal hell for its stars as well as many involved. When one producer finally made up with Kirkwood and proclaimed, "Well, we had quite a good year out of it, didn't we?" the playwright thought:

"*Good*? No director, a star who couldn't remember her name, one producer dead [the renowned Cheryl Crawford], another down with AIDS, robbed in Portland, all manner of feuds, a stack of dreadful reviews. 'Yes,' I finally said, 'a really great year. One more like this and I quit!'"

Not unlike the Davis-Crawford feud, this one featured two veteran contenders. As always, there would be one victor—in both cases, the younger one. Like Davis, Channing had more stamina as well as greater chutzpah, due partly to not being tied to a perpetually ladylike image. Martin was used to occasional catty or ignorant remarks, like one Palm Beach socialite's praise (which Mary did not overhear) about how wonderful of the Broadway legend to be touring the country "at practically eighty." Such comments, in person or in print, were and are part of the territory for an older working actress. Same for Carol Channing, who toured in *Hello, Dolly!* for the last time in her seventies—it was widely known as "the death tour."

But Martin was alarmed as well as hurt by the "playful" Channing's comments, even in front of the media. At the end of their opening run in Dallas

(Martin was from Texas), prior to playing LA, the city honored Carol Channing, who was immediately asked where her costar was? The *New York Post*'s Page Six column chortled, "Quicker than you could say 'putdown,' she quipped, 'She is in her hotel room learning her lines.' As Carol stoked the fires, a spokesman for the show hastened to assure one and all, 'Miss Martin has been word-perfect from Day One.'"

Carol reportedly resented that unlike Mary Martin she had to hide her blondeness (actually a blonde wig) onstage beneath a dark wig. Martin's blonde hair was via peroxide. Though eight years younger than Mary, Channing was playing her contemporary. Martin was, of course, more sensitive about the numerous age jokes, and used her clout to veto more lines than Carol did. America's Broadway Sweetheart would have been very uncomfortable saying a Channing line like, "And Ethel Merman opened her purse and said, 'Well, babe, here's five bucks—go fuck yourself!'" (The punchline to an apocryphal story about Loretta Young, who kept a swear box on her movie sets to collect coins each time somebody used foul language.)

After Carol's public crack in Dallas, Mary toughened up. Kirkwood related, "She was suddenly acting quite the queen. She no longer wanted to lose lines to Carol; she wanted to think about changing the final curtain," etc. "She no longer had the little-girl-lost look or the 'I'll do anything anyone wants' attitude." She simply started decreeing what she would and especially what she wouldn't do or say. Kirkwood believed it was Mary's way of getting back at Carol, even though it was directed at him and the management. When Mary began taking her time doing bits of stage business, Carol grew incensed, but at Jimmy, not Mary. When he tried to be neutral, it often backfired. At one point Channing "gave me a look that would have frozen Joan Crawford" before rehearsals could resume. "If I didn't automatically side with one lady, she made it clear—not so much in words—that I was siding with her rival."

The house of cards inevitably collapsed. Jimmy's pal James Leo Herlihy (author of *Midnight Cowboy*) noted, "Mary Martin wasn't about to limp into New York, her town of habitual triumph, with Carol Channing in the ascendant. She'd sooner take down the whole ship with her, and that's what she did." The fact that she was able to was due to Channing's illogical ultimatum that if Mary went, she went too. Official *Legends!* photographer Kenn Duncan theorized, "Carol liked working with Mary, to the extent that she could sometimes almost get away with murder. Carol's a lot funnier than Mary, and *Legends!* is nothing if not a comedy, at times a farce.

"Mary also brought prestige to the project. . . . With Mary out, Carol would have had to work harder to sparkle. . . . Then there was the question of billing. If Martin left, Carol would not be willing to take second billing to any-one"—except to an unavailable movie star like Julie Andrews.

"ULTIMATELY, *LEGENDS!* WAS ABOUT EGO," said Herlihy. "The practical lesson it taught is: Don't hire someone too old to retain her lines and too willing to use her age as an excuse to get out of the deal. Oh, and don't hire someone too prudish to play along with the writer and her costar."

Mary Martin's departure, Jimmy Kirkwood unofficially admitted, was a relief. A younger actress was called for, and he was still hopeful. But when Carol Channing soon jumped ship as well, he penned a singular letter to the departed divas (reproduced in its entirety in the 1989 *Diary of a Mad Playwright*). Dated November 16, 1986, and addressed to "Dear Mary and Carol and Carol and Mary," it read in part:

"I've known some dummies in my life but you are two of the dumbest white women I've ever encountered. Talented and dear and both a bit crazy in your own very different special ways, but dumb as cat shit.

". . . here you've been breaking your kishkas, to say nothing of your balls, whipping this play and your performances together over one helluva long, torturous, painstaking year. . . . So—now what happens? Well, Mary's tired and doesn't want to come to New York and Carol wouldn't think of doing the play without Mary." He emphasized how audiences ate the play up and how it would sell out during its limited Broadway run—"The show would even pay back. . . . But apparently that isn't important.

"Mary can go back to Rancho Mirage (a retirement community near Palm Springs, aka Death's Waiting Room) and get in the pool and Carol can do *Hello, Dolly!* in Fargo, North Dakota. . . ." He ended with "cc: to almost everyone involved."

Kirkwood returned to his house in Key West. He never received a reply or acknowledgment from Mary, while Charles Lowe telephoned to say Carol and he thought it one of the most hilarious letters they'd ever gotten. "You son of a bitch, how did you know Carol always wanted to play Fargo, North Dakota?" However, Channing would not return to the show or consider a Broadway stint. Not without the humor-free Mary.

Due to management and the media's extreme tact, Martin's defection was not revealed as due to failing memory and ego conflict. Rather, it wound up reflecting poorly on Kirkwood's play, which Carol Channing rejected because she didn't want to be seen as less picky than Mary, or willing to keep touring in Mary's reject with a replacement star.

Legends! closed in January 1987. A year and a half later, James Kirkwood confessed, "I have not spoken to or seen Mary, Carol, or Charles since. I sent them Christmas cards this year, and I received one from Carol and Charles, but no word from Mary." Co-producer Bob Regester died of AIDS in the fall of 1987. Mary Martin, born in 1913, died in 1990 of cancer, a year after

Kirkwood died at age sixty-four, officially also of cancer, although several sources have attributed his death to AIDS.

Lindsay Anderson, one of *Legends!* directors, called it "Jimmy's smashed triumph . . . his last hurrah." The Briton felt it should have opened on Broadway, but the producers and corporate backers saw a chance to rake in big bucks on the road on the strength of Martin's and Channing's names. "So Jimmy and company, in his tour de force, were forced to tour. The two stars had no objections, thanks to their highly remunerative financial arrangements."

Ben Bagley noted, "Kirkwood was, by Broadway standards, a nice guy. Had a spine, but likeable. In the end, though, the two women walked all over him . . . they broke his heart over *Legends!* He was losing weight during the whole ordeal. I think *Legends!* literally helped kill him—that whole sordid experience. Which could have been worth it had it all ended up on Broadway, covered in glory, as originally planned. A Broadway hit makes most anything worthwhile, as most any playwright or diva would agree."

P.S. In 2006, it was announced that *Legends!* would be revived as a vehicle for dueling *Dynasty* divas Joan Collins and Linda Evans. James Kirkwood had told this writer, "As long as there are ambitious, glamorous older actresses, this play *will* have a shelf life."

20

MISS SAIGON

Many operas and classic stories have been updated into modern musicals, from *Romeo and Juliet* into *West Side Story* to *La Bohème* into *Rent*. Perhaps the most ambitious and controversial was *Miss Saigon*, loosely based on *Madame Butterfly*—which also inspired a *South Pacific* subplot about interracial love that ends with anything but "Happy Talk." *Butterfly* was updated to the American war in Vietnam, yet the musical's creators were French, the producer and director Britons.

Alain Boublil and Claude-Michel Schöenberg rejected the more insensitive aspects of Puccini's 1904 opera, whose colonial protagonist Pinkerton abuses the stereotypical Japanese female whose masochism—abandoning her people, converting her religion to her foreign master's, and suicide—matches his callousness. Pinkerton eventually returns only to cart off his half-American child; both versions added dramatic "weight" by making it a son. Boublil and Schöenberg tried to craft a love story of peers.

Miss Saigon unfolds during the final weeks in 1975 before Saigon changed from American control to communist Vietnamese control. The archetypal story still ends tragically—for the woman, of course—but Kim has more dignity and integrity than Cio-Cio-san was given. The non-heel American's wife is fleshed out and gets her own song. As in *Evita*, there is a cynical male commentator on the action, in the form of a half-French Eurasian pimp. Britisher Jonathan Pryce was accused of playing the part completely with a sense of wry irony; theater critic Richard Brestoff advised, "This tool should be used sparingly and balanced with many other elements."

From the onset, the European team made an effort not to offend American theatergoers' sensibilities. Schöenberg explained, "Nobody can say we are either pro- or anti-American." *Newsweek* Vietnam War correspondent Edward Behr was hired as an "honorary consultant" to the musical. Vietnam itself went unexplored on any but a superficial level. *Miss Saigon* would be, for commercial and traditionally biased reasons, Occidentally focused. Schöenberg noted, "It's not a history of the Vietnam War. It's the story of two people lost in the middle of a war."

Although the musical's hero is symbolically named Chris, he isn't a throw-back to the Ugly Missionary. He respects Kim's cultural background (as does she) and her person—although when they meet she's a Saigon bar girl and he's looking for nonmilitary action. "Considering that we were writing for 1989," said Schöenberg, "we tried to improve the human aspect." Unbeknownst to Chris, he gets Kim pregnant. After he departs Saigon, she escapes with her son, Tam, to Bangkok, where she meets her formerly single lover's American wife.

Kim determines that Tam should have a more prosperous and stable future in the United States, and so shoots herself, forcing Tam's father and his wife to take him there. Once again, the East is personified as female, as exotically alluring yet too alien to coexist with—as passive, desperate, even masochistic, and as a victim.

Despite efforts to cast East Asians as Saigon bar girls—they wound up mostly Filipinas—*Miss Saigon* under-represented male East Asian actors, a problem that would cause more resentment in the US than in the UK. When the creative team approached London's Vietnamese embassy for help with décor and costumes, it was politely pointed out that, technically, the show should now be titled *Miss Ho Chi Minh City*. The leading lady, Lea Salonga, seventeen at the time, was discovered in Manila. She almost didn't get the plum part because of her very maternal, omnipresent parent; producer Cameron Mackintosh declared, "Stage mothers frighten me."

Jonathan Pryce, known to UK audiences for local film roles (he was later miscast in the movie of *Evita*), had almost starred in *The Phantom of the Opera* and was a trained singer. He was cast as the Eurasian "Engineer," so-called because he makes things go. The character's "slithering choreography," devised by Bob Avian—Michael Bennett's longtime friend and collaborator—and Pryce, failed to generate much comment in London but would in New York, where *Miss Saigon* made theatrical history with advance ticket sales of over $26 million. Despite—or perhaps in part as a result of—Mackintosh's announcing new ticket prices at an all-time high of $100—$40 higher than for rival shows.

The British Invasion was clearly in full swing, setting the stage for major controversy. Local media charged Mackintosh with "manipulation." He retorted, "The theater is *about* manipulation." Jonathan Pryce's East Asian eyepieces surely weren't going to be used on an American stage? (They weren't.) At least one reporter recycled composer Schöenberg's comment that the Engineer "must be like a sneaky little Oriental mouse," and the enormous Ho Chi Minh statue in *Miss Saigon* was a potential sore point that hadn't resonated in London, but in the United States would remind audiences of America's military non-victory.

THE NEW YORK OPENING was scheduled for April 1991, but Jonathan Pryce, still performing in Britain, hadn't been officially announced for the Broadway run. However, the role was his if he wanted it, according to producer Mackintosh and director Nicholas Hytner—both openly gay men, that openness rarer in the American than British theater. (Hytner directed the acclaimed film of the play *The Madness of George III*.) Once it got out that Pryce, little known beyond the UK, had a virtual lock on the role he'd created, some members of American Actors' Equity Association decided to publicize the fact that the starring part was not open to audition.

A flier distributed in Manhattan cited the habitual practice of giving larger Oriental roles—though in this case a Eurasian—to Caucasian actors, stars or not. "This is the same old story of the same old stories devised by European and American men who depict Asian women as disposable sex objects, use Asian settings only as places to flee from, and portray Asian men as villains or buffoons. . . . As usual, feminine Asian characters are cast for beauty and flesh, while masculine Asian characters—represented as not exactly masculine—are predominantly cast with Caucasian actors. Yet again, Western men demonstrate their discomfort with and contempt for Oriental males."

The charges were difficult to refute (and the Brits scarcely tried). The crucial pimp was written as only half Vietnamese, to diminish his "otherness" and make him more "accessible" to UK and U.S. audiences. And yet the Engineer remains apart from the story's emotionally affective core. Almost invariably, Western entertainments featuring an East Asian theme dwell on an Oriental female—who inevitably comes under the sway of an Occidental male.

In June 1990, three months before final casting decisions would be made, a petition from the Pan Asian Repertory Theatre denouncing *Miss Saigon's* casting hit the news. It stated, "With this action, Equity is sending the following message to its minority members: we will support your right to work so long as your role is not central to the play."

Twelve days later, B.D. Wong, star of *M. Butterfly* (which co-producer Stuart Ostrow felt had been depoliticized by supposedly more commercially minded co-producer David Geffen), wrote to AEA President Colleen Dewhurst to enlist her support "on an issue of racism" and to oppose "a practice I thought was dying." Wong urged Equity members of East Asian descent to join the protest, offering them a form letter to sign. Dewhurst took his side, but the emphasis was on the pending importation of Caucasian non-star Jonathan Pryce, rather than the wider casting issue.

Wong publicly enthused, "Chances to nail the big guys like this don't come often. Let's do it." The comment indicated why the protest gained so much support so quickly: it was Broadway battling the Brits, fueled by more than a little jealousy over such giant successes as *Evita*, *Cats*, *Phantom*, and *Les Miz*.

As often happens with controversial movies, *Miss Saigon* elicited criticism from people who hadn't seen it. One AEA member claimed that Pryce performed in London while "painted yellow," with "taped slit eyes, fake bushy eyebrows, and a wig." In truth, Pyrce didn't wear a wig nor enhance his eyebrows; he employed a Clinique bronzing lotion, and as the protestor should have known, "yellow" is a stereotypical misnomer.

Cameron Mackintosh had to reconsider whether a picketed, media-targeted American production of *Miss Saigon* would be worth it. On the face of $26 million, it would, but British producers were aware how stateside controversy could cut even deeper than dollars. The racial, if not the color, issue was just one aspect—the "fall of Saigon," pregnant bar girls left behind, the towering Ho Chi Minh statue, etcetera, might provoke the type of self-righteousness that had kept major Hollywood filmmakers from treating the Vietnam War for a decade after its end, and then frequently trying to rewrite history in a more gung ho, Rambo-esque way.

A London theater editorial recalled the "limited yet media-intensive protest" versus the 1977 *Nefertiti*, which resulted in its closing en route to Broadway. Protestors had objected to the casting of Andrea Marcovicci, even though Nefertiti was "demonstrably not black—*vide* her world-famous bust in the Berlin museum—although U.S. pickets chose to insist that she was," said the editorial.

Cameron Mackintosh was widely expected to back down, what with the $26 million, a belligerent press, and many AEA protesters of color allying themselves with B.D. Wong and company. Rather, Mackintosh stunned Broadway by taking an ad in the *New York Times* to announce *Miss Saigon's* cancelation. He attacked the opposition to his casting of Pryce, deeming it virtual blackmail and opining that it could lead to casting by quota or via the dictates of actors' unions. Part of the problem was local contention that Pryce wasn't a star and thus was not entitled to take a role that an American actor could perform. Yet *Miss Saigon* in London had elevated Pryce to at least semistardom, and insiders believed that if Mackintosh had taken the issue to arbitration, he would have won his point.

"Cameron didn't want to have to win that way," offered an anonymous associate. "He wanted to win on his own terms, unbeholden to any union, American organization, or special-interest group."

Amazed by the virulence of the protestors and how readily the mainstream Actors' Equity Association had gotten behind them, Mackintosh fumed in a press statement, "Racial prejudice does seem to have triumphed over creative freedom. A sad statement on the current state of the arts in America."

The national media soon weighed in on Mackintosh's headline-grabbing move. Unlike much of the New York media, it generally sided with *Miss Saigon* and the big business it represented. The potential AEA ban on Pryce also threatened international cultural relationships—the general secretary of British Equity denounced its stand, declaring that had Pryce been an American, American Equity wouldn't have been able to prevent his being cast, which "offends us." Besides which, Cameron Mackintosh was easily, at that point, the biggest employer of Broadway actors and technicians!

AFTER AMAZEMENT AT HIS BOLDNESS subsided, Broadway wondered how much of the $26 million refund would spill over to their own shows? British theater columnist Mark Steyn later pointed out what Broadway analysts quickly realized: that most of the refund "would have gone nowhere near the theatre. Had *Miss Saigon* not opened, many of the customers would simply have put their refunds towards a week in Florida or sheet-rocking the garage or enlisting the kids in a drug rehab programme."

The Great White Way concluded that if *Miss Saigon* pulled out before it even started, the loss to Broadway, short- and long-term, would be greater than to Cameron Mackintosh and the musicalizing Europeans. Within days, American Equity reversed itself. Pressure was put on B.D. Wong and others to keep silent for the greater good of Broadway. Jonathan Pryce did "qualify as a star," and the AEA wished "Cameron Mackintosh's production of *Miss Saigon* a long and prosperous run."

The producer delayed his response for several days. He unexpectedly asserted that the show would not go on without Equity's guarantee that members wouldn't campaign against the show, and that all casting and production matters were solely within his jurisdiction—sans criticism. He insisted upon "a positive working environment" and no further press "leaks" that might start the ball of controversy rolling all over again.

Mackintosh got what he wanted, and auditions for unfilled roles in the Broadway production commenced in October 1990.

Miss Saigon became *the* theater sensation of 1991, and its much-ballyhooed (and derided) helicopter replaced the former casting crisis as a topic of conversation. The musical's run—just under a decade in New York, just over a decade in London—didn't match that of, say, *Phantom* or *Les Miz* (nor did the number of non-English-language versions). More difficult and expensive to produce and cast, and despite its re-pedaled love story, *Miss Saigon* was and is nowhere as universal, relevant, or lastingly appealing as other musical imports, though ironically this one was, or seemed to be, the most American of the bunch.

U.S. director-lyricist Richard Maltby Jr. had predicted, "When *Miss Saigon* opens in New York, there's going to be a great sense of pain. This is the kind of show American musicals became great on, a popular entertainment on the major American event of contemporary history. *We* should have looked at ourselves in this way. There'll be a lot of sniffing on Broadway, but in the end a great sadness: this is the show *we* should have written."

P.S. Ironically, the controversy over the casting of this production may have helped it at Tony time. Jonathan Pryce won for Best Actor in a Musical (not his first Tony; he'd won one in 1977 for *Comedians*), and Lea Salonga and Hinton Battle also took home awards.

21

SUNSET BOULEVARD:
NORMA UND DRANG

Imagine a musical of *Sunset Boulevard* starring . . . Gloria Swanson. In 1957, producer Hal Prince telephoned the movie star about the possibility after seeing her on Steve Allen's TV show. She'd already declared, after a humiliating Broadway flop, that she would never return to the stage unless somebody wrote a musical of her classic 1950 screen vehicle.

In 1961, *Variety* announced that Prince had obtained musical rights to the movie, and the project would hit the Great White Way in 1962 starring . . . Jeanette MacDonald (Stephen Sondheim would co-write). Prince envisioned the casting gimmick of MacDonald's on-screen-only romantic partner Nelson Eddy as Max. After the singing diva died in 1965, the project sat on the shelf.

In 1980, Angela Lansbury let it be known that after *Sweeney Todd* she would do the *Sunset Boulevard* musical. Meanwhile, Prince's and Sondheim's *Follies* (1971) had been directly inspired by a famous photo of Gloria Swanson, survivor supreme (born 1899), standing amid the ruins of the Roxy Theatre.

In 1990, *Variety* wondered, "A Musical Version of *Sunset Boulevard*? Andrew Lloyd Webber Is Ready, Mr. DeMille." In 1991 the *New York Daily News* heralded that "Kathryn Grayson, the great MGM singing star of yesteryear, is said to be first in line for the Gloria Swanson role. . . . Sources say she's prepared to lose a lot of weight and get nipped and tucked by a plastic surgeon as soon as the offer is firm." The next year, *Variety* noted, "Meryl Streep, Patti LuPone said to be neck and neck for Norma in the musical." In 1979 the Latin

LuPone had copped the coveted lead in *Evita* from the Nordic Streep who in any case soon left her theater roots behind to follow her movie career (although she has recently returned to the theater in several highly praised performances, including the starring role in the Public Theater's 2006 production of *Mother Courage and Her Children*).

As Meryl's box-office stock climbed, rumors proliferated that producer-director Prince had changed his mind and would replace Patti between *Evita*'s California opening and its Broadway run. Further rumor had it that the rumors had been planted by Hal himself. LuPone told the press, "I've never had doubts about my talents and how I affect an audience. I've been taught to have doubts by directors and producers and critics." She played Eva Peron triumphantly until leaving the show in 1981.

In 1992, Patti LuPone bowed as Norma Desmond in England in a "peek" at the long-awaited musical of *Sunset Boulevard*. It began its London run in 1993, but Patti's new triumph was deeply marred by Webber's company's announcement that the US opening of the show in Los Angeles later that year would star movie star Glenn Close. Why was the American version opening in LA? Because, said Englishman Webber, it was a Hollywood story. Also, LA critics had been kinder—in general—than New York ones.

LuPone publicly questioned the choice, affirming, "I am, after all, a New Yorker." She'd already soured significantly on Webber when he granted Barbra Streisand the right to record the musical's two most famous numbers, "As If We Never Said Goodbye" and "With One Look," on her *Back to Broadway* album before the original cast album was recorded with LuPone. The *New York Times* understatedly declared that Barbra's stealing Patti's thunder "apparently doesn't make Ms. LuPone too happy."

But Patti still had Broadway to look forward to. Glenn Close in LA would be replaced there by Faye Dunaway, an actual faded movie star, and LuPone would play Norma in New York. Then, in London in 1994, around Valentine's Day, just before a performance, Patti received a phone call from her agent back home, with news from Liz Smith's gossip column that Webber had chosen Glenn Close instead of her for Broadway. LuPone's face reportedly contorted "into a strange witch doctor mask." She went on with the show, after memorably trashing her dressing room. (She later admitted, "Things went flying into the street.")

After the curtain fell, news of LuPone's humiliation reached London's theater world. She missed three performances, then settled down to playing out her contract for the remaining weeks.

Patti further vented her rage privately, with lawyers backing her up. Years after, she acknowledged, "The best thing that could have happened was getting fired from that show. I got all this money." Insiders pegged the amount at over

$1 million, more than enough to pay for what LuPone called her "Andrew Lloyd Webber Memorial Pool" at her rural Connecticut home.

A sizable *Sunset Boulevard* ad in the *Los Angeles Times* on May 29, 1994, read, STARRING GLENN CLOSE NOW THROUGH JUNE 26. STARRING FAYE DUNAWAY BEGINNING JULY 5. The Webber-Dunaway association had not begun smoothly. The star had been told to keep quiet, but days before the contract was signed her manager contacted the Associated Press and Faye telephoned *Variety* columnist Army Archerd. Webber's spokesman did not hide his anger. Dunaway then issued a statement saying she would now save her voice—speaking voice too—to "stay in training and prepare for the work ahead."

It was unusual that Webber had chosen non-singer Dunaway for the musical Norma Desmond. (Glenn Close had sung, pre-stardom, and had been Tony nominated for the musical *Barnum*.) Actresses who auditioned for him in Los Angeles or were reportedly eager for the role included Diahann Carroll, Zsa Zsa Gabor, Shirley MacLaine, Rita Moreno, Chita Rivera, Diana Ross, Cybill Shepherd, Meryl Streep, and Raquel Welch, bless her heart. Dunaway had all of three weeks to learn to sing professionally. Neither Andrew Lloyd Webber nor director Trevor Nunn was pleased with the results; each later accused the other of turning thumbs down on Faye—and of wanting her in the first place.

Besides, tickets hadn't sold as well as expected on her name. On June 22, Faye Dunaway heard that the LA production would shut down for good on June 26, Glenn Close's final performance. Glenn and most of the cast would re-open in November, on Broadway. Thus Dunaway wasn't exactly fired; she was made redundant. But of course she was fired.

Dunaway blasted back, deeming the move "another capricious act by a capricious man." At a press conference the done-wrong diva declared, "I hope I am the last in a long line of artists who have come to this man's productions in good faith and have suffered great personal and professional injury at his hands." For good measure, she was suing Webber for $1 million for breech of contract and $5 million on various fraud and defamation charges, also punitive damages.

Webber's spokesman stated from New York, "It's a stickup, and we're not going to tolerate it." Webber himself then added that he planned "the severest action against her insulting, damaging, and defamatory remarks."

By the following January, all legal complications and details were worked out. A joint press release announcement said that "a private settlement was reached today in the dispute between Faye Dunaway and Andrew Lloyd Webber. . . . The agreement stipulates that its terms will remain confidential." This time, Dunaway didn't say an extra word. The amount is rumored to have been between well under $1 million and a mil and a half.

In November 1994, *Sunset Boulevard* opened in Manhattan to great anticipation and robust box office. In March 1995, a tired Glenn Close took two weeks off from the show. *Variety* thereafter allowed, "During that time the industry watched closely to see what impact the star's absence would have at the Minskoff box office." Close would be leaving the show in July, and everyone was curious as to whether *Sunset* would sink without her. No one was more curious than Sir Andrew; his North American employee Edgar Dobie apprised *Variety* that the musical had sold $724,789 of tickets during Close's two-week vacation, when in truth it had sold $569,720, a drop of over $222,000 from Close's last week in the show.

Obviously Dobie, or Webber and Dobie, meant to give the impression that a capable but virtually unknown understudy in Close's place had meant a diminution of only $67,807 in sales over a fortnight. Perhaps Webber and company didn't imagine an actress would have her finger on the box-office pulse of her own vehicle, but Close did. She shot off a single-spaced, two-page fax—which got intercepted and widely publicized—to Webber, asserting:

"I am furious and insulted. I don't think it's an exaggeration to say that my performance turned *Sunset Boulevard* around. I made it a hit. It has existed on my shoulders . . . and yet a representative of your company went out of their way and lied to try to make the public believe that my contribution to this show is nothing, that Karen [Mason]'s performance is equal to mine, and that my absence had absolutely no effect whatsoever on all the thousands of dollars that supposedly kept pouring into the box office. It sickens me to be treated with such disregard.

"If I could leave it in May, when my contract says I can, believe me, I would. At this point, what is making me stay is my sense of obligation to all the people who are holding tickets until July 2."

Although he termed Dobie's action "idiotic," Webber didn't accept his proffered resignation. Webber's company blamed *Variety* for "sensationalizing" the episode. After tremendous publicity that boosted the box office, Webber and Close publicly patched things up, issuing a joint communiqué ruing the fact that "a very private communication between [us] found its way into public hands, especially since the matter has since been completely resolved." Presumably without a large settlement.

The *New York Times* observed that "Nearly every actress to touch the role of Norma Desmond . . . ends up in a public dispute with Sir Andrew." Glenn Close later revealed she'd had additional provocation via Webber's "bad producing. It wasn't only that one incident." A positive review of her understudy was blown up and posted in the theater lobby during Close's absence. "I had an amazingly wonderful understudy [Karen Mason], but what was written in that review kind of cast aspersions on me. I thought that was in incredibly bad taste, since I was getting out there eight times a week and making their money for them."

Veteran Broadway producer Arthur Cantor said of all the bad press, "It can't hurt the show. The next thing is for Betty Buckley to get enraged at [Webber]." Buckley took over for Glenn Close. She cattily advised *New York Daily News* columnist Linda Stasi, "I play Norma *much younger* than Glenn." When Stasi inquired what Betty thought of Glenn's letter to Andrew, she cooed, "It's too bad people's mail goes public. How *does* a thing like that happen?" Just lucky, I guess.

22

THE PRODUCER: DAVID MERRICK

"**W**hy should I give interviews? The facts speak for themselves. . . . Let people guess," said producer David Merrick (1911–2000), also known as the Abominable Showman. "Anyway, the facts are in my career," stated the man born David Margulois, who had renamed himself Merrick after the great British actor David Garrick. Although Merrick projected himself as a ruthless attorney turned producer who was "more interested in theatre in the black than theatre in the round," the son of a salesman loved Broadway more than he let on, and once declared that David Margulois had died and David Merrick had been born on November 4, 1954, the opening night of his breakthrough musical hit *Fanny*.

Stage manager Robert Schear, who began as a production assistant in Merrick's office and worked for him for many years, stated in late 2003, "I get so many interview requests about David Merrick and especially Barbra Streisand," whom the producer kept insisting should be fired because of her looks. "But I'm not interested. It gets twisted and misquoted, and in Mister Merrick's case people want to gossip or condemn and speculate.

"However, as Mr. Merrick said, it's in the facts." So here are several of them, regarding the man whose Broadway producing career will never be equaled:

- David Merrick's theatrical career spanned 1942 to 1996. During the 1963–1964 season alone, he produced eight plays and musicals.

Time magazine estimated in 1966 that he employed twenty percent of Broadway's work force.

- Celebrated British playwright John Osborne told *Women's Wear Daily* that he'd actually enjoyed working with Merrick because unlike other producers, "He didn't have any creative ideas."

- Merrick sometimes denied being Jewish and so hated his hometown of St. Louis that he refused to fly TWA because their flights passed over or through St. Louis. His parents had fought long and loud—"It was like living on the set of *Virginia Woolf*"—and divorced when he was seven.

- Merrick didn't attend his own mother's funeral. He did ask a friend to attend it, in St. Louis. Biographer Howard Kissel theorized that the eventual giving way of Merrick's mind was perhaps the legacy "of his poor, crazy mother. There had always been a screw loose. Now it got looser."

- Merrick first married in 1938. The bride's family refused to attend the wedding. Leonore's inheritance allowed the couple to move to New York in 1939 and David to invest $5,000 in 1940 in an upcoming play that became a hit.

- As a young man, Merrick had such bad ulcers that certain insiders didn't give him long to live. The ulcers excused him from service in World War II.

- "Merrick is profoundly a lawyer," said Reid Shelton, who costarred in the producer's *Oh What a Lovely War!* in 1964. "He loves litigation and uses it, frequently, to manipulate associates and the media. And his other specialty is publicity. He's as much a publicist as a producer."

- Critic Frank Rich noted that Merrick was "chastised not only for his misanthropy and financial ruthlessness, but for being an importer and packager rather than a truly creative producer."

- The producer was famous for affecting a mortician's look of severe black clothes.

    "He looked like Mephistopheles when he glared or sneered at you," said *Hello, Dolly!* leading man David Burns. "Or like a Disney villain. . . . The glasses he wore magnified his enormous pupils. He loved to intimidate and frighten as many people as he can." Merrick's office was done all in red—walls and carpeting—reinforcing the impression of a devil in his lair.

    Though he dressed conservatively, Merrick tried to present a with-it attitude if not a with-it look. When future film and TV producer Joel Thurm, who worked for several years in Merrick's office, came to work one day in platform shoes, bell-bottom blue jeans, and a marine dress uniform jacket, Merrick stared, then stated, "No matter what anybody says, you wear that."

- Merrick's legendary tantrums affected some people more than others. *Hello, Dolly!* composer-lyricist Jerry Herman explained that the producer's out-of-town pre-Broadway rantings "almost did major damage to our costume designer Freddie Wittop, who went through the tortures of the damned." One day, Herman found him at the back of the local theater in tears during a show. Wittop revealed that Merrick had informed him "that the costumes were ugly and he was ashamed to have such wretched rags in his beautiful show." As Wittop explained, Herman's "Put on Your Sunday Clothes" number began with actors strutting about in costume. The combination of clothes and music typically elicited strong applause from audiences. Herman thus pointed out that they were clapping before the music even started.

    "They are applauding your gorgeous costumes." Freddie hugged Jerry and felt better.

- From Kaye Ballard to Streisand, Merrick disliked non-beauties and whenever possible avoided casting them. Talent was a secondary consideration. Unlike the mostly gay men he worked with on *I Can Get It for You Wholesale* (1962)—Barbra's Broadway bow—Merrick didn't believe she had a big future, and failed to put her under contract, to his later fiscal regret when she starred in *Funny Girl.*

- When a reporter asked Merrick what he thought of the women's rights movement, he snapped, "A woman's place is in the oven!"—quite a Freudian slip from the secretly Jewish misogynist. When a notably fat Jewish Canadian critic who had panned several Merrick shows died and was cremated, the producer publicly commented, "The fat's in the fire."

- Unlike his first wife, Leonore, Merrick never wanted children. Five days shy of their 25th anniversary, the marriage terminated because he'd fathered a child via another woman. Eventually he was survived by two official daughters.

- *Gypsy* set designer Jo Mielziner observed, "Merrick has little if any respect for women. He has contempt for unattractive ones and considers all the attractive ones interchangeable." Merrick routinely treated leading ladies badly, excepting a rare Ethel Merman who wouldn't tolerate such treatment. When Anna Maria Alberghetti missed performances in his hit *Carnival* (1961), Merrick publicly stated he didn't believe her claims of poor health and would administer a lie-detector test to her in hospital. Actors in general Merrick considered "unruly children."

• Early on, Merrick displayed a flair for publicity, no matter how outlandish. His 1949 play *Clutterbuck* was boosted by his practice of having bellboys and telephone operators page "Mr. Clutterbuck" during cocktail hour in midtown-Manhattan restaurants and bars. More effective were two-for-one tickets that kept the fiscal failure running for six months.

• It was said that David Merrick liked to be the first to do something, or if need be, the tenth or twentieth. But never the second.

• When a Merrick show took a critical drubbing, he would often sigh and tell an associate, "Time to tack up posters in the men's room again." He meant primarily in the subways, where he pioneered Broadway advertising. After the method and venue proved successful, fellow producers stopped scoffing and followed suit.

• "His ideas are usually cornball and his taste's mostly in his mouth," felt record and revue producer Ben Bagley, "yet his gimmicks have worked surprisingly often." Merrick's idea of wit was embodied by his ad line for his 1980 production *42nd Street*— "The All-Singing All-Dancing Extravaganza with a Cast of 54 (Some Younger)."

• Merrick began publicizing his breakthrough production *Fanny* (1954, co-produced with Joshua Logan) by plastering men's-room mirrors with suggestive stickers asking, "Have you seen Fanny?" He then commissioned a life-sized nude statue of the show's belly dancer and had it erected atop an empty pedestal in Central Park one night—illegally, of course. And of course with enough clues so members of the press and police force could find it the next morning.

• One reason Merrick promoted the hell out of *Fanny* was to make it a hit despite Richard Rodgers having declined to do the music, a fact Merrick never forgave. Rodgers was consistently at or near the top of the producer's enemies list. According to critic Frank Rich, "Such was his detestation of Rodgers that even after the composer's death he took revenge on his elderly widow by seating her in the upper balcony at *42nd Street*."

- When asked by a reporter why he had the reputation of being a mean man, David Merrick logically replied, "Because I *am* mean—what else?"

- When he disliked someone, that person stayed disliked. Merrick taunted *New York Times* critic Howard Taubman more often than most critics, and relished needling him publicly, for instance on Johnny Carson's *Tonight Show*. The insults finally descended to the level of Nazi analogies, at which point Taubman threatened to sue, and Merrick issued a rare apology.

- Taubman's successor at the *Times*, Stanley Kauffmann, was also detested by Merrick, who didn't want him to review a preview of *Philadelphia, Here I Come* in 1966 and prevented him from doing so by canceling that performance after announcing that "a rat" was loose in the theater's generator. The cancellation and its cause made page one of the paper, garnering the show more in publicity than the amount that had to be refunded for tickets.

- Broadway producers often asked a show's creators to give up part of their weekly royalties when business wasn't enough to meet the weekly nut (the amount required before profits commenced). But on *Do Re Mi* (1960), for example, Merrick insisted on such a cut from the creative team and star Phil Silvers during good weeks as well as bad. When Merrick's demands weren't met, he'd cut back on advertising and publicity.

- Merrick didn't like his performers earning outside money. Kaye Ballard was already a Broadway name when she signed to do *Carnival* at $650 a week. Friday afternoons she did a regular appearance on Perry Como's TV show. Merrick had it written into Ballard's contract that should she arrive at the Imperial Theatre one minute late on Friday, she'd have to pay David $750.

- Merrick wasn't intimidated by any actress. He admitted to Carol Channing that initially he didn't want her for *Hello, Dolly!* "I [didn't] want that silly grin with all those teeth that go back to your ears." When Phyllis Newman was Tony nominated for his *Subways Are for Sleeping*, Merrick, seated near her, lied when the list of nominees was read: "Streisand's going to win. I voted for her." Seconds later, Newman won, and the producer "sincerely" congratulated her.

- "Merrick was a sadistic hypocrite," offered lyricist Adolph Green. "He himself went for young girls and was not known for lengthy relationships. But he liked to try and provoke me over the years about my younger wife"—Phyllis Newman, to whom Green was married from 1960 until his death in 2002.

- Merrick often spoke for shock effect, especially to the press. "Homosexuals are taking over the theater" was the theme of one interview he did, after which gay writer-director Arthur Laurents warned that more such verbal bigotry "and we won't work for you." Merrick's "faux-macho general manager—with a penchant for Puerto Rican boys—signaled frantically behind Merrick's back for me to lay off. Merrick wasn't fazed.

   "'It's only for publicity,'" Laurents quoted Merrick as saying. "'I wouldn't have anyone on my staff who wasn't homosexual. They have no one to go home to so they work late and don't complain.'" For the record, Laurents has been wedded to his life partner far longer than Merrick was to any of his contractual wives.

- Jerry Herman, who eventually came out as a gay man, confessed that it took him years to get over the trauma of Merrick's informing him in front of the whole company that his songs for *Hello, Dolly!* were "an embarrassment." Merrick probably really liked them but felt he was encouraging Herman to create better ones. "He really believed he could get better work out of everybody if he frightened them half to death and made them feel two inches tall." Herman rued, "It could have been such a happy time, my first big hit. But I still look back on it with discomfort and trepidation."

   Hello, Dolly! leading man David Burns agreed. "Mr. Merrick is a screamer. Literally. When all else fails and he wants to improve a show, he'll try and scream it into shape." Burns added, "Woe to anyone Mr. Merrick believes to be homosexual. . . . In *Dolly!* he had some unforgettably choice words for Charles Nelson Reilly [a supporting actor], both in front of and behind his very flamboyant back."

- *Hello, Dolly!* was Merrick's most famous and ongoing hit. It cost $440,000 and grossed over $60 million in its original run of 2,844 performances.

- Merrick's ideas didn't evolve with the times. When *Dolly!*'s business fell off after almost four years, he decided to mount an all-black version starring Pearl Bailey in 1967. In 1989, after *42nd Street* finally closed, he announced he would bring it back with an all-black cast. He wasn't able to.

(In the '60s, Merrick had discussed a new *Dolly!* with Jack Benny in drag, opposite Benny's pal George Burns. Benny was willing, but only for one week. Merrick also pursued Bette Davis for the musical title role. She called it "a fifteen-minute show," referring to the famous title number.)

- Merrick married former, but still far younger, flight attendant Etan Aronson, a brunette Swede, twice. The litigation surrounding their second divorce (his fifth) lasted a decade. Their first marriage, in 1969, lasted three weeks before he obtained a Mexican divorce. During their second marriage (which began 1983), at Etan's instigation, she and Merrick adopted two daughters. Eventually he denied in court that he'd been a willing participant in the adoptions.

- "The more his taste and antics are derided," said David Burns, "the more he revels in his outrageousness." For his 1955 *Hello, Dolly!* antecedent, *The Matchmaker*, Merrick hired an old-fashioned black taxicab with dual controls. While a human drove the vehicle from the backseat, a "monkey" sat up front at the dummy wheel, flabbergasting onlookers. The cab's side read: "I am driving my master to see *The Matchmaker*."

- "I think deep down Mr. Merrick is contemptuous of the media and people, even," felt David *Charlie's Angels* Doyle, who appeared in the producer's 1964 flop *I Was Dancing*. "He seems to like the theatre but not theatregoers very much. . . . Some of his p.r. stunts almost seem intended to offend." Such as for the French musical *Irma La Douce* (1960), for which Merrick paid sandwich-board men to walk the streets wearing portable pissoirs.

- On the other hand, Merrick was the first producer to buy full-page newspaper ads for a Broadway show. The practice was criticized as vulgar, trivial, wasteful, and egotistical—until it became commonplace.

- Via the tax dodge of a foundation he set up, Merrick imported a large quantity of quality British fare by avant-garde playwrights, featuring talented actors. Some, like *Marat/Sade* with Broadway newcomer Glenda Jackson, became actual hits.

- Merrick and John Osborne's British drama *Look Back in Anger* (1957) failed to generate much American excitement until

Merrick hired a woman to pose as an affronted theatergoer who got up on the stage and attacked the actor portraying an unfaithful husband. Newspapers duly reported the incident and noted the play's powerful effect on certain viewers. The hoax extended the run by several months (and was revealed weeks after the stunt occurred).

• When Ethel Merman's leading man Jack Klugman sought to invest in *Gypsy*, Merrick replied, "You don't want to invest in this. It's going to be a bomb. If you want to invest in a musical, invest in *Destry*," an ill-fated show starring a pre-TV Andy Griffith and Dolores Gray. Co-producer Leland Hayward and *Gypsy* composer Jule Styne overheard Merrick's typically unflattering remarks about their musical and reportedly got out their checkbooks and asked Merrick, "How much would you take to get out of this show?"

• David Merrick was amazed and intrigued by Woody Allen's open Jewishness. He gave the comic, born Allen Konigsberg, his Broadway debut as a playwright (*Don't Drink the Water*) and as an actor (*Play It Again, Sam*), while predicting, "He's too plain and specialized for television," not to mention the movies.

• "This story may be apocryphal," advised stage and screen costume designer Irene Sharaff, "but it fits David Merrick to a 'T'. . . . Naturally he hated to wait in line, and he had his minions who did everything for him. But sometimes, in later years, he would get out and about, and when he came to a line, he'd march up to the front and tell the first person, 'If you knew what I've got, you'd let me go ahead of you.' He did this many times, and finally one brave person dared to say, 'Excuse me for asking, but what have you got?'

"Merrick cackled and answered back, 'Chutzpah!'"

• When the great caricaturist Al Hirschfeld did a drawing of Merrick as a Grinch-like Santa Claus who steals Christmas, several people thought he would sue. Instead, Merrick turned around and used Hirschfeld's drawing—without permission, of course—on his Christmas cards.

• The most memorable thing about Merrick's 1961 musical *Subways Are for Sleeping* was The Ad, a stunt he'd been planning for years. It had been preceded by thousands of pre-opening posters affixed to subway trains and platforms that bore only the show's title.

Transit Authority officials ordered Merrick to remove the posters, which they believed encouraged homeless people to spend the night underground.

The posters piqued New Yorkers' curiosity, but it was The Ad that extended the disappointing show's run. The stunt was possible because *New York Times* critic Brooks Atkinson, who had a one-of-a-kind name, had retired. His replacement, Howard Taubman, was one of seven critics whose namesakes Merrick found in the telephone book. He invited the seven non-critics to wine and dine at his expense and to agree to the critical praise that would accompany their names and photos in the advertisement, which ran only in the *Herald Tribune's* early edition before editors killed it.

The Ad headlined, "7 Out of 7 Are Ecstatically Unanimous About 'Subways Are for Sleeping.'" For instance, the mock John Chapman called it "the best musical of the century." The mostly rejected ad itself became news and was reproduced nationwide for free. The chutzpah of Merrick's stunt, a cross between exhibitionistic contempt and performance art, was written and talked about and debated, and The Ad quickly took its place as perhaps the greatest publicity stunt in 20th-century theater history. Ironically, it was remembered long after the show that it so lavishly extolled was forgotten.

• "Classy" was, for David Merrick, the ultimate seal of approval. In his mind, it often went together with "English," and the former producer died in his sleep at eighty-eight in a pricey rest home in London. At the same time that he had snobbish tastes and goals, Merrick relished his reputation as "the meanest man on Broadway." "He was conflicted," said Ben Bagley. "His parents were Russian immigrants, it was an arranged marriage, the family was poor and melodramatically unhappy . . . and he bought the dominant culture's stereotypes and propaganda about being Jewish."

Merrick's childhood was described as "Dickensian" by some insiders, and he almost never discussed it. His relief when his battling parents divorced was short-lived, since they briefly remarried before Sam abandoned Celia and David, who then ran away from his mother but had to return for lack of funds. Late in life, Merrick admitted that two of his least favorite adjectives, which in his mind went together, were "poor" and "Jew" (the latter, of course, a noun).

- Besides strongly objecting to Barbra Streisand's looks, Merrick was aghast at her undisguised Brooklyn accent and "blatant Jewishness." He also resented how well liked the nineteen-year-old initially was by his associates. When *I Can Get It for You Wholesale* casting director Michael Shurtleff stood up for her, Merrick retorted, "I want you to take her out and kill her."

  When *Wholesale* composer-lyricist Harold Rome pointed out that the Broadway newcomer could be hired "for scale," Merrick exploded, "You're the most anti-Semitic guy I know. You've hired every ugly Jew in town for this show, and now you want me to hire this *meeskite*."—Yiddish for an unattractive person; Merrick normally avoided Yiddishisms, except in the heat of the moment.

  Rome later disclosed, "Merrick had it very tough coming up, as a Jewish youth and a future producer. It galled him that Barbra, whom he genuinely cannot stand, rose to major stardom by her second Broadway show, *Funny Girl*." When she departed for Hollywood and the movie version of *Funny Girl*—never to return to the stage—Merrick was both relieved and dumbfounded by film producers clamoring for her services.

- Merrick's Midas touch did not translate to Hollywood, where he produced four pictures between 1972 and '80, the most notable being the much-ballyhooed *The Great Gatsby*, toplining Robert Redford and Mia Farrow, a costly flop. While in LA, Merrick picked up a cocaine habit.

- Choreographer-turned-director Gower Champion hired one Karen Prunczik for *42nd Street* (1980) because she was a talented tap dancer. The first day Merrick saw her, he informed Champion, "That girl is pockmarked and she's ugly. I want her fired." Champion refused. One night, when leading lady Wanda Richert was unable to go on, Prunczik had the opportunity to take her place. But Merrick took it away by canceling the evening's performance.

  Many months later, Merrick married Prunczik. A few months later, he initiated divorce proceedings. Former father-in-law Walt Prunczik later filed court papers claiming that Merrick had "been heard mumbling that he had put out a contract on him." A psychiatrist testified that the producer did have "homicidal impulses" against his ex in-law.

- Merrick's longest creative partnership was with Gower Champion. It started in 1961 and ended in 1980 with the producer's infamous *42nd Street* closing-curtain announcement that Champion had died that morning at 59 of a rare blood cancer. Merrick held back the news partly or primarily for the TV cameras that had been summoned to record the shock and tears, also Merrick embracing a thunderstruck Wanda Richert, Champion's mistress, who'd also been kept in the dark.

David Merrick had met his match in Gower Champion. In the early '60s, via his hit musical *Bye, Bye, Birdie*, Champion joined the top ranks of Broadway director-choreographers—with Jerome Robbins, Bob Fosse, and Michael Kidd. All four "had fearsome reputations as tyrants," said critic Howard Kissel. Playwright Michael Stewart called the diminutive Champion "the Presbyterian Hitler."

Although Merrick professed genuine grief at Champion's passing, in subsequent months he removed the man's name from the *42nd Street* marquee and tried to reduce the royalties to which Champion's estate was entitled.

- In 1983, David Merrick suffered a stroke that left him barely able to speak—mostly grunts—and limited his mobility. Confined to a wheelchair, he stepped up his lawsuits against offenders real and imagined, and was a bizarre sight in a maladjusted wig and crudely applied rouge. He'd long since admitted to being frequently depressed. Despite his penny-pinching ways, the man lived modestly—as a sometime bachelor, even shabbily—and seldom gave or attended parties.

  Adolph Green said, "He had a Rolodex full of associates and acquaintances, but no real friends, least of all his wives."

- No surprise, but Merrick did not mellow with age and still enjoyed planning confrontational advertising. When *Cats* proved a "now and forever" hit, he touted *42nd Street* as being for people allergic to cats. When *42nd Street* had run seven years and looked ready to close soon, Merrick began advertising it as "Broadway's *Latest Hit!*"—pushing back the curtain time to 8:15. His leering face on a giant poster over Times Square announced, "David Merrick is holding the curtain for you!" The musical returned to profit by picking up turn-away business from another hit import, *Phantom of the Opera*, across the street.

- Merrick's last public appearance, according to associate Bob Schear, was closing night of *State Fair* (1996). It was an unsuccessful and downbeat ending to a career that encompassed nearly ninety productions. "However, Mr. Merrick didn't know it was closing night, he was so out of it." At the well-attended memorial for Merrick at the St. James Theatre, where he'd had his famous red office, former Broadway star Dolores Gray was present in a wheelchair but asked Schear, "When's David Merrick going to show up?"

- When he died, Merrick was married to his fifth wife—a younger woman who'd been his spokesperson—but had divorced five times. Bob Schear believed Merrick probably had other wives "we didn't know about," as well as unofficial daughters.

- A nurse who looked after Merrick toward the end summed up his personality and his achievement: "This man has channeled his self-destructive instincts into something positive—his work in the theatre. It is rare that someone with that much destructive energy can find such a constructive outlet."

Dollys!

THOSE NOT UP ON THEIR BROADWAY HISTORY might be excused for imagining that *Hello, Dolly!* (1964) was offered to Carol Channing on a silver platter. The role and actress have become so enmeshed, it's hard to think of one without the other. Yet much of the success of *Dolly!* and its myriad revivals is based on its adaptability to most any larger-than-life female celebrity of a certain age. Only Barbra Streisand, at twenty-six, was technically too young for the widow-coming-out-of-seclusion role—though right by Hollywood box-office standards (and musically, of course).

David Merrick had had a success with the 1955 Thornton Wilder play *The Matchmaker*, starring Ruth Gordon as Dolly Levi, born Gallagher. (Only Streisand rejected the *Abie's Irish Rose* heritage.) That was a revision of Wilder's 1938 non-hit *The Merchant of Yonkers*—notice the titles' difference in gender emphasis. The original source materials were the 1835 English comedy *A Day Well Spent*, by John Oxenford, and the 1842 *Einen Jux Will Er Sich Machen*, by Austrian Johann Nestroy—which had no Dolly!

By the early 1960s, Merrick wanted to musicalize *The Matchmaker* and title it *Dolly: A Damned Exasperating Woman*, which was pretty strong language on or off Broadway. Talented young composer Jerry Herman, with the semi-successful set-in-Israel musical *Milk and Honey* behind him, wrote some songs on spec for Merrick, who liked them and was eager to have Ethel Merman hear them. At the time, starring Merman in a musical was like minting money.

But after her triumphant and lengthy turn in *Gypsy*, Merman asserted that she wasn't listening to anything from anyone; retirement looked too good. Both men were crushed. Herman had written with the Merm's voice and style in mind, two songs so specifically that they weren't used in the show until Merman became the final Broadway Dolly in the original run.

Another major contender was musical star Nanette Fabray, but once Carol Channing heard of the project she put herself into high gear and campaigned strenuously for the comeback role. Though she'd achieved Broadway stardom in *Gentlemen Prefer Blondes* in 1949, she hadn't followed up with any other hits, spending much of the '50s playing nightclubs. She was too tall, flamboyant, and large in every sense of the word save girth to play conventional female leads or drama, onstage or onscreen, and she was too ambitious to settle for secondary roles.

"Carol sort of pestered her way into the part," admitted director-choreographer Gower Champion, who'd worked with her before but initially didn't want her as Dolly. "And how right she proved to be." Channing also won over Jerry Herman, whom Merrick hired to do the score—with reservations. Carol declared, "I hope this won't upset you, Mr. Herman, because a composer usually hears his songs being sung in a certain way. But you know, I sing lower than the men in your show." Jerry tailored the score to Carol's quavering baritone, and the two, for whom *Hello, Dolly!* was a professional turning point, became fast friends.

However, the musical's score didn't come together as smoothly as intended. After *Dolly!* proved a dud in previews in Detroit—audiences actually booed and threw things—David Merrick surreptitiously brought in Bob Merrill, who was working on *Funny Girl*. Merrill contributed the song "Elegance," which may have been originally written for *New Girl in Town*, a 1957 Gwen Verdon vehicle based on Eugene O'Neill's *Anna Christie*. Also the "Motherhood March." In time, both were publicly credited to Jerry Herman.

Meanwhile, Champion brought in Charles Strouse and Lee Adams of *Bye, Bye, Birdie* fame. In Detroit they contributed the showstopper "Before the Parade Passes By." Merrick let Herman "rework" the music, if not the lyrics—which encapsule Dolly's new philosophy and the show's theme.

As often happened during the golden age of Broadway musicals, the chief song was released to radio before the show opened, and via Louis Armstrong's jazzy rendition the title song—after which the musical was named—became a number-one hit. Its success meant everyone heard it—including Mack David (brother of lyricist Hal David), who sued Jerry Herman for allegedly plagiarizing his 1948 song "Sunflower" (coincidentally a hit via Armstrong), to which it bore a strong resemblance. Herman had to pay a $275,000 settlement, but the negative publicity didn't harm *Dolly!*, which proceeded to become

Broadway's longest-running musical until *Fiddler on the Roof* surpassed it as Broadway's longest-running production, period.

DOLLY! OF COURSE RESURRECTED and expanded Carol Channing's stardom and gave her a signature role she could and would return to again and again—*ye-es!* Unfortunately, she wasn't lucky or versatile enough to follow it up with another hit, unlike Angela Lansbury after Jerry Herman's subsequent megahit *Mame*. Following assorted showbiz efforts, Channing in later years did a sequel of sorts to *Gentlemen Prefer Blondes*, titled *Lorelei*, besides touring extensively as Dolly.

Once Channing made a hit as Dolly, everyone wanted to play her, it was so clearly a star vehicle and so easily adjusted to the personality of its diva-of-the-month's run. Ginger Rogers was flashy and arrogant. Martha Raye was droll but not enough in character. Betty Grable was charming and eager to please—some said too sweet to play the conniving widow. Pearl Bailey got away with stereotyping the first black Dolly. Phyllis Diller tried to shake her standup-comedy image by playing it relatively straight.

Ethel Merman was Ethel Merman, and that was enough. She agreed to return for three months only, to close the run. It turned out to be her Broadway swansong.

"Dolly is a star herself," David Merrick had proclaimed, "and she needs a star to play a star." He foresaw an endless procession of Dollys after the formula proved viable.

Expectations were high when Ginger Rogers took over the role, but her swanking and attitude soon turned many in the company off, and she began missing several performances, in contrast to the very professional Channing. At that time, Actors' Equity required posting a notice in the lobby or making a pre-performance announcement if a performer was not going on. Merrick opted for the latter, with the announcer welcoming the audience and stating that the role of Mrs. Levi—the word "Dolly" was not used—would tonight be performed by Bibi Osterwald. Just as Bibi's last name was starting to be said, the conductor gave the downbeat and the box-office window slammed shut.

This became known as The Ginger Rogers Cue. Although patrons who'd come to see Rogers were at first disappointed, Osterwald's performance was said by many aficionados to be the best of all stage Dollys. (She eventually got to star regularly in the show.) Alas, via a non-collision of talent and timing, the singer-actress never became a star. It was Osterwald who complained to Equity about Merrick's ruse, and henceforth a performer's absence had to be made clear both from the stage and in the lobby.

"When Ginger left," recalled a backstage insider, "she was relieved. By then, it was too much for her. And we, the crew and cast, were also relieved. . . . She made some of us homesick for Carol!"

Another ex-movie star, and a much more comedic one, was brought in: Martha Raye, aka The Big Mouth. "Perfect show for me," she cracked. "Set in the 1890s—when I was an ingénue."

Raye's jollity was mostly for show, as Melodye—her only child (who so far hasn't written a book)—could attest. Martha was the only Dolly with whom the affable, almost fatuous Jerry Herman did not get along. When she took over Dolly, he was in hospital with hepatitis. He'd routinely worked on the score with each new actress, rehearsing and changing keys, etc. Herman described himself as "sick as a dog;" he was unable to meet with Raye but sent a "gorgeous telegram" proffering an apology. On her opening, he sent "a magnificent bouquet of flowers" to her dressing room.

Neither the telegram nor flowers were acknowledged, and during her run Raye made no attempt to contact Herman, who when let out of hospital recuperated at his summer home on Fire Island. Still weak and confined to a wheelchair, Jerry was taken to lunch at a local restaurant where sat Martha Raye with three gay friends or associates (her final husband was openly gay and decades her junior).

In his wheelchair, Herman rolled over to Raye's table to introduce himself. She gave him an icy stare, then pouted, "You've never been to see me." He explained, "I just got out of the hospital," where he had been for months. He wondered if Raye had received his wire and flowers, and asked, "Didn't you know that I was very, very ill?"

She snapped, "Well, I thought you could have spared *one* evening."

The amazed and deflated composer wrote, "After that, I *never* went to the St. James Theatre to see her."

PEARL BAILEY DELIBERATELY TRIED TO SLOW Dolly's pace. "She lazily led an all-black cast," observed theater buff Ethan Mordden. She also had attitude to spare. "There's a line in the show," her leading man Cab Calloway later noted, "'a damned exasperating woman.' That is Pearl all over, except I might use a stronger word than 'damned.'" A professional singer, Bailey took fewer liberties with the songs than, say, the offhand Rogers or the idiosyncratic Channing. But one of Pearl's idiosyncrasies was claiming that God was onstage with her during a given performance.

"She carried on as if she was preaching or giving you a revelation," said Calloway assistant Cyril Jackson. "She'd go on at length, never coming to the point, except how she and God were close personal friends and She, He, or It was apparently an avid theatergoer who'd blessed Pearl's interpretation [of Dolly]."

More effective than anticipated was Phyllis Diller. Herman had worried, once producer Merrick made the decision to cast most any female box-office name between forty and death, that the comedienne in the fright wig might make a "wild, crazed" caricature of Dolly. "She could have made funny faces or slipped in a few of her raunchy stories." Rather, she enacted Dolly simply and honestly, if unspectacularly.

Dolly had long since proven less a role than a performance, less a character than a force of nature. It's almost impossible to believe she was ever a retiring, reclusive widow, at least since *The Matchmaker* was musicalized. Possibly the most convincing Dolly of all was Tony- and Oscar-winning actress Shirley Booth in the 1958 *Matchmaker* film (costarring Shirley MacLaine and Anthony Perkins, who briefly donned drag, which he declined to do again in *Some Like It Hot*, thereby handing Jack Lemmon one of that actor's biggest hits). Booth had the maturity, charm, push, and demureness to be credible as a personable (but non-diva) widow returning to life and romance. However, since the advent of *Hello, Dolly!* Wilder's nonmusical play has remained dormant, unrevived due to comparison with its tuneful, exclamation-marked twin. Ironically, though, musical ability is not an absolute requirement for an actress-diva playing Dolly!

When Barbra Streisand nabbed the movie version that she'd gone after, she gave an over-the-top performance at times reminiscent of the ageless Mae West (who paranoiacally threatened to sue) that was widely criticized but now seems apt and inventive. How can you overdo Dolly? Besides, what a change to hear the beautiful music beautifully sung.

Another irony: although Carol Channing had beaten Streisand for the 1964 Best Actress (Musical) Tony, it was Barbra who got the rare chance to reprise her Broadway triumph on the screen, earning a Best Actress Academy Award (split with Katharine Hepburn) for *Funny Girl. Hello, Dolly!*'s record of ten Tony Award wins held until *The Producers* overtook it in 2001, winning 12 Tonys.

Other Dollys in varied venues and productions from London to Vietnam included Mary Martin, who proved typically uncomfortable with the character's aggressive, self-starting qualities, and Eve Arden (*Our Miss Brooks, Grease*), who seemed a bit schoolmarmish and detached in the part. Additional Dollys were former B-movie stars Dorothy Lamour and Yvonne De Carlo, and Joanne Worley from TV's *Rowan and Martin's Laugh-In.*

Assorted songs got dropped along the way. For the movie version, Streisand requested a new opening song, a "list song" with complicated, showy lyrics ("Just Leave Everything to Me"), to establish her hyperkinetic character. Babs also wanted a love song of sorts ("Love Is Only Love") to sing in a romantically lit solo scene that featured her in sexy deshabille and firm young cleavage, which belied the widow's claim that she'd been in seclusion lo these many years since the death of Ephraim Levi. But what Streisand wanted,

Streisand got—directed by Gene Kelly, who added yet more dancing to the lengthy musical film. David Merrick, who had a financial interest in the movie, reportedly agreed to pay big bucks at the last minute if Jerry Herman could quickly compose what became "Love Is Only Love."

After Herman presented the song, everyone was happy. It was beautiful and it didn't even sound rushed. Unbeknownst to Merrick and company, Herman had composed it but never used it for a prior musical. By the time of the 1969 Streisand movie Angela Lansbury was a close friend of Jerry's via *Mame*, and was familiar with the song. She happened to sit next to David Merrick on a cross-country flight when he shared the "new" song and she innocently admitted having heard it some time before, much to Merrick's fury.

IN 1970, SEVEN YEARS into *Hello, Dolly!*'s run, Ethel Merman took over the part that had been created with her in mind. Her three-month engagement stretched to nine, but she was delighted, even relieved, to be back where she belonged—starring on Broadway. When she'd declined Dolly, she'd apprised Merrick, "I have spent my entire life in a dressing room, and I have had it with that life." She wanted freedom, for example, "to be able to go to dinner parties at eight o'clock at night, like everybody else does, instead of always eating in the middle of the night." Eventually the inactivity had palled.

The two songs Herman had specifically tailored to Merman were finally publicly performed: "Love, Look in My Window" and "World, Take Me Back." According to Jerry, Merman played Dolly as "tough and funny, but lovable underneath." Her leading man, Jack Goode, felt, "Miss Merman is the perfect Dolly—a career girl who comes out of retirement and shakes up everybody around her. . . . She's the most exciting thing to ever happen to this wonderful show." Some less-partial observers believed that Merman, like Channing, more than made the role her own, trampling it with the force of her unrestrained persona. Either way, audiences came, eager to see and hear. Carol Channing later wrote of "Ethel's greatness in my part."

Merman revealed that the other reason she'd originally rejected Dolly was that she'd always created the roles she played and feared that if she did *Hello, Dolly!* she'd be viewed as following in Ruth Gordon's *Matchmaker* footsteps. Ethel was well known for her competitiveness with other females. The night of Merman's final performance, Carol Channing and accompanying photographers showed up at the theater for pictures of the first and last Dollys, together, as the record-breaking show came to a close.

"I knew you'd make certain to be here tonight, Carol," glared Ethel before refusing to pose with her and shutting the door on her. (Carol later crowed that the *New York Times* instead ran a photo of her alone, the original Dolly.)

Even though Ethel had said no to Dolly, she resented Carol's success in the part. Channing recalled that once she became Dolly, whenever she'd encounter Merman socially, "I would say, 'Hello, Ethel.' And she would look right and left of me, wondering where my voice came from."

Of course, Carol had the last Dolly laugh, outliving Merman and repeating the role on and on. But at a price. Whereas the ghost of Ethel Merman has lingered over every *Gypsy* revival including that of 2003 with Bernadette Peters, Channing lingered in *Hello, Dolly!*—the only musical most people can associate with her. The inevitable comparisons with newer Roses invariably favor Merman, while each new Channing *Hello, Dolly!* has diminished in everything—including supporting casts (the original featured Eileen Brennan and Charles Nelson Reilly)—everything but chutzpah. Theatre historian Ethan Mordden has termed it "build[ing] an evening around the glamour of guts." It became less about viewing a scintillating star in a dazzling musical than going to see—so you could say you had—Carol Channing in her signature role. Or *Hello, Dolly!* with its signature star.

Mordden, to name one, considered the re-stagings "good show biz, but bad musical comedy." He decried the lack of a curtain fall after the show's end. Rather, the musical reprises, the cast's strutting and posing, and the calculated buildup to Carol's/Dolly's appearance in Her Song insures that the "audience rises in salute as if they, too, have been directed by Gower Champion."

It remains to be seen if *Hello, Dolly!* will survive time and Carol Channing, whose final Broadway run in the part (see accompanying sidebar) didn't last as long as expected. *Gypsy* survived Merman partly due to substance, partly because it challenges actresses and often elevates them to new thespic heights. *Dolly!* doesn't so much challenge as accommodate, and though it's a nostalgic, gaudy musical that serves as a holiday for the senses in an increasingly colorless and cookie-cutter time, much of its substance turns out to be image and public relations. As with the story behind Carol Channing's plate, recounted by veteran columnist James Bacon:

"Do you know about Carol Channing's famous silver plate? She once asked me if I had seen her 'plate,' and I stared at her teeth, then said no. She said, 'My silver plate, diddums, from David Merrick.' So she dragged out this famous plate that everyone had seen but me, and it was impressive, and engraved—'Congratulations, Carol, on the $8 million gross for *Hello, Dolly!* David Merrick.'

"Years later, I'm talking with the producer himself, and I mention his gift to Carol, and he snorted, 'Gift, my eye! I sent her the message, but it was Charles Lowe—her P.R. man and husband—who got the silver plate and had my message engraved onto it.' Whatever that plate cost Lowe, he's gotten over a million dollars in publicity out of it. Maybe $8 million."

Carol, Hello!

"There has never been anything like this before in human society."—BROOKS ATKINSON in 1949 on Carol Channing in *Gentlemen Prefer Blondes* (though "mincing coyly in high-heel shoes," she was also "husky enough to kick in the teeth of any gentleman on the stage")

"Gentlemen Must Prefer Amazons"—a COLUMNIST for the Hearst Syndicate

"Carol Channing is rather disconcerting. You'll notice her looking at you with those big baby-stare eyes. Then eventually it dawns on you that the person behind those eyes is, in show business terms, about 200 years old."
—DANNY LOCKIN, who played Barnaby Tucker in *Hello, Dolly!* on stage and screen

"I knew Carol before, during and after *Blondes*. Everyone assumed she would become, and remain, a big star. Well, she didn't remain one . . . it so disappointed and so hardened her, inside. Until *Hello, Dolly!* finally came along, Carol was a bundle of restless, ruthless nerves. The woman, appearances to the contrary, is no dummy."—director-choreographer GOWER CHAMPION

"Perhaps once in a decade a nova explodes above the Great White Way with enough brilliance to reillumine the whole gaudy legend of show business."—TIME magazine in 1949 on the new star

"Carol Channing is a closet intellectual."—columnist LIZ SMITH

"Carol is a theatre actress. I used to stand in the wings every night and watch her. She was like clockwork. Her closing nights were like her opening nights. I loved going to the theatre knowing that you were going to get the same performance every night."—LEE ROY REAMS

"Carol Channing never really crossed over to doing straight plays. Her whole focus is much bigger. The fact that you have to fill a theatre creates a certain style that does become larger than life."—actor JOE BOVA

"Carol is nobody else, and she craves celebrity like chocoholics crave chocolate."—ROSS HUNTER, who produced *Thoroughly Modern Millie*, for which Channing received a supporting-actress Oscar nomination

"Carol Channing has played Dolly over 5,000 times. She's either done it to perfection by now, or it's done in her ability to do any other, more down-to-earth roles."—EILEEN HECKART

"Carol was crushed when the movie of *Gentlemen Prefer Blondes* went to Marilyn. Carol had so built up the character of Lorelei Lee in her mind and the interviews, as if it was one of the all-time roles, an American Anna Karenina or something. In the movie, Lorelei's just a gold-digger. Well, in the play she's also just a gold-digger. Carol's one consolation was that Marilyn was second-billed to Jane Russell."—JULE STYNE, *Gentlemen Prefer Blondes* composer

"Gower Champion wanted to star Nanette Fabray as Dolly, and she would have been marvelous. But not being outlandish or freakish, she'd have made Dolly normal, as Shirley Booth did in the *Matchmaker* movie—for my money, the best and most lovable interpretation. Maybe Channing helped make the show bigger, more of a stage spectacle, by taking Dolly outside the realm of normalcy and reality."—pop-culture historian MARTIN GREIF

". . . . a part nobody wanted and everybody eventually played."—David Merrick assistant-turned-company-business manager STEVEN SUSKIN on Dolly Gallagher Levi

"It's funny. People think Ethel Merman has this deep, masculine voice. But she can sing two octaves higher than Carol Channing."—critic WYATT COOPER

"Carol once said she knocked the Beatles off of the charts. I thought, with *that* voice? And actors do exaggerate so. But she did. The original cast album of *Hello, Dolly!* did knock the Beatles off the charts when it came out in 1964."—record producer BEN BAGLEY

"I once made the mistake of asking Carol to sing *Hello, Dolly!* That is, the title song. She took about ten minutes to explain that she doesn't sing it in the show. The waiters sing it to her, and she does an answering verse. Then I made the further mistake of saying that in the film version, Barbra Streisand does sing it—the entire song. I got what seemed like a ten-second glare."—critic REX REED

"Is this dud still running? Why?"—a DETROIT CRITIC to Carol Channing in her New York dressing room during *Dolly!*'s second year

"When she comes out during the title number in the red dress and feathers, it is a breathtaking number and a real theatre moment. But over the years Carol has embellished it to the point where I think she almost believes her stories about people dying happy during the big 'Dolly!' number. She also says Lyndon Johnson requested that her recording of 'Hello, Lyndon!' for the Democratic presidential convention be played in perpetuity—like an eternal flame—at his presidential library in Texas."—GWEN VERDON

"One of Carol's proudest memories is when Jackie Kennedy and her two children made their first public appearance after JFK's assassination and funeral by going to see *Hello, Dolly!* and then visiting Carol backstage. Because that's what Carol and that show represent: a coming to life again, a rejoining of the human race."—*Hello, Dolly!* producer DAVID MERRICK

"She wants to be the only one in the show. She and Gower Champion, they were not nice people. You know the famous red dress? The dancers in the dressing room in the cellar had a doll with a black dress like the red dress, with the feathers and beads in black. Hanging by a noose."—*Hello, Dolly!* costar CHARLES NELSON REILLY

"Carol's old-fashioned. She likes to give the impression she defers to her husband, that he's in charge, whether it's Charles Lowe or the new Armenian-American one that got her on the Larry King show [in 2003]."—an anonymous FORMER FRIEND of Carol and Charles

"She always has a lot to say and definite things she won't do—like she won't wear earrings because she thinks her face is busy enough."—designer BOB MACKIE

"Carol Channing is now [the late '90s] the last pure theatre star. This is the medium that made her, and she's remained loyal to it."—playwright JEAN KERR

"Believe it or not, the musicals with Mary Martin, Eddie Cantor, Ethel Merman, and Bert Lahr never got standing ovations. American show biz was then in its glory, and even the biggest talents were taken for granted. . . . It was the 1960s and shows such as *Hello, Dolly!* and *Mame* that created the audience-participation finale [epitomized by] *Dolly!'s* applause-athon." —theater historian ETHAN MORDDEN

"Watch Miss Channing as she descends that famous staircase in the title number: we applaud with relief, as we do when an old nag successfully negotiates a tricky course at a point-to-point. . . . Still, this [1996] production got great notices in New York, for drama critics are a sentimental crowd."—theater columnist MARK STEYN

"Last year [1998] Carol Channing told the press that the public's been clamoring for yet another return as Dolly. You'd have to be very old and very nostalgic or very gay and very fond of musicals to still be clamoring. I think where Carol's concerned, they should rename it 'Hello, Delusion!'—like, Dolly Levi meets Norma Desmond."—HERB RITTS

"Despite the fact that Carol's theme song is 'Diamonds Are a Girl's Best Friend,' she lost all of hers three years ago in her divorce."—"Beverly Hills (213)" columnist CATHY GRIFFIN in January 2002

"She's Miss Channing to me and the world."—manager and penultimate husband CHARLES LOWE in 1966

"Carol Channing certainly is."—WOODY ALLEN

23

BROADWAY FLOPS, REVISITED

PEARL BAILEY, *House of Flowers.* "If that's a failure, honey, just call me madam. . . . It didn't work out too great. They hired me, then sort of ganged up on me. When you hire a star, listen to your star. I wasn't about to play the little newcomer girl for anybody, not even Capote and company. So I didn't have much say. What could have been real special and made a ton of money, well, it just . . . it went *kaput.*"

SHELLEY WINTERS played the Marx Brothers' mother in the 1970 flop *Minnie's Boys.* "I still don't know what the hell happened."

ROBERT PRESTON, *Mack and Mabel.* "You cannot beat Jerry Herman's music in that. And the story was better than in many hits. As far as I'm concerned, *Mack and Mabel* did not disappoint. But the audience did."

BETTE DAVIS, *Miss Moffat.* "I loved the material . . . I'd already made a hit with [the film] *The Corn Is Green*, and I was open-minded enough to see them update it and put it in the South with blacks. [Originally it was set in Wales.] But I should have gone with my instinct about [director] Mr. Joshua Logan. The things I'd heard! I should have had my head examined before deciding to work with him."

RICHARD KILEY, *Her First Roman*, about Cleopatra. "It wasn't the history that did us in. So Cleopatra wasn't black [though played by Leslie Uggams]. American audiences don't know and don't care. It was that . . . nothing jelled right. A mess. It still hurts to remember. Oh, God. Don't mess with historical characters. Maybe they put curses on us—like with King Tut's tomb."

DIANA RIGG starred as *Colette*, a 1982 flop that closed on the road. "A fascinating woman. Too complex for Broadway. Or at any rate for a musical. End of discussion, thank you."

TRUMAN CAPOTE wrote the at-times lyrical *The Grass Harp*, which was musicalized in 1971 and lasted seven performances. "Too many people only want to see a big star emoting, or some flashy showbiz musical *about* a big star. . . . Today's theatre-goers usually want the obvious; subtlety completely escapes them. Most audiences belong at a boxing ring. Or preferably in it."

KENNETH NELSON, best known for *The Boys in the Band*, starred in *Lovely Ladies, Kind Gentlemen*, a 1970 musical from the hit play and film *The Teahouse of the August Moon*. "What's quaint or cute in one decade [the '50s] doesn't necessarily *play* in another. I don't feel the picketing or any boycott threats [by the Oriental Actors of America, who noted the preponderance of Caucasian actors in East Asian roles] hurt us. The war in Vietnam did. *Ladies* was set in Okinawa, but to most people that's the same as Vietnam. By the time we came along, nobody wanted to hear or see anything more to do with that whole part of the world."

JAMES COCO was obviously miscast as Lee the Chinese "houseboy" who helped rear the two sons who are the protagonists of *Here's Where I Belong*, based on John Steinbeck's *East of Eden*, the film version of which made James Dean a star. "Steinbeck was a great writer," Coco said, "but his works are often heavy and depressing. He's not been successfully adapted on Broadway." An understatement. The March 3, 1968, opening night of *Here's Where I Belong* was also its closing night and set a new record for a one-night performance Broadway loss: $550,000.

　　As Dean fans recall, the plot involved a son finding out his "dead" mother is alive and well and running a bordello. When *Belong* wasn't depressing, it was reportedly dull; one song and dance revolved around the packing and shipping of lettuce—the setting is California's agricultural Salinas Valley. The doomed musical was picketed by nineteen members of the Oriental Actors of America due to Coco's casting.

PEGGY LEE's one-woman show *Peg* flopped, unlike that of fellow singer Lena Horne. "Chocolate, or café au lait, was in, not vanilla . . . [in] the '80s. Flavor of the decade, I guess."

JOE LAYTON conceived and directed *Bring Back Birdie*, a 1981 sequel to the smash hit *Bye Bye Birdie* (1960). Both starred Chita Rivera, but in the later musical, Dick Van Dyke's charming and occasionally hilarious place was a lumpish, very middle-aged Donald O'Connor. The sequel was set twenty years after the original. "So many factors. . . . Sometimes technology seduces us. We had umpteen television monitors as a major part of the Look of the sequel. . . . People loved the original and felt warmly about it. This meant if they weren't delighted by *our* show, they'd hate it. And did. . . . Mr. O'Connor was making his belated debut on Broadway. Any sparkle he had was long gone. Along with any slimness or sex appeal."

During one of the final performances (out of four), O'Connor, who had costarred in the celluloid classic *Singin' in the Rain* (1952), forgot the words to his song "Middle-Aged Blues." Embarrassed, he asked the band for help, then angrily exploded, "You sing it! I hated this song anyway!" Theater historian Ken Mandelbaum wrote, "*Bring Back Birdie* may rank as the worst Broadway musical ever to be created by top-level professionals."

TENNESSEE WILLIAMS wrote *The Milk Train Doesn't Stop Here Anymore*. "I think audiences were neutral about a poetic play about death. A play or movie about a violent murder, perhaps. Because death happens to everyone, but murder happens to someone else."

VINCENT PRICE played Abraham Lincoln in *Yours, A. Lincoln* (1942), based on the book *Why Was Lincoln Murdered?* "For whatever reasons, the critics did not accept me as Mr. Lincoln. . . . Years and years later, when I enacted Oscar Wilde, the critics were kind and accepting, either because of my age or they found I was more Wildean than Lincolnesque!" Critic George Jean Nathan wrote in 1942 that "the Price Lincoln, had [assassin] Booth not taken the job himself, would have been shot on the spot by every dramatic critic present in Ford's Theatre on the fateful night."

KAREN MORROW. "*The Selling of the President* was based on a best-selling book. . . . [But] suddenly it was the same old thing. We started with a bad director, and we began getting into trouble. I had no way of knowing how to fix myself. I had the lead. I was the driving force in the show, and I just wasn't a substantial enough actress to know what to do."

GEORGE TYLER produced one of playwright George S. Kaufman's rare flops, *Someone in the House*, an adaptation of a French farce. "Timing can be crucial . . . we opened at the height of the 1918 influenza epidemic that killed more people than the First World War. People were avoiding theatres because they were afraid of catching the disease in any place full of people." Kaufman half-jokingly recommended that his play be advertised, "Avoid crowds—see *Someone in the House* at the Knickerbocker Theatre."

MARTHA SCOTT was a huge success as Emily in *Our Town*, but had a flop with *Design for a Stained Glass Window* (1950), about religious persecution in sixteenth-century England. She played a Catholic who preferred death to forcible conversion to Protestantism. "It was the consensus that I under-acted and the rest of the cast overacted. [But] I felt Margaret, my charac-ter, would be calm . . . very spiritual. I don't know, maybe those were Protestant critics. But I was very surprised. And disappointed. I thought it would be both lofty and a success."

Charlton Heston, not yet a screen name, was in the cast. George Jean Nathan deemed him "a pretty fellow whom the moving pictures should exultantly capture without delay, if they have any respect for the dramat-ic stage. [He] duly adjusts his chemise so the audience may swoon over his expansive, hirsute chest, and conducts his prize physique about the plat-form like a physical-culture demonstrator." (Shades of Schwarzenegger.)

MAUREEN STAPLETON. "If people knew what makes a flop, there wouldn't be any. How can you ever tell? You do your best and hold your breath." In 1953 Stapleton acted in *The Emperor's Clothes*. George Jean Nathan felt, "Miss Stapleton played the part as though she had not yet signed the con-tract with the producer."

ROBERT VAUGHN is best known for the TV series *The Man From U.N.C.L.E.* and most recently for *Hustle*. In 1977, he played President Roosevelt in *F.D.R.* "One-man shows were not as popular or commonplace as today. Political shows were, and are, even trickier. . . . This was also a sequel of sorts to a very popular show. Perhaps it was too simple." *F.D.R.* was penned by former MGM chief Dore Schary as a follow-up to his hit *Sunrise at Campobello* (1958), which was not a one-man show. *Variety* com-pared the Vaughn show to "listening to only one end of a telephone con-versation."

ROSEMARY HARRIS starred as Eleanor of Aquitaine in *The Lion in Winter*, one of the 1965-1966 season's best plays. James Goldman's take on a Plantagenet family gathering in 1183 was brilliantly written, as was the popular 1968 film version with Katharine Hepburn (for which she shared the Best Actress Oscar—with Barbra Streisand (*Funny Girl*)). "How can I answer," said Harris when asked why the play didn't draw patrons. A his-tory and a mystery, for the *Herald Tribune*'s Walter Kerr dubbed Harris's Eleanor one of the ten or twelve best performances any theatergoer would likely see in a lifetime.

CHARLES MACARTHUR and Ben Hecht cowrote several hit plays, including *The Front Page*. One of their few flops was *Ladies and Gentlemen*, in 1939, starring MacArthur's wife Helen Hayes. Screenwriter Anita Loos, a close friend of Hayes, later explained, "A certain critic of homosexual persuasion took strong exception to the play and to Helen starring in her husband's play. . . . Charlie was much more upset than Helen. It ate at his masculine pride." So when his lunchmates inquired what he planned to do about the gay critic, he cracked, "I'll take care of him, guys. I'm going to send him a poisoned choirboy."

GYPSY ROSE LEE is best remembered for her memoirs, *Gypsy*. Before that, the stripper penned an autobiographical comedy play titled *The Naked Genius*. "Our producer, Mike Todd, finally decided that if the play was lousy, he'd capitalize on it, and actually advertised it that way. Imagine, truth in advertising! One of Mike's ads said, 'Guaranteed not to win the Pulitzer Prize.'"

JULES FEIFFER'S *Little Murders* had a lengthy Off-Broadway run, but first played Broadway—for seven performances. During intermissions, friends would sincerely congratulate the cartoonist-playwright on what they believed would be a big hit. Feiffer later recalled, "If the audience was happy at the first act, if the actors started playing the jokes and didn't play the characters, we were finished. When they played the characters, there was a kind of tension." He felt the play had a future once audiences stopped enjoying the first act so much and after they didn't tell him halfway through that he had a hit on his hands.

JEAN ARTHUR attempted a comeback via a 1967 comedy aptly titled *The Freaking Out of Stephanie Blake*, produced by Cheryl Crawford (one of three founders of the Group Theatre in the 1930s). A shy, reluctant star, Arthur had abruptly left the hit-play-in-the-making *Born Yesterday* to be replaced by future star Judy Holliday.

Jean managed to convince Cheryl that she'd matured in the twenty-one years since her notorious "sick" walkout on writer-director Garson Kanin's *Born Yesterday*. But on the third day of *Freaking Out* previews, Arthur stopped the show to confide that her doctor had suggested she not continue to perform.

She informed the audience, "I am told that I must go on, and I'm going to because I believe in the show . . . but if something happens . . ." The play folded that evening, and Crawford told Arthur that the whole investment of a then-hefty quarter-million dollars was going down the drain. Garson Kanin said of the future enemies, "There was no love lost between the two ladies, despite their mutual sapphistry."

VIVIEN LEIGH appeared on Broadway for the last time in John Gielgud's 1966 production of *Ivanov*. She was by then reluctantly divorced from Laurence Olivier and would die of tuberculosis the following year. In the play, she essayed a deserted wife dying of tuberculosis. Many fans complained that Leigh's character died prematurely after the first act, but the still-lovely star half-joked, "That's better than the whole show should die." Gielgud attributed the play's lack of success to "American audiences—they have trouble accepting an English cast playing Russians. Especially as Americans aren't fond of Russians in the first place."

TRUMAN CAPOTE was the "Tiny Terror" with the big mouth. The 1966 musical of his novella *Breakfast at Tiffany's*—five years after the hit movie starring Audrey Hepburn—became a notorious and costly flop. Capote did his bit to sabotage the show by informing *Women's Wear Daily* that he disliked the score and leading lady Mary Tyler Moore. Producer David Merrick was furious and threatened to advertise the musical as "David Merrick Presents in Cold Blood *Breakfast at Tiffany's*."

Though he claimed otherwise, Capote got the title via a friend's story about a wealthy New Yorker who'd spent the night with a man in uniform. The younger man had never been to Manhattan, and when his happy host offered next morning to take him for breakfast anywhere he wished, the out-of-towner suggested the expensive-sounding Tiffany's. Merrick eventually described the musical as "an excruciatingly boring evening." Despite a million dollars in advance ticket sales, he closed the widely panned show and took full responsibility for the financial loss.

GORE VIDAL and Truman Capote began as friends with much in common. Apparently too much. Both young gay novelists were intensely ambitious, and celebrity divided them. Both eventually wrote plays, and their mutual, enduring friend was Tennessee Williams, in whose apartment they had their worst in-person falling out.

For the 1967–1968 Broadway season, Vidal attempted a commercial play that owed inspiration to the recent hit movie *Guess Who's Coming to Dinner*, which was about an affluent young white woman bringing home her black fiancé.

"Gore's play was dull as well as derivative," crowed Capote. "He just switched the genders, which Gore is good at—look at *Myra Breckinridge*. He had a white boy bringing home his black girlfriend. Or mistress, because Gore is never subtle. And since he's too permanently in a rage to avoid politics, Gore made it be the son of a presidential candidate. . . . It flopped for the same reason Gore was defeated both times he ran for Congress: no substance!"

PETER ALLEN starred as gangster *Legs Diamond* in the eponymous 1988 musical flop. The Australian singer-songwriter, a popular concert performer, was unprepared for the venomous personal attacks surrounding his bid for Broadway stardom. He recalled in San Francisco, where he went after being diagnosed with AIDS, "I never said I was a great actor . . . but no one believed Harvey Fierstein's idea of making *Legs* a dancing gangster. . . . What it really was, was homophobia. I was as out as a non-out celebrity could be then, and while the press tolerated me in my own shows, they drew the line when I tried to crash their mainstream party. How dare I aim so high or try and impersonate a butch hoodlum?"

ANTHONY NEWLEY enjoyed more success onstage than in movies, via *Stop the World—I Want to Get Off* and *The Roar of the Greasepaint—The Smell of the Crowd*. Eventually he also became known as one of the ex-husbands of Joan Collins, whom he reviled in print often while she was on *Dynasty*. He flopped big in a comeback stage project he thought couldn't miss: the 1983 musical *Chaplin*, which closed on the road. Newley identified with Charlie Chaplin, as both were reared fatherless and were Cockneys from London's East End.

Besides charisma, *Chaplin* lacked action, with most of the screen legend's exciting life occurring offstage and Newley announcing rather than showing what was happening. Then too, three actors played Chaplin—sometimes all onstage at once—and the show had three narrators, including Newley as "himself." The music was described as so-so or less, and another actor tried to recreate the memorable and beloved Stan Laurel, Chaplin's former associate and rival.

Anthony Newley revived *Chaplin* briefly in 1985 but thereafter toured in his prior, more successful musicals.

LIV ULLMANN, movie-critics'-darling-turned-director, starred in one of the biggest flop movie musicals, *Lost Horizon*, in 1973. Six years later she headlined the ballyhooed, costly flop Broadway musical—Richard Rodgers' last—*I Remember Mama*, based on the screen classic. Ullmann, being Norwegian, was considered perfect casting to play the Norwegian immigrant, though she couldn't sing. Universal Pictures supplied half the $1.25 million budget, convinced that the family-centered story had big-screen potential, like *The Sound of Music*.

Despite Ullmann's placid image, there were clashes before and during New York. Director-lyricist Martin Charnin of *Annie* fame was fired after *Mama* got poor reviews in Philadelphia. Charnin announced, "Ms. Ullmann and I do not see 'I to I' about how musicals are made. To make a long and ugly story short, there's no longer a fjord in my future."

Charnin later admitted he'd irked the star by wanting to replace her. (Florence "Brady Bunch" Henderson was one candidate.) "Singing," he revealed, "frightened her, and she couldn't memorize her lines . . . I had thought of it as an ensemble piece, she thought of it as a vehicle for her." Richard Rodgers, seventy-six and ailing, was upset by the goings-on but didn't try to get involved. When Charnin then suffered a serious heart attack, he publicly attributed it to his being fired. Liv Ullmann told the press, "I hope that Martin Charnin will start doing something more constructive than blaming his failures and illnesses on other people."

The musical lost $1.5 million, and Richard Rodgers died four months after its closing.

GINGER ROGERS did two Broadway musicals before Hollywood snapped her up. The second was in 1930. In 1959, her Tinseltown heyday behind her, she returned in *The Pink Jungle*, a musical set in the beauty industry, which closed on the road—Rogers herself campaigned against bringing it into New York. By then she was upset that costar Agnes Moorehead (later most widely known for TV's *Bewitched*) had received nearly all the good notices. Rogers, as was her wont, was too old for her role as a beautician. Since Moorehead was both a draw and the critics' favorite, she was in a secure position for the run of the show. Rogers had to content herself with her fourteen lavish Jean Louis outfits.

Original director Joseph Anthony opined after his firing that audiences were attending for three things—Rogers's wardrobe, Moorehead as a cosmetics tycoon, and the impressive sets—and in spite of one thing: Ginger Rogers. The once-superstar was given two dance numbers for old times' sake, but didn't carry her songs very well. She realized, "We would have been foolish [Ginger more than Agnes] to face the seven New York critics. They would have shot us out of the water." Post-*Pink*, Rogers appeared in several safe musicals, in roles created by genuine musical-comedy stars.

Drownings

MEREDITH WILLSON of *The Music Man* fame tried six years later to wring another megahit, out of the 1963 musicalization of the much-loved motion picture *Miracle on 34th Street*, which had made a child star of Natalie Wood in 1947. The leads of *Here's Love*, Janis Paige and Craig Stevens, were ably supported by comic actors Fred Gwynne and David Doyle. The latter would become best known as Bosley on TV's *Charlie's Angels*, while Gwynne would earn small-screen immortality as Herman Munster on *The Munsters*.

During rehearsals for *Here's Love*, Fred Gwynne's baby daughter died by drowning. The trouper, though brokenhearted, returned to the show for its opening. (Ironically, Natalie Wood later died by drowning off Catalina Island in 1981 at forty-three.) Of her dozens of movies, probably Wood's most popular and widely seen remains *Miracle on 34th Street*. None of its remakes—not the stage musical, a TV movie, nor another feature film—ever approached the original's acclaim or perfect casting.

Señorita Streisand?

ALMOST NOBODY REMEMBERS a 1962 flop musical titled *We Take the Town*, based on the screenplay *Viva Villa!* about Mexican revolutionary Pancho Villa. The show, which never made it to New York, starred Robert Preston, post–*Music Man* and long before the movie musical *Victor/Victoria*. Preston's costars were John Cullum (much later of *Urinetown*), Carmen Alvarez, and Kathleen Widdoes. *We Take the Town* might or might not have been a hit had its star not rejected casting a young singer then performing in boîtes around town.

Producer Stuart Ostrow was "knocked out" by this aspiring actress's singing voice but informed her, "The part calls for an aristocratic Mexican lady."

"So what?" replied Barbra Streisand. "When I sing, there is no nationality."

Ostrow was sold, but couldn't convince Preston, who insisted on a more experienced actress. Streisand later recorded "How Does the Wine Taste?" from the show's score—its only song that more or less endured. As Pancho Villa had been in 1923, *We Take the Town* was shot down—by Philadelphia critics. It didn't reach New York, where it had been booked for the Broadway Theatre. John Shubert returned Stuart Ostrow's $20,000 deposit for the theater, with a note: "Try again, kid; we need new producers."

Looking back in 1999, Ostrow noted, "Today, symptomatic of the theatre's bottom-line mentality, the Shubert empire is run by its former lawyer, who, I can assure you, would not have returned my $20,000 deposit."

One Flops, the Other Doesn't

STAIGER OR STREISAND . . . which one would become a star?

So near, and yet so far apart. It's often presumed that hit musicals must be better works than flop musicals. It ain't necessarily so. The difference, occasionally, is negligible. Sometimes it's timing. Sometimes, especially when a biographical musical revolves around one character, it's who plays her. *Sophie* and *Funny Girl* were both about singing Jewish comediennes who became stars against the odds and despite their looks. For, Sophie Tucker and Fanny Brice both had talent and fascinating personas and life stories.

Both shows opened at the Winter Garden Theatre—*Sophie* on April 15, tax day, 1963. (How much did that timing hurt?) They had much in common, including a proverbial Jewish mother, an unhappy husband overwhelmed by his mate's blossoming success, an "Irish hoofer sidekick" and a kindly black maid. Each show starred a relative newcomer with a highly praised voice, each a potential Broadway star. Both shows endured rough going out of town en route to Broadway. The Brice musical had several titles, among them *My Man*, *A Very Special Person*, and *The Luckiest People*, before producer David Merrick came up with *Funny Girl*.

A pet project of agent-turned-producer Ray Stark, Fanny's son-in-law, the Brice musical had five opening-night postponements and forty rewrites of the final scene alone. Yet it was the Tucker musical, starring Libi Staiger, that folded within a week and is virtually forgotten, like its subject and certainly its star. Fanny Brice might be forgotten too, but for the 1964 *Funny Girl*, which launched Barbra Streisand. (Of course, the hit musical became a hit movie, in 1968—starring Streisand, unusual in that films of musicals typically jettison the Broadway star. That movie later yielded a sequel, 1975's *Funny Lady*.)

Sophie the hit would have launched Libi Staiger. But *Sophie* the flop stopped her career in its tracks. Its music was deemed second-rate; of Steve Allen's oeuvre of 1,000-plus songs, only one, "This Could Be the Start of Something Big," became a major hit (other hits of his include "Picnic," "Impossible," "Gravy Waltz," and the Dixieland tune "South Rampart Street Parade"). Staiger had a following, but not a cult, like the fourteen-years-younger Streisand. She had more stage experience than Barbra, including supporting roles on Broadway in *Wonderful Town* and *Destry Rides Again* with Andy Griffith in 1959. *Sophie* was her fifth and final major production, followed by occasional guest TV and film roles.

Twenty-one-year-old Barbra Streisand had a lot riding on her unproven shoulders. Her only previous Broadway role was Miss Marmelstein the secretary in *I Can Get It for You Wholesale* in 1962. Her future was by no means assured. Talent alone—a Staiger's or a Streisand's—is never enough in show business, which *is* a business. When a costly, much-anticipated musical centers on one performer, she'll either win big or lose big. Second chances are rare—rarer for female performers.

"You know," explained Vera Caspary, who wrote the screenplay for the pre-musicalized *I Can Get It for You Wholesale* (1951), starring another Brooklynite, Susan Hayward, "so many myths invariably grow up around the people who become stars. From most of what I heard about [the musical] *Wholesale*, Miss Streisand was good, but she was not this legendary standout talent and budding superstar that everybody now claims to have instantly recognized.

"And the fact of her standing out had as much to do with her bizarre looks and posturing as her singing talent. Some people did feel that her singing verged on wailing. Today that may be a sacrilege, but the beauty of Miss Streisand's voice was not, then, a universally foregone conclusion."

Caspary, best known as the author and screenwriter of the '40s classic *Laura*, pointed out that *Funny Girl's* producers had initially sought Mary Martin, Anne Bancroft, or Carol Burnett to shoulder the box-office burden. Composer Jule Styne strongly favored young Streisand, who was finally given a very big chance. Had the show been a flop, the producers and indeed the showbiz establishment would have been quite unforgiving. Barbra might have moved on to a solid singing career, but as an actress she almost certainly would not have enjoyed star parts on big or little screen, nor in future Broadway endeavors, if any. (Just how close *Funny Girl* came to bombing—people actually walked out during out-of-town pre-Broadway engagements—is chronicled in Ethan Mordden's book *Open a New Window*, about '60s musicals.)

Had things been different back in '63 and '64, today we might be reading about la Staiger (aka Libs) and her latest project or political endorsement, and asking "Barbra who?" while playing a game of Broadway trivia.

24

GOOD MOVE/
BAD MOVE

Bad Move: Broadway producer Cheryl Crawford was given the chance to present Arthur Miller's 1948 drama *Death of a Salesman* but declined, saying, "Who would want to see a play about an unhappy traveling salesman? Too depressing."

Bad Move: Producer-director Hal Prince said no to *Hello, Dolly!* for a logical but untheatrical reason. "Put it this way. I was asked to direct *Hello, Dolly!* They played me this title song, and I said, 'This for a scene where a woman who doesn't go out visits a restaurant?'" Of course the title number wow-wow-wowed Broadway audiences and was the highlight of a show that became the longest-running musical of its time.

Bad Move: The chief of the ad agency handling *Grease* advised after its Off-Broadway opening in 1972, "I don't think we can do anything with these reviews. It's a disaster. Close it." The show's producer ignored him, and the public ignored the reviews. The popular musical moved uptown, and when *Grease* closed in 1980 it was the longest-running show in Broadway history.

Bad Move: In 1961, Nanette Fabray got a telephone call from Irving Berlin inviting her to play the First Lady in his new musical *Mr. President*. A major disappointment, it was Berlin's swansong. To do the role, Fabray declined a movie role as well as a chance at pop-culture immortality as the voice of Wilma Flintstone in *The Flintstones*. "When I heard that title, I thought, no contest. An Irving Berlin musical . . . or some little cartoon thing with a crazy name that not even a child will remember in two years?"

Bad Moves, Good Move: George Bernard Shaw's acclaimed play *Pygmalion* was eventually made into a classic 1938 English movie. On the other side of the Pond, there were various attempts at a musical version. Rodgers and Hammerstein gave it a go, then announced it couldn't be done. Next, the team of Leonard Bernstein, Betty Comden, and Adolph Green was called in. Comden explained, "We saw the film, and at the end we said, 'Gee, it's such a great movie, why turn it into anything? It's too good. Leave it alone.' That wasn't such a smart move." Frederick Loewe and Alan Jay Lerner gave it a whirl and came up with *My Fair Lady*, such an enduring success on stage and screen that to most people today *Pygmalion*—the film or the play—is simply *My Fair Lady* without music.

Good Move: After her fanciful autobiography was published, Gypsy Rose Lee received four offers for the dramatic rights. Far from rich, she was tempted by MGM and Warner Bros., which each offered about $200,000 to turn *Gypsy* into a motion picture. (The eventual Warners movie of the stage musical, starring Rosalind Russell and Natalie Wood, was a flop.) Gypsy's son, Erik, was incredulous when his mother instead sold the rights to producer David Merrick, who wanted to turn the book into a Broadway musical via the team of Lerner and Loewe. Merrick offered her $4,000 against a percentage of the box-office gross.

"It's a risk," explained the former stripper. "But if the show is success-ful, I'll get royalties from it for the rest of my life, as well as at least that much ($200,000) when it's sold for a film."

Of course *Gypsy* became an ongoing hit as well as an instant classic. There would also be royalties from touring companies, the original cast recording, stock and amateur rights, the movie sale, and eventual revivals.

P.S. Post–Lerner and Loewe, the musical was to have been composed by young Stephen Sondheim, but Ethel Merman didn't want a newcom-er crafting her songs. She accepted Sondheim as a lyricist but asked for and got veteran Jule Styne to create the music.

Bad Judgment: Following *A Chorus Line*'s first night Off-Broadway at Joseph Papp's Public Theater, Bette Midler—who'd done a Broadway stint in *Fiddler on the Roof*—went up to *Line* co-author James Kirkwood. "She said to me, 'It's such a pity. You almost had a hit. But that awful song—what was it? Something about what they did for love?—that threw it right down the toilet. Oh, well.' She was trying to be sympathetic."

Bad Judgment: Depending on the source, producer Mike Todd (Elizabeth Taylor's third husband) or an assistant to columnist Walter Winchell famously dismissed the new musical *Oklahoma!* with "No legs, no jokes, no chance." The show lacked chorus girls and guffaws but wowed audiences with its Rodgers and Hammerstein score (their first together) and Agnes de Mille's innovative choreography. A near-instant classic, it went on to break all Broadway attendance records and become possibly the most-often-produced musical in American high schools.

Good Move, inadvertently: Alan Sues ironically played a homophobic bully in *Tea and Sympathy* on Broadway in 1953. He later gravitated toward comedy onstage and in nightclubs. In 1966 he appeared Off-Broadway in *The Mad Show*, which led to his being signed for *Rowan and Martin's Laugh-In*. But the TV series took a long time to jell, and meantime Sues did a play written by costar Elaine May, *A Matter of Position*. Directed by the renowned Arthur Penn, it opened pre-Broadway to middling reviews. Sues, however, was singled out for praise. To his chagrin, he had to leave the production, being legally committed to *Laugh-In*, which bowed in 1968. The play folded, never reaching Broadway, while *Laugh-In* went on to become a smash hit and cultural phenomenon.

Alan's most notable character on the show was Big Al, the nellie sports reviewer modeled on film critic Rex Reed. Sues stayed with *Laugh-In* the first four years, then left in favor of a Broadway-bound revival of the musical *Good News*. A bad move: it folded on the road. To Sues's dismay, after *Laugh-In* he was seldom hired for anything but comedy—certainly not for bully roles.

Good Move: "In 1966 I signed to host a new TV game show for 13 weeks. I saw it as a paid distraction, a gig in between Broadway musical shows, which were my first love," explained Peter Marshall, born Ralph Pierre LaCock. "So I was anxious to get back to New York. . . . I didn't for a moment believe that *Hollywood Squares* would last beyond the 13 weeks. But it and I lasted, together, 16 years."

Good Move: Charles Strouse, who co-wrote the score of *Bye Bye Birdie* (1960), recalled its star Dick Van Dyke's coming to him with a dilemma. "Buddy, I got an offer to do a television series." Strouse reminded the former Atlanta TV talk show host that *Birdie* was a hit; Dick had just won a Tony and now had his choice of future Broadway roles. He asked how long the TV offer was for? "Twelve or thirteen weeks."

Strouse advised, "Right now you're on top. Stay with Broadway. A television series would be a big mistake." But DVD opted for the little screen and a bigger public. Thanks to his eponymous series, he also became a 1960s movie star (*Mary Poppins*, etcetera).

Good Move: Though it's hard to believe now, in the late 1950s Andy Griffith looked poised to become a Broadway and/or movie star. Television? Who knew? In 1955, Griffith landed on the Great White Way in the comedy hit *No Time for Sergeants*, directed by Morton Da Costa of *Auntie Mame* fame. Coincidentally, Don Knotts, later of *The Andy Griffith Show*, had a small role.

Griffith's second and final Broadway outing, in 1959, was a much-ballyhooed musical: *Destry Rides Again*, (The classic film had starred Marlene Dietrich and James Stewart.) David Merrick produced and Dolores Gray played Frenchy. At 473 performances, it wasn't a flop, but nowhere near the success—nor personal showcase—that *Sergeants* had been. First wife Barbara Griffith allowed, "Andy is usually easygoing, so long as he is the center of attention. . . . Life with a comedian is no joke." Griffith felt the dancers dominated *Destry*.

The year before the 1958 hit film of *Sergeants*, Andy made his screen debut in the riveting *A Face in the Crowd*, directed by Elia Kazan. He portrayed an appealing, two-faced rube who moves from country musician to would-be political powerhouse via the influence of television. Critical reaction was very supportive, and many observers were dismayed that the actor wasn't Oscar nominated. However, his third movie, *Onionhead*, was neither a commercial nor critical hit, and in 1960, Andy began the eponymous TV series which he co-owned thanks to the leverage film and Broadway had given him. It ran until 1968 and made Andy Griffith a household name, though the small screen's gain was the loss of the two other media in which he'd proven his charm and talent.

Bad Move: *A Funny Thing Happened on the Way to the Forum* (1962) was intended to star comic Phil Silvers. He passed on the risky project—an ancient-Roman-style farce. (Fellow TV star Milton Berle also refused.) When *Forum* became a smash hit starring Zero Mostel, Silvers keenly rued his decision. He did retain hopes of starring in the 1966 film version, but by then his name meant nothing on a movie marquee, and Mostel got to reprise his Broadway triumph. Silvers did manage to land a supporting screen role as flesh peddler Marcus Lycus, and nearly stole his scenes with fellow ham Mostel. Alas, the film was a flop. In 1972, Phil Silvers got to star in a *Forum* revival, but, sadly, its run was cut short by his poor health.

Good Judgment, Bad Judgment: Mary Martin was an early choice to play Fanny Brice in *Funny Girl*. Wrong for the wry, comedic, and ethnic part, she was artistically smart to turn it down, less smart to forego the lead in a future hit musical that made a star of Barbra Streisand. Martin would also have been all wrong for Eliza Dolittle in *My Fair Lady*, which made a star of Englishwoman Julie Andrews. But Martin wasn't offered the role, since after listening to Lerner and Loewe's sublime score, the Texan told her manager-husband—who told the composer and lyricist—"How could it have happened? Those dear boys have lost their talent."

Bad Move: Columbia Records' Goddard Leiberson was famous for recording original cast albums of quality. Writer Arthur Laurents was directing the musical *I Can Get It for You Wholesale*, featuring newcomer Barbra Streisand, and sent her to sing for Leiberson, who sent a note to Laurents: "Barbra Streisand is indeed very talented, but I'm afraid she's too special for records." Later he recorded the cast album of *Wholesale* and eventually signed her to a Columbia contract, but at a much higher price than if he'd signed her earlier.

Bad Move: Harold Clurman, asked to direct Carson McCullers's 1949 play *The Member of the Wedding*, begged off with the comment, "It won't make a dime." The admittedly quirky work won the Drama Critics Circle Award for best play, toured for a year, and sold to the movies for a then-huge six-figure advance. *Member* of course made a star of the radiant and unique Julie Harris.

Good Move: Humorist, celebrity wit, and father of Peter "Jaws" Benchley, Robert Benchley was asked by millionaire John Hay Whitney whether he ought to invest in a forthcoming play titled *Life with Father*. Benchley answered, "I could smell it [the play manuscript] as the postman came whistling down the lane. Don't put a dime in it." Whitney, far richer than Benchley, did invest. The 1939 play ran seven and a half years on Broadway (3,224 performances), the longest-running play ever up to that time.

Bad Move: Dean Jones was for a time a movie leading man, especially in Disney pictures. Then he got fundamentalist religion. He also got the lead in Stephen Sondheim's innovative, stunning musical *Company* (1970). Jones played Bobby, the single guy surrounded by married friends urging him to wed. Over the years, the rumor persists that Bobby is a closeted character—played post-Jones by gay actor Larry Kert of *West Side Story*, and in the yearlong tour by gay ex-dancer George Chakiris (from the screen *West Side Story*). Jones left the *succès d'estime* within a month of its Broadway opening, purportedly for health reasons or possibly due to a sticky divorce or over his reported discomfort in the role, which whether it was closeted or not, could have opened up a major post-Hollywood theater career for the actor. Jones later returned in a partially right-wing-funded religious musical (*Into the Light*) that flopped big.

Bad Move: "We're going to run for two years," said Yul Brynner of his musical *Home Sweet Homer*, based on Homer's *Odyssey*, which bowed on Broadway with a Sunday matinee on January 4, 1976. The book and lyrics were by then-hot *Love Story* author Erich Segal, a classics professor at Harvard. Brynner had toured the show for almost a year and believed his standing ovations augured another hit of *The King and I* proportions. Of course the movie star received ovations because he was a star, and many who went to see him as Odysseus were disappointed that he wasn't the King. In one scene he wore long hair and a beard and didn't look at all "Siamese."

As the musical traveled from city to city, major chunks were cut. The show, generally deemed poor to begin with, got worse and worse. When finally it reached New York, it had to face the critics, who were merciless. And New Yorkers were less impressed by a star. *Home Sweet Homer* closed the same day it opened on Broadway, not even playing a nighttime performance. Brynner, no longer box office on the silver screen, thereafter returned to touring in *The King and I* until his death.

Bad Move: A favorite dramatic presence in Edward Albee's plays, Marian Seldes turned to the musical stage for what seemed a sure bet, *Annie 2*. Its creators called it "a continuation," not a sequel. However, it followed in the wake of the 1977 smash *Annie*, which ran nearly six years. (A continuation of profits was doubtlessly hoped for.) *Annie 2* officially opened in Washington, D.C., in 1990. "I smile when I remember it," said Seldes, "because my first reaction to the script was so positive, and I had to sign a very long contract. I thought, I suppose the only problem I'll ever have is finding a way to leave this, because it's going to be such a hit!"

But where *Annie* had had a happy ending and its theme had been hope, *Annie 2*—subtitled *Miss Hannigan's Revenge*—seemed redundant and cold. Dorothy Loudon reprised her Hannigan, and Seldes played a character called Marietta Christmas. This time, Annie was somewhat backgrounded, while Miss Hannigan was placed center stage. The plot was too improbable, as well as mean-spirited. Hannigan's goal is to wed Daddy Warbucks, become Annie's adoptive mother, then kill both and become the world's richest widow. The show didn't make it past D.C. to Broadway, where $4 million in advance tickets had sold in anticipation of a warm, upbeat sequel akin to the original.

P.S. The original Sandy was not rehired in 1989. Deemed too old for the part, he died the year that the "continuation" opened and closed.

Good Judgment: Director–choreographer Bob Fosse was known for consistent attention to the details of his shows, including revivals and tours. His health was often consciously placed second to his work. Michael Cone, a member of the national tour of *Sweet Charity*, recalled a particular rehearsal in Washington, D.C. "He was different that day. I remember I had a line, and I was actually begging for a laugh on it, and he gave me a note, and told me, 'You don't have to work that hard. The line's not that good, and you're better than that.' . . . That night the line came up that I had been pushing so hard on, and I just said it—and it got a bigger reaction than it ever had before. I didn't think about it, I just did it his way. After the curtain came down, they called us all back on the stage and told us that Bobby had died" of a heart attack.

Bad Judgment, Good Move: "What the hell do we know? I'm the girl that read the end of *West Side Story* and said, 'My lord, a musical that ends with a dead body being carried over their heads? I mean, that's just not going to work.'" Yet Chita Rivera took the role of Anita, and she and the musical took Broadway by storm.

25

RUMORS

Rumor(s): *The stories about how actor-playwright Harvey Fierstein got his whiskey-soaked gravel voice, some of them obscene.*

Reality: Fierstein ruined, or terminally deepened, his voice on stage, before breaking through in his own *Torch Song Trilogy.* He'd appeared in an Off-Off-Broadway play titled *Xircus, the Private Life of Jesus Christ.* "I had to deliver a five-page monologue over a recording of Kate Smith singing 'God Bless America' at full blast. The director refused to turn the volume down, and I wanted *every* word heard."

Rumor: *Talented and attractive Florence Henderson costarred in the 1954 musical hit* Fanny, *but never became a Broadway star because she declined producer David Merrick's advances.*

Reality: Henderson, aka Carol Brady from TV's *The Brady Bunch,* denies the rumor. The mystery remains why the singer–actress didn't hit it big in musical comedy. It *is* true, on Broadway and in Hollywood, that many careers have stalled or failed to take off because performers (mostly female) crossed powerful—and vengeful—figures.

Rumor: *Mary Martin never allowed Julie Andrews nor* The Sound of Music *movie to be mentioned, and certainly not discussed or praised, in her presence.*

Reality: Martin starred in the Broadway *Sound of Music* to great acclaim (winning a Tony against Ethel Merman in *Gypsy*). But the screen version went to the younger Andrews, also a better singer. Martin's success in *Music,* her final big hit, was almost totally eclipsed by the record-shattering success of the beloved movie, which made Andrews an international superstar. But Martin did not personally ban the sight or sound of Julie.

Rumor: *Before turning over her dressing room to her* Woman of the Year *replacement, Raquel Welch, Lauren Bacall stripped it completely bare, not even leaving the younger, more buxom performer any toilet paper in the loo.*
Reality: So said several *Woman of the Year* insiders.

Rumor: *Rock Hudson was offered the "butch gay role" in the Broadway musical* La Cage aux Folles *and wanted to accept, but felt it was too close to home.*
Reality: Hudson already had musical stage experience, and hugely enjoyed *La Cage*. But like most closeted movie stars, he only played straight. (Heterosexual actor Gene Barry, who accepted the part, advised fellow actors that it was okay to play gay—*once*. Best known for TV's *Burke's Law*, Barry—born Eugene Klass—isn't generally known to be Jewish.)

Rumor: *Eight-times-married lyricist-librettist Alan Jay Lerner (*My Fair Lady, Camelot*) was bisexual.*
Reality: Three men reportedly had sex with Lerner, including—by his own admission—actor Felice Orlandi, longtime husband of comedic actress Alice Ghostley. Another man was a former boyfriend of actor Reid Shelton (*My Fair Lady, Annie*), of whom Shelton said, "He fell for Alan . . . but soon found out Alan only liked *sex* with men, and saved all his relationships for women." Revue and record producer Ben Bagley also offered, "I had a Puerto Rican lover who met Lerner through a mutual acquaintance, then dropped me. I later heard the affair was brief, sweet, and remunerative."

Rumor: *Lyricist Lorenz Hart was gay "because" he was so short—four-feet-nine to barely over five feet, depending on the source.*
Reality: This fanciful and biased apologizing for the man's sexuality has been put forward in print and TV biographies. In 1999, British theater writer Mark Steyn, in a "The Fags" chapter of his book *Broadway Babies Say Goodnight*, declined to categorize the "Bewitched, Bothered and Bewildered" partner of composer Richard Rodgers. "Any guy of 4' 10" winds up making do, regardless of gender." Yet there are heterosexual dwarves and other men shorter than Hart. Alan Jay Lerner opined, "Because of his size, the opposite sex was denied him, so he was forced to find relief in the only other sex left." Tell that to Toulouse-Lautrec, Dudley Moore, Michael J. Fox, or Mickey Rooney, who played Hart in an MGM biomythography.

Larry Hart agonized over being not only short, but Jewish and gay. Or rather, over the discrimination people with such traits encountered from the unkind majority. As stage and screen celebrity Oscar Levant put it when asked whether he was an "unhappy Jew": "No, but I'm not too happy about anti-Semitism."

Rumor: *Composer George Gershwin (1898–1937) was homosexual or bisexual. Or heterosexual.*
Reality: No real proof, any way.

Rumor: *Peruvian songbird Yma Sumac, able to reproduce incredibly high-pitched bird sounds, was really a Brooklynite named Amy Camus (Yma Sumac spelled backwards).*
Reality: Sumac costarred in a legendary musical flop called *Flahooley* (1951), whose program read, "By the time she was eight, she was the favorite ritual singer of the sun-worshipping Andes Mountain Indians." No wonder people thought her persona fabricated. Originally titled *Toyland*, the forty-performance *Flahooley* was Sumac's sole Broadway show. (Later it was restaged as *Jollyanna* and bombed again.)

Sumac was the genuine article, and her mangled English was real. When she returned to Peru, her car was stoned by countrymen who felt she'd become a *gringa*. She moved to the US, doing occasional nightclub performances, her thick accent still evident in the late 1990s.

Rumor: *For his musical* Oliver! *Lionel Bart stole some of Richard Rodgers' melodies.*
Reality: Based on Dickens's *Oliver Twist*, the record-breaking *Oliver!* with book, lyrics, and music by Bart opened in 1960 in London and in 1963 on Broadway, where it racked up "only" 774 performances. The 1968 film version won the Best Picture Academy Award (the last "Best" musical till *Chicago* in 2003). This pervasive rumor, which even found its way into print, is hard to pin down. Bart himself noted, "*Oliver!* is the biggest thing on two continents. They don't bother to criticize or slander you if you don't impress."

British actor George Rose said, "I think it's from a grudge. I understand that some people who couldn't secure rights to one or other of Lionel Bart's projects then concocted this rumor. I imagine they're anti-Semitic as well as disgruntled." Ben Bagley queried, "Don't you suppose Richard Rodgers would have sued if this accusation had any merit? Jerry Herman got sued, and Bart was fairly new on the scene too, as well as a foreigner. If he'd been sued, everyone would have rooted for Mr. Rodgers."

Rumor: *Horror movie star Bela Lugosi was forced to find work in the theater due to political blacklisting.*
Reality: Back in Hungary, Bela Blasko (born in the town of Lugos) had done extensive theater work, usually romantic leads but also varied roles like Jesus Christ. His American breakthrough was in *Dracula*, his only stage hit

ever. He wasn't first choice for the screen version but finally got the role and became a star—a very stereotyped one due to his unique image and accent.

During World War II, Lugosi spoke out against Hungary's pro-Hitler position. He'd always been a liberal and was anti-monarchy, anti-fascist, etc. This came back to haunt him after the Republican-controlled Congress instigated the House Un-American Activities Committee and its resultant witch hunts. From churning out several films a year, he went to one picture annually, then none between 1948 and '52, when he made two, one of them in England, where he had traveled to do theater as well. At the very least, Lugosi was graylisted for his politics, and the pre-emptive letter he'd chosen to write to the notorious HUAC trying to "clear" his name had little effect.

Rumor: *Discriminating theatergoers who caught any of the nine April 4–11, 1964, performances of the early Stephen Sondheim flop* Anyone Can Whistle *still hold annual reunion dinner parties to celebrate the cult show and analyze why it didn't soar.*
Reality: *Still?* Originally titled *The Natives Are Restless*, the show was a satire about blind conformity. It opened and closed on two Saturday nights, playing out George S. Kaufman's famous warning that satire is what closes on Saturday night. Angela Lansbury, then a movie supporting actress, proved in *Whistle*—as the corrupt mayor of a small town—that she was made for Broadway (eventually earning four Tony Awards). Costars Lee Remick and Harry Guardino also had no prior Broadway musical experience.

During tryouts in Philadelphia, one of the actors suffered a heart attack and had to be replaced. The innovative musical, including Sondheim's occasionally very lengthy numbers, was too unusual for the times, but the original cast album, recorded the day after *Whistle* stopped, has kept its memory very much alive, and certain diehards in and out of Manhattan do indeed meet every year for a wake, a bake, and a new take.

Rumor: *Martin Luther King Jr.'s assassination caused the failure of* The Education of H★Y★M★A★N K★A★P★L★A★N *(1968).*
Reality: This rumor was fostered by the musical's creators. The story of a Jewish Russian tailor—played by Jewish-American actor Tom Bosley (TV's *Happy Days*)—studying in night school to become a U.S. citizen was based on a Leo Rosten character popularized by *The New Yorker* in the 1930s. Though Bosley had temporarily become a Broadway star via *Fiorello!*, after *EHM* opened in Philadelphia it did minimal business and its tryout was cut short. In New York it was inevitably and negatively compared with another musical about Russian Jews, *Fiddler on the Roof*, then in its fourth year.

The show was the 110th Broadway production of eighty-year-old director George Abbott, but its timing was unlucky: during the opening-night intermission, audience member and New York Mayor John Lindsay was advised that King had just been assassinated in Memphis. Word spread throughout the theater, and many people fled amid rumors that riots would ensue all over the country. Because Lindsay attended *Education* when the news broke, the show suffered to some degree by association. However, without a true star, with mostly poor reviews, and without good word of mouth, *Education* probably wouldn't have survived much longer than its twenty-eight performances.

P.S. *Education* did indirectly contribute to a huge musical hit, for in 1968 dancer Donna McKechnie contacted *Education's* choreographer to plead for work in the show. He created a dancing part for her, and six years later McKechnie recounted this episode during the taped interview sessions that were the basis of *A Chorus Line*. The situation was incorporated into the new musical, with McKechnie playing the semi-autobiographical part of Cassie.

Rumor: *Edward Albee wrote* Who's Afraid of Virginia Woolf? *(1962) about two male couples but passed it off as a work about heterosexual marrieds.*
Reality: Such a rumor owes much to the misconception that one can only write about what one knows. (Yet don't most gay playwrights have hetero-sexual parents?) Years later when a San Francisco theatrical group put on the play with an all-male cast, Albee obtained a legal injunction that stopped the production after its first performance. "If I wanted to write a play about two homosexual couples," he announced, "I know how to write a play about two homosexual couples." One could reply, "Butcha haven't, Ed, ya haven't." Though openly gay, the senior citizen writes about, like his musical counter-part Stephen Sondheim, hetero characters and lifestyles.

Rumor: *After the flop of his final musical,* Mr. President, *in 1962, Irving Berlin retired in shame and went into seclusion.*
Reality: His previous show, *Call Me Madam* (1950) with Ethel Merman, was a smash hit. Naturally, Berlin's comeback at seventy-four—he would live another twenty-seven years—was eagerly anticipated, especially as its topic, during the Kennedy years, was an inside look at a fictional First Family. However, the stiff, somewhat menacing Robert Ryan was decidedly un-Kennedyesque, and Nanette Fabray was no Jackie in the looks and glamour departments. The nervous Joshua Logan's direction was widely panned; the book was criticized and so were the unattractive sets. *Mr. President's* music—Berlin's first full stage score was composed in 1914—was merely adequate, and the plot went nowhere.

The Jewish composer of *White Christmas, Easter Parade,* and "God Bless America" was disheartened by *Mr. President's* non-hit status. It ran 265 per-formances, only thanks to advance bookings. Blame fell on Berlin because his name no longer guaranteed a smash. Not a fan of "modern music," especially rock 'n' roll, Berlin withdrew from Broadway and did grow increasingly remote from the outside world.

Rumor: *Anne Bancroft was a frustrated Broadway musical star.*
Reality: This one may have started because a costar said in an interview that Bancroft (born Anna Maria Italiano) loved to sing but seldom got to. Then too, Bancroft was a frontrunner to play Fanny Brice in *Funny Girl*, eventually enacted by Barbra Streisand. Before that, Jerry Herman's *Milk and Honey* (1961) had been the first Broadway musical set in Israel. Bancroft was to have starred later that season in another musical: *The Blue Star*, cowritten by Joshua Logan and with a Burton Lane–E.Y. Harburg score. But egotistical producer David Merrick had canceled it, not wanting to be *second* with a set-in-Israel musical.

(Another role Bancroft nearly played was Joan Crawford in the film *Mommie Dearest*. However, she disliked each screenplay draft and finally departed the project, clearing the way for Faye Dunaway's *Grand Guignol* performance.)

Rumor: *Linda Lee, composer Cole Porter's wife, was a lesbian.*
Reality: When they wed, 1919 headlines read, BOY WITH $1 MILLION WEDS GIRL WITH $2 MILLION!! The smart set on both coasts knew that Porter was gay. Lee was an unknown quantity. Most people correctly assumed it was a marriage for Porter's "convenience" and that sex was immaterial. Inquiring minds thus wondered if Lee would miss "it." There's no evidence that Linda was lesbian. Or bi or heterosexual. Perhaps she was asexual or postsexual. At any rate, she was relieved. Her first husband reportedly beat her, before settling a fortune on her. (The tuneful biofilm *De-Lovely* cast a younger Ashley Judd opposite Kevin Kline as Porter, reversing the reality; Linda was several years Cole's senior.)

Rumor: *Gertrude Lawrence, star of Rodgers and Hammerstein's 1951 hit* The King and I, *didn't really die of cancer, but of something more sinister.*
Reality: The rumor derived from Western reaction to Thailand's ban of the anti-factual and irreverent musical that made a star of shaven-headed newcomer Yul Brynner. The ban also took in its nonmusical predecessor *Anna and the King of Siam* and Jodie Foster's '90s flop *Anna and the King*. Some theatrical gossips and tabloids hinted that Lawrence (1898–1952) had been poisoned or otherwise lethally punished for enacting the British tutor who in her memoirs grossly exaggerated her role at the Siamese court and misrepresented the highly educated and able Mongkut, who'd been a Buddhist monk for several years before ascending the throne. Chalk this one up to another "curse of" fantasy inspired by the "exotic" East.

Rumor: *Bisexual Yul Brynner seduced teenaged Sal Mineo, the crown prince (thus the king's son) in* The King and I.

Reality: It's more likely that the two simply bonded in fictional Siam, when Mineo joined the cast in 1952, playing a prince to Brynner's king. Much later they costarred on screen, and who knows what happened then or had happened by then, for Mineo was admittedly gay. The two remained good friends until Mineo's murder by a sadistic robber who happened upon him in his carport when Sal returned home after rehearsals for an LA stage production of James Kirkwood's *P.S. Your Cat Is Dead!*.

Rumor: *"Composer's composer" (according to composer Burton Lane) Frederick Loewe had a protégée named Anna Maria von Steiner who was a "world-famous pianist and [the] inspiration of [sic]* My Fair Lady.*"*

Reality: So said the Palm Springs press, without checking any of the facts. The Viennese-born "Fritz" Loewe was much more private than professional partner Alan Jay Lerner, with reason. The latter, much married and very sexist, once said, "Women should be obscene and not heard." One of Loewe's escapades, included in the book *Palm Springs Babylon*, was passing off his pal Allan Keller as Anna Maria von Steiner. Palm Springs bought the impersonation, but after the cat was out of the bag there was no more print coverage of the man behind la Steiner or about Frederick and Allan's relationship. P.S. your bias is showing.

Rumor: *Montgomery Clift got his big break in the Pulitzer Prize–winning* The Skin of Our Teeth *(1942) via sexual favoritism from playwright Thornton Wilder.*

Reality: Clift, born in 1920, did become close to Wilder, born in 1897, a major playwright in his day. Before that, Clift had become even closer to actor Alfred Lunt, born in 1892, a major actor via his professional and marital association with wife Lynne Fontanne, five years his senior. Whether or not the beauteous youth slept with any of his gay benefactors is unknown. (He did *not* sleep with his *Skin* director, the virulently homophobic Elia Kazan, who made numerous anti-gay comments on into his old age.)

Rumor: *Laurence Olivier, familiar with John Gielgud's habits, arranged for him to be arrested for "importuning" in a London john in 1953 to eliminate him as competition.*

Reality: Gielgud was entrapped and arrested by an undercover police officer, as happened decades later in a Beverly Hills restroom to *Hogan's Heroes* actor Robert Clary and visiting British singer George Michael. Gielgud was then convicted, not long after being knighted. A national scandal ensued, with the homophobic popular press on the warpath. Gielgud seriously considered giving up acting and sought his colleagues' advice. They all urged him to continue, except longtime rival Olivier. (Critic Kenneth Tynan famously declared Gielgud the world's best actor from the neck up and Olivier best from the neck down.) Courageously, Gielgud chose to move forward with his next project, acting in and directing a West End production of N.C. Hunter's play, *A Day at the Sea*. To Gielgud's heartfelt relief, he was warmly received by theatergoers, as opposed to average tabloid readers.

P.S. Leading British playwright Terence Rattigan wanted to dramatize the episode in *Separate Tables*. But the closeted writer was persuaded to turn the character into a man arrested for approaching women in cinemas. When the play moved to Broadway, Rattigan hoped to restore the character's intended sexuality. But closeted British actor Eric Portman and American producer Robert Whitehead vetoed the idea. Ironically, the role won an Academy Award for David Niven in the 1958 film version; the otherwise charming Englishman was far from pro-gay and habitually closeted numerous gay or bisexual celebrities in his books and interviews.

P.P.S. Alec Guinness was also arrested in a men's room, in Liverpool. However, that information only came out posthumously, because Guinness hadn't been famous at the time, hadn't given his real name at the police station, and, unlike Gielgud—who outlived the closetedly bisexual Olivier by fourteen years—Sir Alec covered his true sexuality with a wife.

P.S. III. After his arrest, Sir John was initially refused entry into the United States, to costar in the 1953 all-star film of Shakespeare's *Julius Caesar*, which first-billed (the eventually openly bi) Marlon Brando. Why? Because the Republican administration had recently enacted sterner laws against allowing homosexuals into what tennis champion Martina Navratilova has labeled "the land of the free heterosexual."

26

BROADWAY
BABBLE ON

"After even Off-Off-Broadway revues became costlier to produce, I launched
my legendary series of recordings. Everyone has sung for me, all the
Broadway biggies, and everyone from Katharine Hepburn to Tony Perkins
to you-name-them. I've specialized in offbeat and discarded songs by the
great composers, cut from Broadway shows.

"My record label, Painted Smiles, was legendary too, and sexy, because
the pair of lips in the very center surrounding the hole that goes over and
down on the metal pole of your record player creates a symbolic sex act
each time you played one of my records—now, of course, available on CD.

"Cowrite my memoirs with me—and I've threatened to write them
for years!—and we'll have a regular Broadway Babylon on our gilded but
culturally relevant hands. I've got the down and dirty on everyone in
showbiz, or at least everyone in showbiz in New York, which is those
worth knowing about."—revue and record producer BEN BAGLEY in a
1995 letter to this author. (He died in 1998 at sixty-four.)

"For her two Broadway shows, Barbra Streisand was Tony nominated, for supporting and then for starring. She lost both times. . . . Streisand was
admired for her talent and briefly cheered for overcoming anti-Semitism
and the prejudice against unlovely girls. But what happened is her ego
blossomed along with her stardom, and she treated people quite badly.
Awards are where behavior like that can catch up with you."—columnist
BOYD MCDONALD

"Larry Olivier would talk about the brotherhood or fraternity of actors in front of a group, then turn right around and look through an individual actor like he was a dirty pane of glass."—costar ANTHONY QUINN (*Becket*, 1960)

"I've been offered it. I passed. Everybody musically inclined's been offered it.... It's one of the great Broadway scores, but don't hold your breath." —MADONNA in 1997 on the proposed movie of *Chicago*

"Stabbed by the wicked fairy!"—playwright Jerome CHODOROV's brother, EDWARD, when named as a communist by Jerome Robbins in 1953

"Jerome Robbins complied with the witch hunters because he didn't want them to tell his mommy he was gay."—GREG LAWRENCE, author of *Bullets over Broadway*

"Stephen Sondheim wasn't ready to come out of the closet until his mother died."—MERYLE SECREST, Sondheim's biographer

"Either you're a fireplace person or you're not, and I've never trusted anyone who wasn't. Stephen Sondheim, who lives next door to me, complains because the smoke gets into his living room. A most disagreeable man. I don't think he's a fireplace person."—KATHARINE HEPBURN

"The big shocker [in Tommy Tune's memoir] was one paragraph about the cum facials he and Andy Warhol used to engage in—each using their own. They were inspired by Mae West, who was so young looking. Tommy admitted that they didn't seem to work very well, and wondered if it was more effective with someone else's cum? For, Miss West used that of the muscle-men in her nightclub act."—Tony winner MICHAEL JETER (*Grand Hotel*)

"I don't think a day has passed in the last 15 years that I haven't contemplated suicide. Have I been in a state of depression for the last decade and a half? I don't think so."—TOMMY TUNE in his 1997 book *Footnotes*

"There are always fewer genius directors than there are shows going into rehearsal. Careful—or you'll end up with Garson Kanin directing yours."—writer ETHAN MORDDEN

"David Merrick is a turd in human clothing."—LAURENCE HARVEY, who departed a Merrick musical after the abrasive producer yelled at his star

"In the 1930s, with the Great Depression, jobs were scarce all over, and very scarce on Broadway, as they still are. We were grateful to have jobs there, and we were young but we were responsible. Now I read about how in *Rent*, which is a hit for quite a while already, several of the actors at any one time are out sick or playing hooky. Even when we were sick, we showed up and worked. We never put the audience or our ethics second." —*King Kong* star FAY WRAY, who performed in three Broadway shows in the 1930s, speaking in 2002

"When I saw *Rent* I had a feeling of déjà vu. No, not *La Bohème. Hair.* Think about it . . . so many similarities. The sex and drugs and death and youth and bigotry, the anger and exuberance, and, yes, the still canyon-sized generation gap."—DAVID DUKES, who starred in the 1988 nonmusical *M. Butterfly*

"First they took *Romeo and Juliet* and made *West Side Story* out of it. Okay. I liked the music, anyway. But what did poor *La Bohème* ever do to deserve *this?*"—screenwriter JEFFREY BOAM (*Indiana Jones and the Last Crusade*) on *Rent*

"My audition for the great Harold Arlen [for her first Broadway show, *House of Flowers*] didn't work out very well. It was also rather confusing. He told me, 'You need to go away and live a little.' I was 18, but I was auditioning for the part of a 14-year-old."—DIAHANN CARROLL

"The problem is that most of America thinks the Tony Awards have something to do with hair or hair products. . . . Once the unsophisticated majority finds out the Tonys are about the theater, most of them yawn and watch something else."—anonymous PBS-TV EXECUTIVE in 2001

"I thought B.D. Wong was fabulous in *M. Butterfly.* But then he seemed to disappear . . . not that surprising, as Broadway has few roles for Asian-American actors, let alone gay East Asian ones. . . . I saw him in a spoof of the Charlie Chan [films] called *Shanghai Noon.* Now he has a book out [in 2003] about becoming a father and coming out of the closet."—New York journalist LLOYD GORDON

"As much as I admire him, Stephen Sondheim is not my world. Oscar Hammerstein's are the sort of English lyrics I would aspire to write." —French lyricist ALAIN BOUBLIL (*Les Misérables*)

"They're not Parisians. They're good Jewish boys—like most writers of the theatre. They're in the new tradition of European Jewish writers, which is after all where most of the American musical theatre comes from." —British producer CAMERON MACKINTOSH on Claude-Michel Schöenberg and Alain Boublil (*Miss Saigon, Les Miz*)

"You're revolting, and on top of that you're not even very feminine."—the words from CAROL CHANNING'S MOTHER that Carol said drove her to the stage, where she felt more accepted

"Excuse me, but Mary Martin's charm largely eludes me. Of course she's competent, but unlike Merman who was too big for the screen, Martin was too small for it. . . . Her Pollyanna image fronts a will of iron and a savagely ambitious husband who's become her producer and hatchet man."—playwright JOHN VAN DRUTEN (*I Remember Mama*)

"I knew her better than a husband would."—BEATRICE LILLIE on stage star Gertrude Lawrence (*The King and I*)

"At a certain point, she wanted to be a singer—a mezzanine soprano, as she says. But she's much too funny, and at heart she's an anarchist. Whenever she opens her mouth it's mutiny on the high C's."—stage star IVOR NOVELLO on Bea Lillie

"Musical!"—SIR WINSTON CHURCHILL's succinct reply to W. Somerset Maugham as to what it was like bedding the handsome Ivor Novello. (The statesman claimed the actor-writer-composer-producer was his sole same-sex affair; his mother, a nonpolitician, claimed otherwise.)

"The last I saw of Bea Lillie was her being led away—forever, as it turned out—from a Museum of Modern Art screening in Manhattan after she bared her bosom. If she'd been several decades younger, it would probably have been laughed off; it wouldn't have ended her career and all public appearances."—Tony-winning actor BILL MCCUTCHEON of *Anything Goes* (Lillie lived to ninety-four.)

"You Americans always assume Englishmen are queer anyway—the way we speak, our good manners . . . So we can get away with more. And do." —gay or bisexual stage star CYRIL RITCHARD (originally Australian), Captain Hook in *Peter Pan*, who once declared, "My singing isn't really as bad as it sounds."

"As you may know, the real Chanel was bisexual. But Kate [Hepburn] would be the last to let that come into the open . . . too close to home. What she liked to emphasize was how she and Chanel both idolized their fathers, with whom each woman identified very strongly."—*Coco* costar GEORGE ROSE

"She was a woman who was uncomfortable with being a woman." —ARTHUR LAURENTS on Katharine Hepburn, who starred in the film version of his play *The Time of the Cuckoo*

"Most people do think of me as just another pinko faggot, a bleeding heart, a do-gooder. But that's what I am."—LEONARD BERNSTEIN

"What Lenny did is unheard of in the theatre. Too many people get credit for things they don't do, much less remove their names."—agent FLORA ROBERTS, on client Leonard Bernstein's giving up his credit as co-lyricist for *West Side Story*, which he composed; he gave sole lyrical credit to younger man Stephen Sondheim

"It is very rare indeed what Lennie [sic] did for Stephen. And I know that a great deal of that generous act's motivation was the feeling and camaraderie that one gay man can feel for another."—gay actor MAX ADRIAN, Dr. Pangloss in Bernstein's original *Candide* in 1956

"I won't name him, to protect the talentless . . . an irritating actor who used to come to my parties and drink bottles of gin. Bragged constantly about his nonexistent theatrical triumphs. The last time he ever showed up, he rambled prominently as usual, but I heard an opening and used it. He'd just finished saying, 'And I had the audience glued to their seats.'

"I said, 'Dahling, how fiendishly clever of you to think of it!'"
—TALLULAH BANKHEAD

"I remember Tallulah Bankhead telling of going into a public ladies' room and discovering there was no toilet tissue. She looked underneath the booth and said to the lady in the next stall, 'I beg your pardon, do you happen to have any toilet tissue in there?' The lady said no. So Tallulah said, 'Well, then, dahling, do you have two fives for a ten?'"—ETHEL MERMAN

"After Tallulah appeared in one play for which she was a bit mature, some of the critics took notice. She was devastated. . . . She phoned up one of her more fearless friends and asked, 'Dahling, I don't look 40, do I? Be honest, now.' So he said, 'No, Tallulah, you don't. Not any more.'"—friend and costar ESTELLE WINWOOD

"Estelle Winwood is not Tallulah's best friend! I am! And I've got the scars to prove it!"—PATSY KELLY (*No, No, Nanette*)

"I admire any actress who can clothe the outrageous with style. One of my heroines was the divine Sarah Bernhardt. As everyone knows, she eventually had to have a leg amputated. While recuperating, she received a telegram from the monetarily obsessed head of the Pan-American Exposition in San Francisco. He offered $100,000, an unheard-of fortune at the time, if Bernhardt would allow her leg to be exhibited. She wired back to him, 'Which leg?'"—actress CORNELIA OTIS SKINNER (daughter of actor Otis Skinner), who authored a book on Bernhardt

"I'll tell you who I admire. Not so much these movie stars who come to Broadway and get exorbitant publicity and fees on a silver platter, milady, but women who run things and get in there and make it happen. Imagine the guts and effrontery of a woman theatrical manager with her own troupe back in 1865—yes, that was happening, folks—at a time when no woman could vote or even own property in her own name. *That* is to admire."—EILEEN HECKART

"Carol Channing tries to give forth a positive word about anybody she's asked about, no matter how heinous. But one person you shouldn't bring up is Danny Kaye. Back during *Let's Face It* [1941], his costar was Eve Arden. Carol, her understudy, went on when Eve got sick, and Carol wowed everyone. Except Kaye. Carol was shortly dismissed. Kaye was a prima donna."—showbiz publicist CHARLIE EARLE

"Carol [Lawrence] told me a story about how some performers lose interest during a long run, forcing you to take steps. . . . At the end of *West Side Story*, Maria, disgusted by the violence, threatens a gang member with a gun. Well, this one actor didn't react with fear; rather, he was nonchalant, wasting the moment and ruining it for the audience and for Carol, who, after the performance, demanded what the hell happened?

'I didn't feel it anymore,' he just said. She was furious. But she gave him back his motivation, because the next night her gun was loaded with blanks, and as the guy began to sneer at her, she cocked the gun in his face, and he went pale. From then on, he never went out of character in that scene."—revue and record producer BEN BAGLEY

"Well, the inspiration for the song was a conversation Rex [Harrison] and I had while walking along Fifth Avenue. We were bemoaning our marital woes . . . problems with our assorted wives, when Rex suddenly blurted out, 'Alan, wouldn't it be marvelous if we were homosexual?' People turned to look, but I turned the thought into, 'Why Can't a Woman Be More Like a Man?' [later retitled "A Hymn to Him"]. Shaw would have loved it; he disdained the idea of any possible romance between Henry Higgins and Eliza, but for Broadway we had to include a romance."—*My Fair Lady* lyricist ALAN JAY LERNER, who had eight wives (Harrison had six)

"I have lived, and done it openly for 12 years, with a devoted friend and companion whom I love. I find, however, that most American journalists who have heard of me and wish to write about me try to inquire, quite impertinently, about the nature of the relationship . . . as if they might find a perceived flaw which would allow them to label me less of an actress. . . . But love is love. So enough."—DAME EDITH EVANS (1888–1976), who lived for sixteen years with a female partner

"The profession of acting does attract many emotionally unattractive people. . . . More and more, I find. . . . As I've often said, if a woman wants to act like a man, why can't she act like a *nice* man?"—DAME EDITH EVANS

"Pearl Bailey has an ego that won't quit. She was in *House of Flowers*, and in it she was a madam. Well, fine, that's her persona anyway. But in this musical, she wanted to be a madam without her girls. She didn't want any feminine competition in what she saw as her vehicle, which it wasn't. A potential hit musical, but it closed early."—JAMES KIRKWOOD, a creator of *A Chorus Line*

"Josephine Baker. We were on Broadway together in 1935. They called her the no-clothes horse. That was in France. On Broadway, brother, she had clothes!"—BOB HOPE

"When we costarred [onstage] in *Becket*, I wanted Larry [Olivier] to be my buddy. But he didn't want to know. He just wasn't interested. I tell you, I felt like a schoolboy with a crush on his teacher. I loved and was not loved. I was terribly hurt."—ANTHONY QUINN

"Richard [Burton] is so discriminating, he won't see a play with anybody in it but himself."—then-wife ELIZABETH TAYLOR

"Laurence Olivier is the most overrated actor on earth. Take away the wives and the looks, and you have John Gielgud."—OSCAR LEVANT

"Richard Burton could have been another Olivier, but he met Elizabeth Taylor. He went Hollywood after marrying Dame Fortune."—DAME JUDITH ANDERSON, on Burton's giving up the stage

"Mary Martin was Broadway's biggest closet king. Everyone thought Ethel [Merman] was butch and maybe a lesbian, but she wasn't. And everyone thought that lovely little Mary was Miss Femme, and she was—except next to her gay husband [Richard Halliday]. In other words, don't judge a star by her cover."—BOB FOSSE

"I always heard that Noel Coward wrote that song ["Mad About the Boy"] because of his friend Cary Grant."—DOUGLAS FAIRBANKS JR. in his memoirs, explaining that it wasn't written about *him*

"I was at a benefit rehearsal with Ethel Merman, the queen of Broadway herself. She kept wanting them to add more songs from *Gypsy*, her latest triumph. I dared to suggest another song from *my* show, *West Side Story*, and she reacted as though I were leading a palace revolution. . . . There were others present that day, including an actress whom I won't name, but she's the only one who really stood up to the Merm, and very effectively too. Ethel backed down immediately when this actress fixed her with her gimlet eye and said, 'Don't you dare get manly with me!'"—LARRY KERT

"Honey, I'm a singer from day one. Carol's a comedienne. If I have a natural gift for comedy, I can't take the praise—God gave it to me. But I don't think too many folks outside Carol's immediate circle can claim she has a divinely inspired voice. . . ."—PEARL BAILEY, comparing her and Carol Channing's turns in *Hello, Dolly!*

"Rod Steiger's the worst actor that ever lived. The very name makes me throw up. He's so terrible. He's one of the world's worst hams. A real *jambon!*" —TRUMAN CAPOTE

"Oscar Hammerstein was a city boy, and lyricists are not infallible. In the song 'Oh, What a Beautiful Morning' he wrote, 'The corn is as high as an elephant's eye,' unaware that Oklahoma is *not* part of the Midwestern corn belt."—Midwestern playwright WILLIAM INGE

"With the single exception of Homer there is no eminent writer, not even Sir Walter Scott, whom I despise as entirely as I despise Shakespeare when I measure my mind against his."—GEORGE BERNARD SHAW, critic turned playwright

"I can forgive Alfred Nobel for having invented dynamite, but only a fiend in human form could have invented the Nobel Prize."—GEORGE BERNARD SHAW

"It is his life's work to announce the obvious in terms of the scandalous." —writer H.L. MENCKEN on Shaw

"David Mamet strikes me as a pretentious, macho-er-than-thou Norman Mailer clone, a poseur in the vein of Hemingway, who were he alive today would no doubt be writing plays and screenplays and directing. . . . I find Mamet's writing has a closet-y quality. . . . I don't like bluster, bravado, or berets on non-Frenchmen's fat heads."—New York columnist BOYD MCDONALD

"He really showed great promise. But it wasn't acting he was as interested in as stardom. Acting was the means. . . . He wanted it fast; perhaps he had a sense of feeling doomed. He only did what he had to do in the theatre until Hollywood paid attention to him."—GERALDINE PAGE, who starred in *The Immoralist* on Broadway, in which Dean played a supporting role

"If he'd lived, they'd have discovered he wasn't a legend."—HUMPHREY BOGART, who began onstage, on James Dean

"Young men are the least self-disciplined of actors . . . the least dedicated to craft. Take a talent like Brando. After he took the easier route of camera acting, not having to show up more often for less money and more memorizing, he never returned to the stage. That was just a stepping stone. . . . Believe me, Marlon's sole abiding interest is Marlon."—writer TRUMAN CAPOTE (Brando once allowed, "An actor's a guy who, if you ain't talking about him, ain't listening.")

"In the theatre, you were more wary of reading reviews. The praise of a Walter Kerr or a Brooks Atkinson meant more and less than a more casual, less influential movie or TV review. . . . I got so much praise for *The Miracle Worker* that eventually I got sort of numb to it. Until one of my sons, when he was three or four, saw the movie of it and asked, 'Mom, when did you get over being blind?'"—PATTY DUKE, who earned an Oscar for the screen version

"There is a writer, Robert Brustein, a critic—assassin—who tried to destroy me. He came close. If ever I were to commit suicide, I'd want him within ten feet of me."—playwright WILLIAM INGE, whom Brustein attacked in a venomous article that temporarily shattered Inge, who much later took his own life

"So-so on stage, *Dreamgirls* would make a less than so-so movie, but it *will* eventually be filmed, simply because it's a black showcase, and of course they will hire some gay white male director to do it, and he'll be so *thrilled*. Too sad."—author DAVID SHIPMAN

"I was not turned off by Miss Merman's famous belt nor her hard-as-nails demeanor. I found her voice and personality occasionally refreshing. No, what I found off-putting was her tendency to perform robotically. In any given show, her performance on opening night was the same performance she'd give eight months later. She didn't vary by a hair. That's nonhuman!"—critic WYATT COOPER (the same was said of Carol Channing)

"I contend that the most rabid human species is the minority member who's trying to pass. I refer specifically to Grace Kelly's gay uncle, George Kelly. The playwright. He hated gays, Jews, most women, blacks, liberals, of course. He was a royalist, sided with the king against the people in the French Revolution. When his niece became Princess Grace, he almost burst a gut in rapture. . . . I recall that someone at our table disagreed with George, and George did what was apparently a habit: called the man a liar, then said, 'You've told so many lies, it's a wonder your face hasn't turned black!' . . . By the time I met him—the once—he hadn't had a Broadway success in I don't know how many decades."—writer JAMES LEO HERLIHY (*Midnight Cowboy*)

"The worst part of Broadway success has to be the inevitable film version inevitably casting someone else in your role. It can wound egos and create enemies, even ruin friendships. . . . After Rosalind Russell got the movie of *Gypsy*, Merman busied up and spread innuendo about the sexuality of Roz and her producer husband, whom [Russell] met when he was involved with Cary Grant."—ANN MILLER

"Maybe Hollywood is on to something. We were all pleased as punch to get the chance to be in the movie (of *The Boys in the Band*). It was anything but a hit . . . even so, legions more people see a movie than a play. Among them the movietown movers and shakers. I should've said no to doing the movie, instead of being limited by it. Of course if I hadn't been in it and it had been a hit, it would personally have killed me."—KENNETH NELSON, star of the original *The Fantasticks*

"The wonder is that [Broadway producer] David Merrick's movies bombed. Because his taste was always on the Hollywood level."—British director JACK CLAYTON, who helmed one of them, *The Great Gatsby*

"Way back when, nudity in and of itself was classed along with pornography. It was also often, between two people, a sign of contempt. [Director-producer] Jed Harris had great contempt for his fellow man and he could express it, insultingly and without a word, by appearing semi-nude or jaybird naked in front of someone. . . . When he received his colleague [playwright] George S. Kaufman completely in the nude, Kaufman, unhappily for Harris, didn't bolt and didn't flinch. And when he left, after the long business meeting, Kaufman merely added, 'By the way, Jed, your fly's open.'"—JACK GILFORD (*A Funny Thing Happened on the Way to the Forum*)

"Beatrice Arthur reprised her Vera Charles characterization in the motion picture of *Mame* that starred Lucille Ball in place of Angela Lansbury. . . . Bea later said it was one of her all-time lows, professionally and personally. It drove her back to drinking. . . . I remember when Lucy had Madeline

Kahn fired, and a few of us went over to Bea on the set to ask what she thought about the shenanigans. Bea just rolled her eyes. Then when I asked who *she* thought should be playing Mame, she silently indicated—herself!"—Hollywood columnist LEE GRAHAM

"I hope the publicity isn't going to be on the order of: he's playing Liza Minnelli's first gay husband. Or questions like, Isn't it daring of you to play an openly gay man? I hope that in theatre, at least, such attitudes are passé."—Australian HUGH JACKMAN (Curly in *Oklahoma!* in London in 1998) in 2003, preparing to play Peter Allen on Broadway in *The Boy from Oz*

"It is a mystery why of all of my plays on Broadway, only *Dracula* ran more than a few weeks. . . . Today, interviewers come out of the woodworks . . . [but] can you believe that during the entire run of *Dracula*, no one asked me for an interview? Not in New York, where they are blasé. But later, in California, where they are most impressed by New York plays, there was considerable interest. And then even more after the movie became the big sensation of 1931.

"Two years after the war, I was in a rather charming play (*Three Indelicate Ladies*, 1947). In Boston I received excellent reviews, but they criticized the play, said perhaps it needed some rewriting. Instead, before arriving on Broadway, the stupid producer closed up the show!"—BELA LUGOSI in 1952

"Helen Hayes was so proud to have a theatre named after her. Eventually it was torn down . . . but then they named another one after her, and for the first time ever, she made me laugh when she said, 'Oh, it's wonderful to be a theatre again!'"—theatrical producer ROBERT WHITEHEAD

"Poor old Vincente Minnelli. He was directing too late in life. All he cared about were colors and costumes, not action or performances. David Merrick hired him for his name value . . . he knew he could run Minnelli like a puppet. Because by then his mind had slowed to a turtle's gallop." —JO MIELZINER, set designer of the 1967 flop *Mata Hari*

"The man [David Merrick] thinks his wit is sharper than a hummingbird's beak. But he's still, au fond, a lawyer, and the part of him that does resemble a hummingbird's beak is securely hidden from view."—director ROBERT MOORE, former actor who appeared in Merrick's *Cactus Flower*

"Paul Lynde, it turned out, was anti-Semitic, later blaming 'the Jews' for his failure to become a top-ranking star in Hollywood or New York. . . . He may have been funny to audiences, but he was very unfunny to me, and we

avoided each other as much as possible."—concentration-camp survivor
ROBERT CLARY on his *New Faces of 1952* costar

"Back in 1969, I flew to New York to audition for Kate Hepburn, who was
going to play Chanel in *Coco* the musical. I couldn't sing, but hell, neither
could she! I wanted the part of her assistant, Sebastian. . . . If I may say so,
I gave a brilliant audition . . . I flew back to San Francisco, and René
Auberjonois got the role—and eventually a Tony. If Miss Hepburn didn't
much care for gay actors, butch though she assuredly was, she loathed gay
actors who impersonated females, as I was famous for doing. Regardless
that offscreen, she virtually never wore a skirt and never high heels."
—impressionist CHARLES PIERCE

"I thought Alan Cumming was excellent in *Cabaret*. I thought, 'What a daring,
gender-bending performance.' Until I saw him give the same performance
in a movie, and then another movie, and another, and. . . ."—actor-coach
GUY STOCKWELL

"The way I heard it, Hal Prince hired this English blonde nobody ever heard
of [Jill Haworth] to play Sally Bowles in [the original] *Cabaret* because she
was untalented, which the character is supposed to be. Apparently, Liza
Minnelli had wanted the part, but Prince and his cohorts said she was too
talented for Sally. That baffles me. Audiences love to see and hear talent,
even if we understand that the character's supposed to be lacking. It's just,
how dumb do producers think audiences are?"—costume designer
HERMAN GEORGE

"What's sad is the passing [in 2002] of Adolph Green. Socially, I could take
or leave him. But when he partnered professionally with Betty Comden,
that was a match made in heaven, a boon for Broadway. . . . The giants
are all dead or in retirement, and all I see coming up are dwarves and
ordinary though sometimes very mercenary people."—publicist
MICHAEL LUTZ

"Well, *Cats*. Hmm. What a concept. But a director? All it requires is a costumer,
a choreographer, makeup, and lights. . . . Is the direction innovative?
Exciting? Even logical? The answer has to be: Nunn of the above."
—composer SIR MICHAEL TIPPETT, referring to *Cats* director Trevor
Nunn

"I won't identify the bodies or names, but you can bet if *The Full Monty* had
been about females, all those bodies would have been nice. . . . Couldn't
they have chosen more hunks and no fats?"—Los Angeles–based British
musicologist PHILIP BRETT

"I don't see much point in transsexual stories. There are thousands of gay and lesbian stories waiting to be told. . . . *Hedwig and the Angry Inch* left me cold. Also rather queasy . . . that 'inch' reference. All a transsexual is, is a closeted homosexual who cops out and realigns their body so they can become an opposite-sex heterosexual."—playwright ANTHONY SHAFFER (*Sleuth*)

"Charles Ludlam and Marian Seldes are the best and most interesting actresses working regularly on Broadway, or thereabouts, in the 1980s. This speaks volumes about the condition of the once brimming and bubbling American theatre."—HERMIONE GINGOLD

"Marian Seldes is the luckiest Broadway actress in recent history. Thanks almost entirely to Edward Albee's plays, she's become a major personality and presence—a tall woman, even—of the theatre. . . . It is good to see a woman of a certain age prominently included. She is also slim and elegant, which at that age is nearly as important as talent."—celebrity publicist CHEN SAM

"Nathan Lane has a wonderful sensibility for comedy . . . I'd say a gay sensibility. I would like to see him, for a change of pace, in a Tennessee Williams or Edward Albee [play]. . . . It does rather surprise me that as a gay man he participates in that degree of homophobic humor in *The Producers*. They couldn't have known ahead of time it would be such a hit."—MADELINE KAHN

"David Mamet really thinks he's great. But if he can't grab you in the Arthur Miller or Tennessee Williams way, he'll grab you by the balls with endless foul language. He's like a terrorist of words."—actor-director JOSÉ FERRER on the playwright of *Glengarry Glen Ross* (1984)

"A man of the theatre died last night."—acting coach STELLA ADLER in 1982 to her class, about estranged Stanislavskian colleague Lee Strasberg. After the class sat down again, she added, "It will take 100 years before the harm that man has done to the art of acting can be corrected."

"I was married to a true devotee of the theatre, Helen Menken. She created a sensation in the title role of *The Captive* (1926). . . . I urged her to take on the role; I knew a shiny bit of press bait when I saw it. You see, I'd knocked around on Broadway myself before moving out to California and Warner Bros."—late bloomer HUMPHREY BOGART, whose more-famous-then wife's character was "captivated" by a lesbian in the imported stage hit by Edouard Bourdet

"Yes, it was ahead of its time and failed. Even so, I'm proud my wife [Gladys Lloyd] costarred in it. . . . It might have had a better chance in New York, where *The Captive* was a smash hit until the authorities shut it down. . . . Chicago audiences didn't take to the play, and the press there gave it as little publicity as they could."—EDWARD G. ROBINSON on *Sin of Sins*, a lesbian-themed 1926 play formerly titled *Hymn to Venus*, which one local critic deemed "a horrible thing of soul leprosy"

"Rock Hudson could have been the toast of Broadway in *La Cage aux Folles*. He was offered the more husbandly part and he'd seen and loved the show, but he couldn't say yes . . . too contrary to the ingrained habit of publicly avoiding everything gay-associated, except as a spectator, and even then."—friend and TV-costar NANCY WALKER

". . . I was starting to get worried because I wasn't nervous. I always think of Ethel Merman when it comes to nerve. She once told me, 'I never get nervous. I know what I'm going to do. The audience should be nervous, they don't know what they're gonna get!' I've never forgotten that." —ROSE MARIE (*The Dick Van Dyke Show*), who did four Broadway shows

"The Gospel According to Barbra relates a battle with me over the staging of 'Miss Marmelstein' that went like this: Barbra wanted to use a chair on casters, I fought her; she wanted to roll around the stage on the chair during the song, I fought her; she won the battle and stopped the show cold opening night in Philadelphia, I capitulated.

"In point of fact, 'Miss Marmelstein' was staged by Herb Ross and very inventively. It was his idea to use a chair on casters and it was he who directed the rolling around the stage. If she really had stopped the show cold opening night, David Merrick would never have wanted to fire her, but she couldn't have: it was dead before she came on."—*I Can Get It for You Wholesale* director ARTHUR LAURENTS on what Laurents calls Streisand's "invented story" that has received "credence and acceptance as fact merely by being repeated in interviews, articles, and celebrity biographies"

"It's not very long [eighty minutes], but it's a clever play, from an unexpected source—a film actor named Daniel Stern (*Home Alone, City Slickers*) . . . about the different levels of fame, and lost fame, so crucial to most American performers. It's quite trenchant and amusing, actually."—EMMA THOMPSON in 2003 on Stern's *Barbra's Wedding*, about a former TV supporting actor coming unhinged at being reduced to a stargazer on the day of his Malibu neighbor Barbra Streisand's wedding

"If you are what you eat, then Richard Stilgoe must eat a lot of arseholes."
—a UK TELEVISION COMEDIAN on the lyricist of *Starlight Express*

"When someone first mentioned this new show to me, I thought the title was *You're in Town*. I didn't get around to seeing *Urinetown*, but I possibly may because in the meanwhile it's won [in 2002] Tonys for best music and lyrics and book! To me, the shocking thing is I'm not shocked anymore."
—TV (*The Honeymooners*) and stage (*Take Her, She's Mine*) star ART CARNEY

"One of my favorite musicals—the story, the music, everything—was *On a Clear Day You Can See Forever* [1965]. John Cullum and Barbara Harris were so good in it. What happened? For a while, she was in several movies, then she disappeared—she must still be alive. And John Cullum disappeared, until he made a big comeback on Broadway in—can you believe it?—*Urinetown*. Good for him, but God help us."—movie director GEORGE SIDNEY (*Show Boat, Kiss Me, Kate!*)

"Late the night before *West Side Story* went into rehearsal, Lillian Hellman called me. . . . 'This is Lillian.' (No 'Lillian Who'; certainly no 'Hello, how are you?') 'You are in for the worst experience of your life. Leonard Bernstein is a megalomaniacal monster. He will destroy every word you write. Good night.' Click."—writer ARTHUR LAURENTS (Hellman had worked with Bernstein on *Candide*.)

"I'd like to say here that it was Nanette Fabray who took all my good clothes away [in *Mr. President*, 1962]. She didn't want my dresses to be better than hers. [Costume designer] Theoni Aldredge told me years later, when . . . I said to her, 'Remember that beautiful dress? Why did it get cut?' and she said, 'Miss Fabray requested it.' Oh, well!"—actress ANITA GILLETTE

"It was difficult working with Ray [Bolger, the Scarecrow in *The Wizard of Oz* film]. He never really looked at you. He was sort of off on his own. . . . He just had no contact and never paid any attention to you. And that [*By Jupiter*, 1942] was my first lead and I really needed support."—NANETTE FABRAY

"I thought Ray Bolger was nice to me, early on. Whatever motives he may have had, he seemed kind. To me, anyway. Years passed . . . I realized he didn't like me, and I never knew why. I'd never done anything to him. . . . I ended up loathing him. He's dead now, so I can say that."—actress GRETCHEN WYLER

"His big thing during *All American* [1962] was to sing [his old hit] 'Once in Love with Amy' after the curtain call while we all stood onstage watching. We finally had to get up a petition that said if he wanted to do his nightclub act that was fine, but we wouldn't have to stand there every night for his number and curtain speech."—ANITA GILLETTE on Ray Bolger

"There was one time during rehearsals [for *The Pajama Game*, 1954] when I didn't feel comfortable in a certain place in the show. I questioned something [George Abbott] was doing. So I asked to see him, and I went up to his office. There he was, sitting behind that huge desk, and he said, 'What is it, Janis?' and I said, 'Mr. Abbott, I'd like to talk to you about this scene. I don't feel it. I can do better.'

"He said, 'Janis, you have five minutes to make up your mind. That's the way it is. That's the way it's going to be. Now, you want to stay in the show, or you want to leave? You go outside and stand there for five minutes, and make up your mind.' Well, I burst into tears, which I'd had no intention of doing. . . . Then I dried my tears and . . . walked back and said, 'Mr. Abbott, I'm staying.' He said, 'Good. Get back to work.'"—JANIS PAIGE

"Andrew Lloyd Webber is to be thanked for making scenery the star of hit musicals. *Phantom*'s crashing chandelier, *Miss Saigon*'s helicopter, *Sunset Boulevard*'s enormous staircase . . . and the allegedly feline costumes in *Cats*."—CHARLES GRAY (*The Rocky Horror Picture Show*)

"*Cats*, the empty musical . . . powerfully demonstrates the popular appeal of cats and the wild freedom they represent. The authors of the show took T.S. Eliot's anthropomorphism more seriously than he did, notably in the case of pathetic Grizabella, a once-beautiful cat who mourns her lost youth and ascends into heaven at the end; they give her a lamentation, the song 'Memory,' from one of Eliot's poems about *humans*. One longs for the honesty of Don Marquis's weather-beaten Mehitabel, who like any normal cat is blissfully unaware that she is no longer attractive in human terms."—PROFESSOR KATHARINE M. ROGERS, author of *The Cat and the Human Imagination*

"Andrew Lloyd Webber's music is everywhere. But then so is AIDS."—MALCOLM WILLIAMSON, Master of the Queen's Musick [sic] in 1992 (he later apologized . . . to People With AIDS)

"Did you hear the latest *Cats* joke? After *Aspects of Love* bombed, an associate told Lloyd Webber it was time to face the future. Because you can't live on memories. Webber said, 'I can.'"—theatrical producer JOAN LITTLEWOOD ("Memory," of course, was *Cats'* sole hit song.)

"It's not true that [we] are no longer speaking. I saw his last show. At least I hope it was his last show."—TIM RICE on former collaborator (*Evita, Jesus Christ Superstar*) Andrew Lloyd Webber

"The sickness of jealousy is more intense in the arts and media because people's successes and failures are so public there. You are most hated when you are most successful."—BARBRA STREISAND

"Shallow . . . very pretentious. . . . That's like saying, 'Entire part of mother played by Lizzie Flop.'"—GEORGE ABBOTT, commenting on the *West Side Story* billing—"Entire production conceived, choreographed and directed by Jerome Robbins"—of his former assistant

"Madonna is currently, in the wake of her latest and one hopes final movie disaster [*Swept Away*, 2002], looking for a Broadway project, preferably a musical, since her fans expect her to sing but even they know that she can't act her way out of a paper condom."—critic REX REED

"Mitch Leigh and Joe Darion don't really have a true success on their hands with *Man of La Mancha*. It's not only a one-song show, it is completely overshadowed by the song. The proof is all the people calling up for tickets to what they call 'The Impossible Dream' or the 'Impossible Dream musical.'"—revue and record producer BEN BAGLEY on the musical adapted from Cervantes' *Don Quixote* which ran nearly six years on Broadway

"Don Black honed his craft . . . in the theatre. His first show was a musical about premature ejaculation, which, predictably enough, came off very quickly."—theater columnist MARK STEYN on the lyricist of *Sunset Boulevard* and *Aspects of Love*, also movie songs like "Born Free" and "Diamonds Are Forever"

"You never know who'll go from the stage to Hollywood stardom. It happened to Richard Gere . . . he was in a [1971] rock opera I was in, *Soon*. Three Broadway performances was all it lasted. He was flat and aimless, often rude, and pretty much talent-free. Very one-dimensional. But that's part of the Hollywood requirement."—PETER ALLEN

"Jack Cole was a genius of the dance. He did a lot for Broadway, then he did a lot for Hollywood. He's the one who finally got a studio [Columbia] to start a dance unit where they would train dancers for the movies instead of bringing them in from New York. Jack also helped shape the moves and personas of Rita Hayworth, then Marilyn Monroe. He was gay and a part-time bastard, he was a perfectionist, and we engaged in fistfights from time to time."—GWEN VERDON, Cole's pupil and then his assistant, pre-stardom

"I enjoyed doing *Pippin* [1972] and being in a hit. I did not enjoy those critics who felt disappointed that I didn't give them Granny from *The Beverly*

Hillbillies. I'm an actress, and there's all sorts of grandmothers in this world, and I'll whoop the tar out of anyone who wants to argue with me on that!"—IRENE RYAN

"I did not get to act with Bette Davis in *The Night of the Iguana*. I simply shared a stage with her. The lady embodies that unfortunate cinematic habit of playing to the audience rather than to and with her professional colleagues."—British actress MARGARET LEIGHTON

"They say there's no fool like an old fool, and there's certainly no ham like an old ham. The allegedly lovable Bert Lahr [the Cowardly Lion in *The Wizard of Oz* film] was a spoiled eccentric who got to overindulge in show after show. He'd been very popular, so he got away with it still. Then I worked with him in *Foxy* [1964], or tried to. Lahr fully intended to hog the entire thing, to make a wreck and a failure of it rather than play just his role and stop chewing the scenery. . . . The man was *impossible*. Which is putting it as politely as I know how, since the old fart is dead."—LARRY BLYDEN

"Katharine Hepburn was selfish, as well as a liar from A to Z about her private life, even giving out a false birthdate—day, month, and year—for most of her life [that of her late, reportedly gay brother]. But, oh, Ginger Rogers made Kate look kind! What can I say about her? And they say one should only speak good of the dead. In which case, I'll just say: Ginger Rogers is dead—*good*!!"—actor TONY RANDALL

"Miss Hepburn is an acquired taste. Like Greek olives and Sapphic poetry." —HERMIONE GINGOLD, who in 1969 refused to say "lavatory" onstage; the same year, Katharine Hepburn became the first star to utter a four-letter word ("Shit!") on Broadway, in *Coco*

"Let me see . . . what was your dear mother's name?"—GEORGE BERNARD SHAW's teasing reply when playwright Clare Boothe Luce (*The Women*), who idolized him, met him and gushed, "Oh, Mr. Shaw, if it weren't for you, I wouldn't be here!"

"Excellent. Greatest!"—telegram from GEORGE BERNARD SHAW to actress CORNELIA OTIS SKINNER in 1935 when she scored a hit with a revival of his *Candida*
> "Undeserving such praise."—she cabled back
> "Meant the play."—cabled Shaw
> "So did I."—cabled Skinner

"I used to think Shaw was God. Literally. I was that young when *My Fair Lady* came out; its record album bore the show's logo: Shaw, up behind a cloud

. . . Julie Andrews as a puppet being manipulated by Rex Harrison, and both being manipulated by Shaw, with a snowy beard. He looked like what we were told a male God looked like, and was English besides." —songwriter SHARON SHEELEY (Hirschfeld's famous caricature, which included Shaw, who was Irish, was used for the hit musical's posters, programs, and cast albums.)

"I've had people tell me they thought they'd seen a particular Broadway show, then realized they'd only seen my drawing of its cast members. . . . A famous actor at a party insisted he'd hated *Chicago*, until he was reminded he'd seen my caricature, only. That made me wonder if he'd hated my artwork, since he thought he'd hated the show?"—master caricaturist AL HIRSCHFELD

"I loved Kander and Ebb's music in *Chicago*, but [the show] was kind of depressing. Then when the O.J. [Simpson] thing came along and *Chicago* was back, everyone said how right it was for the times, about a murderer becoming a star from killing. Then I read it was based on a real-life story, so it was always true to life and the times. But I personally prefer the record album to the show itself."—NELL CARTER (*Ain't Misbehavin'*)

"Everyone's a critic, right? I did a musical that was ahead of its time. It was *No Strings* [1962], an interracial romance. So I did *not* get the girl [Diahann Carroll]. Even so, I was informed that Senator Strom Thurmond wanted to make a political issue out of it. However, for some reason he desisted. Even though he hated the show, though of course he never saw it." —RICHARD KILEY (*Kismet*)

"Pearl Bailey as an Irish-American, Jewish by marriage (in *Hello, Dolly!*). It's stunt casting. . . . Pearl told a friend of mine that the reason she joined the Republicans was that when the Democrats were in power she was just one in the crowd, but when the Republicans were in, she and Sammy Davis Jr. were the only black celebs they could tap for public appearances and White House dinners."—TRUMAN CAPOTE, who wrote *House of Flowers*, in which Bailey starred

"Spare me homophobic Jews who as a minority should know better. I heard about [Tony Awards show producer] Alexander Cohen disparaging any and all Tony winners who dare to thank their same-sex partners in their acceptance speeches. He won't have them on again. You know, one reason I moved to England is the hypocritical extent of prejudice back home, from the mainstream as well as this, that, and the other minority. It's still

liberty and justice for most."—KENNETH NELSON (*The Boys in the Band,*
The Fantasticks)

"I do wish I'd seen that legendary [1931] Broadway staging of *Private Lives*
with its all-gay, all-British cast . . . [of] Noel Coward, who wrote it; his
protégé and reported lover Laurence Olivier; Olivier's wife Jill Esmond,
who later left him for a woman and moved to Wimbledon; and bisexual
Gertrude Lawrence, Coward's best friend. . . . I imagine there was plenty
of subtext in *that* production."—SIR NIGEL HAWTHORNE, star of stage,
TV (*Yes, Minister* and *Mapp and Lucia*), and film (the first openly gay Best
Actor Oscar nominee, for *The Madness of King George*)

"The motion picture we did was a classic. Burt Lancaster in it gave a classic
performance, and I don't think John Lithgow doing his part [in a 2002
musical version], or the new project itself, really merits discussion on my
part, or certainly not comparison."—TONY CURTIS, costar of *The Sweet*
Smell of Success (1957)

"Miss De Havilland was ushered in as we all stood as though for military
inspection. 'Well! Isn't it something!' volunteered the Hollywood superstar
as she shook hands with the group. Then she quickly turned and left the
cast gaping. Isn't it something? Something is what? We all put our heads
together pondering Olivia's enigmatic statement, giving it every inflection,
every intonation, accenting first one word, then another. Finally we decided it was like gazing at someone's newborn child in its crib and, wanting
to be polite, cooing, 'What a beautiful bassinet!'"—JOAN FONTAINE,
who'd taken over the female lead in the hit play *Tea and Sympathy*, which
her Paris-based sister deigned to attend while in New York

"The day will come when James O'Neill will be remembered only as the
father of *Eugene O'Neill*."—the reply of the then-famous actor's son and
future playwright to a journalist who scolded him, "If you weren't James
O'Neill's son, you'd be down in the gutter with all the rest of the bums."

"Julie [Andrews] is good at playing Eliza as a guttersnipe. She's still learning
how to portray her as a lady."—REX HARRISON on his *My Fair Lady*
stage costar (Audrey Hepburn did the screen version)

"Even though he was English, Rex Harrison didn't try to hide his occasional
displeasure with doing a stage [project]. He was washed up in pictures and
he was insecure about playing Henry Higgins. Naturally he didn't know it
would make him a bigger star than ever, topped off with the movie [ver-
sion] and his Academy Award."—REID SHELTON of the *My Fair Lady*
original cast

"I worked with Shaw. I've worked with them all. . . . Now [the 1950s] the latest rage is the work of Tennessee Williams. He's terribly daring. Maybe people need to be shaken up a bit. But I find life dark and dramatic enough without enduring his plays."—ESTELLE WINWOOD, who lived to 101

"I see Miss [Claudette] Colbert has in her post-film, post-prime career returned to the stage. She is interesting to watch, if not to work with. Stubborn as a mule. I once, in a pique of frustration, told her that I'd wring her neck if she had one."—SIR NOEL COWARD

"Maggie Smith is very good, very technically proficient. However, she tends to be unvarying on the stage, more so than on the screen where makeup can achieve a lot, and to punctuate as much with her wrists as her voice." —DAME CELIA JOHNSON, Smith's costar in the film *The Prime of Miss Jean Brodie*

"In this show, you come out humming the fur."—theater director DEREK ANSON JONES (*Wit*), on *Cats*

"In England it doesn't happen. But *here*, they confuse me with *her*, and because we share the same first name I've even been asked if we're related. . . . When I was asked if I was Hermione Baddeley I said, 'No, she's the fat one.' I remember she was in a play called *Diary of a Nobody*. I think she wrote it herself."—HERMIONE GINGOLD (*A Little Night Music*)

"Why don't you sue for nonsupport?"—DOROTHY PARKER to an actress who'd not worked in twenty years but kept insisting, "I loathe the idea of leaving the theatre, I'm so wedded to it."

"Even though his reputation was about crass commercialism, [producer] David Merrick did have one classy idol—[playwright] Arthur Miller. He met him one day, while Miller was accompanied by [wife] Marilyn Monroe. David, who was totally and even obnoxiously straight, only had eyes for Miller. For years, Merrick would recall, 'I just couldn't stop staring at Arthur Miller.'"—writer MORDECHAI RICHLER

"Anita Morris was no dumb blonde. She was a dumb redhead. Very proud to be a sexpot. And very ambitious. She admitted, during *Nine*, that she'd marry any kind of man to get into the limelight. I once asked her what about using talent, and she said a famous movie actress had advised her, 'Get under a man who's established in the business, and work up.'" —Broadway star DOLORES GRAY

"I once told [agent] Leland Hayward a joke. He claimed he had a great sense of humor. He didn't appreciate this one. Anyway, at a cannibal market they were selling brains by profession. Plumbers' brains cost so much, teachers' brains cost so much, etcetera, but most expensive of all were agents' brains. This, the cannibal could not figure out, so he asked a salesman why? The guy says, 'Do you know how many agents it takes to produce a pound of brains?'"—ZERO MOSTEL

"When we worked live performances, Gracie [Allen] often asked afterwards how many people had been in the theatre. She never asked how much the take was. Money matters didn't concern her. Gracie thought there was no business in show business."—GEORGE BURNS

"Some [audience members] just honestly forget [to turn off their cell phones during the play]. But there are others who simply don't care whether or not they ruin the experience for everybody around them. Some night I'd like to stop the play, bring down the curtain, and tell everybody to get their refund from the guy with the phone, and walk off the stage."—EDWARD NORTON, in *Burn This* (2002)

"An associate once asked Irving Berlin if, due to his great reputation, he wrote songs for posterity? Irving answered, 'No, for prosperity.'"—composer JULE STYNE (*Gypsy*)

"A hand upon your opening and may your parts grow bigger."—opening-night telegram from DOROTHY PARKER to actress Uta Hagen

"Fritz [composer Frederick Loewe] was possibly the last person to see [lyricist] Larry Hart alive. He knew how Larry had suffered from being short, which in the opinion of Fritz's partner [lyricist] Alan Jay Lerner was why Lorenz Hart was homosexual. Well, the man had been killing himself with drink, out of remorse. It was a slow if not unexpected death, but Fritz said he had to check himself from admonishing his petite colleague, 'You're killing yourself by inches.'"—JULE STYNE (*Funny Girl*)

"That's the risk an actor takes. I was shocked, in the revival of *Nine*, to see how short Antonio Banderas is. Movies really deceive. But I commend him. It's just that the stage is so much more—real!"—Monaco columnist DELPHINE ROSAY

"I'm doing a limited-run show, *Bill Maher: Victory Begins at Home* [2003], because New York and the stage afford me more freedom of speech than you get on TV. And because on Broadway, the bigots stay home."—*Real Time* host BILL MAHER

"You haven't lived until you've seen Rosie O'Donnell impersonating the Cat in the Hat. She loved the [2000 musical] *Seussical* and took over the role for a month. I pictured her as more of a puppy."—harmonica virtuoso LARRY ADLER

"Every time [Ed] Begley came to the word, he broke into a jig and sang, 'Oh, the cat woman can't, but the cat man do.' He couldn't say the unfamiliar word with a straight face."—playwright SOL STEIN, in whose *A Shadow of My Enemy* Begley had an important speech containing the word "Katmandu" (the capital of Nepal). Despite the playwright's having final say according to the Dramatists Guild, the speech had to go during out-of-town tryouts because the Broadway-bound star (an Oscar-winner) wouldn't alter his behavior

"What keeps Neil Simon from being great is . . . he never quite lets go of the shtick."—playwright ANTHONY SHAFFER

"Broadway actors can be awful hammy. You ever see Merman or Ray Bolger in a play or musical? They can hardly wait for the other guy to shut up. Same today. I saw Madonna in a play—yeah, I said play. Same thing. And Jason Alexander from *Seinfeld*. Et cetera. On film, the desperation and greed don't show, anyway."—actress BIBI OSTERWALD (*The Golden Apple*)

"What opinion would you have if someone kidnapped *your* baby? My baby was *Hello, Dolly!* Streisand and her agent went after it hard for Barbra. . . . The *Dolly!* set of the Harmonia Gardens is still there on the [20th Century] Fox lot. Every time I went by it to do an episode of *The Love Boat*, I did a Dance of Death, enjoying it abandonedly."—CAROL CHANNING, who incorrectly described the film version as the studio's biggest-ever bomb

"Back around the 1950s, before directing and before touring as a Shakespearean actor, I earned decent reviews Off-Broadway in a Strindberg play, *The Creditors*. . . . [Costar] Beatrice Arthur was very good, but too *strong*. I didn't truly think she'd get very far in the theatre. . . . Ethel Merman was comparably strong, but she sang. And she tried to be sexy, though it came off as brassy instead. . . . Singing tends to feminize a performer, especially a female one."—GEORGE ROY HILL, who helmed the musical *Greenwillow*

"A certain deep-closeted actor reportedly met his mate . . . performing in *Cats*. Ironic. Because how can you tell the gender, pro or con, of anybody acting in *Cats*?"—publicist BILL FEEDER

"It's none of your business!"—GYPSY ROSE LEE to her son by Otto Preminger when he inquired who his father was (she finally told him at twenty-two)

"Miss [Gypsy Rose] Lee and I were discussing a fellow actor who used to pray before every performance. If it was for talent or stardom, it didn't work. Miss Lee said, 'Well, praying is like a rocking chair. It gives you something to do, but it doesn't get you anywhere.'"—RODDY McDOWALL, who won a supporting Tony for *The Fighting Cock*

"I have white ancestors too, and I carry some red Indian blood. . . . I think my racial mix stimulates my creativity as a poet, writer, playwright . . . and citizen of the world."—LANGSTON HUGHES (1902–1967)

"It takes a tirelessly resourceful actor, not an exploding mushheap like Richard Harris or a has-been wannabe like Robert Goulet."—writer ETHAN MORDDEN, preferring Richard Burton, the original star of *Camelot*

"Steve Allen's books, which most people have no idea exist, have one redeeming feature: you can put them down. Sophie Tucker's estate should have sued when he wrote the score for *Sophie*. That music had about as much to do with her as I do with Alfred Hitchcock. It was a terrible show, bitterly disappointing in relation to what it could have been. Allen's music, unlike his books, could not be put down, stuffed under a sofa, or flung at the wall."—TRUMAN CAPOTE

"Admittedly, my score was not up to the sometimes sublime standard of Jule Styne and Bob Merrill in *Funny Girl*. But it wasn't chopped liver, either, and it wasn't fair that Libi Staiger seemed to lose all hope for stardom because our show took a nosedive—no pun, and I'm not comparing Miss Staiger with Miss Streisand, who is more talented, even, and certainly has a bigger nose.

"As to how talented and big a star Libi might have become, sadly we will never know."—STEVE ALLEN on *Sophie*, about Sophie Tucker (by contrast, *Funny Girl*, about another offbeat Jewish singer-comedienne, Fanny Brice, was a hit and a star-maker)

"After the extraordinary achievement of *West Side Story*, Leonard Bernstein just stopped. . . . He spent the last years of his life tinkering with *Candide*, a Voltaire operetta whose characters include a woman with only one buttock—but, then, the whole show is half-assed."—MARK STEYN, North American correspondent of *The Spectator*

"I briefly met this famous actress. Very talented. Very promiscuous. At a party, her agent told us all in front of her that in her new drama she would be playing a virgin. I blurted out, 'Will she be playing it from memory?' If looks could kill, she'd have murdered me on the spot."—stage and film actor JASON ROBARDS JR.

"Angela Lansbury as a lunatic and a Southern tramp? I saw *Prettybelle* [1971] strictly for her, but she was so blatantly miscast. Since then, I've never assumed that even a talented, intelligent performer necessarily knows best what roles are right for her."—playwright N. RICHARD NASH (*The Rainmaker*)

"The fact that inconsistency is a part and parcel of art really struck home when I heard the music in *Prettybelle*, a flop musical that starred Angela Lansbury. The story was idiotic, but it's the music that struck me speechless. This was from the same two guys [Jule Styne and Bob Merrill] who'd done all that fantastic music for *Funny Girl*, so many good songs that several weren't kept in the movie [version], for space. Their music for *Prettybelle* was the palest shadow of wonderful. That's when I learned there are no guarantees, even from artists."—composer-actor PAUL JABARA

"Where Anthony Newley went wrong [in *Chaplin*, 1983] was imagining he had anything in common with the comic genius. That is what prior Broadway acclaim can do: swell your head and shrink your reason. . . . He and Charlie Chaplin both came from England. Period."—producer STAN MARGULIES (TV's *The Thorn Birds*)

"Bea Arthur's Meg makes Mama Rose look like Little Miss Muffet."—*Gypsy* composer JULE STYNE on Arthur's monstrous mother character in the 1968 flop musical *A Mother's Kisses*

"What was Bea thinking? She went from *Mame* into *that* (*A Mother's Kisses*)? It was her bid to move over from supporting to leading lady? Go figure. It must have seemed like a good idea at the time . . . I should be glad. If she hadn't done that, she wouldn't have had to go into television."—Arthur's *Golden Girls* costar ESTELLE GETTY

"The stage has its own magic. It softens, even beautifies. Somebody strident, like Ethel Merman or like Bea Arthur in *Mame*, can be amusing, even charming, upon the stage. But not usually on the screen, so magnified. And a truly homely woman like Lotte Lenya . . . in *From Russia with Love* she looked like a toad. But on Broadway in *Threepenny Opera*, she's a national treasure."—LARRY KERT (*West Side Story*)

"You have to be big to come across inside a theatre. To be a star there you need big features. I was lucky with my eyes . . . the mouth one can always enlarge. . . . I loved the theatre, and when I initially flopped in pictures, I was preparing to go back to New York. But I was summoned back, just in time, by the great British actor billed as 'Mr. George Arliss' who saw something in me. However, I'd have been quite content to become the American Duse and live my career on the stage."—BETTE DAVIS

"The thing is, Betty Buckley was *good* in *Carrie* [1988]. But she must have known even a good performance of a demented [mother] character in a super-mess of a project could in no way salvage it. Barbara Cook realized this [in England] and left *Carrie* before America ever got *wind* of it, if you know what I mean."—playwright BOB RANDALL (*The Magic Show*)

"If *Titanic* did one good thing, it's kept Leo DiCaprio off Broadway. . . . Horrible thought: Do you think we'll ever see Tom Cruise on Broadway, around 2015 or 2020? With any luck, by then I'll be dead."—RICHARD HARRIS (*Camelot* on screen and stage, in that order)

"I liked Nathan Lane in Terrence McNally's plays. Wonderful stage talent. Then he had this spell of trying to become a movie star and edging back into the closet. Now he's back to normal and Broadway's better off." —BEN BAGLEY

"It's sad. Broadway was a big enough, great enough venue that it grew its own stars. Big people with big talents. Now, for the most part, they must import from movies or TV—big people with big salaries and follow-ings."—theatrical photographer KENN DUNCAN

"Who could ever forget Whoopi Goldberg in *A Funny Thing Happened on the Way to the Forum*? Many, however, have tried. . . . It's a *man's* role, not a gender-bender. Heaven forbid someday they do *Man of La Mancha* as 'Woman of La Mancha.'"—RICHARD KILEY (*Man of La Mancha*)

"He's not short, and I hear he did fine in *The King and I*. But good or adequate is not what it's about, not what it's supposed to be about. And Lou Diamond Phillips, after Yul Brynner, is *small*."—KIM HUNTER (*A Streetcar Named Desire*, on stage and screen)

"Jonathan Pryce is Caucasian but landed the star part in *Miss Saigon*. Obviously there is a big-time push from English stage and screen powers to try and make him a star . . . in movies like *Brazil* and *Evita* as Juan Peron. They're trying to make a leading mountain out of a molehill."—publicist BILL FEEDER

"Two of the worst ideas I have ever heard about for musicals are from the autobiographies of Boy George and Rosie O'Donnell. . . . By all means come out of the closet. But whatever your orientation, keep your life sto-ries to yourself, or at least on the bookshelf. Don't make us hear you *sing* them."—nightclub owner TAMMI GOWER

"At $90 a seat, you don't want to just hear me sing."—ROSIE O'DONNELL in 2002 about her upcoming musical based on her book *Find Me*, and why she was adding a second person to it

"I passed on the play about the gay baseball player (*Take Me Out*) that later got the Best Play Tony [in 2003]. Who knew? Then I didn't see that crazy new British show *The Play What I Wrote*. I was offered tickets for when Roger Moore guest-starred. Didn't go, and then he collapses on stage, almost has a heart attack—I read he's 75. I miss all the excitement, staying at home. Nowadays, my back goes out more often than I do."—BUDDY HACKETT in 2003

"Tovah Feldshuh played Yentl on stage before Streisand musicalized her for the screen. Decades later, Feldshuh is amazing as Prime Minister Meir in *Golda's Balcony* . . . accents galore—Meryl Streep would die—and a Henry Kissinger impression you have to hear to believe."—Monaco radio personality DELPHINE ROSAY

"You re-evaluate people when their talent conflicts with what is fair. Like with David Rabe. In the late '90s he's done an AIDS-themed play (*A Question of Mercy*). I just saw it at the New York Theatre Workshop. Here's a straight man writing about gay men and demonizing one of the two main gay men in it and making a hero out of the straight doctor, in such a biased way that if he'd done this with or to any other minority, he'd have been lambasted for it. Yet the average reaction goes, 'Isn't it wonderful of David Rabe to write a play about AIDS and even include a gay couple.'"—SUSAN STRASBERG (Broadway's *The Diary of Anne Frank*)

"In the end, he was only about getting straight black men into the fold. At one point someone in the audience asked, 'What about women?' and he answered, 'I mentioned my mother, didn't I?' And he was serious! He didn't care about the dramatic lack of women playwrights or other people of color, and he absolutely didn't care about lesbian and gay voices in the theatre."—lesbian Jewish playwright SARAH SCHULMAN on black playwright August Wilson at a 1997 Town Hall debate about more equitable representation in American theater

"Society, or the media, focus much more on divisions of race, but the biggest divisions are of gender, and entertainment really shows this up. For every play or movie by a black man, how many, or any, are there by a black woman? For every gay play, how many lesbian plays? Men like to keep the power within their sacred masculine circle."—actress LYNNE THIGPEN

"One reason I became an actor was because I heard you could meet queers in the theatre."—SIR IAN MCKELLEN

"I don't mean to sound flippant. But eight marriages can do that to a man. Actually, your question is itself rather flippant."—composer FREDERICK LOEWE, when asked why his former partner, lyricist Alan Jay Lerner, seventeen years his junior, had died first

"I did. I have believed thirteen was my lucky number. I'm re-evaluating that."—ALAN JAY LERNER, whose thirteenth musical, *Dance a Little Closer* (1983), closed in one night and was his Broadway swansong

"Michael Crawford was in the movies of *Hello, Dolly!* and *A Funny Thing Happened on the Way to the Forum.* I've seen him on stage in *Phantom of the Opera.* The critics say now he has all this dramatic weight to bring to the part, but I don't buy it. He has more weight, but not dramatic."—BEN BAGLEY

"No denying Lauren Bacall has presence. She brings glamour and star power to whatever she does. But when I saw her in two musicals, . . . she is a very unmusical person. She would stand or sit there while the people all around her sang and danced. And when she did actually sing, or talked-sang . . . well, don't ask."—ROBERT PRESTON (*The Music Man*)

"Joan Rivers has tried more than once to make it on Broadway. She's even directed a movie—she's done it all. But in a play, she gives the impressi on she's annoyed that the other people on the stage get to talk too." —MADELINE KAHN

"In 1961, when I directed my play *Invitation to a March*, Shelley Winters, the star, complained to [producer] Lawrence Langner that her leading man was gay. This was the same Shelley who tried to come between Farley [Granger] and me when we were living together, but she wasn't good in the play and she knew it. . . . 'Miss Winters,' Langner said, 'Mr. Laurents wanted you for this play. I did not. I said he could have you on one condition: that I never have to talk to you. Good day.'"—writer-director ARTHUR LAURENTS (Granger had gone on studio-arranged dates with Winters during her pre-flab days.)

"We're not allowed to get married in this world—I don't know why. But I'd like to declare in front of millions of people, 'I love you and I'd like to live with you the rest of my life.'"—2003 Tony winner MARC SHAIMAN to fellow *Hairspray* winner and life partner of twenty-five years Scott Wittman

"It was the gayest Tony Awards show ever, including composer Marc Shaiman kissing his love and lyricist. . . . But why did Shaiman say gay people aren't allowed to marry 'in this world'? Has he never heard of France, Holland, Denmark, Sweden, a growing number of others, including soon Germany? The United States is *not* the world."—DELPHINE ROSAY (and, in 2005, Great Britain.)

"Out of every musical I ever saw, the one thing that stands out most for me was from *The Fantasticks*, when the heroine says the line, or prayer or mantra: 'Don't let me be normal!' You don't expect that sort of forward thinking and validation in a musical, but it was written, someone said it, I heard it, and it became my bit of hope, my mantra, ever since then." —author HELENE HANFF (*84 Charing Cross Road*)

"The blacklists didn't affect Broadway much, due to the fact that where TV was beholden to sponsors and corporations, theatre producers were and are self-employed. No sponsors, nor the banks to which the film studios were so indebted."—stage actress turned Congresswoman HELEN GAHAGAN DOUGLAS (wife of two-time Oscar-winner Melvyn Douglas)

"I'm honored to help recreate the memory of a great writer and humanitarian like Dalton Trumbo."—RICHARD DREYFUSS in 2003; a different actor starred in *Trumbo*, an Off-Broadway play, each week—e.g., Alec Baldwin, Tim Robbins, and Chris Cooper—in the portrait of the most famous of the Hollywood Ten, adapted by Christopher Trumbo from his late father's letters

"I'm aghast that such Red-sympathetic types as Dalton Trumbo and a mob of others could continue to make a living off our American theatre. But now he gets hired to script A-list pictures such as *Spartacus* and *Exodus*. Disgraceful!"—archconservative columnist HEDDA HOPPER, who urged a boycott of *Spartacus* (1960), which President Kennedy made a point of attending

"I'm polite. I always insist on good manners. I remember one party at which I had a chat with a rather nice man, but after he got up and left, I turned to my hostess and inquired *why* she'd invited that uncouth hick? She was, of course, surprised. I explained that although I sometimes forget a face, I do not forget a back—not one that got up and walked out on a stage performance I'd given a few nights before!"—JONATHAN HARRIS (*Lost in Space*)

"Miss Merman is a great broad . . . that is, she's a great Broadway star." —MARY MARTIN

"Mary Martin? Oh, she's all right, if you like talent."—ETHEL MERMAN

"Mr. George Abbott and other Broadway producers have from time to time approached me about starring in a 'vehicle' . . . however, I am afraid that because I enunciate and speak English, American audiences might not understand me."—DAME EDITH EVANS

"One doesn't always know what to make of Broadway or what it expects of us. As a newcomer in the 1960s I was taken to New York's collective bosom. But when I returned in the 1980s in what had been a significant hit in the West End, New York was underwhelmed and *Rose* was counted as a complete failure. . . . Broadway can be quite unstable for a foreigner."—GLENDA JACKSON, actress turned politician

"Theatre is miles from pictures, entirely different. Yet the brotherhood [gay actors] who work in New York on the stage seem as terrified to keep their little secret as their Hollywood counterparts. I shan't name any names, but only because one can be sued for telling the truth, which in the States is a controversial thing."—British comedy actor KENNETH WILLIAMS

"It's awful. We begin in the theatre, then the pictures spoil us. Spencer Tracy once told Charles and me, 'Don't bother with plays. Stick to pictures. Why make a fool of yourself on a nightly basis?' Charles liked doing theatre; I prefer to do revues, skits, and my own comic specialities."—ELSA LANCHESTER, wife of closeted film star Charles Laughton

"The theatre is no place for a man who bleeds easily."—Irish playwright SEAN O'CASEY's advice to Canadian actor Hume Cronyn

"One of the early unsuccessful plays that I was in was back in 1938 . . . I believe for six performances. Its title was *Eye on a Sparrow*, and the director was Antoinette Perry, now known as the 'Tony' of Broadway's Tony Awards. The reviews were so bad that she took her real name off [the credits] and used a masculine alias instead [John M. Worth]."—MONTGOMERY CLIFT

"Gore Vidal did a satirical play called *Visit to a Small Planet* that became a Jerry Lewis movie. He also did *The Best Man*, a very safe, rather pretentious, and quite homophobic political play—ironic, in that Vidal is homosexual and twice ran for political office."—Broadway costume designer MILES WHITE (*Oklahoma!*)

"I'm sure critics have nothing so practical as a union nor as dignified as a guild. If they did, Kenneth Tynan should resign from it. The gall of setting oneself up as an arbiter of good taste in regards to the theatre, then helping stage a pornographic, all-nude revue passing itself off as a play or even social commentary—his dreadful *Oh! Calcutta!* I'd like to assassinate him."—HERMIONE GINGOLD (*A Little Night Music*)

"Then Hal Prince went to my wife and asked why I wouldn't do (*A Funny Thing Happened on the Way to the Forum*), and she came to me and said, 'I heard you turned down *Forum*. And I said, 'Oh, yes, I forgot to tell you.' And she said, 'If you don't take it, I'm going to stab you in the balls.' So I said, 'All right, but this is the last time I'm gonna do something for money for you!'"—ZERO MOSTEL

"Katie [Hepburn] was a tough customer even when young. In one of her early plays, *Death Takes a Holiday*, the producer didn't like her in the part and went backstage to give her the option of resigning. This infuriated her. 'I'm not going to take that privilege,' she answered coolly, 'so if you wish to fire me, do so. But get out of here, because you'll be lucky if I don't kill you.'"—movie director GEORGE CUKOR, who began in the theater

"I'm resigned to the fact that those of us who have lived our professional lives mostly on the stage—myself, Katharine Cornell, Eva Le Gallienne, Edith Evans, Geraldine Page, many others as well—will not be as vivid in the memory of future generations as those who have made dozens of motion pictures or even done television."—HELEN HAYES, two-time Oscar winner

"It was my mother who helped push me into the business, having recognized my budding genius at an early age. . . . She took me to a children's audition at a theatre where I did my little act and got hired immediately. The stage manager then took me back to my mother and said to her, 'Shall we say three pounds a week?' and my mother replied, 'I'm sorry, but we couldn't possibly afford to pay that much.'"—SIR NOEL COWARD

"Talk about ego. George White was like Ziegfeld—not quite as famous. But big shows, lots of girls, legs . . . cheesecake made him rich. But the cheese went to his head. He genuinely believed that they nicknamed Broadway—New York's oldest thoroughfare—after him: the Great *White* Way."—composer JULE STYNE (*Bells Are Ringing*)

"Publicity, in the woist sense of the woid, has always been the life's blood of show business! Flo Ziegfeld would deliberately ignore his bills so his creditors would sue him, take him to court, and get his name in the papers. Publicity at any cost. Or none at all!"—JIMMY DURANTE

"Clare Boothe, the socialite who became a playwright and diplomat, was distantly related to the acting Booth family, which included Lincoln's assassin, John Wilkes Booth. To unrelate themselves, the family added an *e*. . . . Her second marriage was to [Time-Life] publisher Henry Luce, so from then on she had power as well as wealth. Clare was not only extremely opinionated, but vengeful, and if she disliked you she was apt to try and destroy your reputation."—actor-coach ROBERT LEWIS

"[Ray Bolger's] wife was finally banned from the theatre. He'd be in rehearsal and he'd be fine, but then his wife would tell him about the other performers and performances and, well, his wife was real trouble. I had to rehearse my one remaining number, [the showstopper] 'Nightlife,' in one of the bathrooms, with [director] Josh ([Logan] sitting on the sink and me standing in front of the johns, because they were afraid to let Ray see it."—ANITA GILLETTE, the ingénue in *All American* (1962)

"My grandmother always told me when I went into the business to beware of the casting couch. I realized six months into the road on this show that the girls didn't have to worry about it. It was the guys who had a problem."—TERPSIE TOON of *Sugar Babies*, later a director-choreographer

"I remember Jack Barrymore cared about the details, before the drinking took over. . . . When he did *Hamlet*, he reminded the girls who would carry on the dead Ophelia in the burial scene that they were playing virgins. Whereupon one of them said, 'Mr. Barrymore, we're extras, not character actresses.'"—TALLULAH BANKHEAD

"When Irish eyes are smiling, beware."—Welsh actress SIAN PHILLIPS (who enacted Marlene Dietrich on stage) on ex-husband Peter O'Toole

"I showed my appreciation of my native land in the usual Irish way by getting out of it as soon as I possibly could."—GEORGE BERNARD SHAW

"In the *Gypsy* company, [Ethel Merman] was famous for a sexual joke she didn't get. When she asked Jack Klugman, her leading man, whether Tab Hunter was gay, Jack replied, 'Is the Pope Catholic?'
    "'Yes,' said Ethel, still waiting for the answer.
    "Not bright, no, but endearing and despite a life spent in saloons, childlike."—ARTHUR LAURENTS, who wrote the musical *Gypsy*

"Richard Rodgers—beautiful music, ugly sentiments. He wound up not doing the music for *Coco*, which André Previn did instead. When colleagues pointed out that Coco Chanel had collaborated with the Nazis, Rodgers told them he knew something even 'worse' about her: she was bisexual."—WARREN CASEY, co-creator of *Grease*

"As far as I know, he's never made mention, but I wonder how Stephen Sondheim feels now about the various anti-gay lyrics he wrote when he was still in the closet?"—RON VAWTER, stage and screen (*Philadelphia*) actor

"Sondheim insists his shows aren't at *all* autobiographical. Why so vehemently, I don't know. But he's still never done anything with a gay theme or major gay character, and . . . suppresses gay content from his work. Contrast this with Jonathan Larson, who was apparently heterosexual but did include quite a bit of gay content in his first and last big show, *Rent*. You tell me who's 'the better gay.'"—stage director JOSÉ QUINTERO

"Critics have their own agendas, often fueled by green—money and jealousy. Or insecurity. . . . Some critics even write books. One is Martin Gottfried, who described *Who's Afraid of Virginia Woolf?* in print as 'the most successful homosexual play ever produced on Broadway.' An out-and-out homophobe. Years later he does a biography of Danny Kaye, and because he likes Kaye, he pretends Kaye was not homo- or bisexual. Facts be damned."—Beverly Hills columnist and former Warner Bros. executive RICHARD GULLY

"Fritz Loewe's music was among Broadway's most ravishing. But he created his own biography like a novel. He was a mystery figure, and two of his persistent claims cannot be verified: that he started composing at age seven and at 13 was the youngest pianist to appear with the Berlin Philharmonic. . . . He said he'd written a European song named 'Katrina' that sold millions of copies. Likewise his first decade in the U.S. is largely unaccounted for. Actors and writers are not the only ones who abuse imagination."—Broadway set designer JO MIELZINER

"Most successes in show business have less to do with talent than sheer, dogged, persistent sticking around."—actor-playwright-producer-director GEORGE ABBOTT (1887–1995)

"Strictly overrated!"—CHARLOTTE RAE (TV's *The Facts of Life*) on George Abbott, who replaced her early on in his hit *The Pajama Game* (1954) with Carol Haney, who thus became a Broadway star

"If not for Broadway, I might never have made it to Hollywood. Look at the female movie stars then, how different I was from them. But via Broadway, you could still become a movie star, and I owed it to Carol Haney's broken leg (in *The Pajama Game*). I went on for her, and in those days you had major movie directors and producers in the audience, so."—SHIRLEY MACLAINE, who began as a dancer

"Working for Mr. Abbott at that early stage of my career was not easy . . . not pleasant. I needed direction, and he was a man of few words. A lot of things, he didn't care about. He'd delegate a lot. He'd rather have been playing golf or tennis each afternoon. He was more of a traffic cop at times than a director, and I thought he was old *then*—he was in his seventies. But he's still a great man."—GWEN VERDON in 1991; she became a star in Abbott's *Damn Yankees* in 1955

"When he's not working, he's golfing, and when he's not golfing, he's dancing."—GEORGE ABBOTT'S SECRETARY when Abbott was ninety-five (at the 1987 Tony Awards ceremonies he asserted, "It's because I love the theatre so much that I thought I'd stick around.")

"I only stopped playing in my late eighties because my last tennis partner died. It was only natural I then turn to golf."—GEORGE ABBOTT at ninety-four

"When my husband was 104 he was playing golf, and one day he fell down and I got in a panic—he was turning pale and his eyes shut and his breathing slowed down. I wasn't sure if he'd hear me, but I yelled, 'Darling, I'll go get help. Just lay there.' He spoke up and corrected me, 'You mean *lie* there.'"—George Abbott's wife JOY

"I'm seventy-seven but I'm still beautiful. I'm not gay, though I have had very close gay friends. And I never had to do the casting couch bit, never had to kiss anyone or anything. I just worked hard and became a superstar. Now I'm taking it easy. Theatre's a big thrill for me, and . . . I don't mind playing gay. I played Laurence Olivier's lover in *Spartacus*. But I'm not gay myself—unlike the last guy who played this role . . . that English guy from *Peter Pan*."—TONY CURTIS during the 2002 fifty-city tour of *Some Like It Hot*, in which he played Osgood (as did Australian Cyril Ritchard in the 1972 *Sugar*)

"Remember when Streisand spoke about doing Shakespeare and Russian plays, maybe even Greek drama? Some people laughed. Some naively believed her. We're overall too materialistic a society for big stars to do theatre while they're big stars. Money comes first, art a distant second. In England there's more training and craft, less money and greed, and there's a smaller distance between the so-called superstar and the supporting player . . . they may have a monarchy over there, but among actors it's much more democratic."—REID SHELTON (Daddy Warbucks in *Annie*)

"I always wanted to do a Noel Coward play, but I never really got the chance."—JOHN WAYNE

"Then I thought to myself, 'Darn it, maybe I can't do what Vanessa Redgrave can. But can Vanessa Redgrave do what I can do? Who's kidding who here?'"—RAQUEL WELCH, who occasionally ventured onto Broadway, taking over for musical stars

"I've never known anyone in Hollywood as talkative as Miss [Geraldine] Page. I suppose that is why she lives in New York. With theatre, you get to repeat yourself every night."—film star LAURENCE HARVEY

"Gerry Page is a superb Method actress. I once asked what method she used. She said, without batting an eyelash, 'Talent.'"—HELEN HAYES

"To this day, people will ask me how on earth I managed to play Chinese in *Flower Drum Song* (1958). An even dumber question I get now and then is how come I wasn't in the screen version, which was all Oriental actors. You can't cheat the camera like you can on stage. Anyway, I've had plenty more difficult assignments. Such as playing Barbra Streisand's fiancé in [the movie of] *On a Clear Day You Can See Forever*."—LARRY BLYDEN

"It was funny, because she really wasn't a singer. When the album came out she said, 'I sound like Donald Duck!' And in fact she does."—*Coco* costar RENÉ AUBERJONOIS on Katharine Hepburn

"It is rather a mystery. Florence Henderson might have been an American Julie Andrews. At least on the stage. She had the voice and looks . . . but her only starring Broadway musical was *The Girl Who Came to Supper* [1963]. Why nothing came of it, and with her great reviews, who can say? Then of course she sealed her fate by going on TV and playing Mrs. Brady in *The Brady Bunch*."—RODDY McDOWALL, who costarred in the stage but not film *Camelot*

"People who only know him from *Law & Order* on TV are sometimes surprised to discover that Jerry Orbach had this big Broadway career behind him . . . a talented musical entertainer. He was brilliant in the original production of *Chicago*. Much better than Richard Gere in the movie. Gere used a funny, nasal, almost clownish voice for his songs that indicated he wasn't comfortable with his own voice, and he was the only main actor who did not get an Academy Award nomination for it. He did . . . a fraction of what Jerry Orbach did in *Chicago*."—nightclub owner TAMMI GOWER

"I think our show [*Over There!*] was the last one John Travolta did before the movies took him. I remember how popular he was with the chorus boys. He was having lots of fun, loved the backstage life. But Hollywood . . . who can compete with that money and mystique? . . . Others too. Richard Gere—I think *Bent* was his last play. Such good work, and such a profound play. . . . We three loved all the movies we did, but we never lost the love of working in front of real, live audiences."—MAXENE ANDREWS of the Andrews Sisters

"Timing has so much to do with it. The two most influential choreographers Broadway ever had were Jack Cole and Agnes de Mille. Jerry Robbins and all those who came after learned from them. The younger ones endured, and they didn't give credit, and eventually they became more highly rated than their actual work merited."—dancer-instructor FRED KELLY, who taught brother Gene to tap dance

"Jerome Robbins was a shark. He had no scruples . . . on *West Side Story* he'd pit the Sharks against the Jets. He wanted hatred to flow. He never trusted in the performers' ability. He'd whisper to one cast or 'gang' member, 'So-and-so's going around saying your mother's a hooker.' There were actual fights and injuries on that show. Jerry didn't mind a bit."—ANONYMOUS ORIGINAL CAST MEMBER in 1987

"Well, of course it's a shame about Abraham Lincoln [being shot] in 1865. But in 1800, there was an assassination attempt on George III in one of *our* theatres [London's Drury Lane]. It would have been an even worse tragedy, for we only get one monarch in a lifetime, while you get a new president every four years or so."—REX HARRISON during the American bicentennial year of 1976

"Talk about nerve and presumption. Andrew Lloyd Webber has made known his opinion that the great Richard Rodgers never really fulfilled his potential because—get this—he never created a 'sung-through' musical à la Webber [sic]. That English pipsqueak! He is Andrew Lloyd Webber rolled into one!"—BUDDY HACKETT

"Among celebrities, at least, white marriages where neither partner is attracted to the opposite sex tend to last longer. The relationship doesn't turn bitter or disappoint due to sexual stagnation, and kids don't usually strain it. They also have the strongest incentive to stay together—other than true love—which is business and image."—CHRISTOPHER HEWETT, gay stage and TV actor (*Mr. Belvedere*), referring to Alfred Lunt and Lynne Fontanne, contractually married fifty-five years, and producer-director Guthrie McClintic and actress Katharine Cornell, forty years

"You'd imagine stage biographies [to be] on a higher plane of truth than movie-star ones. Not when it comes to homo- or bisexuality. One biographer of Lunt and Fontanne says they never had kids because they were 'too busy' acting. What about all the busy straight actors who had children? . . . A book about Kit Cornell gives every detail about her working relationship with her documentably gay husband, then skimps over her living with another woman during the 14 years between his death and hers [Cornell's]. Deceit, thy name is biographer.'"—KEN DICKMANN, writer and Los Angeles Filmex affiliate

"I was in a play with them [Alfred Lunt and his older wife, Lynne Fontanne]. Lynne was carrying on something frightful about her devotion to Alfred. Mostly for show, of course. It finally got on my nerves. One day, during a dress rehearsal, during the break, she wailed at me, wringing her hands, 'Oh, where-oh-where would I be without Alfred?' I decided to tell her, for she wasn't getting any younger. I said, 'You'd be right here, where I am—playing your mother.'"—ESTELLE WINWOOD

"Lynne Fontanne *might* have become a luminary, *sola*. Alfred Lunt, less likely. He was too ordinary and yet too fey. As a team, they could succeed on stage together. Their one motion picture was a flop. But as a marital institution, they rose to new heights on Broadway the longer they were together. Put wife next to husband, and the audience no longer sees feyness or ordinariness, they see a reflection; they see what they want to see, and what the publicity tells them: a matrimonial model."—EILEEN HECKART

"The Lunts liked to give the impression they encouraged young talent mightily. That is to say, Alfred Lunt encouraged young male talent. Mightily. Their, or his, most famous protégé was Monty Clift. Who knows what really went on; who cares. Point is, once it became known, after Clift was a Hollywood star and unlike Lunt didn't take a wife, that he was homosexual, Lunt—and Lunt and Fontanne—dropped him like a hot potato."—REID SHELTON (*My Fair Lady, Annie*)

"One of the more unusual stories about stage fan worship is Bram Stoker, the author of *Dracula* (1897). His vampire is the most frequently depicted fictional character in film history. But in his own lifetime, Stoker was besotted with [actor] Henry Irving. In his twenties, Stoker 'found' Irving and although he married, as tradition decreed, he dedicated the next three decades of his life to Irving, who used him as a servant. It was a happy relationship and helped Irving's career. Poor infatuated Stoker could never have known he would create something more popular and lasting than Henry Irving, then the most famous actor on earth, ever did."—composer and critic VIRGIL THOMPSON

"One morning shortly after Neil [Simon] and I were married, Neil announced to me that he didn't want to be married to an actress. My immediate but unvoiced response was, gee, I wish you had mentioned that *before* we got married, and *before* I was in rehearsals playing Lady Anne [in] *Richard III* at Lincoln Center!"—MARSHA MASON (the playwright wanted her to give up her career to raise his two daughters)

"There [have] been a number of successful plays about alcoholics. Men alcoholics. But audiences and particularly critics don't care for plays about women alcoholics. Not even when Neil Simon writes one. We did *The Gingerbread Lady*, and it ran short of 200 performances, which for him is a flop."—MAUREEN STAPLETON (the screen version featured Simon's then-wife Marsha Mason)

"I love the way the English have taken the thing over and spent all that money on it. It wasn't that we didn't have the money, we didn't have the *thought*. The English were backward, we thought. They knew nothing about musicals. Now we're eating out of their hand."—producer-director GEORGE ABBOTT in the early 1990s

"Alan Bates was working with an American actor who'd recently found out that in England young boys are addressed as Master so-and-so. He didn't know it's used with the first, not the last name. He innocently asked Mr. Bates, 'So you were called, all those years, Master Bates?' The star didn't speak to the young man for the remainder of the run."—JEREMY BRETT, Bates's pal and TV's Sherlock Holmes

"Well, it's no one *I* know."—actress CORAL BROWNE, upon laying eyes on a thirty-foot-tall golden phallus that decorated the set of Peter Brooks's 1968 production of *Oedipus Rex* at London's National Theatre. Its star was John Gielgud (who reportedly said, "I feel as if we should give the set designer a big hand")

"It impressed me how offhand Sir James Barrie was about his popular reputation resting chiefly on one rather juvenile play. . . . I understand when a dinner companion once mentioned that not all of Barrie's plays enjoyed long runs, the playwright answered, 'True. Some of them Peter out and some Pan out.'"—SIR JOHN GIELGUD

"Larry had a terrible fault as an actor, early on. He was a giggler. No schoolgirl in church was worse. I heard he'd been fired from one play due to giggling, and almost lost another because of it. It was Noel [Coward] who, with my help, determined to cure Larry of this disastrous affliction." —GERTRUDE LAWRENCE (*The King and I*) on her *Private Lives* costar, Laurence Olivier

"They asked me to star in the movie of the [British lesbian-themed] play *The Killing of Sister George*. I went to see the play, and I had to say no. It's a very good play, but I told Beryl Reid, the actress who starred in it, that *she* had to star in the movie version. And she did. That role was absolutely *her*."
—BETTE DAVIS

"One wouldn't ordinarily praise a tremendously successful theatrical producer. But this one had class—he even answers his mail [and] he has looks, youth, audacity, economic acumen . . . and heart—he's openly gay, a rare and inspiring role model. In fact, he's now the highest-paid individual in Great Britain, an all-Britannic success story."—BEN BAGLEY on Cameron Mackintosh, producer of *Cats*, *Phantom*, *Les Miz*, etc.

"Robert Stigwood became super-rich before I did . . . from stage musicals and their record albums, like *Jesus Christ Superstar* and *Evita* and so on. . . . Among producers, he's sort of a Howard Hughes. Just because we're similarly inclined in our private lives doesn't mean we have much else in common. Like, he loves the stage and I love movies."—gay producer ALLAN CARR, who teamed with Stigwood to make the film of *Grease*

"It's fairly well known in my circle that I have the same [suit] tailor as Marlene Dietrich. But it should be obvious to anyone that unlike the movie glamour girls I don't wear *décolleté*. After all, I am a producer, and it's a question of business and confidence."—at one time, Broadway's leading female producer, the closeted CHERYL CRAWFORD (*Porgy and Bess*, *Sweet Bird of Youth*)

"I have to give credit to Cheryl Crawford. In 1954, she gave me *The Diary of Anne Frank* to read. She passionately believed I could play it, and that my being Jewish could only enhance the performance and veracity. It was my stage debut [in 1955]. . . . When it came time to cast the movie, Audrey Hepburn was first choice, and my not being a big name counted against me. It also, and I didn't talk about this for years, did *not* help that I was Jewish. Hollywood wanted someone non-Jewish . . . it would reassure the audience and supposedly, and most ironically, make them more sympathetic to the Anne Frank they were watching."—SUSAN STRASBERG in 1975

"Why does theatre attract more gay actors than the movies? I think it's due to the camera. Not that the camera doesn't lie—it does, often. But California people are more apt to place stereotypes in front of the camera. Theatre has more leeway, more faith in an actor's ability to make believe. Casting for the stage is nowhere as rigid and discriminatory."—stage and screen actor

DAVID WAYNE (*How to Marry a Millionaire*), Marilyn Monroe's most frequent leading man

"I have a friend who's straight and acts 'soft,' to use casting-director parlance. So he never gets big roles on screen—and he's not old enough to play sexless authority figures. Meanwhile, a friend of a friend is gay, quite butch, and yes, a movie star. With a wife and all that. He was a star before her, but to *continue* his stardom, which was fading, the wife was worked in."—heterosexual stage (*Bent*) and screen (*Gods and Monsters*) actor DAVID DUKES

"Yeah, that's cool. Everyone knows Harvey Fierstein's gay, and why shouldn't he play Tevye (in *Fiddler on the Roof*, 2004)? It is called acting, after all. And I hear most men that produce only daughters are gay-inclined anyway." —JERRY ORBACH

"No question that theatre takes up more of an actor's time than working in movies or on TV. That is, once you're hired; getting hired can be full-time work in itself . . . I know of several actors and playwrights who have practically no social life or sex life, no time for nurturing relationships because they're so dedicated to and involved in the theatre."—BEATRICE ARTHUR

"Yes, okay, it's true. I was a virgin till my thirties. I'm a creature of the theatre. Next question."—ELAINE STRITCH

"Of all the presumptuous announcements. Miss Helen Hayes, who was very married at the time, left a hit play [*Coquette*, whose screen version won Mary Pickford her Oscar] of Jed Harris's in the 1920s by stating she was pregnant by an act of God! That's the type of announcement they usually make hundreds of years later about the mothers of founders of major religions."—DAME JUDITH ANDERSON

"Neil Simon used to create such original and clever plots. Now an audience has to plotz through his latest reminiscence about dead wives, ex-wives, and former marriages. . . . This play, which I think is his 30th [*The Dinner Party*], is . . . is it fiction or nonfiction? Either way, it's so personal, *he* should pay audiences."—PHILIP BRETT, musicologist and Grammy-nominated conductor

"I made a prediction, when I was starring for her in *Toys in the Attic*, that if her boyfriend Dashiell Hammett ever died, she'd never write another play. She never did and never could after her editor and her advisor weren't around anymore. She needed Hammett and [producer] Herman [Shumlin] to come up with her biggest hits."—ANNE REVERE, who'd costarred in Lillian Hellman's *The Children's Hour*, won an Oscar for *National Velvet*, then was politically blacklisted

"I was telling a young actor who was considering doing a play about one particular play where the audience stayed away in droves. He nodded gravely, then asked, 'Is droves like carriages or something?'"—an ICM AGENT in Los Angeles

"When you're a minor actor or not very talented, yet you persist in show business anyway, you usually wind up either a talk-show host, a game-show host or, sometimes, an actor's coach like Lee Strasberg."—Broadway set designer JO MIELZINER

"A charlatan."—MONTGOMERY CLIFT on acting coach Lee Strasberg, with whom he studied for a while

"I was thinking how it was just within the last ten years that [critic] John Simon felt free to call a play 'faggot nonsense' in *New York* magazine." —playwright CRAIG LUCAS (*Prelude to a Kiss*) in 1993 on persistent homophobia

"Lesbians and gay men are the only citizens of the United States considered so despicable and heinous that they couldn't even be depicted on stage. . . . No matter how anti-Semitic the country was, you could present Jewish characters. . . . You could show gangsters, murderers, and prostitutes, but you could not present lesbians or gay men on stage for fear they might be emulated or somehow be infectious."—former publicist KAIER CURTIN, author of *We Can Always Call Them Bulgarians: The Emergence of Lesbians and Gay Men on the American Stage* (1987)

"Joseph Papp was a strange man in some ways . . . a huge ego for an initially noncommercial producer. . . . He could get very personal with you, yet he'd seldom discuss his gay son [who later died of AIDS]. . . . And he discomfitted a lot of people with his strange way of trying to break the ice: he'd try and guess people's weight!"—actor and acting coach (to James Dean, Jack Nicholson, etcetera) JEFF COREY (before turning to theater, Papp had worked in carnivals guessing people's weight)

"A friend asked if I wanted to share a unique theatregoing experience. Who's in it, I asked? Two Australians. What's it about? The ancient Australian art of gentle origami. That's what I *thought* I heard . . . but origami is Japanese, and why 'gentle'? So we get to the theatre, and the poster says 'The Ancient Australian Art of Genital Origami.' Oh-oh. And a banner says,

'The Penises Are Coming! The Penises Are Coming!' Too late: the show's starting. . . .

"Well, it was not *paper* they folded that evening. I never knew scrotums were so . . . flexible. It just goes to show what lengths men will go to for entertainment in Australia's Outback. Unforgettable!"—*Newsweek* senior editor SARAH PETIT on the 2001 Off-Broadway hit *Puppetry of the Penis*

"I do think it'll have a long run. Some people say a musical they can't pronounce won't run in the U.S.A. But *Les Misérables* has a universal theme that transcends its Franco-English roots. . . . It is not a star-making vehicle—that may or may not affect its run."—PETER O'TOOLE in 1987, the year *Les Miz* opened in New York (its Broadway run was later exceeded only by *Cats* and *Phantom*)

"If an actress pushes with finesse and backs it up with talent, sometimes she doesn't have to take an audition 'No' for an answer. The classic example was Mildred Dunnock in *Death of a Salesman*. The playwright and director saw her strictly as refined. But Linda Loman was strictly a housewife. Irregardless [sic], Dunnock *had* to play the part—she'd even understudy. So she kept returning to auditions, wearing different housedresses, shifts, even padding . . . finally inhabiting the right dowdy look and nailing the character. Dunnock earned the part, and critics said she was born to play it." —ROSE MARIE (*The Dick Van Dyke Show*)

"I have been a victim of blacklisting. . . . This happened in a democracy, people targeted because of their private and peaceful political beliefs. People were hurt, even destroyed, because a small group of malicious and lying politicians decided to increase their power via irresponsible exaggerations, lies and scapegoating. . . . Fear and propaganda are alarmingly easy for politicians to spread. They're even better actors than we are."—selfdescribed "liberal Democrat" MILDRED DUNNOCK (1901–1991)

"One very large waste of talent and humanity was a victim of the McCarthy witch-hunts . . . Margaret Webster, a big-time stage director. She was the daughter of that old actress Dame May Whitty. Margaret was pro-Russian back when they were our allies [in WWII], so José Ferrer the actor fingered her. And he told the Congressional inquisition she'd employed a known communist who was Paul Robeson, a black man. They ruined Robeson—blacks weren't supposed to have political opinions—and they tried to ruin his friends and coworkers; they almost got Lena Horne because she'd been Paul's friend.

"So naturally Webster was ruined, all her career and future, after she had to go before McCarthy's henchman, who was Roy Cohn, a gay Jew but a Republican first and last. . . . The only ones who were immune to the blacklisting were conservative white men."—dancer-choreographer ALVIN AILEY (Webster, called "the ablest woman in our theatre" by critic Brooks Atkinson, was the first female to direct Shakespeare on Broadway.)

"The mean-spirited ignorance of too many politicians should not be downplayed. When a rabidly anti-communist Congressman was trying to kill the Federal Theatre and somebody quoted Christopher Marlowe, he demanded to know if Marlowe, present tense, was a communist. This ignoramus who hoped to obliterate theatre for the masses during the Great Depression when few people could afford theatre tickets had never heard of the immortal Elizabethan playwright."—activist American playwright CLIFFORD ODETS in 1939

"I don't know what was on her mind, but [Marie Christiansen] misread the end of her line. She said to us, 'Now, as you've all been good today, children, Mr. Thorkelson will read to you from the book 'A Sale of Two Titties.'"—MARLON BRANDO, recalling an early stage experience in *I Remember Mama*

"I knew [stripper] Gypsy Rose Lee was an intellectual when she said that men weren't attracted to her by her mind—they're attracted by what she doesn't mind."—boyfriend and producer MIKE TODD

"My husband took me to see the X-rated, all-nude play *Oh! Calcutta!* At intermission he turned to me and asked, 'How come there are no erections?' 'Dummy,' I told him, 'these are professionals.'"—JOAN RIVERS

"I thought he was an underrated actor. I once suggested he play Hamlet. He said, 'I prefer New York to them small towns.'"—JOHN BARRYMORE on Jimmy Durante

"The worst actress I saw on Broadway didn't get there. *Mata Hari* closed in [Washington,] D.C., en route to Broadway. Anyway, she was imported by David Merrick, who cast for looks, not talent. . . . In this show, after she's been executed by all these rifles, the curtain descends slowly. But as it's coming down, Marisa Mell lifts her head to see what's the Mata."—actor JAMES GREGORY (TV's *Barney Miller*)

"There's a terrible yet delicious story about [actress-producer] Eva Le Gallienne's 1980 production of *Alice in Wonderland*. During rehearsals, the costumes, which were made of Naugahyde, kept changing due to conceptual revisions. Finally, one cast member gave his opinion to a colleague:

'That old dyke doesn't care how many naugas have to give their lives for this show!'"—occasional stage actor VINCENT PRICE

"Sandy Dennis virtually ruined my London production of *The Three Sisters* [in 1965]. Everyone there was looking forward to it . . . it was a showcase for the Method. . . . [Dennis's] nervous tics were more than to laugh at, and made it unwatchable. Her stuttering took away from the suspension of disbelief, from everybody else's lines. In the third act, when she says, 'Oh, it's been a terrible evening,' somebody in the audience shouted, 'It sure has been!' When the show ended, there were boos, hisses, rude words, and noises. An incomparable catastrophe."—LEE STRASBERG

"Some investors felt it might as well not have played, because thanks to [director] Tommy Tune *The Will Rogers Follies* didn't make money. Tune chose and pushed through a set design which could not be seen from side seats, which therefore could not sell. . . . Some backers even blamed Tune when the show's very popular dog act was locked inside a van which caught on fire, incinerating the dogs. That hurt some investors almost as much as the loss of profits."—theater director DEREK ANSON JONES (*Wit*)

"I do not speak ill of the hand that feeds me, but oh, yes, it is good to be back in the theatre. . . . The theatre is typically more straightforward than Hollywood . . . I remember when Warners bought *The Man Who Came to Dinner*, which Monty Woolley made such an enduring success in. They then proceeded to rewrite it for Cary Grant—just sabotaged the play! . . . I told them I'd do it if they restored it to the original and cast Woolley in the lead. They did, and we did it, and it was a great hit."—BETTE DAVIS in the 1970s (in the screen version she was first-billed though playing Sheridan Whiteside's secretary)

"When Bette Davis came [to see the show], Anne was a wreck, and she went up on her lines. But there was Eve Harrington at last being Margo Channing and having to face the first Margo—it was really too much." —costar LEE ROY REAMS on Anne Baxter in *Applause*, the musical of the film *All About Eve*

"She'd be wearing her mink coat, and a couple of times, when something was going wrong with the show, she'd say, 'I'm a very gifted actress. I've won two Academy Awards.' I thought, this is so sad she has to say this. But she had to do it to bolster her confidence."—actress JULIE KURNITZ of *Minnie's Boys* (1970), starring Shelley Winters as the Marx Brothers' mother

"When it came to undisciplined, unprofessional behavior . . . that was Jennifer Holliday in *Dreamgirls*, which I choreographed [with director Michael

Bennett]. The reason they put up with her was that her solo was a stand-out . . . not hummable and a hit tune, but she performed the shit out of it. But I wonder if it justified all she put us through."—MICHAEL PETERS (best known for Michael Jackson's "Thriller" video)

"Well, I don't really like to criticize him. I mean, I'm not sure if he's really alive still. . . ."—*Fiddler on the Roof* librettist JOSEPH STEIN on producer David Merrick

"When I first met Yul Brynner in 1949, he was producing wrestling shows for one of the [TV] networks [and] his only accent was straight out of the South Bronx."—columnist JAMES BACON (Brynner became a star via *The King and I* on Broadway, then a "foreign" star in films.)

"I've been openly gay for nearly 50 years . . . I've been acting for almost 47 years, and I've played all but six of Shakespeare's plays."—DANIEL DAVIS (Miles on TV's *The Nanny*), costarring in the 2004 revival of *La Cage aux Folles* with also openly gay Tony winner Gary Beach (Broadway's *The Producers*)

"Kevin Spacey has a refreshing lack of the masculine acting tricks most young actors still cling to. . . . He does tend toward smugness and defensiveness too often, I think, to be effective in plays over the long run."—*Lost in Yonkers* costar IRENE WORTH

"In the first scene I'm on the left side of the stage, and the audience has to imagine I'm eating dinner in a crowded restaurant. Then in scene two I run over to the right side of the stage and the audience imagines I'm in my own drawing room."—actress RUTH GORDON, describing her new play

"And the second night you have to imagine there's an audience in front."—playwright GEORGE S. KAUFMAN's response

"When I die, I want to be cremated and have my ashes thrown in Jed Harris's face."—the last wish of playwright GEORGE S. KAUFMAN

"I don't dislike hardly anybody, but he's one exception. But I'm not going to say why at this time."—stage actor turned game-show host (*Hollywood Squares*) PETER MARSHALL on stage actor (*Cabaret*) turned game-show host Bert Convy

"You like old movies? Then you owe a huge debt to Broadway. A mighty percentage of the movies Hollywood made were from Broadway plays. That's where Hollywood looked first, for stories and stars. Now, too often, it looks in the gyms, gutters, ghettoes, and high schools."—movie director GEORGE SIDNEY (*Show Boat, Bye Bye Birdie*)

"Broadway has something for everyone. It's not all high-brow, it's not all musicals. You could go see Anne Heche of *Ellen* [DeGeneres]fame in a play, or now see Elizabeth Berkley of *Showgirls* fame or infamy in a revival of *Sly Fox*, based on a play from the 1500s but starring Richard Dreyfuss. That's variety!"—theater columnist VICTORIA NEWTON in 2004

"Somehow, the most memorable thing about this less than starry but revved-up *Cabaret* revival is Scotsman Alan Cumming's darlin' nipple ring. It seems yet the focus and the symbol of this provocatively pansexual actor's show-stealing performance in a non-lead role."—critic MURA T. FALCO (*Going Out*)

"I did have one homosexual husband. At least. Guthrie McClintic. He was an extremely famous Broadway producer who loved his fellow man—often. I wasn't the only actress he married. He married Katharine Cornell. But it was different for her than me—like her husband, she was attracted to her own kind. You know: Birds of a feather fornicate together."—ESTELLE WINWOOD on her second of four husbands

"One day Eugenie Leontovich, who was the star of *Grand Hotel*, asked me if I would like to meet Katharine Cornell, whom I had much admired. There were some very sordid stories about her husband, Guthrie McClintic, carrying on—even something about having [male lovers] in the back of the balcony while she was performing—but I had never heard anything about Cornell.

"We went to her house on the East Side, and watching Leontovich and Cornell together—there was a certain subtle intimacy in their rapport from which I was excluded—I understood why she would be married to a man like McClintic."—HERMAN SHUMLIN, producer of *Grand Hotel* and *The Children's Hour*

"That was a really strange group of people. I think Ethel [Shutta] was 75, and Fifi [D'Orsay] was 80, and they both needed a babysitter. They really acted like kids. . . . Alexis [Smith] was really the Ice Goddess . . . if we all cracked up onstage—and we did—she'd never participate. . . . Yvonne [De Carlo] was famous for being great in rehearsal. She would tap dance her little heart out and then change her shoes, go on stage, and lose it. She also used to put all these hairpieces on, and they'd fly all over the stage."—SHEILA SMITH, *Follies* (1971) actress and understudy

"Barbra has the voice and talent. I just don't think she'll ever come back to Broadway. . . . She strives for technical perfection, but she doesn't really relate to audiences, and that's so important when you work live."—LIZA MINNELLI on Streisand

"May I go down on you?"—JOHN BARRYMORE's greeting, with arms open and ready to bow, in the dressing room of any given star whose performance he'd greatly admired

"Wouldn't that be rather difficult at the same time?"—JERRY HERMAN to officially bisexual Liz Smith when she bowed and told him and Carol Channing after an admirable benefit performance, "May I go down on you?"

"I can't do this show . . . I've never been that poor, and I've never even *known* a Puerto Rican!"—STEPHEN SONDHEIM's initial reaction when asked to write the lyrics for *West Side Story*

"John Waters says *Hairspray* is *Cats* for fat people. I think John Waters is Woody Allen for gay people."—ROBERT DOWNEY JR.

"Somebody forgot to tell Bobby Short he was black. But he forgot to tell he was gay. At least he kept his own nose."—DON RICKLES

"Completely all voice and no internals. I left that show because I said, 'The play is lost in your palate. I'm an acting teacher. I can't have my name involved with this kind of exterior performing. You have only this 'This is CNN' voice.'"—CHARLES NELSON REILLY on James Earl Jones in *Paul Robeson*

"She was a little troublesome. She didn't like working with other people. She was much more comfortable alone when she wrote her little ditties."—CHARLES NELSON REILLY on his former acting pupil Lily Tomlin

"Ever since they costarred in that movie *Stage Door*, Katharine Hepburn and Ginger Rogers have been rivals, with Rogers always upstaged and outraged. . . . Ginger also followed her in touring *Coco* on the straw-hat circuit. Her Chanel portrayal was deliberately more feminine, and was written up as 'less strident' than Katharine Hepburn's."—GEORGE ROSE, costar of the Broadway *Coco* starring Hepburn

"As yet, [George] Bernard Shaw hasn't become prominent enough to have any enemies, but none of his friends like him."—OSCAR WILDE on a fellow Irish playwright

"I saw your *Private Lives* the other night. Not very funny."—actress DIANA WYNYARD to Noel Coward
     "I saw your Lady Macbeth the other night—very funny!" —COWARD's reply (not funny at all was the result of Wynyard's realistic playing of the sleepwalking scene with her eyes closed: she fell over a parapet and broke several bones)

"You *couldn't* have been better."—actor ERNEST THESIGER'S (Dr. Pretorius in *The Bride of Frankenstein*) backstage greeting to a not-very-talented colleague

"Claire Trevor once went back to see Judith Anderson after a performance of *Medea*. She had been truly bowled over and she said, 'I simply can't find the words to tell you how superb you were.' Judith Anderson just said, 'Try.'"
—ROCK HUDSON

"If you don't have a rod of steel in your spine, you're never going to survive in the arts in this country. . . . I tell my students, 'If you can find anything else in your life that will make you happy, do it. Because in the theatre, virtue is not its own reward. But if you'll be unhappy if you're not in the theatre, if you like swimming in polluted water with sharks, come on in.'"—playwright EDWARD ALBEE

"Darling, I don't care what anybody says—I thought you were marvelous."
—BEATRICE LILLIE to a rival performer

Costume designer ORRY-KELLY: "[Tallulah Bankhead] gives these grand cocktail parties, invites the finest people, and then when she opens the door to usher them in, she's wearing a large black garden hat, a strand of pearls, and her black pumps. That is all. And, you know, it isn't pretty."
CAROL CHANNING: "What isn't, Orry?"
ORRY-KELLY: "It looks like an old Chinaman's mustache. . . . It's food stained . . . and it's on the bias. It has a sneer."

"I did wonder if [his] career would come to a grinding halt with this crazy, almost subversive play. [*MacBird!*, 1966] was based on a character based on our president, LBJ, played by Stacy [Keach]. He arranges the murder of his boss, named John Ken O'Dunc, which is avenged by his brother, Robert Ken O'Dunc. You couldn't have had anything like this in the '50s, under the Republicans. . . . *MacBird!* was written by a Barbara Garson. . . . That was Off-Broadway, about 25 years ago. I hope Ms. Garson is still alive and well."—STACY KEACH SR.

"You know, for all her work on *Oklahoma!* Agnes de Mille only got $1,500. True, she wasn't famous before, but without her choreography there was no *Oklahoma!* The producers knew they had to do something or there'd be a scandal. Instead of giving her any kind of future percentage, which in time could come to millions, they paid her an extra $50 a week for the duration of the Broadway run."—GWEN VERDON

"I never played myself or even my own mother in *Gypsy*, but I played another part closer to myself, darling. It was far from Broadway, someplace in

Ohio. I starred as *Auntie Mame*. That part was *much* more me."—GYPSY
ROSE LEE

"I'm not related to Ken Mandelbaum, whose musical-theatre writing I admire.
Years ago I was introduced to Carol Channing, who thought I was Ken.
She talked so much and so quickly that I never got a chance to correct
her."—HOWARD MANDELBAUM, photographic entrepreneur

"How *dare* you call yourself an actor? You're not even a bad actor. You can't act
at all, you fucking stupid hopeless sniveling little cunt-faced cunty fucking
shit-faced arsehole."—LAURENCE OLIVIER to Laurence Harvey at a dinner party after Harvey criticized John Gielgud's acting, as quoted by
Harvey's biographer and sister-in-law, Anne Sinai

"What a lucky child to have two fairy godfathers!"—actress DAME MAY
WHITTY at the baptism of the son of bisexual actor Emlyn Williams, whose
former lovers Noel Coward and John Gielgud attended the ceremony

"In an agent's office, I overheard an actor say Margaret Sullavan was having an
affair with the producer Jed Harris. . . . I'd lean against the fence and I'd
stare up at our apartment with the lighted windows on the second floor.
More nights than I care to remember I'd stand there and cry. . . . I
couldn't believe my wife and that son of a bitch were in bed together. But
I knew they were. And that just destroyed me."—HENRY FONDA on his
first wife, who like the mother of Jane and Peter eventually took her
own life

"I agree with my confederate Peter Cook. He was the first to say he preferred
musicals, because when it came to plays about sex, sodomy, and substance
abuse, you can get all that at home."—DUDLEY MOORE

"Shakespeare's plays are bad enough, but yours are even worse."—novelist
LEO TOLSTOY (*War and Peace, Anna Karenina*) to fellow Russian Anton
Chekhov, after viewing *Uncle Vanya*

"I could play her better than that."—American theater star JULIE HARRIS to
a fellow actor while waiting in line at the Kennedy Center in Washington,
D.C., to be presented to Queen Elizabeth II

"I won't name any names, but I do owe a personal raspberry to each person
who said I was a fool to go to Broadway, do theatre, and play a gay character. . . . You know, Hollywood is worldwide; you can do a Hollywood
film Down Under. But only Broadway can do a Broadway musical."
—Australian film star HUGH JACKMAN, who won a 2004 Tony for *The
Boy from Oz*

"I don't think doing a dastardly thing can be excused by any amount of talent. I don't judge Elia Kazan. However, nor do I associate with him."—lyricist CAROLYN LEIGH on the McCarthy-era director who named names

"The irony was, I was playing a man who was dying, and the star of (*Grand Hotel*), David Carroll, really was dying. . . . I saw the bottle [of AZT in Carroll's hotel room] and just burst into tears. David made me vow not to tell a soul. And I didn't."—costar MICHAEL JETER, who later died of AIDS himself

"Thanks to a theatrical agent and good friend, Mr. and Mrs. Greenberg finally got tickets to see *The Producers* on Broadway. This was the most sold-out show of the year, especially after it won 12 Tony Awards. Scalpers were retiring on this one.

"They'd actually lucked into front-row seats. But they noticed that in the row behind them, there was an empty seat. When intermission came and no one had sat in that seat, Mrs. Greenberg turned to the woman sitting next to it and asked, 'Pardon me, but this is such a sold-out show, and in such demand. We were wondering why that seat is empty.'

"The woman said, 'That's my late husband's seat.'

"Mrs. Greenberg was horrified and apologized for being so insensitive. But a few minutes later she turned around again.

"'Without meaning to be rude or anything—surely you must have a friend or a relative who would have wanted to come and see this show?'

"The woman nodded, but explained, 'They're all at the funeral.'"
—comedian-actor ALAN KING, who played (Samuel) *Goldwyn* Off-Broadway

"Why do people take an instant dislike to me?"—ANDREW LLOYD WEBBER, to Broadway fixture Alan Jay Lerner, from whom he sought advice about *Phantom of the Opera* in 1986; Lerner's reply: "It saves time."

"I think [Thornton Wilder's] real problem is he's . . . never had a good lay."
—TENNESSEE WILLIAMS on the gay playwright behind Dolly Levi and *Our Town*

"Yes, Charles Nelson Reilly was in the original cast of *Hello, Dolly!* In fact, he was the most original one."—CAROL CHANNING

"Broadway . . . you have to say the same lines night after night. How boring that is!"—BARBRA STREISAND, who forsook the theater for film in the late '60s

"I don't like that they're [the audience] allowed to look wherever they want to look."—actor-director JODIE FOSTER on why she hasn't done any stage work since attending Yale

"Yes. But he was only an emperor."—stage legend SARAH BERNHARDT, replying to an American who observed that her US visit was receiving more publicity than the recent one of Dom Pedro of Brazil

"My last [Broadway] show folded on the road in 1995 [after] I broke my foot. . . . Broadway has changed—now it's like answering to a board of directors. I don't know how to do that and be in charge of a show. . . . It's like telling a painter how to paint a picture."—TOMMY TUNE in 2006, starring in and directing the musical *Dr. Dolittle* after spending most of the prior decade performing in concert and Las Vegas

BIBLIOGRAPHY

Abbott, George. *Mister Abbott*. New York: Random House, 1963.

Atkinson, Brooks. *Broadway*. New York: Macmillan Company, 1970.

Amacher, Richard E. *Edward Albee*. New York: Twayne Publishers, 1969.

Banham, Martin. *The Cambridge Guide to Theatre*. New York: Cambridge University Press, 1992.

Bankhead, Tallulah. *Tallulah—My Autobiography*. New York: Harper & Bros., 1952.

Barrow, Andrew. *Gossip 1920–1970*. New York: Coward, McCann, 1979.

Beaton, Cecil. *Cecil Beaton's Fair Lady*. New York: Holt Rinehart & Winston, 1964.

Belasco, David. *The Theatre Through Its Stage Door*. New York: Harper & Bros., 1919.

Behr, Edward, and Mark Steyn. *The Story of Miss Saigon*. Madison, WI: Arcade Publishing, 1999.

Bell, Marty. *Broadway Stories*. New York: Limelight Editions, 1993.

Bergreen, Laurence. *As Thousands Cheer: The Life of Irving Berlin*. New York: Viking Press, 1990.

Bernhardt, Sarah. *The Art of the Theatre*. Trans. by H.J. Stenning. New York: Dial Press, 1925.

Billington, Michael. *Theatre Facts and Feats*. Enfield, Middlesex: Guinness Superlatives Ltd., 1982.

Block, Geoffrey. *Enchanted Evenings: The Broadway Musical from "Show Boat" to Sondheim*. New York: Oxford University Press, 1997.

Brady, Kathleen. *Lucille: The Life of Lucille Ball*. New York: Hyperion, 1994.

Brandreth, Gyles. *Great Theatrical Disasters*. London: Granada, 1982.

Brantley, Ben, editor. *The New York Times Book of Broadway*. New York: St. Martin's Press, 2001.

Brown, Jared. *Zero Mostel*. New York: Atheneum, 1989.

Brown, John Russell. *The Oxford Illustrated History of Theatre*. Oxford, England: Oxford University Press, 1995.

Burton, Jack. *Blue Book of Tin Pan Alley*. Watkins, Glen, NY: Century House, 1950.

Channing, Carol. *Just Lucky, I Guess*. New York: Simon & Schuster, 2002.

Cottrell, John. *Laurence Olivier*. London: Weidenfeld & Nicolson, 1975.

Curtin, Kaier. *We Can Always Call Them Bulgarians*. Boston: Alyson Publications, 1987.

Crawford, Mary Caroline. *The Romance of the American Theatre*. Boston: Little, Brown & Co., 1913.

de Mille, Agnes. *Speak to Me, Dance with Me*. Boston: Little, Brown & Co., 1973.

Dennis, Patrick. *Auntie Mame*. Chicago: Harcourt & Brace, 1958.

Drennan, Robert E. *The Algonquin Wits*. Secaucus, NJ: Citadel Press, 1968.

Engelbach, Arthur H. *Anecdotes of the Theatre*. London: Grant Richards, 1914.

Ewen, David. *The Life and Death of Tin Pan Alley*. New York: Funk and Wagnalls, 1964.

Faderman, Lillian. *Scotch Verdict*. New York: Morrrow, 1983.

Feibleman, Peter. *Lilly—Reminiscences of Lillian Hellman*. New York: Morrow, 1988.

Flinn, Denny Martin. *What They Did for Love*. New York: Bantam Books, 1989.

Fontaine, Joan. *No Bed of Roses*. New York: Morrow, 1978.

Frommer, Myrna Katz, and Harvey Frommer. *It Happened on Broadway—An Oral History of the Great White Way*. New York: Harcourt Brace & Co., 1998.

Gam, Rita. *Actress to Actress*. New York: Nick Lyons Books, 1986.

Gammond, Peter. *The Oxford Companion to Popular Music*. New York: Oxford University Press, 1993.

Garebian, Keith. *The Making of* My Fair Lady. Toronto: ECW Press, 1993.

Garfield, David. *The Actors Studio: A Player's Place*. New York: Macmillan, 1980.

Gelb, Arthur, and Barbara Gelb. *O'Neill*. New York: Harper & Row, 1962.

Gelderman, Carol. *Mary McCarthy—A Life*. New York: St. Martin's Press, 1988.

George, Daniel. *A Book of Anecdotes*. London: Hulton, 1957.

Gorelik, Mordecai. *New Theatres for Old*. New York: Samuel French, 1940.

Green, Stanley. *Broadway Musicals*. Milwaukee, WI: Hal Leonard, 1985.

Greenberger, Howard. *The Off-Broadway Experience*. Englewood Cliffs, NJ: Prentice-Hall, 1971.

Grobel, Lawrence. *Conversations with Capote*. New York: New American Library, 1985.

Grossman, Barbara W. *Funny Woman: The Life and Times of Fanny Brice*. Bloomington, IN: Indiana University Press, 1991.

Gussow, Mel. *Conversations with Arthur Miller*. New York: Applause Books, 2002.

_____. *Edward Albee: A Singular Journey—A Biography*. New York: Applause Books, 2001.

Hadleigh, Boze. *Bette Davis Speaks*. New York: Barricade Books, 1996.

_____. *Celebrity Feuds!*. Dallas, TX: Taylor Publishing, 1999.

_____. *Hollywood Babble On*. New York: Perigee, 1995.

_____. *Sing Out!*. New York: Barricade Books, 1997.

Harris, Andrew B. *Broadway Theatre*. London: Routledge, 1994.

Harris, Jed. *A Dance on the High Wire*. New York: Crown Publishers, 1979.

Harris, Roy. *Conversations in the Wings—Talking About Acting*. Portsmouth, NH: Heinemann, 1994.

Harris, Warren. *Lucy and Desi*. New York: Simon & Schuster, 1991.

Harrison, Rex. *Rex: An Autobiography*. New York: Morrow, 1975.

Havoc, June. *Early Havoc*. New York: Harper & Row, 1980.

_____. *More Havoc*. New York: Simon & Schuster, 1959.

Hay, Peter. *Theatrical Anecdotes*. New York: Oxford University Press, 1987.

Hayman, Ronald. *John Gielgud*. Random House: New York, 1971.

Hemming, Roy. *The Melody Lingers On*. New York: Newmarket Press, 1986.

Henry, Louis C. *Humorous Anecdotes about Famous People*. Garden City, NY: Halcyon Press, 1948.

Herman, Jerry, with Marilyn Stasio. *Showtune: A Memoir*. New York: Donald I. Fine Books, 1996.

Hirschfeld, Albert. *The American Theatre as Seen by Hirschfeld*. New York: George Braziller, 1961.

Huggett, Richard. *The Curse of* Macbeth*, with Other Theatrical Superstitions and Ghosts*. Chippenham, England: Picton, 1981.

Isherwood, Christopher. *The Berlin Stories*. New York: New Directions, 1945.

Jackson, Arthur. *The Best Musicals: From "Show Boat" to "A Chorus Line": Broadway, Off-Broadway, London*. London: Webb & Bower, 1977.

Johns, Eric. *Dames of the Theatre*. New Rochelle, NY: Arlington House, 1974.

Kander, John, Fred Ebb, and Greg Lawrence. *Colored Lights*. New York: Faber & Faber, 2003.

Kiernan, Robert F. *Gore Vidal*. New York: Frederick Ungar, 1982.

Kirkwood, James. *Diary of a Mad Playwright*. New York: E.P. Dutton, 1989.

Kissel, Howard. *David Merrick—The Abominable Showman*. New York: Applause Books, 1993.

Laurents, Arthur. *Original Story By: A Memoir of Broadway and Hollywood*. New York: Alfred A. Knopf, 2000.

Lawrence, Greg. *Dance with Demons—The Life of Jerome Robbins*. New York: G.P. Putnam's Sons, 2001.

Lee, Gypsy Rose. *Memoirs of Gypsy Rose Lee*. New York: Harper, 1957.

Lees, Gene. *Inventing Champagne: The Worlds of Lerner and Loewe*. New York: St. Martin's Press, 1990.

Lerner, Alan Jay. *My Fair Lady*. New York: Coward McCann, 1957.

Lewis, Arthur. *Those Philadelphia Kellys (With a Touch of Grace)*. New York, Morrow, 1977.

Lillie, Beatrice, with James Brough. *Every Other Inch a Lady*. Garden City, NY: Doubleday, 1972.

Little, Stuart W., and Arthur Cantor. *The Playmakers*. New York: W.W. Norton, 1970.

Logan, Joshua. *Movie Stars, Real People, and Me*. New York: Delacorte Press, 1978.

Long, Robert Emmet. *Broadway, the Golden Years*. New York: Continuum, 2001.

Mandelbaum, Ken. *"A Chorus Line" and the Musicals of Michael Bennett*. New York: St. Martin's Press, 1989.

_____. *Not Since "Carrie": 40 Years of Broadway Musical Flops*. New York: St. Martin's Press, 1991.

Marks, Edward B. *They All Had Glamour*. New York: Julian Messner, 1944.

Matlaw, Myron. *Modern World Drama: An Encyclopedia*. New York: E.P. Dutton, 1972.

McGovern, Dennis, and Deborah Grace Winer. *Sing Out, Louise!* New York: Schirmer Books, 1993.

Merman, Ethel, and George Eells. *Merman: An Autobiography*. New York: Simon & Schuster, 1978.

Mordden, Ethan. *The Fireside Companion to the Theatre*. New York: Simon & Schuster, 1988.

_____. *The Hollywood Musical*. New York: St. Martin's Press, 1981.

_____. *Open a New Window: The Broadway Musical in the 1960s*. New York: Palgrave, 2001.

Morley, Sheridan. *A Talent to Amuse*. Boston: Little, Brown & Co., 1985.

_____, and Ruth Leon. *Hey, Mr Producer! The Musical World of Cameron Mackintosh*. New York: Back Stage Books, 1998.

Myers, Eric. *Uncle Mame*. New York: St. Martin's Press, 2000.

Nolan, Frederick. *Lorenz Hart: A Poet on Broadway*. New York: Oxford University Press, 1994.

Oppenheimer, George. *The Passionate Playgoer*. New York: Viking, 1962.

Ostrow, Stuart. *A Producer's Broadway Journey*. Westport, CT: Praeger, 1999.

Phillips, Gene D. *The Films of Tennessee Williams*. Berkeley, CA: Art Alliance Press, 1980.

Plimpton, George. *Truman Capote*. New York: Doubleday, 1997.

Preminger, Erik. *Gypsy and Me*. Boston: Little, Brown & Co., 1984.

Raymond, Jack. *Show Music on Record: From the 1890s to the 1980s*. New York: F. Ungar, 1982.

Redfield, William. *Letters from an Actor*. New York: Viking, 1967.

Rhodes, Gary Don. *Lugosi*. Jefferson, NC: McFarland & Co., 1997.

Richards, Dick. *The Wit of Noel Coward*. London: Leslie Frewin, 1968.

Rigg, Diana, compiler. *No Turn Unstoned*. London: Hamish Hamilton, 1982.

Rodgers, Richard. *Musical Stages: An Autobiography*. New York: Random House, 1975.

Rose, Brian. *Televising the Performing Arts*. Westport, CT: Greenwood Press, 1992.

Rosenberg, Deena. *Fascinating Rhythm*. London: Lime Tree, 1992.

Rossi, Alfred. *Astonish Us in the Morning: Tyrone Guthrie Remembered*. London: Hutchinson, 1977.

Sagalyn, Lynne B. *Times Square Roulette: Remaking the City Icon*. Cambridge, MA: MIT Press, 2001.

Sanders, Coyne Steven, and Tom Gilbert. *Desilu*. New York: Morrow, 1993.

Santopietro, Tom. *The Importance of Being Barbra*. New York: Thomas Dunne Books, 2006.

Schanke, Robert A., and Kim Marra, editors. *Passing Performances: Queer Readings of*

Leading Players in American Theatre History. Ann Arbor, MI: University of Michigan Press, 1998.

Schulman, Sarah. *Stagestruck: Theatre, AIDS, and the Marketing of Gay America*. Durham, NC: Duke University Press, 1998.

Secrest, Meryl. *Stephen Sondheim: A Life*. London: Bloomsbury, 1998.

Seldes, Gilbert. *The Seven Lively Arts*. New York: Sagamore Press, 1957.

Sheward, David. *It's a Hit! The Back Stage Book of Longest-Running Broadway Shows, 1884 to the Present*. New York: Watson-Guptill, 1994.

Sinfield, Alan. *Out on Stage—Lesbian and Gay Theatre in the 20th Century*. New Haven, CT: Yale University Press, 1999.

Skinner, Otis. *Footlights and Spotlights*. New York: Blue Ribbon Books, 1924.

Skolsky, Sidney. *Times Square Tintypes*. New York: Ives Washburn, 1930.

Spignesi, Stephen J. *The Cat Book of Lists*. Franklin Lakes, NJ: New Page Books, 2001.

Stein, Joseph. *Fiddler on the Roof*. New York: Pocket Books, 1965.

Stevens, Gary, and Alan George. *The Longest Line: Broadway's Most Singular Sensation—"A Chorus Line"*. New York: Applause Books, 1995.

Steyn, Mark. *Broadway Babies Say Goodnight*. New York: Routledge, 1999.

Suskin, Steven. *Show Tune*. New York: Dodd, Mead & Co., 1986.

Taylor, William R., editor. *Inventing Times Square*. Baltimore: Johns Hopkins University Press, 1991.

Teichmann, Howard. *George S. Kaufman: An Intimate Portrait*. New York: Atheneum, 1972.

Toll, Robert C. *On with the Show*. New York: Oxford University Press, 1976.

Trager, James. *The New York Chronology: The Ultimate Compendium of Events, People and Anecdotes from the Dutch to the Present*. New York: HarperResource, 2003.

Traubner, Richard. *Operetta: A Theatrical History*. New York: Oxford University Press, 1983.

Trewin, J.C. *The Night Has Been Unruly*. London: Robert Hale, 1957.

Tune, Tommy. *Footnotes*. New York: Simon & Schuster, 1997.

Turner, Mary M. *Forgotten Leading Ladies of the American Theatre*. Jefferson, NC: McFarland & Co., 1990.

Underwood, Peter. *Karloff*. New York: Drake Publishers, 1972.

Van Hoogstraten, Nicholas. *Lost Broadway Theatres*. New York: Princeton Architectural Press, 1997.

Viagas, Robert, and Baayork Lee and Thommie Walsh. *On the Line: The Creation of "A Chorus Line"*. New York: Morrow, 1990.

Vorlucky, Robert, editor. *Tony Kushner in Conversation*. Ann Arbor, MI: University of Michigan Press, 1998.

Voss, Ralph F. *A Life of William Inge*. Lawrence, KS: University Press of Kansas, 1989.

Walsh, Michael. *Andrew Lloyd Webber: His Life and Works*. New York: Harry N. Abrams, 1989.

Warde, Frederick. *Fifty Years of Make Believe*. New York: International Press Syndicate, 1920.

Watkins, Maurine Dallas. *Chicago*. New York: Alfred A. Knopf, 1928.

Webster, Margaret. *The Same, Only Different*. New York: Alfred A. Knopf, 1969.

Wilder, Alec. *American Popular Song*. New York: Oxford University Press, 1972.

Wilder, Thornton. *The Matchmaker*. New York: Samuel French, 1985.

Wilk, Max. *OK! The Story of* Oklahoma!. New York: Grove Press, 1993.

Williams, Tennessee. *Memoirs*. Garden City, NY: Doubleday, 1975.

Willson, Meredith. *But He Doesn't Know the Territory*. New York: G.P. Putnam's Sons, 1957.

Winecoff, Charles. *Split Image: The Life of Anthony Perkins*. New York: E.P. Dutton, 1996.

Wodehouse, P.G. *Author! Author!* New York: Simon & Schuster, 1954.

————. *Performing Flea*. London: Jenkins, 1953.

Woollcott, Alexander. *The Portable Woollcott*. New York: Viking, 1942.

Wright, William. *Lillian Hellman*. New York: Simon & Schuster, 1986.

Zadan, Craig. *Sondheim and Company, 2nd Edition*. New York: Da Capo Press, 1994.

Zolotow, Maurice. *No People Like Show People*. New York: Random House, 1951.

INDEX